GLOBAL PERSPECTIVES ON PRESS REGULATION

In this ground-breaking two-volume set, world-leading experts produce a rich, authoritative depiction of the world's press, its freedom, and its limits.

We want press freedom but we also want freedom from the press. A powerful press may expose corrupt government or aid it. It may champion citizens or unfairly attack them. A vulnerable press may lack supporters and succumb to conformity. It may resist, and overcome tyranny. According to common belief, press freedom involves social responsibilities to equip public debate and render government transparent. Is this attitude valid given that the press is usually a private, commercial actor?

Globally, the health, authority, and viability of the press varies dramatically. These patterns do not conform to traditional divisions between North and South, East and West. Instead, they are much more complex. How do we measure successful press regulation? What concessions can the state and/or society demand of the press? What constitutes the irreducible core of press freedom?

The contributions in Volume 1 look at key jurisdictions in Europe; whereas Volume 2 goes beyond Europe to analyse the situation in key jurisdictions in Asia, Africa, the Americas and Oceania. Each volume can be used independently or as part of the complete set.

This work will be incredibly valuable to policy makers and academics who seek to capture the global picture for the purposes of effecting change.

Volume 2: Asia, Africa, the Americas and Oceania

Global Perspectives on Press Regulation

*Volume 2: Asia, Africa,
the Americas and Oceania*

Edited by
Paul Wragg
and
András Koltay

·HART·
OXFORD · LONDON · NEW YORK · NEW DELHI · SYDNEY

HART PUBLISHING

Bloomsbury Publishing Plc

Kemp House, Chawley Park, Cumnor Hill, Oxford, OX2 9PH, UK

1385 Broadway, New York, NY 10018, USA

29 Earlsfort Terrace, Dublin 2, Ireland

HART PUBLISHING, the Hart/Stag logo, BLOOMSBURY and the Diana logo are
trademarks of Bloomsbury Publishing Plc

First published in Great Britain 2024

A catalogue record for this book is available from the British Library.

A catalogue record for this book is available from the Library of Congress.

Library of Congress Control Number: 2023019968

ISBN: HB: 978-1-50995-039-3
       ePDF: 978-1-50995-041-6
       ePub: 978-1-50995-040-9

Typeset by Compuscript Ltd, Shannon

To find out more about our authors and books visit www.hartpublishing.co.uk.
Here you will find extracts, author information, details of forthcoming events
and the option to sign up for our newsletters.

Global Perspectives on Press Regulation

Volume 2: Asia, Africa,
the Americas and Oceania

Edited by
Paul Wragg
and
András Koltay

•HART•
OXFORD • LONDON • NEW YORK • NEW DELHI • SYDNEY

HART PUBLISHING

Bloomsbury Publishing Plc

Kemp House, Chawley Park, Cumnor Hill, Oxford, OX2 9PH, UK

1385 Broadway, New York, NY 10018, USA

29 Earlsfort Terrace, Dublin 2, Ireland

HART PUBLISHING, the Hart/Stag logo, BLOOMSBURY and the Diana logo are
trademarks of Bloomsbury Publishing Plc

First published in Great Britain 2024

Copyright © Paul Wragg and András Koltay, and Contributors severally 2024

A catalogue record for this book is available from the British Library.

A catalogue record for this book is available from the Library of Congress.

Library of Congress Control Number: 2023019968

ISBN: HB: 978-1-50995-039-3
      ePDF: 978-1-50995-041-6
      ePub: 978-1-50995-040-9

Typeset by Compuscript Ltd, Shannon

To find out more about our authors and books visit www.hartpublishing.co.uk.
Here you will find extracts, author information, details of forthcoming events
and the option to sign up for our newsletters.

To Sam, Daniel and Joey (PW)
To Orsi, Zalán and Zétény (AK)

PREFACE

This two-volume set invites readers to assess the conceptual, practical, and doctrinal issues arising in realisation of a press freedom ideal in which the press may act as public watchdog without undermining the rights of others. Through careful, systematic evaluation of the differing perspectives on this ideal, as it relates to the various political, cultural, and social climates around the world, this collection presents an unparalleled catalogue of world thought on the problem.

Volume 1 focuses on the European experience, in which, blighted by its history, a complex series of soft and hard law provides the press with the means to challenge state power whilst seeking to restrain it from unduly interfering with hard-fought human rights. In this ecosystem, we see that voluntary press regulatory schemes are common, such that the question becomes how far the state may go to enforce human rights norms without compromising press freedom.

Volume 2 provides viewpoints from the larger world, in which regulation is viewed with justified suspicion, from the USA, whose historic experience of suppression under oppressive colonial rule colours its view of press freedom to this day, to China, Latin America, and Africa, where repressive regimes continue to hold considerable influence. Even in those commonwealth countries, lacking the same overt histories of repression, we find stubborn resistance to regulation despite a more general embrace of human rights culture. Here, then, we see the continuing challenges that realisation of the press freedom ideal must face.

ACKNOWLEDGEMENTS

The editors would like to thank to all the contributors to this volume. Thanks are also due to our colleagues who helped with the publication of the book, especially Édua Reményi, who did a sterling job editing it. We are also grateful for the enormous support of the publisher. Without them this work would never have been born.

TABLE OF CONTENTS

Preface.. vii
Acknowledgements ix
List of Contributors xiii

1. *The Scope of the Regulatory Ideal: Vertical Freedom, Horizontal Restrictions* 1
    Paul Wragg

PART I
ASIA

2. *Between Politics and Commerce: Media Governance in China*..........................23
    Hualing Fu

3. *The Uncommon Law in the Hong Kong SAR: The Shifting Norms of Press Freedom under the National Security Law*..............................47
    Anne SY Cheung

4. *Regulation of Press in India – An Overview of the Legal Framework and Related Concerns* 75
    Annappa Nagarathna

5. *Israeli Perspectives on Press Freedom and Regulation* 99
    Tehilla Shwartz Altshuler

6. *Freedom versus Regulation: An Evolving Free Press in South Korea*...............129
    Ahran Park and Kyu Ho Youm

PART II
AFRICA

7. *Transforming Information and Communication Technologies from Infrastructures of Freedom to Architectures of Political Repression: The Case of Internet Shutdowns in Egypt and Cameroon* 153
    Lyombe Eko

8. *Free Expression of the Traditional Media in South Africa and the Constraints Imposed by Law* 177
    John Campbell and Suhail Mohammed

PART III
THE AMERICAS

9.   *Why is Freedom of the Press Adjunct to Freedom of Expression
     in Canada?* 205
     David Mangan

10. *Media Regulation in Chile: Authority and Liberty Compounded* 225
     John Charney

11. *The US Press: A Legal Framework of Complexity, Contradiction and
     Uncertainty*...245
     Lili Levi

PART IV
OCEANIA

12. *Media Regulation and Press Freedom in Australia: Problems without
     Resolution*...273
     David Rolph

13. *One Body to Rule Them All: Press Regulation in New Zealand* 303
     Ursula Cheer

14. *Conclusions* 329
     András Koltay

Index 335

LIST OF CONTRIBUTORS

John Campbell is a Barrister at The 36 Group in Field Court, Gray's Inn London and an advocate from The Bridge Group, Johannesburg specialising in Defamation and Privacy

John Charney is an Associate Professor at Pontificia Universidad Católica de Valparaíso

Ursula Cheer is the Professor of Law at University of Canterbury, New Zealand

Anne SY Cheung is Professor of Law at the University of Hong Kong

Lyombe Eko is a Professor of Media Law, Comparative and International Communication at the College of Media and Communication, Texas Tech University

Hualing Fu is Warren Chan Professor in Human Rights and Responsibilities at the University of Hong Kong

Kyu Ho Youm is a Professor and the Jonathan Marshall First Amendment Chair at the University of Oregon

András Koltay is Research Professor at the University of Public Service (Budapest) and Professor of Law at the Pázmány Péter Catholic University (Budapest)

Lili Levi is Professor of Law at the University of Miami School of Law

David Mangan is Associate Professor at Maynooth University (Ireland), Adjunct Professor at Osgoode Hall Law School (Toronto), and Global Professor at KU Leuven (Belgium), Faculty of Law & Criminology

Suhail Mohammed is a practising member of the Johannesburg Bar and a member of Group One Advocates, Sandton, South Africa

Nagarathna Annappa is an Associate Professor of Law & the Chief Co-ordinator at Advanced Centre on Research, Development and Training in Cyber Law and Cyber Forensics, National Law School of India University, Bengaluru, India

Ahran Park is an Assistant Professor of Journalism and Media Law at Korea University Seoul

David Rolph is Professor of Law at the University of Sydney and a Fellow of the Australian Academy of Law

Tehilla Shwartz Altshuler is a senior fellow at the Israel Democracy Institute

Paul Wragg is Professor of Law at the University of Leeds

1

The Scope of the Regulatory Ideal: Vertical Freedom, Horizontal Restrictions

PAUL WRAGG*

1. Introduction

Press regulation is not a popular topic for academic debate. At least, not amongst legal commentators. The established literature, such as it is, is dominated by media and communication scholars and political scientists,[1] rather than lawyers.[2] This may be due to the dynamics of the intellectual debate in which free speech and press freedom, as conceptual matters, is dominated by the US market, where the leading modern-day scholars such as Seana Shiffrin, Robert Post, C Edwin Baker, Frederick Schauer, and Martin Redish, have extended the work of Alexander Meiklejohn, Thomas Emerson, and Zechariah Chafee Jr, who came before them. For Americans, steeped in the rhetoric, if not the reality, of a First Amendment that, ostensibly, admits of no reasons to manage free speech production, the idea of a regulatory body, independent of government or not, overseeing journalistic standards, is so unpalatable as to be heresy of the highest order.

For reasons like this, there is, it seems, deep distrust of the idea that press regulation is legitimate and can operate effectively whilst leaving press freedom untouched. This hostility is not confined to the academic community, of course. After the British Government drew up plans for a tougher, independent regulatory body to tackle rampant press malpractice in the industry, the press, led by a right-wing tabloid chorus, descended into hysteria: 300 years of press freedom

---

* Special thanks to Agastya Nehra, University of Leeds, LLB graduate 2021, for his supreme research assistance in preparing this chapter.

[1] See, eg, L Fielden, 'Regulating the Press: A Comparative Study of International Press Councils' (Reuters Institute for the Study of Journalism, 2012); D McQuail, *Media Performance: Mass Communication and the Public Interest* (New York, SAGE, 1992); J Curran and J Seaton, *Power Without Responsibility*, 8th edn (New York, Routledge, 2018).

[2] See P Wragg, *A Free and Regulated Press* (Oxford, Hart Publishing, 2020).

were about to end, they screamed.[3] Accordingly, the Government, beholden to the press for its stay in power, backtracked furiously.

Nevertheless, despite negativity and suspicion, regulatory bodies monitoring press standards, are common around the world. As we saw, in Volume 1, such bodies are prevalent in Europe. Almost every country, with the notable exception of France, has a regulatory body in place, albeit the models of regulation vary, from self-regulation to co-regulation, from voluntary schemes to mandatory ones. Sometimes, these bodies have coercive or quasi-coercive powers to fine or recommend fines, as in the United Kingdom (UK) and Denmark, respectively, but these are the outliers. Typically, the regulatory body can do no more than issue an adverse adjudication, which offending newspapers are expected to publish. Whether these rebukes are taken seriously or not depends upon the underlying cultural traits at play. In places like Finland, adverse adjudications are received with shame and regret; in the UK, they are worn as badges of honour.

In this volume, we explore the social, legal, and political cultures of countries beyond Europe. Our reason for collecting the papers in this way was to illustrate the diversity and disparity of the institutional norms. For, whereas, in Europe, the political systems as well as legal and cultural norms surrounding press freedom are broadly homogenous (with the obvious exception of Russia), the same is (obviously) not true for the rest of the world. Here, we find a broad spectrum of political regimes and social histories that have influenced legal norms concerning the press, from the Juntas of Chile to the British sovereignty of Hong Kong, from the US influence in Korea to the British Mandate in Israel and British rule in India, from the Commonwealth influences in Canada, Australia, and Aotearoa New Zealand to the war of independence from British rule in the United States of America (USA), from the influence of Roman-Dutch law in South Africa to the Arab Spring in North Africa. Despite this great diversity, there are common themes that emerge from the excellent papers produced by the commentators in this volume. In this introductory chapter, I draw out some of these themes to illustrate both the concerns, and promise, inherent in press regulation as a means of safeguarding rights across the spectrum of legitimate interests at stake in various entrenched press practices.

2. The Press as Instrument of Government

2.1. Terminology

To begin with, we should be clear on terminology. The term 'press' is fraught with uncertainty. Personally, I tend to distinguish 'press' from 'media' to distinguish

---

[3] See, eg, 'Press Freedom in Britain is under Attack – Again', *The Spectator* (31 December 2016); 'Daily Mail Comment: After 300 Years, the Freedom of Britain's Press is in Peril. YOU can Save It', *The Daily Mail* (9 January 2017); G Rayner, 'Investigative Journalism to be "Stopped Dead in Tracks" by "Menacing" Laws After Leveson Inquiry', *The Independent* (15 October 2015).

the traditional print medium from modern forms of broadcast, through radio, television, and the internet.[4] In keeping with the absence of uniformity in the larger literature, our authors were free to use the terms as they saw fit, and typically, they did so by using them interchangeably. Nevertheless, as will be seen, there is a tradition, especially in Europe, but also globally, of operating different regulatory regimes for the printed press and the broadcast media. So it is that we find these differential schemes in Chile, India, Aotearoa New Zealand, Israel, South Africa, Canada, Australia and, to some extent, the USA. The reasons for this differential treatment are, in an important sense, technological (at least, historically), relating, as it does, to the avoidance of the sort of bandwidth chaos that cannot happen in a print context. The obligation to serve the public, then, is justifiable against broadcasters as a lost opportunity cost, for the installation of one broadcaster deprives other potential entrants in a competitive market from occupying that channel or frequency. This reasoning explains why a broadcaster may be obliged to act impartially in respect of factual or news-related items when the (printed) press has no such obligations, at least not in a legal sense. Yet, we also find that models of voluntary self-regulation, of the type that is common in Europe, exist around the world, for example, in Aotearoa New Zealand, Chile, South Africa, Israel, Korea and Canada, as well as a mandatory scheme operating in India.

Press regulation can, and does, have differential aims. As we saw, in Volume 1, these aims speak to three distinct interest groups: those of victims or objects of press speech; society at large; and the readership.[5] Across this spectrum of interests, those aims can be distinguished, alternatively, between that which regulates conduct (that is, the newsgathering process) and that which relates to content. For example, a provision insisting on minimum standards of accuracy can speak to all three interest groups, from the reputational rights of victims, to the contractual rights of readers, to the indirect interest of wider society when public decision-making is affected by partisan press coverage. Similarly, provisions relating to privacy can speak to a victim's rights, as part of the newsgathering process, not to be harassed by journalistic enquiries, especially if they are vulnerable or in a place in which heightened vulnerability can be expected, for instance, hospitals, funerals, etc, as well as rights to privacy accruing in undue privacy-invading expression.

In this sense, the contested nature of the term 'press freedom' is apparent. Yet, there is no reason why even the strongest regulatory provisions should be thought automatically anathema to press freedom. For example, as we also saw in Volume 1, it is common for regulatory provisions to contain exceptions that disapply or otherwise reduce prohibitions when matters of public interest are at stake. In this way, the label of 'victim' may be inapplicable to organs of the state and even individual office holders. Similarly, private organisations and office holders may be ineligible to regulatory protection if the speech unearths instances of fraud or other such criminal matters or civil wrongs that affect the public in sufficient numbers.

---

[4] See Wragg (n 2) 1–4.
[5] See, further, ibid 173–254.

2.2. The Role of the Press

Nevertheless, the literature invites problems in its near universal insistence that the press performs a public service rendering it an integral part of the political system. For it is commonly said that the press is the 'cornerstone of democracy' or that it has a duty to act as a public watchdog. This trope is common in both the literature and the legal jurisprudence, as we saw in Volume 1, and as we shall see in this volume too. For example, we see it said by courts in Korea, Israel, India, and Hong Kong. We are entirely familiar with the importance of this principle, for a government that can suppress criticisms of its own actions can act against its own people's interests with impunity. Similarly, as John Charney says of Chile, 'the press was [also] seen … as an instrument of social cohesion, which, backed by the principles of autonomous government, would be able to dismantle the colonial authoritarian heritage'.[6]

Nevertheless, the argument has two dimensions. In one sense, it can be understood in purely negative terms: that, in those instances when the press discovers wrongdoing in public office, it should be free to expose it, thus bringing it to the attention of the populace with a view to agitating for justice and/or political change. Wrongdoing, in this sense, can be moral as well as legal, such that the press is empowered, or ought to be, to chastise government for incompetence or negligence as much as for fraudulent or other deviant activity. In this negative sense, the press operates without expectation; in fact, we see no conceptual difference between the press as institutional speaker or the journalist – or, indeed, anyone – as an individual (or 'unqualified') speaker. If they should stumble upon some public interest matter, the law will protect them from a vengeful government. This is the classic sense of free speech as an agenda-less enterprise that law is generally uninterested in, in an important sense; it is concerned only to address acts of state overreach (that is, illegitimate uses of power).

The alternative understanding, though, attributes to the press some positive dimension. We see this, clearly, for example, in the work of Cass Sunstein and Owen Fiss who, during the late 1980s and early 1990s, agitated for an agenda-driven understanding of press freedom, as an institution that *must* deliver positive benefits for electoral decision-making. Of these, Sunstein's is the more potent of the two, but both are united in their insistence that, without regulatory intervention of some kind, public debate is not 'uninhibited, robust, and wide-open'[7] and that a 'well-functioning deliberative process increases the likelihood that political outcomes will respond to people's desires and aspirations'.[8] Given that such efficiencies do not arise organically, according to our lived experiences, then some

---

[6] See J Charney, 'Media Regulation in Chile: Authority and Liberty Compounded' ch 10, section 2 in this volume.

[7] OM Fiss, 'Why the State?' in J Lichtenberg (ed), *Democracy and the Mass Media* (Cambridge, Cambridge University Press, 1990) 147.

[8] CR Sunstein, *Democracy and the Problem of Free Speech* (New York, Free Press, 1995) 244.

sort of artificiality must be added to the system so as to realise this outcome. The question, though, is what?

In the UK, Dame Onora O'Neill has argued that the missing ingredient is public trust (in all public-facing institutions, not simply the press).[9] If the public had greater trust in the press, then the epistemic process underpinning informed public decision-making would be optimised, or otherwise much improved, because they, the public, would have confidence that the underlying information on which they act is reliable. To achieve *this* end, she says, the press itself must improve its own culture such that 'careful inquiry' and 'fact-checking' become ingrained in their working practices to a much greater degree than of late.[10] For commentators like Sunstein, Fiss, and O'Neill, the 'duty' to fulfil this function is but the 'price' of constitutional protection from undue state interference.[11]

Public trust in the press plays an important role in our innate sense, at its most essential, of whether the press is an instrument for us, the people, against them, the government – and so works (or wants to work) for our benefit. Or whether, instead, it is an agent of the state working, in the final analysis, *against* us. For we can also say that in Soviet Russia and Communist China under Mao that the press was *also* vital to the political system, just not in the sense that the democratic process theorists have it. Hualing Fu highlights this problem in the Chinese context. As he says, the *neican* was (and still is) 'the ideological apparatus of the Party', which played a role in 'proactively discovering and guiding public opinions'.[12] Accordingly:

> For the official press, the task to guide and educate the public is as important as to inform and advise the government, and it is the back-door communication that gives journalists special access to power and significant influences in society. It is well known that, in contentious cases, it may be more important to know a good *neican* journalist than a good lawyer, for a leader's potential responses to a *neican* report is weighty and influential in court decisions.[13]

For reasons such as this, as Tehilla Shwartz Altshuler reports, public trust in journalism is low in Israel whereas,[14] as David Rolph notes, public trust in the national broadcaster, the Australian Broadcasting Corporation, is consistently high.[15]

Yet, the idea that the press has a *duty* to perform this public service goes well beyond the vital principle that public interest expression should be protected *when* it arises, for it carries the weight of a communitarian burden that trumps

---

[9] O O'Neill, *A Question of Trust* (Cambridge University Press, 2002).

[10] O O'Neill, 'Ethics for Communication?' (2009) 17(2) *European Journal of Philosophy* 167, 172.

[11] See, eg, G Robertson, *People Against the Press* (London, Quartet Books, 1983) 158; J Barron, *Freedom of the Press for Whom?* (Bloomington, Indiana University Press, 1973) 340.

[12] HL Fu, 'Between Politics and Commerce: Media Governance in China' ch 2, section 2 in this volume.

[13] ibid.

[14] T Shwartz Altshuler, 'Israeli Perspectives on Press Freedom and Regulation, ch 5, section 6 in this volume.

[15] D Rolph, 'Media Regulation and Press Freedom in Australia: Problems Without Resolution', ch 12, section 2 in this volume.

the individual interests of the journalist herself and, in the final analysis, the property and commercial interests of an owner and her shareholders. If we pare back the romanticism that informs that principle, we shall see that the concept of duty invokes greater intellectual difficulties than romance alone can either reveal or solve. For, if we are honest, we see that the imposition of a duty must carry with it, as a logical premise, the creation of a corollary right or interest in enforcement of that duty. In my own work, I have sought to emphasise that this right-duty nexus deserves greater intellectual attention than it receives. To my mind, the idea is so problematic that it ought to be dispensed with; that we should think of press freedom solely in negative terms, as a right against state interference when it (the press) conducts public interest journalism but which is regulatable when it commits wrongdoing, especially against non-state actors: this is why I argue that we should think of the press as something that should make good not do good.[16]

To insist, though, that the press, as a series of private enterprises with shareholders to satisfy, is an organ of government, on which the whole political system *depends*, invites the sort of difficulties that both Fu and Anne Cheung highlight so persuasively in their chapters on the situation in China and Hong Kong, respectively. For the sort of argument that, say, Sunstein, Fiss, James Weinstein,[17] have made, and which, long before them, the Hutchins Commission endorsed, that the press undermines the political system through the dissemination of false information, is but the other side of the same coin used by Lenin, Pinochet, and, more recently, Putin and Xi.

To be sure, there are important differences between what the established US literature says about press freedom as a facet of democratic society and that which authoritarian regimes proclaim. Nevertheless, there is an underlying commonality that is not easily avoided unless we are clear on the separation of individualism and communitarianism as the base units of the language of freedom. For the logic of communitarianism, as communism has it, is that the grand vision of the ideal communist state can be achieved, through the dictatorship of the proletariat, only by means of central planning. This, of itself, presupposes not only that the ends but also the means of achieving it are indubitable and known only (or best) by the ruling party. Accordingly, Putin and Xi can say, as Lenin, Stalin, and Mao could, that overt criticism of state action corrupts the vision and undermines the realisation of the vision through the taint that such criticism creates. Thus, they can say that unbridled criticism *is* a national security threat. For speech that undermines public confidence in the current government will have wider economic effects that, in its ultimate form, unsettles markets, deters foreign investment and, so, jeopardises the realisation of power and influence on the world stage.

---

[16] See Wragg (n 2).

[17] See, eg, A Bhagwat and J Weinstein, 'Freedom of Expression and Democracy' in A Stone and F Schauer (eds), *The Oxford Handbook of Freedom of Speech* (Oxford, Oxford University Press, 2021) 82, for details of his work and a summary of his key claims.

Admittedly, the unbridled censorship apparent in the worst ideological regimes of, say, North Korea or the Soviet Union at its peak, is an extreme form of communitarianism, but subtler forms may be as subversive, especially in the wrong hands. Certainly, the manipulation of facts to serve political ends is not a phenomenon confined to the propaganda machinery of a Goebbels or Mussolini. The West knows it affectionally as 'spin' and it has driven left- as well as right-leaning governments in the immediate past, most notably, in the UK, in the media campaigns of Alastair Campbell as Director of Communications and Strategy for New Labour at the turn of the Millenium. Recently, of course, such 'spin' has been developed into more overt forms of propaganda that has seen a marked resurgence of populist ideology in Europe and, of course, in Donald Trump's presidency. This propaganda is characterised by a culture of blame in which the dynamic of 'us' and 'them' figures centrally, and in which the othering inherent in 'them' serves as an egregious (though ethereal) threat to realisation of the political agenda that populists pursue for 'us'.

Although it is incredible that such subversions of truth should not only exist but also thrive at the highest level of office, in mature democracies like the USA, or even the UK (which has suffered its own inimitable period of collective self-delusion and no less self-harm caused by Brexit), there is an inevitability about it given our conflicted sense of individuality that informs our understanding of press freedom. For if, as we maintain, the press is entitled to form its own opinions, but not its own facts, then the rampant partisanship that has emerged is bound to impact, detrimentally, the public sphere in which collective decision-making takes place. Given that such decisions involve the allocation of finite resources to complex economic, social, and political issues, in circumstances where a high degree of risk and uncertainty abound (for, to paraphrase Oliver Wendell Holmes, democracy is an experiment, as all life is), the distinction between fact and opinion is often much slighter than it would otherwise appear. Moreover, when issues depend, for their ultimate fact pattern, on levels of esoteric expertise, in which nuance and subtly abound, there is bound to be a loss of understanding, let alone misapprehension, in whatever is produced.

Accordingly, even the most self-reflective journalist can find themselves hamstrung by the sheer complexity of separating fact from opinion – and once the reality of chronic time-pressure is added into the mix, we see how hopeless the communitarian ambitions may seem. Nevertheless, we must add a further complexity into our analysis by recognising that a partisan press is an interest-led entity. Whether these interests manifest directly in the owner's wishes for his newspaper or appear in the diluted form of individual (conscious or subconscious) biases and worldviews, a serious problem arises in the expectation of communitarians that the press act as politically-neutral conduits interested only in serving her fellow woman. Indeed, the dilemmas that have faced the Republican party, in the USA, and the Conservative Party, in the UK, are apt. For when the figure-head is (apparently) popular with the public despite the vocal misgivings of those that know them, the will to power can be blinding. So it is that owner, editor, and individual journalist, united by their deep-seated political affiliations, may be driven by the urge to put suspect political aptitude for leadership in its best possible light (to communicate figurehead actions and decision-making positively when negativity seems more appropriate) is entirely understandable if not quite forgivable.

Once we have this dilemma firmly within our grasp, and have married it to the individualism inherent in the liberal constitutions of mature democracies, we may see that the problem we are describing here is not a question of what is *said* but what is *believed*. Thus, we may see that what is usually tacit in communitarian thought is not that the public is being protected from the *press*, so much as being protected from *themselves*. It is common for scholars to describe interventions in the epistemic process as a necessity borne from the 'bounded rationality' of voters – a connotation that, although faintly condescending, is more than justified by our shared histories of popular authoritarian regimes, brought about by electoral will, from Hitler's rise to power in Germany to Robert Mugabe's rule in Zimbabwe. Typically, commentators argue that some state intervention is necessary so that voters have access to a diverse range of opinions either for the purposes of election or, more generally, for the reasons of self-governance, of which Jürgen Habermas's[18] and Robert Post's[19] work is most notable. Yet, whereas for Habermas, the scheme for greater pluralism is purely ethical ('the democratic constitutional state depends on motivations oriented to the public interest that cannot be legally enforced, however modest their scale may be'),[20] for Post, and his followers, obligations to promote pluralism, etc, are not merely ethical; they form part of the complex matrix that *is* press freedom. Thus, Post can say, as Habermas cannot, that the press is a mere 'fiduciary' or 'intermediary' in the formation of public opinion, whose interests, therefore, are only indirectly concerned with self-governance, for they are not of a form that can have *direct* interest in self-governance *per se*.[21]

This view reflects that of the Hutchins Commission, who conceived of the press as 'a forum for the exchange of comment and criticism'; to 'present' and 'clarify' society's 'goals and values'; to provide 'full access to the day's intelligence' and 'a truthful, comprehensive, and intelligent account of the day's events in a context which gives them meaning'.[22] Objectives such as these are common, and familiar, in broadcasting laws. For example, as we shall see, obligations of 'objectivity' exist in Chile, Aotearoa New Zealand and Israel. Further, these viewpoints are reminiscent

---

[18] See, eg, J Habermas, *Between Facts and Norms* (New York, Polity, 1996).

[19] See, eg, R Post, 'Reconciling Theory and Doctrine in First Amendment Jurisprudence' (2000) 88 *California Law Review* 2353.

[20] J Habermas, *Philosophical Introductions* (New York, Polity Press, 2018) 130.

[21] See, eg, R Post, 'Participatory Democracy and Free Speech' (2011) 97(3) *Virginia Law Review* 477, 486–87.

[22] The Commission on Freedom of the Press, *A Free and Responsible Press* (Chicago, University of Chicago Press, 1947) 20–29. It should be noted that the Hutchins Commission concluded that these were obligations only in an ethical, not legal, sense.

of a popular view amongst commentators that the imposition of burdens upon the press – essentially, to serve public discourse through reliable information and pluralistic opinion – is a corollary of the special benefits that the press receive as a matter of law.[23] Whether such special laws exist is a different matter.[24]

Post is not unaware of the problems in using law to 'equalize' influences on public debate, for, as he sees it, it would be 'tyrannical'.[25] Nevertheless, there is a major problem here which, to my mind, Post's scheme cannot overcome, and that is how, by means of law, his plans for press freedom are to be achieved without the law overreaching.[26] Others have attempted to overcome this problem in more convincing, if less visionary, ways. One of the most compelling, recently, is to be found in Andrew Kenyon's work, which has produced some wonderful schematics for realising a better-informed society, chiefly through judicial supervision of pluralism obligations in public broadcasting.[27] Nevertheless, there is an inescapable but depressing futility about all this. If the ambition of democratic process theory is to create an information repository of reliable information and pluralistic opinion, then the obvious question that arises is to ask: to what end?

The most cherished principle of democratic self-government is, of necessity, its greatest weakness: maximal enfranchisement, captured by the principle of one person, one vote, means absolute equality between voters without exception. Yet, this also means that the most thoughtful, careful, responsible choice in public decision-making counts exactly the same as the most rash, irresponsible and ill-conceived.[28] To give the voting public access to the more exceptional repository means nothing if the public fails to engage with it. Worse still, it means nothing if the public cannot understand or otherwise misinterpret the information and opinions that they receive. For there is every possibility that the public, although compulsorily educated, lack the optimal cognitive abilities or, even, the luxury of time, to perform the externally-imposed obligation of due diligence inherent in responsible public decision-making. This is a serious problem but one which admits no obvious solution unless we are to sacrifice our most cherished principles. We do not monitor the cognitive performances of citizens for public

---

[23] See, eg, J Lichtenberg, 'Foundations and Limits of Freedom of the Press' in Lichtenberg (n 7)128; Robertson (n 11) 157–58.

[24] See Wragg (n 2) 113–18. The US Supreme Court, for example, has always denied that it treats the press differently from any other speaker (see, eg, *Citizens United v Federal Election Commission*, 558 US 36 (2010)), and we find similar statements in the UK apex court decisions (eg, *AG v Observer Ltd* (1990) 1 AC 109, 201) and the Strasbourg jurisprudence as well (eg, *Magyar Helsinki Bizottság v Hungry*, App no 18030/11, [168]).

[25] Post (n 21) 484.

[26] See, further, the critical comments of John Charney in his exceptional book, *The Illusion of the Free Press* (Oxford, Hart Publishing, 2018).

[27] See, eg, AT Kenyon, *Democracy of Expression: Positive Free Speech and Law* (Cambridge University Press, 2021).

[28] Martin Redish makes a similar point: 'For if an individual wishes to buy a car because he believes it will make him look masculine, or to vote for a candidate because the candidate looks good with his tie loosened and his jacket slung over his shoulder, who are we to tell him that these are improper acts?' M Redish, 'The Value of Free Speech' (1982) 130 *University of Pennsylvania Law Review* 591, 619.

(or private) decision-making. We do not assess their epistemic reasoning prior to the casting of votes. Clearly, we do not: hence, Brexit. Thus, in assessing the role of the press, as part of our analysis of press freedom's meaning, we must ask a deeper question: what can *law* do?

2.3. The Role of Law

John Stuart Mill's much-maligned thesis, in *On Liberty*, is that although the state may interfere with other-regarding activity when unjustifiable harm arises, it has no right to tackle harmful self-regarding activity. One facet of this view has obvious application to the dynamic just described. If an individual acts upon misunderstood information or, even, misguided intentions, then that is a matter for her alone, and not the state. This holds true even if the outcome of those self-directed actions has negative impact upon the public sphere. In this way, for example, Mill defends drunkenness, albeit not if the drunk has children which, through her drunkenness, she neglects.[29] Although Mill does not draw the distinction so finely, we can distinguish the difference through the principle of remoteness as an aspect of causality. The damage done to her children's welfare is sufficiently direct and immediate that the state has legitimate interest in regulating her actions. Properly speaking, they are other-regarding and cause sufficient harm to warrant intervention. The damage done to the public purse, through the diminished, perhaps negligible, income tax receipts that her drunkenness generates is too remote to count. The state cannot compel her to embrace sobriety even though her upstanding citizenry would be in its interests and, no doubt, her immediate community's.

This principle has application to our understanding of the state's legitimate interests in managing public discourse. Clearly, although criticisms of state performance is other-regarding speech, the 'harm' done to society resides not in the speaker's actions, in bringing the incompetence or corruption to our attention, but in the state's actions itself. Accordingly, suppression does not address harms arising from the other-regarding activities but, instead, prevents the harm caused by its own actions from being remedied or otherwise mediated by further action, be that through the populace or other state agencies intervening. All of this is obvious and demonstrates that we do not want for the analytical language that helps us identify clear threats to press freedom, nor do we want for a language to condemn such actions.

Accordingly, we can say, with Lyombe Eko, that state shutdowns of the internet, to suppress criticisms of government, are both draconian and repressive. For, as he explains in his chapter, 'in Africa north and south of the Sahara, the fundamental tension is between the right of freedom of the press and authoritarian

---

[29] JS Mill, 'On Liberty' in *Collected Works of John Stuart Mill* (edited by JM Robson) (Toronto, University of Toronto Press, 1977) vol XVIII, 295.

governmental censorship and persecution of the defiant, independent private press for political and ethical reasons'.[30] The examples he discusses of shutdowns in Egypt and Cameroon are subversive applications of national security rhetoric to justify censorship of political speech.

Nevertheless, we should be attuned (more than, I think, we are) to the parallel danger of the susceptibility of the term 'duty' to just this sort of subversion. For the language of 'duty' also let this subversive rhetoric in and allows it to thrive unless we are careful. Accordingly, we see the importance of the contributions that Fu and Cheung make to this discussion. The promise of a more liberal environment for the Chinese press, prompted by the post-1989 collapse of Communism, and the relaxation of Party control over the press, through the commercialisation of the media, has diminished in recent years under President Xi's premiership. In this way, the legacy *neican* press still retains something of its importance as an organ of the state that gathers information and reports public opinion back to the Party.[31] As Cheung reports, there is growing concern that China's rhetorical commitment to 'one country, two systems' policy to Hong Kong, following China's resumption of sovereignty over the province in 1997, is being eroded through the imposition of repressive national security measures.[32] As she says, 'the law was drafted in language and style of the PRC's [People's Republic of China] Soviet-inspired Socialist legal tradition, which is fundamentally different from that adopted in local legislations drafted by common law lawyers' and which is available publicly only in Chinese, which 'could make it more difficult for the law to be subject to international criticism'.[33]

Similarly, as Shwartz Altshuler reminds us, Israeli policy towards journalists also struck this sort of authoritarian note in its application of the British mandated Press Ordinance (1933) which required newspapers to obtain a licence for publication and which was used divisively 'against Israeli-Arab journalists and media outlets'.[34] The Israeli Supreme Court sought to restrict state use of this repressive measure, which was only repealed, by the state, in 2017. Even so, the Government Press Office still retains the power to restrict access to 'official press conferences, access [to] government buildings, and [permission to] cross Israeli military checkpoints' through its power to issue press cards to recognised journalists.[35] Clearly, this has the power to chill press freedom. Moreover, it is redolent of the apparent policy, during Trump's presidency in the USA, of the selective, preferential

---

[30] L Eko, 'Transforming Information and Communication Technologies from Infrastructures of Freedom to Architectures of Political Repression: The Case of Internet Shutdowns in Egypt and Cameroon', ch 7, section 2 in this volume.

[31] HL Fu, 'Between Politics and Commerce: Media Governance in China', ch 2, section 2 in this volume.

[32] ASY Cheung, 'The Uncommon Law in the Hong Kong Special Administrative Region: The Shifting Norms of Press Freedom under the National Security Law' ch 3, section 2.3 in this volume.

[33] ibid.

[34] T Shwartz Altshuler, 'Israeli Perspectives on Press Freedom and Regulation', ch 5, section 2.4 in this volume.

[35] ibid.

treatment of journalists during White House briefings.[36] This exclusionary policy is but a subtler but no less troubling instance of the state malpractice that Eko alerts us to. For, just as he can say that 'selective internet disconnectivity' by the state acts as a 'barometer of the level of democracy and respect for freedom of expression in specific political dispensations',[37] so we can say that selective press access to state briefings is a comparable corruption of the public sphere.

3. The Protection of Individual Rights on the Horizontal Plane

Whereas regulatory oversight of the public watchdog role is problematic, the overall notion of state-driven regulation is not.[38] As outlined above, there are three discernible interest groups in respect of press regulation, of which society is only one. Whereas society has an interest in accurate information dissemination by the press, its ability to compel the regulation of inaccurate information is weak if the principles outlined in the previous section are to be maintained. This does not mean that a regulator cannot include an accuracy obligation within its code, but it does – or, rather, should – limit its regulatory options when inaccurate information is published. Since the use of coercive measures, such as financial penalty, would be contrary to the liberty principle as other-regarding activity tending to produce harm only remotely (see previous section), then the most that should follow, at the regulatory level, is an adverse adjudication notifying the readership, and wider society, of the fact of inaccuracy (which we might say, with Habermas, is of supreme ethical value to the public sphere).

Compulsory press regulation can also provide an important societal function in bringing to light corrupt or immoral practices within the press industry itself. For, whereas, the press is an exceptional vehicle for exposing industrial-scale wrongdoing in other private sector activities, it tends to be less likely (or, perhaps, more unwilling) to shine a light on its own foibles. Shwartz Altshuler draws attention to just such a problem in her chapter, in which she shows the ingrained levels of corruption and machinations between the press and high-ranking officials in Israel, including indictments on bribery, allegations of duress, and fraud.[39] Regulatory provisions concerning transparency, especially transparency of ownership, bring to light the sort of 'biased, incomplete, and sometimes false coverage'

---

[36] See discussion in T Zick, *The First Amendment in the Trump Era* (Oxford, Oxford University Press, 2019).

[37] L Eko, 'Transforming Information and Communication Technologies from Infrastructures of Freedom to Architectures of Political Repression: The Case of Internet Shutdowns in Egypt and Cameroon', ch 7, section 3 in this volume.

[38] To be sure, the term 'state-driven' needs careful handling. It is legitimate for the state to insist that the press is regulated so long as it is not responsible for its oversight.

[39] T Shwartz Altshuler, 'Israeli Perspectives on Press Freedom and Regulation', ch 5, section 5.1 in this volume.

that arises when media owners use their newspapers to promote their own business interests and advance their personal interests.[40]

Yet, by far, the most significant benefit of compulsory press regulation is to provide an independent forum by which victims of press malpractice may experience (a sense of) justice when the press exceeds its law-given freedom and so breaches the rights of others. In this way, regulatory codes of conduct are legitimate where they mirror existing legal obligations that the press is under not to, say, unduly harm a person's reputation or their rights to privacy. Of course, if the regulator operates a code that is no more than a series of legal obligations so that it can perform a quasi-judicial oversight of press interactions with others, one might wonder what value regulation adds that the judicial system does not. This is an important point, for we must see that the true value of such regulation is to provide quick, cheap, and efficient outcomes that the legal system either cannot (for want of public funding, say) or does not (through the inherent complexity of the litigation process).[41] It is legitimate, then, for the regulator to use coercive measures against press activity that causes unjustified harm to the victims of press malpractice and, conceivably, breaches the legal (contractual) rights of readers (albeit I shall ignore readers' rights here).[42]

Yet, as we shall see, there are no compulsory, comprehensive schemes of press regulation outside of Europe (and, even then, there is really only the Danish scheme that is truly mandatory, as Volume 1 demonstrated). This is not to say that there are no compulsory schemes as such. The broadcast press is subject to such regulation in Aotearoa New Zealand, Chile, Israel, Korea, and Australia. Although such regulation tends to focus on structural rather than content requirements, interestingly, several countries enforce strict right to reply requirements. Charney discusses the broadcasting regulatory regime, for TV and radio, at length in his chapter, in which he evaluates the compatibility of Consejo Nacional de Televisión and Asociación de Radiodifusores de Chile with notions of press freedom. He notes that the Chilean Press Act 2001 'contains the right to reply whenever a person or legal entity has been offended or unfairly mentioned by the media' (including the printed press).[43] In Korea, the Press Arbitration Act 2005 contains not only the right 'to request a correction of inaccurate factual news and to reply to factual assertions' but also 'a right to demand a follow-up story to a previous report about a suspect in criminal proceedings if the suspect has been acquitted of criminal charges'.[44] The strength of this right to reply is notable for its

---

[40] ibid.

[41] See discussion in Wragg (n 2) 278–83.

[42] There is an interesting discussion to be had about whether accuracy clauses are, in fact, legitimate objects for coercive regulation if it can be said the reader has paid for accurate information. See discussion in Wragg (n 2) 230–41.

[43] J Charney, 'Media Regulation in Chile: Authority and Liberty Compounded', ch 10, section 4 in this volume.

[44] A Park and K Ho Youm, 'Freedom Versus Regulation: An Evolving Free Press in South Korea', ch 6, section 4.1 in this volume.

comparable uniqueness. As Rolph says, attempts to strengthen the right to reply in Australia were met with such opposition that the plan was dropped almost as soon as it was mooted.[45] In Aotearoa New Zealand and South Africa, rights to reply exist but not, strictly speaking, as rights *per se*. Instead, the act of providing an opportunity of a right to reply counts in mitigation in civil claims when outlets defame individuals.[46]

Typically, though, the printed press is subject only to voluntary regulation, where regulation exists at all. India represents a fascinating exception to this rule. As Annappa Nagarathna explains, the Press Council of India operates a mandatory scheme in that all journalists at newspapers and news agencies are captured by their regulatory remit.[47] Accordingly, under the Press Council Act 1978, the Council is empowered to hear complaints concerning any breach of the code. Nevertheless, this generous remit is somewhat constrained by the pronounced inhibitions on its ability to deal with breaches effectively. Thus, although the Council has the power to both 'warn, admonish, or censure' unethical journalistic conduct or content, and may, if it is 'necessary or expedient in the public interest to do so', instruct an outlet to publish 'any particulars relating to any inquiry', these powers have a symbolic quality given that the Act provides the Council with no punitive powers as such to enforce these provisions should they be ignored by the wrongdoer. In this sense, the 'mandatory' quality of the Indian Press Council has an unavoidable tokenism about it.

Admittedly, the fashion for voluntary schemes of self-regulation is defensible, especially in regions with fragile or emerging democratic political systems in play. As John Campbell and Suhail Mohammed explain, this is certainly the case in South Africa where the harsh censorship of apartheid government has left its mark. The Internal Security Act 1950, for example, permitted state prohibition of:

> any publication calculated to further the objects of communism, or which conveyed information calculated to endanger the state or the maintenance of public order and, from 1960, these prohibitions were extended to the objects of the African National Congress and the Pan-Africanist Congress, and their members.[48]

Such repressive measures are apparent in other jurisdictions. As we have seen, the restrictive Press Ordinance (1933) operating in Israel was only repealed in 2017 despite severe judicial criticisms, as well as restrictions, on its usage following the

---

[45] D Rolph, 'Media Regulation and Press Freedom in Australia: Problems Without Resolution', ch 12, section 2 in this volume.

[46] See J Campbell and S Mohammed, 'Free Expression of the Traditional Media in South Africa and the Constraints Imposed by Law', ch 8, section 4.3.3 in this volume; U Cheer, 'One Body to Rule Them All': Press Regulation in New Zealand, ch 13, section 6 in this volume.

[47] See A Nagarathna, 'Regulation of Press in India: An Overview of the Legal Framework and Related Concerns', ch 4, section 5.2 in this volume.

[48] J Campbell and S Mohammed, 'Free Expression of the Traditional Media in South Africa and the Constraints Imposed by Law', ch 8, section 3.3 in this volume.

decision in *Kol Ha'am*.[49] We find similar reactions to such oppressive measures in Korea which, as Ahran Park and Kyu Ho Youm explain, has taken successive liberalising steps to counteract the 'press law [that] existed in Korea primarily as the dictatorial leaders' tool against the news media'.[50] Likewise, the Chilean experience speaks to such concerns, albeit, perhaps with greater rhetorical zeal than doctrinal certainty. As Charney explains, Chile has a rich history of cherishing press freedom that extends back to the formation of the Republic in its Constitution of 1823.[51] These efforts were buttressed by further reinforcements in 1970 'in order to alleviate the anxieties of a parliament that saw in Salvador Allende's presidential inauguration a threat to the free press'.[52] India's scheme is fascinating in this light given that journalists, themselves, are empowered to bring complaints to the Council if the state interferes, or seeks to, with the fulfilment of their public watchdog function. Certainly, this is an unusual provision.

Nevertheless, the existence of voluntary schemes does at least signal recognition, if not entirely enthusiastic willingness, within the press industry that standards are important, especially on the horizontal plane, that is: the relationship between the press and its objects of critical scrutiny. An inevitable limitation of this voluntary arrangement is the less than total coverage that it entails, for those who willingly submit to the regulator's purview is usually less than the total of those that should.

This is a common theme in the chapters that follow. We see this pattern in Israel, where standards are governed by the Israeli Press and Media Council, which, unusually, is 'authorised to hear ethical complaints even against non-members of the council'.[53] Depressingly, however, 'the tribunal's decisions regarding such journalists are not perceived by media owners as well as journalists as having importance'.[54] Likewise, the Korea Press Ethics Commission is a self-regulatory body established by the media which oversees an ethics code relating to 'reporting suicide, the rules for reporting disaster and the rules for reporting general election opinion polls'[55] amongst other things. In Chile, there is the Consejo de Ética de los Medios de Comunicación Social, an 'independent self-regulatory body whose members are elected by the Federation and has as its central goal guaranteeing respect for journalistic ethics' and which operates a complaints-handling service.[56]

[49] See discussion in T Shwartz Altshuler, 'Israeli Perspectives on Press Freedom and Regulation', ch 5, section 4.1 in this volume.
[50] A Park and K Ho Youm, 'Freedom Versus Regulation: An Evolving Free Press in South Korea', ch 6, section 1 in this volume.
[51] J Charney, 'Media Regulation in Chile: Authority and Liberty Compounded', ch 10, section 2 in this volume.
[52] ibid, section 3.
[53] T Shwartz Altshuler, 'Israeli Perspectives on Press Freedom and Regulation', ch 5, section 6 in this volume.
[54] ibid.
[55] A Park and K Ho Youm, 'Freedom Versus Regulation: An Evolving Free Press in South Korea', ch 6, section 4.2 in this volume.
[56] J Charney, 'Media Regulation in Chile: Authority and Liberty Compounded', ch 10, section 4 in this volume.

South Africa, meanwhile, has a similar self-regulatory system, the Press Council of South Africa, which is empowered to hear complaints and issue adverse adjudications but whose sanctions are limited to 'reprimand or correction' rather than fines or damages.[57] This is comparable to the situation in Canada, which has, since 2015, the National NewsMedia Council, 'a voluntary ethics body for the news media ... [which] 'publishes decisions made in response to complaints'.[58] In Aotearoa New Zealand:

> the print media regulates itself through the New Zealand Media Council, a private body funded by newspaper proprietors and journalists through their unions. The Council does not have total coverage of the print media nor does it have any legal powers.[59]

The same is true in Australia, albeit the position is, in some respects, worse. As Rolph tells us, 'a key feature of the [Australian Press Council's] complaints handling process is that a complainant has to waive their right to take legal action before a complaint ... can proceed'.[60]

Historically, at least, one of the difficulties in monitoring press standards has been the difficulty in determining who should count as 'the press' especially given the industry's reluctance to define itself as a 'profession'.[61] In an important sense, this problem has become more pronounced in the digital age as increases in 'citizen journalism' has proliferated.[62] Nevertheless, as we saw in Volume 1, this problem is not insurmountable, as, certainly, the Danish experience illustrates. Moreover, as Park and Ho Youm explain, this has not been a problem in Korea, which requires all news outlets, be that print or online, to register with the local mayor's or governor's office.[63] Despite its sinister appearance (my words), this system serves a functional purpose not dissimilar from that operating in Denmark (see Volume 1). In this way, the mechanics of regulation are served by identifying those obliged (legally or ethically) to observe the codes of conduct that prohibit press malpractice.

Admittedly, the need for compulsory press regulation depends upon the adequacy not only of the voluntary scheme (for if the press were sufficiently responsive to it then the necessity for tougher regulatory schemes would be diminished) but also qualities within the legal system itself. For if access to justice presents little

---

[57] J Campbell and S Mohammed, 'Free Expression of the Traditional Media in South Africa and the Constraints Imposed by Law', ch 8, section 3.1 in this volume.

[58] D Mangan, 'Why is Freedom of the Press Adjunct to Freedom of Expression in Canada?', ch 9, section 1, fn 5.

[59] U Cheer, 'One Body to Rule Them All: Press Regulation in New Zealand', ch 13, section 4 in this volume.

[60] D Rolph, 'Media Regulation and Press Freedom in Australia: Problems Without Resolution', ch 12, section 2.

[61] See discussion in Wragg (n 2) 129–133.

[62] See discussion in P Coe, *Media Freedom in the Age of Citizen Journalism* (Cheltenham, Edward Elgar, 2021).

[63] A Park and K Ho Youm, 'Freedom Versus Regulation: An Evolving Free Press in South Korea', ch 6, section 4.1 in this volume.

practical difficulties, which may be achieved through sufficient public funding for litigation, and the law is sufficiently robust, then those that are wronged would have little or no need for a formal regulatory scheme. Australia, for example, which has little in the way of formal constitutional protection for press freedom, is known for its defamation laws which are said to operate with sufficient (or at least tolerable) reliability such that the absence of a formal law of privacy is not an impediment to justice (at least, in theory).[64] This may be contrasted with the situation in the USA where the absence of formal press regulation is compounded by tougher defamation and privacy laws that make it virtually impossible for public figures (widely defined) to obtain justice for even egregious attacks on both reputation and private life. Allied to this, of course, is the journalistic culture in any given jurisdiction. For if the press operates with sufficient propriety that attacks on individuals (rather than the state) is always confined to a narrow sense of public office holder then, once again, detrimental impacts on personal reputation and private life would be at least understandable if not always excusable.

Nevertheless, it must be recognised that, even on the horizontal plane, the interest in public interest expression can, and does, arise. As Lili Levi demonstrates, the strategic lawsuits against public participation (SLAPPs) phenomenon is of direct concern. Amongst other things, SLAPPs are characterised by threats to litigate on what are unmeritorious claims, usually on spurious grounds of defamation, against instances of (genuine) public interest journalism. The US is unusual, but not alone,[65] in having anti-SLAPP legislation in place (across 32 states). These laws 'are designed to deter meritless lawsuits brought ostensibly over the defendants' exercise of their First Amendment rights but in fact to deter protected speech'.[66] There are signs that other jurisdictions recognise SLAPPs as a problem deserving state attention. In South Africa, 'the Constitutional Court has, for the first time, expressly acknowledged that such suits can be defended where they are an abuse of process',[67] while, in Israel, there is judicial 'recognition' of the problem, but no proffered solutions as yet: the courts 'have refrained from adopting an anti-SLAPP legal doctrine and, on several occasions, have urged legislators to amend the Defamation Law so that they may contend with the chilling effect of these lawsuits'.[68]

Although we can recognise SLAPPs as a problem, we must be careful with our usage of it, for the term has an opaqueness that permits ready application

---

[64] See discussion in Rolph's chapter (ch 12). See, further, P Wragg, 'Enhancing Press Freedom through Greater Privacy Law: A UK Perspective on an Australian Privacy Tort' (2014) 36(4) *Sydney Law Review* 619.

[65] See position in Canada, discussed by D Mangan, Why is Freedom of the Press Adjunct to Freedom of Expression in Canada?', ch 9, section 2.3.

[66] L Levi, 'The US Press: A Legal Framework of Complexity, Contradiction and Uncertainty', ch 11, section 2.4 in this volume.

[67] J Campbell and S Mohammed, 'Free Expression of the Traditional Media in South Africa and the Constraints Imposed by Law', ch 8, section 4.3.5.

[68] T Shwartz Altshuler, 'Israeli Perspectives on Press Freedom and Regulation', ch 5, section 7.2 in this volume.

to circumstances that should make us decidedly uncomfortable. For example, consider the facts of *Snyder v Phelps*,[69] in which the bereaved Snyder family sued members of the notorious Westboro Baptist Church in tort when they staged a protest about homosexuals in the army at the funeral of Lance Corporal Matthew Snyder, a gay serviceman killed in the line of duty. At first instance, the Snyders were awarded US$10.9 million in damages (which the judge reduced to US$5 million). The US Supreme Court, though, overturned that decision on appeal. For, according to the Court, Phelps and his brethren were 'peacefully picketing … on a matter of public concern' and, accordingly, the first instance decision was a violation of their First Amendment rights.

Superficially, these facts bear no relation to the sort of claim that SLAPPs campaigners have in mind. Neither does it easily fit the circumstances described by the originators of the term SLAPPs, Penelope Canan, a sociologist, and George Pring, a lawyer, who invented it in 1988.[70] The archetypal SLAPP dispute, according to them, concerned civil society petitioning government to enforce sanctions for breaches of environmental law. The stultifying legal action, then, was of corporations issuing vexatious motions against those citizens on spurious grounds. For example, 'When a woman asked her city council to delay the annexation of land to benefit a real estate development, the developer sued her for conspiracy'.[71] Although Canan and Pring located the nub of the SLAPPs phenomenon in threats to the First Amendment, it was actually the element protecting the right to petition government for redress of grievances that they had in mind. In their original findings, defamation accounted for remarkably little of the threatened legal action. Moreover, it was not press speech but public protest that they had in mind when they did speak of threats to free speech.

Nevertheless, the phrase 'SLAPPs' has enjoyed a renaissance of late but in terms not entirely faithful to its original. The United Nations, the Council of Europe[72] and various governments around the world have championed state intervention to tackle what has been described as a 'significant increase'[73] in SLAPPs tactics being used to silence dissent. In this way, the paradigm has shifted to an almost exclusive focus upon threats to press freedom. No doubt these threats are concerning, especially where powerful outfits suppress, or seek to suppress, discussion of serious public interest matters. We see an instance of this, for example, in the Council of Europe's report highlighting the threats of violence and intimidation against journalists, especially Daphne Caruana Galizia,

---

[69] *Snyder v Phelps* 562 US 443 (2011).

[70] P Canan and G W Pring, 'Strategic Lawsuits Against Public Participation' (1988) 35 (5) *Social Problems* 506.

[71] ibid.

[72] See Commissioner for Human Rights, 'Time to Take Action Against SLAPPs' (Strasbourg, 27 October 2020), www.coe.int/en/web/commissioner/-/time-to-take-action-against-slapps.

[73] See United Nations Human Rights, 'SLAPPs and FoAA Rights' Info Note, www.ohchr.org/Documents/Issues/FAssociation/InfoNoteSLAPPsFoAA.docx.

who was murdered amid her extensive investigations into organised crime.[74] The Conservative UK Government, led by former Minister for Justice, Dominic Raab MP, has also promised to tackle SLAPPs through legislation although, rather enigmatically, Raab singled out Russian 'oligarchs' as the insidious threat in need of state action.[75] This is surprising given that several Russian 'oligarchs' are known Conservative donors,[76] including Evgeny Lebedev, who was appointed to the House of Lords by disgraced former Prime Minister, Boris Johnson, and whose business interests include ownership of London's *Evening Standard*, whose editor, from 2017–2020, was former Chancellor of the Exchequer, and Conservative MP, George Osborne. Meanwhile, Lebedev's father, Alexander, was a former KGB operative who acquired London's *The Independent* and *The Independent on Sunday* in 2010.

We must take the SLAPPs problem seriously, but in doing so, we need to develop a suitable methodology to distinguish what might be called genuine SLAPPs from genuine disputes. Returning to the *Snyder v Phelps* litigation, consider this: the Snyder family had filed suit against a non-government organisation with the aim of suppressing or otherwise penalising the exercise of First Amendment rights on a matter of 'public concern' (or public interest). That suit had been for what Raab would label 'sky-high' damages.[77] Some of those claims were unmeritorious. For example, the original motion included defamation, which the first instance court dismissed as baseless. Ultimately, the Court found that the interference with the First Amendment right had no legal merit.

It may be that the problem of SLAPPs is ameliorated, if not eliminated, by careful judicial scrutiny of the underlying facts. Certainly, to return to an earlier point, we do not want for legal language to distinguish outrageous abuses of process from meritorious disputes. Nevertheless, the legal system is rarely the problem in discussions on SLAPPs for the underlying wrong is, in an important sense, pre-legal. It happens when claimants *threaten* legal action. The chilling effect, then, may well happen long before the legal system is properly engaged. Accordingly, legislative or judicial measures designed to penalise SLAPPs tactics, such as punitive costs orders, only have real power if the defendant is sufficiently robust, financially and psychologically, to retain her faith in the legal system through to the end of the process, or, at the very least, to an interim hearing in which a judge *might* have sufficient access to the facts to know if the litigation is meritorious or not at an early stage in proceedings (for if the dispute relies on a contested fact pattern, the judge may have little choice other than to let the matter

---

[74] See Commissioner for Human Rights (n 71).

[75] See Ministry of Justice, 'Strategic Lawsuits Against Public Participation (SLAPPs)' (20 July 2022), https://consult.justice.gov.uk/digital-communications/strategic-lawsuits-against-public-participation/results/slapps-call-evidence-response.pdf.

[76] S Murphy, 'UK Report on Russian Interference: Key Points Explained' *The Guardian* (21 July 2020); O Bullough, 'The Toxic Relationship Between Britain and Russia Has to Be Exposed' *The Guardian* (13 November 2019).

[77] See Commissioner for Human Rights (n 72) 4.

20   *Paul Wragg*

play out). What it cannot tackle, though, are *successful* SLAPPs tactics that cause the defendant to settle the claim prior to issue or, worse, retract her published statements *before* the legal process is engaged.

Ironically, given the sinister overtones that press freedom campaigners tend to read into greater regulatory oversight, enhanced press regulation could play an important role in tackling the SLAPPs problem, at least as it relates to serious investigative journalism. For, to combat the exorbitant costs and chronic anxiety caused by the *mere* prospect, let alone the actuality, of lengthy litigation and the delaying tactics that often accompany them, press victims with access to a regulatory arbitration scheme can frustrate these characteristic SLAPPs strategies by challenging their opponent to settle the matter through cheap, efficient arbitration. This puts the SLAPPs claimant in an awkward position, for the unwarranted refusal to engage in that process jeopardises their prospects of pursuing further litigation, not least for the adverse costs position it puts them in (depending on the underlying civil procedure rules of that jurisdiction, of course). The threat, by the defendant, to challenge the claimant to arbitrate the dispute has real power in exposing SLAPPs tactics by bringing them into the open prior to, or instead of, lengthy litigation, with its attendant cost risks, and so goes some way to redressing the imbalance of power between her and the SLAPP tactician.

4. Conclusion

Our aim, in bringing together these commentators from a diverse range of legal systems and political cultures, was to shed light on the regulatory framework as it exists around the world. We do not pretend that these pictures represent a comprehensive picture. There were some countries that we would have liked to include but, understandably, could not convince scholars in the region to engage with the project, not least for the career risks it may pose (or which they perceived it to pose). For those of us accustomed to the protections that robust institutions of academic freedom afford, we may easily forget the dangers that our colleagues overseas face. We are mindful of those challenges and grateful to all commentators for the work they have done. For, in the pages that follow, you will find a collection of thoughtful, rigorous, and sustained scholarship that speaks to the passion to protect press freedom and the overarching, transcendental interest in ensuring that the rule of law always prevails and that justice is done, and seen to be done, whenever injustice occurs, and by whomever is the cause, be that the state, powerful corporations and individuals, or the press itself.

PART I

Asia

2

Between Politics and Commerce: Media Governance in China*

HUALING FU

1. Introduction

'The surname of Chinese media is (Communist) party', declared President Xi during a propaganda conference held on 19 February 2016.[1] President Xi's statement may seem extreme, but it is not new. It is well understood that the Chinese Communist Party owns and controls the media, using it as its mouthpiece. Media is defined by its party-nature and serves as a propaganda platform for the Party. President Xi's statement challenges an alternative view of the media that suggests a people-nature, according to which, the media should have relative autonomy in supervising the Government on behalf of the people. President Xi's speech was an attempt to reclaim the Party's absolute control over political narratives in Chinese society. The Party regards the alternative view of the media as unsuitable for China, believing that the media not under the total control of the Party may obstruct the Party's governance strategy and be used by hostile forces to subvert the socialist system.

This chapter argues that, in spite of the increasing assertiveness of the Party's control over the media, China's powerful propaganda state continues to face significant challenges, including those posed by commercialisation of the media, demand of public opinion, and technological advancement. Chinese media under the Party's control is not a monolith. Rather, it is composed of a range of stakeholders with diverse identities and of different and even competing interests. In fact, China's media governance is torn between two contradictory imperatives of centralisation and decentralisation, with the former pointing towards an increasing Party control, often couched in the language of absolute and comprehensive

* The author would like to thank Sida Liu, Han Zhu and the editors for their valuable comments on the earlier versions of the chapter, and KT Ouyang for his research assistance.
[1] XM Zeng, '如何把握"党媒姓党"三个关键' ('Three Keys to Understand "Party Media" Following the Surname of the Party') (*CPC News* 9 March 2016), http://theory.people.com.cn/n1/2016/0309/c40531-28185505.html.

control, and the latter driven by the force of market, social demand, and technological innovation.

Censorship and indoctrination will remain the principal agenda of the propaganda state, but China's social and economic ecosystems have changed and continue to evolve, making the Party's totalising control strategy unsustainable. The Party may have hardwired these challenging considerations into the overall media system, through reforms it initiated in the past decades, in commercialising the press, in legitimising public opinions supervision (POS) or simply media supervision, and in embracing information and communications technologies (ICT), social media in particular. Those reforms may have created an intrinsic space in the media that allows plural voices and diverse interests to survive and even thrive in certain circumstances, all within the existing political system, hence the possibility of alternative media narratives and practices even in the highly politicised and repressive period we are currently witnessing.

2. Media Control in a Leninist Party-State

According to existing scholarship, China's media governance is characterised by three core features. Firstly, it is intrinsically political, as the Party controls the media for propaganda purposes, deploying it to shape public opinion, maintain power and justify its actions.[2] This is reflected in the Constitution of the People's Republic of China (hereinafter 'Chinese Constitution'), which defines China as a 'Socialist system' based on the 'alliance between workers and peasants' and 'democratic dictatorship', and in a 2018 amendment that defines socialism in China as the leadership of the Chinese Communist Party.[3] Media control and governance is a hard-core political issue, and remains 'the first imperative' of China's media governance, as pointed out by Perry Keller.[4] Historically, taking a Leninist instrumental view, the Party took the strategies of fighting for press freedom and democracy as long as the enemy was in control, but curtailed them once victory had been achieved. The Party is keenly aware of the value of propaganda and the importance of monopoly of information,[5] insisting that the media must develop a

---

[2] Scholarly research on Chinese media include: A-M Brady, *Marketing Dictatorship: Propaganda and Thought Work in Contemporary China* (Lanham, Rowman & Littlefield, 2008); YW Lei, *The Contentious Public Sphere: Law, Media & Authoritarian Rule in China* (Princeton, Princeton University Press, 2018); DC Lynch, *After the Propaganda State: Media, Politics, and 'Thought Work' in Reformed China* (Stanford CA, Stanford University Press, 1999); M Repnikova, *Media Politics in China: Improving Power under Authoritarianism* (Cambridge, Cambridge University Press, 2017); D Stockmann, *Media Commercialization and Authoritarian Rule in China* (New York, Cambridge University Press, 2013).

[3] The Constitution of the People's Republic of China, art 1.

[4] P Keller, 'Privilege and Punishment: Press Governance in China' (2003) 21(1) *Cardozo Arts & Entertainment Law Journal* 87.

[5] Press and the freedom of the press were Western ideas that were introduced to China since the 1830s, mostly via Japan, and indigenised according to cultural tradition and political need. This

Party consciousness so that it follows the Party's instructions and serves the Party's interest, and the Party spirit should permeate the entire media sector, making the Party the soul of media in China.[6]

Organisationally, the Party has built its own governance structure and institutions independent of the Constitution, exercising its prerogative powers in controlling the state.[7] In the broadly defined media sector, the Propaganda Ministry of the Party is responsible for the control and management of the broadly defined media sector, including the press, television, radio, publication, film, and social media.[8] The Propaganda Ministry operates through a hierarchical structure, with local branches in every province, city, and county in the country. These branches are responsible for implementing the Party's media policies and ensuring that all media outlets in their jurisdictions adhere to the Party's instructions. Given the political significance of the media and the ownership structure, the Party has direct control over the appointment, transfer, and removal of all senior officials in all media outlets as it sees fit. The Party's external control is reinforced through the political mechanism within the media outlets. There is a parallel Party mechanism within every media organisation, implementing Party news policies and monitoring news work from within.

In regulating the vast media empire, there is necessarily a degree of separation of functions and division of labour between the Propaganda Ministry and the Government, as well as a separation of powers between central and local authorities. Before the Party and state organisational restructuring in 2018, media governance had four elements: first, unified leadership of the Party, as stated above; second, a two-tract control mechanism by which the Party organ and the executive Government shared power over media governance, with the Party making decisions with excessive hands-on management power, and the executive agency (currently the State Administration of Press, Publication, Radio, and Television) serving as the Party's executive arm; third, provincial control of local media, while delegating control over local media to the corresponding local Party committees and government departments, reflecting the resilience of China's fragmented political structure; and, finally, departmental responsibility, whereby a particular party or government department that created and thus controlled a media outlet was made responsible for supervising that media outlet.[9] These four mechanisms,

historical process shaped a particular view about freedom of the press – a statist view that sees press and the freedom of press as a collective right to be used by political authorities for China's salvation, rather than an individual right based on personal autonomy and free will. This view continues to impact contemporary conceptualisation and practices in China under the leadership of the Communist Party. See Y Guo, *Freedom of the Press in China: A Conceptual History, 1931–1949* (Amsterdam, Amsterdam University Press, 2020).

[6] Zeng (n 1).

[7] K Lieberthal, *Governing China: From Revolution Through Reform* (New York, WW Norton, 1995).

[8] For details of the organisational chart and job description of the Ministry, see Brady (n 2) ch 2; Keller (n 4). For a survey of the literature on the evolving role of Party in propaganda, see D Shambaugh, 'China's Propaganda System: Institutions, Process and Efficacy' (2007) 57 *The China Journal* 25.

[9] The Party of course does not 'own' a newspaper as such. Different levels of Party and state organ creates, and thus 'own' its own newspapers and exercise control over them. The Party's highest organ,

characterised by Party-state division and local separation of power, formed an interconnected, yet fragmented, control web that constituted the backbone of China's media governance.[10]

However, these regulatory features have been regarded as an unnecessary hurdle in the Party's exercise of absolute control of the media. Since 2018, the Party, through a series of decisions, has decided to shift a significant range in media management from the Government to the Party and to be placed under the direct control of the propaganda system, with the rationale of rationalising governance and maximising efficiency under the overall and absolute leadership of the Party.[11] Under the reform, the Party's Propaganda Minister has taken over from the Government the authority of managing news, publications, and films at their operational level, reflecting a powerful trend of centralisation and politicisation.

The second feature relates to the unique political functions that Chinese media serves. The truly political features of the Chinese propaganda state are not merely the negative power of censorship, deletion, or blockage of information perceived to be sensitive but the aggressive gathering of information and surveillance to inform decision-making and the positive act of moulding and directing public opinion. It is those positive acts that make the Chinese press uniquely political. Its textbook function includes serving as the mouthpiece (literally the tongue and the throat) of the Party, a function that has been well noted, and it is also the eyes and ears of the Party that monitor public opinion and supervise local officials, a role that has often been neglected. The Chinese media plays a double function of a public-facing propaganda as well as an official-facing 'internal reference' (*neican*), an internal press, which is attached to a major newspaper, designed to bring stories too sensitive to the public, but too important to be ignored, to the attention of the Party and government leaders of the respective levels and ranks on a confidential basis.[12]

---

the Central Committee 'owns' the People's Daily, for example. Newspapers thus are hierarchical, reflecting the ranking of the organ that creates it. And the newspaper is thus ranked accordingly and is a government department by rank and status but managed as a business.

[10] Keller (n 4) 98; Lynch (n 2).

[11] For the 2018 reform, see 中共中央关于深化党和国家机构改革的决定 (Decisions of the Central Committee of the Chinese Communist Party on Deepening the Reform of the Party and State Organisational Institutional Reform), PRC Government, 4 March 2018, www.gov.cn/zhengce/2018-03/04/content_5270704.htm; 中共中央印发《深化党和国家机构改革方案》(Plan for the Reform of the Party and State Organisations), PRC Government, 21 March 2018, www.gov.cn/zhengce/2018-03/21/content_5276191.htm#1. For the 2022 reform, see 中共中央關於深化黨和國家機構改革的決定 (Decisions of the Central Committee of the Chinese Communist Party on Deepening the Reform of the Party and State Organisational Institutional Reform), PRC Government, 4 March 2018, http://big5.www.gov.cn/gate/big5/www.gov.cn/xinwen/2018-03/04/content_5270704.htm; 中共中央国务院印发《党和国家机构改革方案》(Plan for the Reform of the Party and State Organisations), *People's Daily* (17 March 2023), http://politics.people.com.cn/n1/2023/0317/c1001-32645833.html.

[12] ZY Hao, '做好内参工作当好耳目喉舌 – 以陕西工人报内参编发工作为例' ('Do Well in the Work of Internal Reference and Become an Effective Mouthpiece: The Case of the Internal Reference for *Shan'xi*

Neican has been an integral part of the Chinese press under the leadership of the Party; it has been institutionalised, allowing journalists to play a significant role in collecting information for the Party and state. The *neican* press regularly gathers intelligence and collects public opinion for the Party, compensating for the information deficit that often characterises authoritarian states,[13] and offering a partial solution to 'the dictator's dilemma'.[14] Journalists, relatively detached from the Party and government apparatuses, have been entrusted to bring problems of respective sectors to the attention of leaders of various ranks to inform their decisions. For the official press, the task to guide and educate the public is as important as to inform and advise the Government, and it is the back-door communication that gives journalists special access to power and significant influences in society. It is well known that, in contentious cases, it may be more important to know a good *neican* journalist than a good lawyer, for a leader's potential responses to a *neican* report is weighty and influential in court decisions.[15]

Another significant political function of the media is its relentless pursuit of social and political impact through positive reporting and proactive engagement with the public to mould public opinion, highlighting the role of the media as the ideological apparatus of the Party. As the Party demands, the media should not only have the will to struggle in controlling the narrative powers but also be strategic and effective in exerting control, particularly in proactively discovering and guiding public opinion.[16] A particularly repressive role relates to the political use of media in silencing different voices, vilifying dissenters, and shaming political offenders, usurping the legal system, especially that of the court, in allocating criminal responsibilities and punishment, as the frequent use of naming and shaming through public confession in mass media in the Xi era demonstrates.[17]

The third feature is the visible lawlessness in China's media governance and the absence of judicial remedies on key issues such as licence, censorship and routine penalties imposed for rule violations. It does not mean that China is short of legislation to impose criminal punishment; the laws of subversion, state secrets, espionage, and ordinary criminal law provisions, in particular public order offences, have been in place. Indeed, China has imprisoned a large number of

---

Workers News) (2016) 8 新闻知识 (*Media Knowledge*) 107; W Xu, '运用内参报道推动政法工作升级' ('Upgrading Political Legal Work Through Internal Reference') (2017) 23 中国报业 (*China Newspaper Industry*) 50; MK Dimitrov, *Dictatorship and Information: Authoritarian Regime Resilience in Communist Europe and China* (Oxford, Oxford University Press, 2023).

[13] Repnikova (n 2).

[14] Dimitrov (n 12) ch 8.

[15] For research on the relationship between court and media in China, see BL Liberman, 'Watchdog or Demagogue? The Media in the Chinese Legal System' (2005) 105(1) *Columbia Law Review* 1.

[16] SW Chen and C Zhang, 'From Suppressive to Proactive?: Chinese Governments' Media Control Strategies in Popular Protests' (2019) 17(2) *China: An International Journal* 1.

[17] E Pils, 'The Party's Turn to Public Repression: An Analysis of the "709" Crackdown on Human Rights Lawyers in China' (2018) 3(1) *China Law Society and Review* 1.

journalists, professional or lay,[18] and the practice is continuing.[19] China is also at the forefront of legal protection of cyber security and regulation of data, creating a range of legislation on that emerging area that has a direct bearing on media and media governance.

It is lawless largely because there is a visible legal vacuum to govern censorship, and filling the vacuum are *ad hoc* political directives and instructions that have been issued for expediencies. Article 35 of the Chinese Constitution offers sweeping protection of 'freedom of speech, the press, assembly, association, procession, and demonstration',[20] which is qualified by a series of constitutional duties in subsequent articles and the catch-all national security laws and criminal offences. Given the dominant position of the state media and the politicisation, there is little room left for legal regulations. Law is clearly absent and silent in an area where politics prevails. Instead, the State Council, China's executive branch, stepped in and passed administrative regulations to manage the broad media field, including newspapers, television and radio, films, publishing houses and so on. The governing law is the State Council Regulations on the Management of Publications, enacted in 2001, which defines publications broadly to include newspapers, periodicals, books, audio-video products, and electronic publications and which manages their entire editorial cycle from publication, printing or copy, import and export.[21]

There are also separate regulations and rules to govern newspapers, television, and film, supplemented by more detailed implementation rules on particulars and details. Those rules dictate state monopoly, central planning of the media sectors and state control, and supervision over content. Provisions in these administrative instruments are particularly concerned with standard government approval procedures and equally standard prohibitive rules for violations devoid of any substantive rules on rights and remedies.[22] Those regulatory rules were mostly made in the 1980s and 1990s and amended from time to time, but the basic structure remains largely unchanged.[23] In Keller's terms, China's media governance was defined by granting privileges to state operators and imposing punishment against challenges through censorship and punishment.[24] The focus is on the provision

---

[18] Reporters without Borders, 'The Great Leap Backwards of Journalism in China, Reporters Without Borders', https://rsf.org/sites/default/files/2021-01-31_china_report_en__3.pdf.

[19] H Davidson, 'Chinese Journalist Arrested on Charges of Espionage' *The Guardian* (25 April 2023), www.theguardian.com/world/2023/apr/25/chinese-journalist-dong-yuyu-arrested-on-charges-of-espionage.

[20] The Constitution of People's Republic of China, art 35.

[21] The State Council, The People's Republic of China, 'Regulations on Publication Administration' (23 August 2014), http://english.www.gov.cn/archive/laws_regulations/2014/08/23/content_281474983043721.htm.

[22] Keller (n 4).

[23] For a survey of the regulatory framework in English, see HL Fu and R Cullen, *Media Law in the PRC* (Asia Law and Practice, 1996); Keller (n 4). For Leading Chinese texts of media law, see YZ We, 新闻传播法教程 (Textbook of Media Law) 中国人民大学出版社, 2019).

[24] Keller (n 4) 100.

of licences to eligible operators and prohibitive rules rather than on the rights of citizens, journalists, or newspapers, not least for providing legal remedies.

Censorship is imposed largely through informal means, situational and particularistic. Indeed, a key feature of media governance in China is its informality, flexibility, secretiveness and thus uncertainty.[25] As Chan Yik puts it: 'Propaganda work targets constantly changing domestic and international situations and public opinions, [it] needs to follow the Party's unified deployment and rapidly, timely, flexibly, and appropriately manage the propaganda work … be policy-oriented, random and flexible'.[26] What governs the media in its daily operations are not rules, which are often vague, subject to interpretation, and not able to respond to the particularistic demands of the Party in the context of a particular issue. Rather, it is the routine meetings, confidential memos or frequently oral instructions in briefings or even through telephone calls that have become the building blocks of China's media law.

These pictures become more nuanced once censorship and media control is placed in a longer historical span, and examined not only top-down from a political viewpoint but also bottom-up and inside-out from a social and economic viewpoint.

Over the more than four decades since the late 1970s, China has been pursuing a policy of gradual market reform and social and economic liberalisation while maintaining an authoritarian political system. The Party state has been managing the tension between an overarching demand for political stability focusing on order and expediency in its order maintenance, and the imperative of economic and social development prioritising rights and legal certainty for their protection. The result of that tension is the formulation of a dualistic strategy: increasing rights recognition and protection and thickening legality in civil and commercial fields, with serious and not insignificant attempts to endow rights to citizens in a broad range of social and economic matters, to create a legal framework to govern interpersonal relations with an enhanced institutionalisation of private dispute resolution in the legal system. Alongside the Party's prerogative power in controlling the media politically, there is nonetheless a growing legal sphere based on private law of reputation, privacy and personal information that has been able to place the media under some legal framework to regulate and protect the media.[27]

---

[25] ibid 96.

[26] CY Chan, 'The Legitimation of Media Regulation in China' (2018) 3 *Chinese Political Science Review* 172.

[27] China has been described as a dual state in a Fraenkelian sense, in that there is a prerogative domain defined by 'unlimited arbitrariness', and in the Chinese case, controlled absolutely by the Party according to Party rules in core and sensitive political areas, and an emerging normative domain that is more legal-rules based, rights-oriented and courts-centric to regulate interpersonal relations in social and economic areas, under the guidance of and with the support of the Party. The prerogative state is superior to the normative state and determines which matters are reserved for political decisions and what is left alone to be processed by the legal system. The lack of firm and clear boundaries between the domains defines a dual state, and in Ernst Fraenkel's words, the prerogative state has 'jurisdiction over jurisdiction'; see E Fraenkel, *The Dual State: A Contribution to the Theory of Dictatorship*

A key point to note is that, although the media itself is anchored on and woven into the one-party state and, in essence, is based on institutionalised lawlessness in the macro political sense, media reform over the past four decades has created a significant and thick social and economic dimension, which is associated with an economic logic that commercialised media must follow, public opinion that the media reflects and from time to time defers to, and technologies that the media is embedded in, all requiring some legal regulation and protection. The next part of the chapter identifies the key reform initiatives and core challenges to the prevailing governing model of media. The force of commercialisation, the reliance on media by the Party to solve its agency difficulty and the problem of democratic deficit, and the impact of ICT, social media in particular, have worked together to reduce the incentives, feasibility and indeed necessity of political censorship. Those forces have been at work in exposing the vulnerability of the Party's censorship regime from the margins and placing the existing control mechanism under significant stress tests.

Facing the challenges, the Party has adapted itself in adjusting the control strategies. Under the new design, the Party allowed commercialisation of the media without privatisation, opened up the media sector for competition without liberalisation, introduced transparency and accountability without democratisation, and created a degree of legality without the rule of law.[28] The Party has remained in firm control of media governance, but also allowing legal regulation to play a role within a larger realm of tolerance and freedom.

3. Commercialisation without Liberalisation

When China embarked on its incremental market reform in the 1990s, the press that was created by the gigantic propaganda state became a huge financial liability for the Party and was placed under enormous stress. It was also fundamentally discredited as China slowly progressed out of the political chaos of the Cultural Revolution in which the press played an instrumental role. Unable to continue to pay for the discredited mouthpieces, the Party felt the pain and need to reform the media outlets, or most of it outside the core, such that they could survive on their own financially and also regain its credibility, while allowing the Party to maintain political control. The entry point to achieve the goal was to force commercialisation of the vast media sectors to reduce financial burdens

---

(Oxford, Oxford University Press, 2010) 67. For the application to China, see E Pils, 'China's Dual State Revival Under Xi Jinping' (2023) 46(3) *Fordham International Law Journal* 339; HL Fu, 'Between the Prerogative and the Normative States: The Evolving Power to Detain in China's Political-Legal System' (2022) 16 *The Law and Ethics of Human Rights* 61.

[28] ME Roberts, *Censored: Distraction and Diversion Inside China's Great Firewall* (Princeton, Princeton University Press, 2018).

on the state.[29] Or in Daniela Stockmann's words, it was to put the Party's propaganda for sale.[30]

The marketisation involved a plethora of initiatives and innovations which brought a sudden and significant challenge to the structure and propagandist nature of the press in China. The Party allowed commercial advertisement in 1981 to benefit the media; and it ordered the reduction of a number of newspapers as part of a larger exercise to reduce the financial burden on the local governments; it created a dualistic structure by separating the political, propaganda-geared press (the so-called institutional press) from the commercialised, market-oriented press, with profits generated from the latter to subsidise the former. As Qian Gang and David Bandurski observed, commercialisation witnessed the emergence of 'a myriad of metro newspapers (commercially oriented daily tabloids or broadsheets) spiced up official news with consumer-relevant lifestyle entertainment and sports coverage'.[31] Or in Anne-Marie Brady's words, while Party papers remain propagandistic and thus politically correct, 'their subsidiary papers are the real money-spinners, publishing tabloid-style scandal sheets which appeal to a mass audience'.[32]

Instead of a total domination of the *People's Daily* and the China Central Television (CCTV), there has emerged a degree of diversity in the media sector, characterised by local control, local news and local dynamics, all geared to compete for revenues and influences.[33] There are also more commercially sophisticated reforms. The Party consolidated the commercial outlets and formed gigantic media amalgam through acquisitions or policy interventions to become commercially competitive domestically and internationally; it corporatised and securitised media conglomerates subjecting the media to the market; it piloted on contracting out of non-editorial functions to private partners to attract investment and management skills; it even allowed, for a short period of time, overseas investment to improve management, professionalise journalists, and enhance the competitive edge.[34]

Commercialisation brought a harbinger of change, causing a significant shift in media governance regarding the Party–media, media–reader and media–journalist

---

[29] G Qian and D Bandurski, 'China's Emerging Public Sphere: The Impact of Media Commercialization, Professionalism, and the Internet in an Era of Transition' in SL Shirk (ed), *Changing Media, Changing China* (Oxford, Oxford University Press, 2011); SL Hu, 'The Rise of the Business Media in China' in ibid; D Miao, 'Between Propaganda and Commercials: Chinese Television Today' in ibid. See also Lynch's rich analysis of the commercialisation process and its social consequences, Lynch (n 2).

[30] Stockmann (n 2).

[31] Qian and Bandurski (n 29) 41.

[32] Brady (n 2) 83.

[33] Stockmann (n 2) 5.

[34] YZ Zhao, 'From Commercialization to Conglomeration: The Transformation of the Chinese Press within the Orbit of the Party State' (2000) 50(2) *Journal of Communication* 3. The wide-ranging reform also caused political alarm on the political risk a free-wheeling media may pose. Of course, commercialisation decisively did not lead to the privatisation of the press. After a brief experiment of semi-private press in Shanghai in the late 1980s, and in Guangzhou in the early 1990s, the press was put under the firm control of the Party, which has remained the case to this day.

relations. The first and foremost change was a new and alternative logic that a commercialised press must follow. Having been pushed to the market to survive, largely on its own, the commercialised media had to prioritise its bottom line, and to allow it to take readers' preferences seriously. Once the market became a key consideration, newspapers developed deference to the hands that feed them, and those outlets which were dependent on commercialisation had to shift their priorities from propaganda to reader-preference. For the first time in the People's Republic, for a large part of the press, political propaganda was no longer the only function, and was not even the principal function. Newspapers that were market-conscious were less politically alert or politically relevant, for a newspaper that relied on advertisement revenue necessarily had to rebalance political loyalty and popular taste.[35]

A commercialised media encouraged competition in multi-faceted ways to improve its management, readership, and profitability, bringing choices to readers, forcing newspapers to produce content that could attract readers, increase circulation, and draw advertisement, hence the development of a reader-focused and circulation-driven press, similar to overseas counterparts at the operational level, thus opening the door for learning from foreign practices in managing media as a business. As the media treaded the commercialising path, it shifted its focus and priorities in resource allocation from the editorial department to the advertisement department. As the newspaper got thicker in its daily edition, and also became more specialised in its target reader groups, it also became more informative, educational and entertaining, if not exciting. In highly commercialised settings where competition is intense, censorship was a secondary concern outside the highly politicised zone of strict prohibition. Reduced censorship and specialisation in turn enhanced credibility, leading in a common perception that commercialised press was 'unofficial', therefore more credible in the eyes of readers.[36]

A commercialised newspaper was more decentralised and placed firmly under local control and management. As a result, the media became localised, reporting on local news and commenting on locally relevant matters. They became more responsive to local circumstances, decisively overcoming the highly centralised, politicised and standardised press that used to characterise China. It was sarcastically stated that newspapers across China were all the same except for the names of the papers! Commercialisation certainly flattened the Chinese media, in content if not in ideology, transforming it from a hierarchy to a horizontal structure with regional diversity and competition.

Decentralisation created the possibility and incentives for different regions and cities to prioritise, specialise, and develop their comparative advantages.[37] The

---

[35] Lynch (n 2); Stockmman (n 2).

[36] Stockmann (n 2) 12.

[37] Examples include social media in Shenzhen, critical press in Guangzhou, popular television in Hunan, and the Chinese Hollywood in the Huanzhou and Shanghai region. See Lei (n 2) 75.

most commercialised and successful newspapers were and continue to be located in the three metropolises of Guangzhou, Beijing, and Shanghai with a higher level of economic growth, higher level of internationalisation, and longer tradition of commercialised press. Guangzhou has enjoyed the most vibrant press in China due, to a significant degree, to its adjacency to Hong Kong and the direct and tacit influences of Hong Kong's free-wheeling press.

Those successful news metropolises in turn created a vibrant market for journalists and journalism. Many young and talented reporters swamped the big cities where commercialised press thrived, working on contract terms and were paid on a piece-work basis and depending on the readability of their publication.

The market produced its own problems for the media sector that called for action and re-regulation. Once the Party loosened its political grip over the media, all hell broke loose, leading to a near 'narcotisation' of society in which political control and legal regulation were equally absent.[38] The chief concern was by far not the ideological nonconformity or a journalist-led rebellion. There were significant concerns over unregulated advertising, defamation and vilification, violation of copyrights, prevalent obscene, and violent materials, or otherwise 'uncivil' speeches,[39] while the Party devotes most of its scarce resources to control political speech, leaving commercial speech and other non-political types of speech largely 'free'.[40]

The chief challenge was corruption within the media profession.[41] As it happened, commercialisation of the media sector was part of the larger political drive for further marketisation in the aftermath of the crackdown in 1989, and corruption had since emerged as a pervasive problem common to all the sectors in China. The media was no exception, and the pursuit of profits in the emerging market, without political discipline or legal control, provided ample opportunity and incentive for corrupt and unethical journalistic conduct. Corruption in the news media became such an important issue that regulatory attention shifted from political compliance to ethical journalism. The question was how unruly and corrupt journalism could be reined in and made accountable. The 2005 Newspapers Rules, for example, pay more attention to the ethical standing of media organisations and the journalists, requiring compliance with advertising rules, a clear separation of journalists from the advertising team, and a strict prohibition of paid-for news in any form, compulsory prescription of newspapers,

---

[38] Lynch (n 2).

[39] GB Yang, 'Co-Evolution of the Internet and Civil Society in China' (2003) 43(3) *Asian Survey* 405; Min Jiang, 'The Co-Evolution of the Internet, (Un)Civil Society, and Authoritarianism in China' in J deLisle, A Goldstein and GB Yang (eds), *The Internet, Social Media, and a Changing China* (Pennsylvania, University of Pennsylvania Press, 2016).

[40] R Cullen and HL Fu, 'Seeking Theory from Experience: Media Regulation in China' (1998) 5 *Democratization* 155.

[41] R Li, 'Media Corruption: A Chinese Characteristic' (2013) 116 *Journal of Business Ethics* 297; D Bandurski, 'China Leads the World in Media Corruption, Says Expert' (*China Media Project* 23 January 2015), https://chinamediaproject.org/2015/01/23/expert-chinas-leads-the-world-in-media-corruption.

and other unethical and prohibition of requesting and accepting any money, property or any other interest in the news-gathering process.[42]

Market reform within the media has continued, and corruption prevention has also become an emerging media law in China in the form of a code of conduct, ethical standards and legal regulations. Commercial interest has a foot inside the door, and the Party has accepted the necessity for civil and commercial law, such as contract, employment or intellectual property rights and professional conduct to regulate the media Leviathan, and also create some order, based on legality on the political margins. In sum, all the commercial initiatives and innovations dilute the political control of the propaganda mechanisms and subject a significant part of the Chinese press to the force of the market and legal rules, which in turn created a fresh space for a new and dynamic press that proved to be consequential in many aspects.

4. Accountability without Participation

Parallel to the commercialisation of the press, there was also a Party-initiated process to transform the media from a mouthpiece to a watchdog, subjecting the Party and government (at the lower end) to the broad POS, also referred to as media supervision.[43] If commercialisation introduced an element of freedom through market to Chinese media, POS empowered citizens to exercise the positive right to monitor government through the development of legal rights.[44] POS started in the late 1980s as part of the larger political reform in the pre-1989 era, and evolved into different streams of thought. First, POS was a democratic input and an agent of political transformation as part of a top-down process when reform-minded Party leaders called for the separation of powers suitable to the Chinese political system and used the media as an entry point for political change. As Qian and Bandurski noted, a visible change occurred when the Party started 'to treat the media and internet as the voice of the public and to respond to it accordingly'.[45] To respond to the call, Chinese journalists developed a unique identity in the political system, and openly referred to the press as the Fourth Estate, and themselves as kings without crowns,[46] proudly claiming supervisory power not only on behalf of the Party but also on the Party itself. Commercialisation brought foreign media and its ideas to China, producing enduring impact among young journalists. The idea of a transformative press quickly vanished after 1989

---

[42] The Constitution of the People's Republic of China, arts 38–40.
[43] Repnikova (n 2).
[44] Stockmann (n 2); Lei (n 2) 35.
[45] Qian and Bandurski (n 29) 39.
[46] H de Burgh, 'Kings without Crowns? The Re-Emergence of Investigative Journalism in China' (2003) 25(6) *Media, Culture and Society* 801; H Wang and FLF Lee, 'Research on Chinese Investigative Journalism, 1978–2013: A Critical Review' (2014) 14(2) *The China Review* 215.

and was replaced by the second role, which is a more facilitative function of solving the problem of information asymmetry that the Party faced in the process of market reform and political decentralisation.

Accountability institutions, such as courts with limited independence or press with managed freedom, not only survive but also thrive during periods in authoritarian states. POS was a governance idea that the Party promoted in the late 1980s in response to dual reform challenges: an enduring bureaucratic resistance to reform initiatives and emerging corruption practices that were closely associated with economic reform. To discipline a vast bureaucracy and party apparatuses at a time of social and economic change, the Party was resorting to the media to put officials in the media spotlight and expose abuses and corruption in public.[47] There were strong incentives for the Party to use the media to supervise their subordinates through mobilising public opinion. It was often said that the Chinese central Party state, lacking democratic input, faced an acute agency problem, and lacked information and enforcement tools in confronting increasingly autonomous local states and disciplining its own bureaucrats. In that sense, a managed freedom of the media could serve as a feedback mechanism in identifying and solving hidden social problems.[48] A media that is partially free is far more effective in serving the Party's interest than an oppressive and propagandistic press.[49]

Finally, public opinion was strategically used to serve as the utilitarian safety valve. A limited freedom of the press was allowed not for the sake of satisfying the democratic pursuit nor for reining in local governments and their bureaucrats, but for more effective social control to maximise stability – that was, to give the masses, directly or via their representatives, lawyers or journalists, a limited opportunity to air their grievances and state their claims in public. Freedom of expression, when managed and well-controlled, could channel grievances to institutions for resolution, and in the process, legalise and individualise conflict – thus preventing a large scale problem at a later stage. It also offered a procedure, legal or otherwise, that effectively absorbed and captured public demands, provided certain satisfactions to those who expressed critical views, and reproduced legitimacy for the Party state. China in the first decade of the new millennium witnessed annual protests in the hundreds of thousands and extra-legal petitions in the millions; they could all be seen as an exercise of the managed freedom of expression as part of China's smart governance, often dubbed as developing what many have referred to as the Chinese responsive authoritarianism.[50] There was a significant shift in the control strategy, and the focus was no longer to supervise bureaucrats in the local state but

---

[47] D Chen, '"Supervision by Public Opinion" or By Government Officials? Media Criticism and Central-Local Government Relations in China' (2017) 43(6) *Modern China* 620, 624.

[48] Repnikova (n 2).

[49] Stockmann (n 2).

[50] R Qiaoan and JC Teets, 'Responsive Authoritarianism in China – a Review of Responsiveness in Xi and Hu Administrations' (2020) 25 *Journal of Chinese political Science* 139.

to monitor public opinion themselves to control the society, which were no longer means to an end but the end itself.[51]

POS has ebbed and flowed in practice in response to the change in larger political circumstances, but it was a legitimate governance tool in the political discourse for decades before 2013. Indeed, the Party was successful in creating popular programmes of investigative journalism in the Party-controlled national network, the well-known and impactful focus of the national network, CCTV, for example, in the heart of the propaganda state, to expose maladministration and corruption.[52] The political signal from the central level was soon picked up and replicated at the local levels. When a managed exposure of minor corruption was taken as a proxy for good governance as it did, local officials will naturally be incentivised to use those mechanisms to advance their own interests.[53]

With the convergence of central policy and local interest, investigative journalism prospered. As Wusan Sun points out, because of decentralisation, the local government makes the local media a 'tool for local administrations to promote their economic policies, improve public relations and affirm their own validity'.[54] Local governments can push back media criticisms if the criticism is regarded as damaging to their reputation, and that is easily achievable given the local political control over the local media. To achieve the conflicting purposes of both launching media criticisms to satisfy central demand and not offending local agents, local media has to improvise, adapt and be tactical. Therefore, for media criticism to bypass local censorship, media outlets focus their firepower on criticisms targeting officials and government in different jurisdictions.

POS did not merely serve the central interest in a mechanical way. The local press also developed its own identity and interest in the dynamic central-local rivalries and coped with forces coming from above and below. Rather, POS was possible in China because of 'strategic alliances' among governments, media outlets and journalists. Any analysis of the phenomenon would need to take into consideration the tensions and mutual reliance between different levels of government, the interests of media outlets and the aspirations to be free and speak for the people among journalists.[55]

Chinese journalists also demonstrated their eagerness and capacity to expose scandals and some the willingness to do so at great risk to their personal lives and

---

[51] P Lorentzen, 'China's Strategic Censorship' (2014) 58 *American Journal of Political Science* 402; G King, J Pan and ME Roberts, 'How Censorship in China Allows Government Criticism but Silence Collective Expression' (2013) 107(2) *The American Political Science Review* 326; Roberts (n 28).

[52] XP Li, '"Focus" (Jiaodian Fangtan) and the Changes in the Chinese Television Industry' (2002) 11(30) *Journal of Contemporary China* 17.

[53] D Chen, *Convenient Criticism: Local Media and Governance in Urban China* (State University of New York Press, 2020).

[54] WS Sun, 'Alliance and Tactics among Government, Media Organizations and Journalists: A Description of Public Supervision in China' (2010) 7(1) *Westminster Papers in Communication and Culture* 43, 50.

[55] ibid. For a forceful elaboration of the deliberative community between lawyers and journalists, supported by non-governmental organisations and information technologies, see Lei (n 2).

careers.[56] Coupled with the autonomy that commercialisation of the press brought about, the critical culture, as endorsed (and limited) by the Party, and the idea of a free profession serving as the Fourth Estate, inspired by US counterparts, all instilled a sense of journalistic professionalism. Without challenging the political system head-on, a group of savvy journalists doubted and challenged the traditional mouthpiece role by 'pushing the boundaries of what is politically acceptable to publish'.[57] While a socialised legal profession led to the emergence of public interest and human rights lawyering, a critical and autonomous press nurtured a spirit of freedom in the two decades before 2013.

Critical journalism was managed by the Party to serve its political agenda. As such, it had its intrinsic limits and had to control any possible excesses that could implicate the central authority and the entire political system. The end message had to be a positive one for the Party. The Party's tolerance was thus highly selective, limiting to matters of social and economic rights, and follows China's political protocols. As a general rule, the media is not allowed to criticise a party organ of the same rank, and media criticism can only be unleashed by a particular media outlet with a higher rank against officials or their offices with a lower rank,[58] or by press located outside the jurisdictions where alleged scandals were placed under investigation. Local agents, who enforce unpopular policies on the ground and are at the receiving end of grievances, are, of course, easy targets of media criticism and local protests.[59] When pressed to locate causes, allocate liabilities and assign blame, criticisms targeted 'bad apples' within a largely healthy orchard, with fingers pointing at individual officials without implicating the institutions, not to mention the larger political system in which institutions embed themselves. As a matter of rules, the system had to be presented as part of the solution rather than part of the liabilities.

There are legal empowerments for POS. Journalists are assisted in their investigative journalism by the enactment of the equivalent of the Freedom of Information Act in China in 2007, called the Open Government Information Regulations (OGIR). Under the OGIR, all government departments are duty-bound to proactively, promptly, and accurately disclose information that they have 'produced or acquired … in the course of their performance of administrative management functions'.[60] Most importantly, it also authorises citizens to apply to obtain a range of government information from a government department upon request; imposes a duty on the government department to acknowledge receipt of the request in a timely fashion, and reply to the request according to different

---

[56] Lei (n 2) 84.

[57] Brady (n 2) 81.

[58] Chen (n 47) 628.

[59] ibid 634.

[60] Open Government Information Regulations of the People's Republic of China 2019, art 2. For the English translation, see 'Open Government Information Regulations of the P.R.C. (2019)' (*China Law Translate*, 15 April 2019), www.chinalawtranslate.com/en/open-government-information-regulations-of-the-p-r-c-2019.

statutory circumstances. The OGIR also provides follow-up legal remedies in the form of both agency review and judicial action if the request for disclosure is declined.[61] The OGIR proves to be one of the most frequently used legal tools to create transparency in government and ensure government accountability. It is easy to use, low in cost and clear in procedure. Lawyers, civil society actors and, to a lesser degree, journalists have resorted to the Regulations in a variety of circumstances to advance their interests. It is a mechanism that can shed light on an otherwise opaque system, and, not surprisingly, it has attracted a large number of applicants, many of them organised and repetitive. OGIR has been commonly regarded as a highlight of China's effort to build transparency and accountability, resulting in a degree of legal action and the mobilisation of a broad rightful resistance based on legal rights.[62]

The operation of OGIR has led to two criticisms.[63] From the perspective of the applicants, the system has failed to achieve the substantive goal of opening up the Government and improving access to government information. Government departments can easily deny access to information requested, and legal remedies are largely ineffective for applicants when access was declined. Legal action produces inconvenience and harassment rather than accountability. From the Government side, the OGIR, with its low cost and easy procedure, has led to abuse leading to repetitive applications by the same applicants over the same issues and the resulting wastage and inconveniences. In sum, the OGIR system is either useless for people who need it or abused by people who have no need for it. In response to the latter concern, the State Council amended the Regulations in 2009. For frequent applicants, a requested government may ask the applicant to provide an explanation for the reason behind the request and may refuse to handle the application if it is regarded as unreasonable.[64] In addition, the Government may also choose to impose a fee for processing an application in the circumstance where the number or frequency of the applications of an applicant 'clearly exceed reasonable limits'.[65]

One significant achievement in press freedom in China was made in 2003, in the aftermath of the SARS pandemic when the Government took disasters,

---

[61] For an OGIR database, see Open Government Information in China, Paul Tsai China Center, Yale Law School, https://law.yale.edu/china-center/resources/open-government-information-china; F Lin, 'Authoritarian Transparency: A Comparative Survey on Open Government Information Regulations in China' in XW Zang, *Handbook on Public Policy and Public Administration in China* (Cheltenham, Edward Elgar, 2020); HL Fu, XC Zhang and M Palmer (eds), *Transparency Challenges Facing China* (Wildy, Simonds & Hill, 2019).

[62] H Zhu and HL Fu, 'Transparency As an Offence: Rights Lawyering for Open Government Information in China' (2017) 12(2) *The Journal of Comparative Law* 417.

[63] C Peng, 我国政府信息公开制度的宪法逻辑 (The Constitutional Logic of the Open Government Information System in Our Country) (2019) 2 法学 (*Legal Studies*) 94.

[64] OGIR, art 35.

[65] ibid art 42. For an empirical study on the strategic use of OGIR to deny access to justice to repeat litigants, see J Kim, RE Stern, BL Liebman and XH Wu, 'Closing Open Government: Grassroots Policy Conversion of China's Open Government Information Regulation and Its Aftermath' (2022) 55(2) *Comparative Political Studies* 319.

natural or man-made, off the list of state secrets. This allowed journalists, legally speaking, to report on disasters as they happened rather than waiting for standard news lines, as they used to do. International press and commercial incentives with the press establishment were at work to make the declassification happen. It is true that the Government has continued to resort to criminal law, including that on secrecy and intelligence, to punish reporters for exposing scandals and disasters. There are also other subtle political or administrative means to impose effective constraints. However, lifting disasters from secrecy opened a large space for active journalism, especially on social media. Prior to the lifting of the ban, Chinese readers first learned about domestic disasters in overseas media, especially those from Hong Kong and Taiwan, before any authorised domestic publication. This was an embarrassing censorship that always backfired and has since been reduced.[66]

What are the legal challenges to POS? While the introduction of commerce into the press has invited law into the media field to (re-)regulate those multifaceted private law relations, the initiation of POS generates a set of questions that require answers from public law, such as the legal consequences of newspaper criticisms and the type of remedies, if any, that are available for victims; legal tools that would be available to facilitate investigative journalism, the fluctuations of forbidden zones in media coverage, and risks of the boundary spinning activities. Law has entered the media field again, both to empower and constrain the media and journalists.

The law of defamation and its application to media organisations and journalists have produced a mixed result. POS-generated news critique is subject to the rules of defamation, which have been commonly practised since 1986 when China's civil law first created the right to reputation and a resulting tortious liability.[67] Defamation has always been a criminal offence in private action.[68] With all its immaturity and limitations, the law of defamation has worked reasonably well and, on the face of the legal record, has developed a pro-plaintiff reputation, holding the press and journalists accountable for their expression. While POS encourages investigative journalism, it does not offer any additional protection for journalists who exercise their power.

---

[66] HL Fu, 'The Secrets about State Secrets: The Burden of Over-Classification' (2019) 14 *Journal of Comparative Law* 249.

[67] There is a body of literature on defamation in China, see HL Fu and R Cullen, 'The Law of Defamation in China' (1998) 11 *Transnational Lawyers* 1; BL Liebman, 'Innovation Through Intimidation: An Empirical Account of Defamation Litigation in China' (2006) 47(1) *Harvard International Law Journal* 33; XY Chen and PH Ang, 'Defamation Litigation and the Press in China' (2008) 12 *International Journal of Communications Law and Policy* 53; X He and F Lin, 'The Losing Media? An Empirical Study of Defamation Litigation in China' (2017) 230 *The China Quarterly* 371; Mei Ning Yan, 'The Chinese Defamation Law Four Decades on (1979–2019): Legal Rules Versus Political Uncertainties' in A Koltay and P Wragg (eds), *Comparative Privacy and Defamation* (Cheltenham, Edward Elgar, 2020).

[68] MN Yan, 'Criminal Defamation in the New Media Environment: The Case of the People's Republic of China' (2011) 14 *International Journal of Communications Law and Policy* 1.

When China was preparing for the new Tort Law, journalist associations and legal scholars, influenced by the American public figures doctrine, proposed to introduce the defence of actual malice on the part of a defendant to China, but to no avail. Without legislative support, courts in major cities in China nevertheless adapted the principle to support POS by protecting critical reports that have relied on reasonable sources and properly worded or requiring 'serious inaccuracies' in reporting on the part of journalist defendants or whistle blowers, thus creating a breathing space for POS in China.[69] However, without direct legislative support or support from the Supreme People's Court, isolated cases are of limited value in a system where precedents are not followed.

Laws have been amended and made to offer special protection of the reputation of China's revolutionary heroes and martyrs. In responses to occasional doubts and critiques of some of the official narratives, in the form of political satires, casual comments or investigative journalism, that were regarded insulting or inflammatory, the Government took a number of legislative initiatives, including the enactment of the Law on the Protection of Heroes and Martyrs and the amendment of Criminal Law, to provide civil and criminal tools to protect the reputation of anyone who had been officially named a revolutionary hero or martyr,[70] leading to a series of criminal punishment of opinion leaders.[71]

5. Technologies for Freedom, Technologies for Control

ICT has had a general empowering and emancipative impact on readers and citizens, allowing them to break through the myriad of government censorship to exercise their freedom of expression. From radio, telephone, telegram, fax, satellite, Weibo to WeChat, and Douyin among other powerful social media platforms, ICT has without exception empowered citizens to access information, communicate with each other, form communities, express critical views on current affairs, and organise collective action, even when an ICT is under tight government control and surveillance. Even the tiniest enhancement, as primitive as an audio-cassette, had exerted its freedom-enhancing power in China's unique historical moment of the 1980s, and those progressive impacts were visible and impactful as ICT has evolved over the decades. ICT has a general emancipatory power.[72] The Government has struggled to place ICT under some political control while

---

[69] Yan (n 67) 449.

[70] HL Fu, 'Duality and China's Struggle for Legal Autonomy' (2019) 1 *China Perspectives* 3.

[71] D Bandurski, 'Honoring China's Heroes' (*China Media Project*, 10 May 2022), https://chinamediaproject.org/2022/05/10/honoring-chinas-heroes.

[72] A Esarey and Q Xiao, 'Political Expression in the Chinese Blogosphere: Below the Radar' (2008) 48(5) *Asian Survey* 752; YW Lei, 'The Political Consequences of the Rise of the Internet: Political Beliefs and Practices of Chinese Netizens' (2011) (3) *Political Communication* 291.

maximising its social and economic utilities, only to discover that ICT evolves so fast and becomes more powerful and popular that it has to learn to live with its social and political impact. By 2023, China has over one billion social media users and over one billion internet users,[73] a force that is an integral part of the society that the Party has to reckon with.

ICT is particularly useful for people in authoritarian states where access to independent sources of information is severely restricted, and forums of expression are dominated if not monopolised by the Government, where ICT can deliver a much-demanded shortcut.[74] Historicising the impact of ICT on politics,[75] ICT has provided unique challenges to the censorship regime in China. Each generation growing up in China since the late 1970s battled with the Government on the use of the technology of the day to gain access to information that the Government wanted to control, and develop capacity of expression that the Government is keen to censor. From short-wave radio to listen to the Voice of America and the British Broadcasting Corporation, roof-top antennas in Shenzhen to watch the TV programmes of Hong Kong, telephone and fax machines to improve communications, and of the internet and social media to construct autonomous social communities, each ICT tool helped to bring a new element of freedom to society while the Government explored its economic potentials and limited its political risks.

In the age of Artificial Intelligence (AI), social media platforms, such as WeChat, Douyin, Little Red Book, among many others, continue to provide technological tools to improve state and society communications,[76] and to form new sites of contention in a new and more sophisticated round of cat-and-mouse, anti-censorship warfare, making POS an unstoppable social accountability mechanism and often an essential part of the Party's symbiotic relationship with ICT.[77] At the same time, the dark side of social media, including disinformation, deception, bigotry, among others, necessitates government intervention and effective regulation. The nature of the Chinese political system may have given China some comparative advantage in reining in technological giants, imposing social accountability, and becoming a regulatory leader.[78]

---

[73] S Kemp, 'Digital 2023: China' (*Data Reportal*, 9 February 2023), https://datareportal.com/reports/digital-2023-china.

[74] GB Yang, *The Power of the Internet in China: Citizen Activism Online* (Columbia, Columbia University Press, 2009).

[75] Y Zhou, *Historicizing Online Politics: Telegraphy, the Internet, and Political Participation in China* (Stanford, Stanford University Press, 2006).

[76] A Fung and YY Hu, 'Douyin, Storytelling and National Discourse' (2022) 9 *International Communication of Chinese Culture* 139.

[77] ZZ Yu, JX Hou and O TY Zhou, 'Short Video Activism *With* and *on* Douyin: An Innovative Repertoire of Contention for Chinese Consumers' (2023) 9(1) *Social Media + Society*; XT Gao, 'The Impact of Douyin (Chinese TikTok) On The Socialization of Chinese Youth' (2023) 155 (01013) *SHS Web of Conferences*, www.researchgate.net/publication/367078114_The_Impact_Of_Douyin_Chinese_TikTok_On_The_Socialization_Of_Chinese_Youth.

[78] E Hine and L Floridi, 'New Deepfake Regulations in China Are a Tool for Social Stability, But at What Cost?' (2022) 4 *Nature Machine Intelligence* 608; A Hemrajani, 'China's New Legislation on

What is unique about social media? First of all, social media is privately owned, and the ownership structure defines the DNA of the ICT platforms, which exist for profits, and political loyalty is intrinsically and logically a secondary consideration. Property rights that the Party has been promoting and largely respecting shield the companies from direct and wanton political intervention. In that sense, private law legal protection matters to a significant degree even in that politically sensitive matter, explaining the historical reluctance of the Party to allow even a small degree of private ownership of the print press.

Facing the growing power of the privately owned ICT sector, the Party has acted decisively to impose an orderly and state-driven development strategy, superimposing political accountability on the market. The measures it has taken tend to be law-compliant and implemented within the legal framework, as demonstrated by the anti-monopolistic regulatory actions against ICT giants in China.[79] They are often learned from overseas, experiences, ranging from oppressive fines to force ICT giants to comply with political imperatives to legal requirements to the taking of 'golden shares' in the companies to allow Party officials to secure key positions.[80] As long as private ownership remains, the Party would have to rule the social media from a distance and through a legislative framework. The mantra of managing the official press as a business, but controlling it as a government, simply does not apply to ICT-based social media.

Second, social media is designed to evade state control and enhance freedom, and the control problem is exacerbated due to the sheer size of netizens who are active internet and social media users. The internet, because of its anonymous features by design, speed, interactivity, and autonomy, which are bugs for the hierarchical, authoritarian government system, can bypass the traditional regulatory mechanisms and compromise their countermeasures, and prove to be resilient in expanding the realm of freedom, the freedom of speech in particular, and in making the Government more accountable to the people.[81] As such, social media is often given more credibility than official media. Within a system with state monopoly of news and their interpretations, social media is an alternative source of information, regarded as more neutral, authentic, and trustworthy. It often develops different narratives on developing events, putting the authority and legitimacy of the state media at risk.[82]

Deepfakes: Should the Rest of Asia Follow Suit' *The Diplomat* (8 March 2023), https://thediplomat.com/2023/03/chinas-new-legislation-on-deepfakes-should-the-rest-of-asia-follow-suit.

[79] AH Zhang, *Chinese Antitrust Exceptionalism* (Oxford, Oxford University Press, 2021); AH Zhang, 'Agility over Stability: China's Great Reversal in Regulating the Platform Economy' (2022) 63 *Harvard International Law Journal* 457.

[80] R McMorrow, Q Liu and C Leng, 'China Moves to Take 'Golden Shares' in Alibaba and Tencent Units' *Financial Times* (13 January 2023), www.ft.com/content/65e60815-c5a0-4c4a-bcec-4af0f76462de.

[81] Yang (n 74).

[82] Lei (n 2).

The true challenge of social media, with its connectivity and autonomy, is an associative power. It is particularly impactful in creating a virtual civil society, mobilising social forces, and organising collective actions. The emerging public sphere, powered by social media, based on legal rights, encouraged by increasing foreign support, and centred around an emerging rights complex that included journalists, lawyers and non-governmental organisation (NGO) leaders, citizen activists, advocated online and offline, first for social and economic rights relating to labour, equality, and environmental, but then moved to more sensitive areas, such as religious freedom, police accountability and disclosure of personal assets of party and state officials.[83] As Ya-Wen Lei forcefully argued, the combination of legal rights, journalistic freedom and powerful technologies constructed an emerging deliberative space on a limited scale.[84] For a brief moment, there appeared the possibility of a path 'toward greater freedom of expression, association, and political participation that would gradually erode and transform the authoritarian state'.[85]

The empire struck back. Upon President Xi's ascent to power, the Party panicked and regrouped to build a new framework to control social media. When the internet first arrived in China, the Party managed its impact by extending pre-existing control mechanisms.[86] However, as technology evolved, the Party realised that social media could no longer be contained within the existing regulatory framework. The Party adapted its control strategy to bring social media under a new model of control.[87] Starting in 2013, the Party silenced opinion leaders in social media through criminal punishment. The Party has effectively removed opinion leaders, human rights lawyers, NGO leaders and investigative journalists through criminal prosecution, disciplinary action, and mobilisation of fear.[88] It also put official media and their journalists under tight control, effectively severing any ties between official journalists with their citizen peers. It has also gone on the offensive, tapping into the power of technology to undergird its control. It has grown sophisticated and effective in monitoring and surveillance, censorship, manipulating information, and recruiting netizens to promote its agenda.[89] It has resorted to legality, often highly authoritarian in its nature,

---

[83] HL Fu, 'The July 9th (709) Crackdown on Human Rights Lawyers: Legal Advocacy in an Authoritarian State' (2018) 27 (112) *Journal of Contemporary China* 554.

[84] Lei (n 2).

[85] XG Zhou, 'Social Media and Governance in China' in T Fingar and JC Oi (eds), *Fateful Decisions: Choices that Will Shape China's Future* (Stanford, Stanford University Press, 2020) 136; Ya-Wen Lei and D X Zhou, 'Embedding Law into Politics in China's Networked Public Sphere' in deLisle, Goldstein and Yang (n 39).

[86] R Creemers, 'The Privilege of Speech and New Media: Conceptualizing China's Communications Law in the Internet Age' in deLisle, Goldstein and Yang (n 39).

[87] ibid 96.

[88] Fu (n 83); Pils (n 17); Pils (n 27).

[89] TC Chen, *The Making of a Neo-Propaganda State: China's Social Media under Xi Jinping* (Brill, 2022); Q Xiao, 'The Road to Digital Unfreedom: President Xi's Surveillance' (2019) 30(1) *Journal of Democracy* 53.

to improve and enhance its control over social media. Chief among them are a plethora of legislation and regulations on cyber security, data sovereignty, privacy of personal information and promotion of ICT, AI technologies in particular, making China the regulatory pioneer in those cutting-edge areas. While the Party leaves the control of official media largely to its prerogative power, it has turned to legality in managing the social media.

While the control over the official press in the Xi era may be watertight, the censorship of social media is at best porous,[90] even with a massive amount of money spent to make it work, as the powerful white paper movement force-fully demonstrated.[91] The social media in China is so interwoven into the digital economy and AI initiatives that any attempt to separate the regime-supporting and the regime-threatening aspects is challenging. It has been the clearly stated policy that the Party embraces new technologies and promotes digital economies, while at the same time softly managing the side effects that those technologies would necessarily bring about. On the political side, political propaganda has shown its vulnerabilities, and proves to be limited in either supressing or guiding public opinion. But public opinion can be managed. The Party is now an active participant in social media, having invested heavily to create public and personal accounts. Indeed, the Party has immersed itself into social media so deeply and pervasively that it has become part of the social media eco-system, taken for granted by netizens as partners. For the Party, the economic freedom that social media brings about will continue to be enhanced, but the associated political freedom will be placed under an effective but proper level of control. The Party struggles to bring the two contradictory imperatives to a proper equilibrium.[92] The tension between the imperatives of innovation and those of control would necessarily create ample space in social media for the Party to exercise some control, for law to regulate some activities, and for netizens to enjoy some rights and freedom.

6. Conclusion

China has gradually tightened the political space for the media since 2013 under President Xi's leadership. The Party has become less tolerant of dissenting politi-cal views and any discussion of socially contentious issues. It has enhanced its capacity to control, monitor, and shape public opinion. The Party is moving

---

[90] Roberts (n 28).

[91] GG Wu, 'Breaking out of Xi's Great Prison' (*Journal of Democracy*, December 2022), www.journalofdemocracy.org/breaking-out-of-xis-great-prison.

[92] M O'Shaughnessy, 'What a Chinese Regulation Proposal Reveals About AI and Democratic Values' (*Carnegie*, 16 May 2023); H Roberts et al, 'The Chinese Approach to Artificial Intelligence: An Analysis of Policy, Ethics and Regulation' (2021) 36 *AI & Society* 59.

towards the far statist end of the media freedom spectrum, characterised by centralised political control, extensive censorship, and instrumental use of the press for propaganda and repression. For social media, political control is more embedded, inside-out, and intrusive.

Seen through an increasingly political lens, the media is nothing but a tool in the Party's overall control over the state, economy, and society. In a polity where the separation of powers and other liberal constitutional designs are treated with hostility and decisively denied in public, and the press's narrative as 'the Fourth Estate' is now viewed not only as a cheap Western importation unsuitable for Chinese society but also as a conspiracy to undermine China's political system. Many have argued that China has returned to an upgraded neo-propaganda state and media freedom is impossible.

At times of pervasive cynicism, it is essential to look at the media beyond mere politics and high-pitched political rhetoric. There is a tendency in the literature to focus on the impact of commercialisation and technologies on a free media and the free media's impact on political transformation, asking whether the commercialised media and technological advancement would lead to democratisation. There remains the possibility that what the Party demands and what the majority of readers, audiences, netizens, and ordinary people expect may still converge on the possibility of a reasonable level of free flow of information and good governance of media, without imagining where improved governance may lead them politically. The Party control of media that is credible and effective cannot be and should be absolute and totalising. At the same time, effective and fair government intervention and regulation are needed in the age of AI-supported disinformation and deception, a common challenge that faces all regime types.

A commercialised press, an integral part of China's market economy, will continue to dominate China's media landscape, placing readers, that is, people, at the centre of journalistic attention. The Party continues to maintain political power without popular elections and is bound to seek popular legitimacy through alternative means, with the media playing an indispensable role in facilitating that legitimation process. Social media will continue to evolve to produce new tools to challenge censorship and empower journalists, lawyers and activist citizens in continuing and resuming their critical journalism. Foreign influences, subtle but enduring and powerful, cannot be ignored in shaping the culture of mass media in China, given the high level of continuing international exchanges of people, goods and services and common technological challenges, creating a powerful convergence force to pull China's media towards some common standards, all under the watchful eyes of the Party.

All of the above are moving pieces that require legal regulations of the media. Law has a meaningful role to play in mediating the complex relations between the Party and the (social) media, and between the media and society and in regulating commercialised and ICT-based media. These multifaceted relations demand legal certainties and protection, involving a wide range of legal issues, such as privacy, reputation, data, property and the more general civil and commercial law matters, alone with the issues of national security. None of these are novel nor politically sensitive that cannot be reconciled with the core interest of the Party.

3

The Uncommon Law in the Hong Kong SAR: The Shifting Norms of Press Freedom under the National Security Law

ANNE SY CHEUNG*

1. Introduction

Few legal expressions have ever gained general consensus among Hong Kong people on its importance, yet generated fundamentally different understandings of what it entails as has the term 'common law'. Although it is widely believed that much of Hong Kong's remarkable success as a capitalist city and an international financial centre is due largely to the common law system, there may be little common ground on what the common law entails. At one end of the spectrum, the common law refers merely to the formalistic aspect of judge-made law and the system of binding precedent.[1] At the other end, it encompasses the entire legal and judicial system, including what were perceived to be the values and procedures of the English legal legacy, in particular, the ideology of the rule of law, the procedural rules of the common law (eg, presumption of innocence), the developed rules of statutory interpretation, and the impressive range of human rights.[2] Equally important for the thriving of this liberal but non-democratic city is freedom of the press – the freedom of the newspapers, broadcasters and other branches of the media to report and discuss matters of public interest.[3] Hong Kong used to be a 'rambunctious media hub', enjoying much political freedom and free

* The author would like to thank her colleagues Professor Eric Ip for his detailed and valuable comments, and Michael MK Cheung for his helpful research assistance.
[1] M Eisenberg, *The Nature of the Common Law* (Cambridge, Harvard University Press, 1988) 1: 'The common law … is that part of the law that is within the province of the courts themselves to establish.'
[2] Y Ghai, 'The Intersection of Chinese Law and the Common Law in the Hong Kong Special Administrative Region: Question of Technique or Politics?' (2007) 37 *Hong Kong Law Journal* 363, 371.
[3] E Barendt et al, *Media Law: Text, Cases, and Materials* (London, Pearson, 2014) 1.

flow of information.[4] The Hong Kong Government used to proudly parade the number of media outlets and news establishments in its annual reports.

Expectedly, the continued survival of the common law and press freedom is seen by many as one of the litmus tests for the success of the unprecedented social and political experiment of 'one country two systems' when the People's Republic China (PRC) resumed its sovereignty over Hong Kong on 1 July 1997. The continued application of the common law is guaranteed under Article 8 of the Basic Law, the mini constitution of the Hong Kong Special Administrative Region (HKSAR).[5] Freedom of expression is protected under the Bill of Rights (BOR),[6] with freedom of the press entrenched under Article 27 of the Basic Law. Since then, for around two decades, the HKSAR had continued to prosper as a capitalist city, an international financial centre and a vibrant media hub enjoying much political freedom.

But the tide of events turned in recent years. In 2014, the city was embroiled in the Umbrella Movement and came to a standstill for 79 days when hundreds of thousands camped on the streets fighting for the direct election of the Chief Executive.[7] In 2019, one million people reportedly took to the streets to protest an Extradition Amendment Bill that could have sent Hong Kongers to stand trial in the mainland.[8] Although the Bill was withdrawn after months of violent protests,[9] the PRC directly legislated for Hong Kong the National Security Law (NSL) on 30 June 2020.[10] Law and order have been seemingly restored, but things are never quite the same. According to the World Press Freedom Index, Hong Kong was ranked 148th out of 180 regions in 2022,[11] a sharp fall from 18th place in 2002.[12] This is indeed alarming and worrying as the respect for the press sheds light on

---

[4] D Weisenhaus, *Hong Kong Media Law: A Guide for Journalists and Media Professionals*, 2nd edn (Hong Kong, Hong Kong University Press, 2014) 1.

[5] Article 27 of the Basic Law of the Hong Kong Special Administrative Region of the People's Republic of China, adopted at the Third Session of the Seventh National People's Congress on 4 April 1990, promulgated by Order No 26 of the President of the People's Republic of China on 4 April 1990, effective as of 1 July 1997.

[6] Hong Kong Bill of Rights Ordinance (Cap 383) (HKBORO), s 8(16).

[7] J Kaiman, 'Hong Kong's Umbrella Revolution – the Guardian Briefing' *The Guardian* (30 September 2014), www.theguardian.com/world/2014/sep/30/-sp-hong-kong-umbrella-revolution-pro-democracy-protests.

[8] The Bill was formally known as the Fugitive Offenders and Mutual Legal Assistance in Criminal Matters Legislation (Amendment) Bill 2019; 'China Extradition Bill: More Protests in Hong Kong over Law Change' (*BBC*, 17 June 2019), www.bbc.co.uk/newsround/48573125.

[9] H Chan, 'Explainer: Hong Kong's Five Demands – Withdrawal of the Extradition Bill' *Hong Kong Free Press* (23 December 2019), https://hongkongfp.com/2019/12/23/explainer-hong-kongs-five-demands-withdrawal-extradition-bill.

[10] Law of the People's Republic of China on Safeguarding National Security in the Hong Kong Special Administrative Region (NSL), LN 136 of 2020, B2345 (in Chinese). An unofficial English translation is available at www.gld.gov.hk/egazette/pdf/20202448e/egn2020244872.pdf.

[11] Reporters without Borders, 'Hong Kong', https://rsf.org/en/country/hong-kong.

[12] Reporters without Borders, 'Reporters Without Borders Publishes the First Worldwide Press Freedom Index', (October 2002), https://rsf.org/en/reporters-without-borders-publishes-first-worldwide-press-freedom-index-october-2002.

how freedom of the ordinary people is respected in other aspects and how tolerant a government is of dissenting voices.

In the seminal work, *Four Theories of the Press*, Fred Siebert and his colleagues argued that the scope of freedom the press will enjoy depends much on the political systems in society.[13] The NSL provides a critical intersecting point for us not only to review the continued operation of the 'one country two systems' model but the exercise of press freedom in the HKSAR. Other than analysing the legal provisions of the NSL and the judicial interpretation of relevant cases affecting the media, the study of press freedom in the HKSAR must be examined in the larger national security roadmap of the PRC. Under the leadership of President Xi Jinping, there was a significant development in the operation of the 'one country two systems' policy in the HKSAR in light of a new holistic approach to national security outlined in a White Paper of 2014.[14] In addition, the PRC enacted a nationwide NSL in 2015, expressly placing responsibility on the HKSAR to safeguard national security.[15] As a result, the HKSAR must follow the new agenda on national security instead of having a dual system of national security as contemplated under Article 23 of the Basic Law.

This chapter argues that the enactment of NSL on 30 June 2020 signifies an important milestone in the development of the 'uncommon' law in the HKSAR: a move towards a system of 'common law with Chinese characteristics', and rendering the common law operating in the HKSAR uncommon among that of other jurisdictions in the democratic common law world. Section 2 of this chapter begins by explaining briefly the historical development of the common law, which was not particularly conducive to the protection of freedom of expression. It is the International Covenant on Civil and Political Rights (ICCPR), implemented through the Hong Kong Bill of Rights Ordinance (HKBORO) and the Basic Law that 'have done more to guarantee protection of fundamental rights than the common law could do unaided'.[16] This is illustrated in a period of 'constitutional common law'[17] actively implemented by the courts between 1991, and the early years after the handover. However, this understanding is undergoing a gradual but fundamental change under the new holistic approach for protecting national

---

[13] FS Siebert, W Schramm and T Peterson, *Four Theories of the Press: The Authoritarian, Libertarian, Social Responsibility, and Soviet Communist Concepts of What the Press Should Be and Do*, 3rd edn (Champaign, University of Illinois Press, 1984).

[14] Information Office of the State Council of the PRC, White Paper, 'The Practice of the "One Country, Two Systems" Policy in the Hong Kong Special Administrative Region' (10 June 2014), http://english.www.gov.cn/archive/white_paper/2014/08/23/content_281474982986578.htm.

[15] See art 11 of the National Security Law of the PRC, adopted at the 15th session of the Standing Committee of the Twelfth National People's Congress of the People's Republic of China on 1 July 2015.

[16] Sir A Mason, 'The Role of the Common Law in Hong Kong' in J Young and R Lee (eds), *The Common Law Lecture Series 2005* (Hong Kong, Faculty of Law of the University of Hong Kong, 2005) 15.

[17] EC Ip, 'The Politics of Constitutional Common Law in Hong Kong Under Chinese Sovereignty' (2016) 25 *Washington International Law Journal* 565. The term 'constitutional common law' was first used by Henry P Monaghan in the US context. See HP Monaghan, 'Constitutional Common Law' (1975) 89(1) *Harvard Law Review* 1–3.

security adopted by the PRC in 2014 under President Xi's leadership. Section 3 then examines the impact on press freedom in the context of the 'uncommon' law in Hong Kong under NSL in three areas: the changing norms of freedom of the press set by the NSL, the protection of journalistic sources, and the freedom to publish, self-censorship and continued survival of media outlets.

2. From Common to Uncommon Law

2.1. The English Common Law Legacy

In 2018, Justice Robert Tang PJ, in delivering his retirement and farewell speech, reminded us that 'unless adequately controlled by the application of human rights law, the common law can be misused'.[18] He urged us to be vigilant in guarding our freedom, including freedom of the press, rule of law and independence of the judiciary.[19] What Justice Tang has highlighted in his cautionary note is the 'protean power' of the common law,[20] which can be used as a double-edged sword – for oppression as well as protection of civil liberties. By nature, the common law made by judges is vulnerable to ordinary legislative repeal. Consistent with the doctrine of parliamentary supremacy long practised in the United Kingdom, it is the legislature that is the supreme law-making body that can make and unmake law. The virtues of the common law are heavily dependent on the political tradition of government restraint, and the underlying principles of that legal tradition, such as free trial, habeas corpus and due process. Scholars have asserted that the common law has provided a poor foundation for protecting civil liberties and curbing the power of the Government. Yash Ghai pointed out that when the common law was transplanted into the former colonies of Kenya and India, one had witnessed only how a system of 'perverse rule of law' was being widely practised, where discrimination and arbitrary use of power were formally endorsed by the legal and judicial systems.[21] Likewise, Peter Wesley-Smith documented the racist and anti-Liberal period of the common law in the colonial days of Hong Kong.[22]

On the specific protection of freedom of speech, Geoffrey Robertson and Andrew Nicol in going through a brief history of the development of this right

---

[18] R Tang, 'Farewell Sitting for the Honourable Mr Justice Tang PJ on 22 October 2018' [16], www.hkcfa.hk/filemanager/speech/en/upload/1217/upload%20-%20Farewell%20Sitting%20Speech%20(Final%20Version).pdf.

[19] ibid [12] and [19].

[20] ibid [16].

[21] Ghai (n 2) 365.

[22] P Wesley-Smith, 'Anti-Chinese Legislation in Hong Kong' in MK Chan and JD Young (eds), *Precarious Balance: Hong Kong Between China and Britain, 1842–1992* (Hong Kong, Hong Kong University Press, 1994).

from the common law in England dating back from 1275 to the Human Rights Act of 1998 have concluded that the common law never adopted a free speech principle.[23] For example, they argued that the crime of sedition has a long history, tracing back to 1476, and was invoked freely against 'aggrieved colonists in America' in the late eighteenth century, indirectly contributing to the American Revolution.[24] While a complete absence of the common law principle of freedom of speech may be a radical claim to some, it is agreed generally that the scope of this common law right, if it exists, was much more limited than the right under the Human Rights Act,[25] which has incorporated into English law the right to freedom of expression under the European Convention for the Protection of Human Rights and Fundamental Freedoms (ECHR).

It was not until the twentieth century and after the Second World War that there was a gradual change in the understanding of the nature of the common law. Much credit is due to the international human rights movement with the adoption of the Universal Declaration of Human Rights by the United Nations in 1948. Following the ICCPR and the ECHR, the human rights spirit was reinvented in the common law in England,[26] and the development of 'constitutional common law' in various commonwealth countries.[27] The common law has now evolved and come to be valued for its libertarian values and protection of human rights, entrenched through various national constitutions. Often, it is the constitution or bill of rights that provides the moral and legal authority to the common law, enabling judges to actively exercise constitutional review powers.[28] Research shows that courts in entrenched parliamentary democracies in the Commonwealth have assumed greater power to protect individual rights.[29]

The development of the common law in Hong Kong closely followed the above pattern.[30] In the context of freedom of expression, criminal prosecutions under libel law were used frequently by the colonial Government against newspaper editors for criticism of government policies in the early days of British rule (1842–1890) in Hong Kong.[31] Sedition law was imported by the British colonial rulers to Hong Kong to criminalise speech likely to incite others to insurrection or public disorder.[32] After the Second World War, there were two notorious cases

---

[23] G Robertson and AGL Nicol, *Media Law*, 5th edn (Mytholmroyd, Sweet & Maxwell, 2007) 7.

[24] ibid 4–5.

[25] Barendt et al (n 3) 2.

[26] Robertson and Nicol (n 23) 40.

[27] Ip (n 17).

[28] S Gardbaum, *The New Commonwealth Model of Constitutionalism: Theory and Practice* (Cambridge, Cambridge University Press, 2013).

[29] EC Ip, *Hybrid Constitutionalism: The Politics of Constitutional Review in the Chinese Special Administrative Regions* (Cambridge, Cambridge University Press, 2019) 1.

[30] J Chan and CL Lim, 'Interpreting Constitutional Rights and Permissible Restrictions' in J Chan and CL Lim (eds), *Law of the Hong Kong Constitution*, 3rd edn (Singapore, Sweet & Maxwell, 2021).

[31] M Ng, *Political Censorship in British Hong Kong: Freedom of Expression and the Law (1842–1997)* (Cambridge, Cambridge University Press, 2022).

[32] For history of sedition law in England, see Robertson and Nicol (n 23) 2. For history of sedition law in Hong Kong, see HL Fu, 'Past and Future Offences of Sedition in Hong Kong' in HL Fu,

of prosecution against the press under the then Sedition Ordinance, and the last prosecution was in the 1960s.[33] Although the common law crimes of criminal libel and sedition were rarely charged in the post war period, the archaic and oppressive side of the common law system unfortunately has been retained in the Hong Kong legal system.[34] The offences of criminal defamation,[35] sedition,[36] and scandalising the court[37] remain in the law books of the HKSAR.

In 1976, the UK Government ratified the ICCPR, and extended those rights to Hong Kong except with various reservations concerning immigration, election, and self-determination.[38] The ICCPR requires state parties to protect citizens' freedom of expression, right to hold opinions and right to hold a peaceful assembly, amongst other rights considered to derive from the inherent dignity of the human person. However, the Hong Kong Government did not give legal effect to the rights and freedoms protected under the ICCPR until 1991 when there were only six years left before Hong Kong's sovereignty was to return to China. In the run up to 1997, the British Hong Kong Government made hasty attempts to liberalise the colony and the law.[39]

In June 1991, the HKBORO was enacted as a means of bolstering the confidence of Hong Kong residents after the June 1989 military crackdown against student protesters in Beijing. The purpose of the Ordinance was to incorporate the ICCPR into Hong Kong law.[40] The Ordinance enjoyed entrenched status through the Letters Patent,[41] a colonial constitutional instrument. Its superior

---

CJ Petersen, and SNM Young (eds), *National Security and Fundamental Freedoms* (Hong Kong, Hong Kong University Press, 2005) 217.

[33] In 1952, *Wen Wei Pao*, a pro-China newspaper, was prosecuted for the publication of libellous material and sedition. *Fei Yi Ming and Lee Tsung Ying v The Crown* (1952) 36 HKLR 133. In 1967, the Leftist newspapers, the *Afternoon News*, the *Hong Kong Evening News* and the *Tin Fung Daily News* were charged and convicted of sedition and false reporting. Apparently the second case was not reported in the official report but was discussed in various writings, see, eg, Ng (n 31) 119.

[34] Under s 5 of the Defamation Ordinance (Cap 21), any malicious publication of a defamatory libel is treated as a criminal offence. Anyone convicted is liable to imprisonment for two years and subject to a fine.

[35] Defamation Ordinance (Cap 21), s 5.

[36] Crimes Ordinance (Cap 200), s 9.

[37] *Wong Yeung Ng v Secretary of Justice* [1999] 2 HKLRD 293.

[38] '4. International Covenant on Civil and Political Rights', *United Nations Treaty Collection*, https://treaties.un.org/Pages/ViewDetails.aspx?chapter=4&clang=_en&mtdsg_no=IV-4&src=IND; updated background brief prepared by the Legislative Council Secretariat for the meeting on 4 January 2018: Reports of the Hong Kong Special Administrative Region in the light of the International Covenant on Civil and Political Rights, Legislative Council Secretariat (2018), www.legco.gov.hk/yr17-18/english/panels/ca/papers/ca20180104cb2-602-4-e.pdf; N Jayawickrama, 'Hong Kong and the International Protection of Human Rights' in R Wacks (ed), *Human Rights in Hong Kong* (Oxford, Oxford University Press, 1992) 120.

[39] For example, all provisions relating to the control and suppression of local newspapers under the Control of Publication Consolidation Ordinance (Cap 268) enacted in 1951 were repealed in 1987, leaving only the offence of publishing false news to be re-enacted as s 27 of the Public Order Ordinance. Later in 1989, the false news offence was removed from the statute.

[40] The purpose was stated in s 2(3) of the HKBORO.

[41] Art VII(3) of Hong Kong Letters Patent 1991 (No 2), passed under the Great Seal of the Realm Amending the Hong Kong Letters Patent 1917 to 1990.

status was repealed by the Standing Committee of the National People's Congress (NPCSC) in February 1997,[42] but the Court of Final Appeal (CFA) has interpreted Article 39 of the Basic Law, which states that provisions of the ICCPR as applied to Hong Kong shall remain in force, as conferring power on the Hong Kong courts to strike down legislation for non-compliance with the ICCPR.[43]

For the first time Hong Kong had a codified, justiciable, legislative provision guaranteeing freedom of expression in the form of Article 16 of the BOR, which is a replica of Article 19 of the ICCPR. Article 16(2) of the BOR defines freedom of expression to include freedom to seek, receive and impart information and ideas of all kinds through any media of one's choice. The general understanding is that this protects freedom of the press. However, Article 16(2) is subject to Article 16(3), which allows restrictions to be imposed on the exercise of this right if clearly provided by law, and if necessary for the protection of reputations, national security, public order, and public health and morals.

The Hong Kong courts have made some audacious attempts to affirm press freedom in this area. Although section 7 of the HKBORO only allows individuals to invoke the Ordinance against the Government, judges have allowed BOR arguments to be used in litigation between private individuals.[44] After 1997, in the early years of post-handover, judges also made a bold move by resetting the standard for common law libel actions arguing broader protection of the defendant's rights in defamation actions under the BOR and the Basic Law, the latter protects explicitly freedom of the press under Article 27. In *Tse Wai Chun Paul v Cheng Alert & Others*,[45] the CFA rewrote the test for fair comment as a defence in defamation law. It is well-established that fair comment is only a valid defence if it involves comment on a matter of public interest based on facts which are true or protected by privilege and the comment must be one which could have been made by an honest person, but such a defence can be defeated if the comment was 'actuated by malice'. The test for malice was, however, unsettled. Lord Nicholls, in writing the leading judgment, replaced the test of 'malice' with 'honest belief'. He held that honesty of belief is the touchstone, and the defence of fair comment is still available even if the comment was actuated by any ulterior motive such as spite, intent to injure or intent to arouse controversy.[46] In his concurring speech, Chief Justice Li highlighted that in a society which greatly values freedom of speech and safeguards it by a constitutional guarantee, it is right that the courts

---

[42] Decision of the Standing Committee of the National People's Congress on Treatment of the Laws Previously in Force in Hong Kong in Accordance with art 160 of the Basic Law of the Hong Kong Special Administrative Region of the People's Republic of China (adopted at the Twenty Fourth Session of the Standing Committee of the Eighth National People's Congress on 23 February 1997). See app II, art 7.

[43] *Ng Ka Ling v Director of Immigration (No 1)* (1999) 2 HKCFAR 4 [78]–[79]. See also *Comilang Milagros Tecson v Director of Immigration* (2019) 22 HKCFAR 59 [24].

[44] *Cheung Ng Sheong Steven v Eastweek Publisher Ltd* [1995] 3 HKC 601.

[45] *Tse Wai Chun Paul v Cheng Albert & Others* (2000) 3 HKCFAR 339.

[46] ibid [75].

when considering and developing the common law should adopt a generous approach so that the right of fair comment on matters of public interest is maintained in its full vigour.[47] The CFA decision was endorsed by the UK Supreme Court in *Spiller v Joseph*.[48]

In fact, in line with the shift in constitutional paradigm, the Hong Kong Government under the British rule amended the Interpretation and General Clauses Ordinance (IGCO) back in 1995 so that the press would have better procedural safeguards against executive search and seizure of journalistic materials.[49] Under part XII of the IGCO, there are specific access conditions governing the applications for production, search and seizure orders of journalistic materials by law enforcement officers, which was meant to provide additional protection to media freedom.[50] Overall, the key features of IGCO include: (1) law enforcement officers must apply before a judge from the District Court of High Court for production or search order (sections 84 and 85); (2) materials seized by officers under a search warrant have to be sealed pending any application to have the material returned by the person from whom the material was seized or anyone claiming to be the owner (sections 85(7) and 87); and higher standard will be required from law enforcement officers for ex parte application and immediate use of journalistic materials (section 85).

Justice Keith of the Court of Appeal explained in *Apple Daily Ltd v the Commissioner of the Independent Commission against Corruption*[51] that the enhanced status given to journalistic materials is to facilitate the important role played by a free and independent press as public watchdog.[52] 'The press should be able to speak out on matters of public interest without fear of reprisal, and journalists need to protect the confidentiality of the sources of the information they receive.'[53] At the same time, he recognised the legitimate requirements of law enforcement agencies may in exceptional cases make it necessary for journalistic materials to be the subject of seizure and inspection. A balance between these competing interests must be carried out.[54] In addition, judicial oversight is required not only at the stage of application but also at the final stage. In *Commissioner of Police v Television Broadcasts Ltd*,[55] the Court of First Instance (CFI) elaborated

---

[47] ibid [3].

[48] *Spiller v Joseph* [2010] UKSC 53.

[49] Interpretation and General Clauses Ordinance (Cap 1). For a background of reform, see Submission dated 23 June 1995 from Hong Kong Journalists Association (1995), https://legco.primo.exlibrisgroup.com/discovery/delivery/852LEGCO_INST:LEGCO/1223860970006976; Legislative Council Brief: Interpretation and General Clauses Ordinance (Chapter 1) Protection of Journalistic Material: Interpretation and General Clauses (Amendment) Bill 1995, https://legco.primo.exlibrisgroup.com/discovery/delivery/852LEGCO_INST:LEGCO/1221384070006976.

[50] MN Yan, 'Other Restrictions on Newsgathering and Reporting' in Weisenhaus (n 4) 186–87.

[51] *Apple Daily Ltd v the Commissioner of the Independent Commission against Corruption* [2000] 1 HKLRD 647.

[52] ibid [10].

[53] ibid.

[54] ibid.

[55] *Commissioner of Police v Television Broadcasts Ltd* [2016] 5 HKC 463.

that after the access conditions under section 84 have been satisfied, the Court still has to carry out the constitutional test of balancing required under Article 16(3) of the BOR, governing freedom of expression.[56] As will be discussed later, the protection of journalistic materials becomes a contentious point under the NSL regime after 2020.

By the time of handover, Yash Ghai wrote that the common law system in Hong Kong 'had achieved robustness, and having shed many of its colonial relics, became the bearer of liberal values'.[57] In reviewing the first ten years after the handover (1997–2007), Johannes Chan considered that the judiciary was 'reasonably Liberal' towards free speech despite a mixed record of upholding press freedom. It has been construing restrictions to the right narrowly, and applying the test of legality, necessity and proportionality dutifully.[58] Eric Ip describes the 'ascendency' of the common law into 'constitutional common law' in the HKSAR courts after the handover.[59] The common law has been strengthened by the BOR and the Basic Law provisions for the protection of fundamental rights, and the judiciary had been assuming an active role of constitutional review.[60] Ip has further highlighted the core constitutional common law doctrines developed by the courts: the Basic Law's supremacy, the living constitution, the separation of powers, the principle of legality, proportionality, the margin of appreciation, and avoidance of judicial reference,[61] which is in line with the modern development of the common law in parliamentary democracies such as the UK, Canada, Australia and New Zealand.

The high watermark in the HKSAR courts' endeavour to develop constitutional common law upon entering the uncharted waters of the PRC's 'one country two systems' experiment is the judgment of *Ng Ka Ling v Director of Immigration (No 1)* in 1999.[62] The case concerned the right of abode of children born of Hong Kong permanent residents in China. What was most controversial about the judgment was that the CFA unequivocally declared that the Hong Kong courts have the constitutional jurisdiction to examine whether any legislative acts of the National People's Congress (NPC) and the NPCSC are consistent with the Basic Law, and to declare such acts as invalid if found to be inconsistent.[63] The justification given by the CFA is based on the design of the Basic Law underpinned by the common law concept of the rule of law, separation of powers and independence of judiciary. As Chief Justice Li explained:

---

[56] ibid [34].

[57] Ghai (n 2) 367.

[58] J Chan, 'Freedom of the Press: The First Ten Years in the Hong Kong Special Administrative Region' (2007) 15 *Asia Pacific Law Review* 163, 189.

[59] Ip (n 17) 568.

[60] S Deva, 'Putting Byrnes and Hong Kong in a Time Machine: Human Rights in 2021 under the Shadow of Beijing's National Security Law' (2021) 27 *Australian Journal of Human Rights* 467.

[61] Ip (n 17) 568–69.

[62] *Ng Ka Ling (No 1)* (n 43).

[63] ibid [61]. For discussion, see Chan and Lim (n 30) 568–70.

As with other constitutions, laws which are inconsistent with the Basic Law are of no effect and are invalid. Under it, the courts of the Region have independent judicial power within the high degree of autonomy conferred on the Region. It is for the courts of the Region to determine questions of inconsistency and invalidity when they arise. It is therefore for the courts of the Region to determine whether an act of the National People's Congress or its Standing Committee is inconsistent with the Basic Law, subject of course to the provisions of the Basic Law itself.[64]

The bold assertion of the constitutional jurisdiction of the CFA plunged Hong Kong into the first constitutional crisis after the handover.[65] Despite the Hong Kong Government's unprecedented application to invite the CFA to clarify its judgment, the CFA in *Ng Ka Ling (No 2)*[66] simply gave a clarification which stated the other side of the same coin (namely, the Hong Kong courts cannot question the authority of the NPC or NPCSC to do any act 'which is in accordance with the provisions of the Basic Law and the procedure therein'),[67] without retracting its earlier bold assertion.

The CFA described the rights and freedoms set out in Chapter III of the Basic Law as 'the constitutional guarantees for the freedoms that lie at the heart of Hong Kong's separate system', and said that the courts should give them 'a generous interpretation … in order to give to Hong Kong residents the full measure of fundamental rights and freedoms so constitutionally guaranteed'.[68] Notwithstanding that the CFA's decision on the right of abode in *Ng Ka Ling (No 1)* was subsequently overturned by the NPCSC interpretation in June 1999,[69] the constitutional jurisdiction asserted by the CFA was left untouched. The principle adopted by the CFA by which Basic Law guarantees of rights and freedoms are interpreted has been repeated and applied in subsequent cases and the Hong Kong courts have continued to strive hard to protect fundamental constitutional rights by adopting a generous approach to the interpretation of the rights and freedoms whilst narrowly interpreting restrictions to them.[70]

In *HKSAR v Ng Kung Siu*,[71] despite the fact that the National Flag Ordinance was enacted by the HKSAR's legislature in compliance with the NPCSC's decision to add the PRC Law on the National Flag to Annex III of the Basic Law, the CFA nevertheless conducted a constitutional review of the statutory prohibition of desecration of the national flag with criminal sanctions and applied the

---

[64] *Ng Ka Ling (No 1)* (n 43) [64].

[65] AHY Chen, 'Constitutional Controversies in the Aftermath of the Anti-Extradition Movement of 2019' (2020) 50 *Hong Kong Law Journal* 609.

[66] *Ng Ka Ling v Director of Immigration (No 2)* (1999) 2 HKCFAR 141.

[67] ibid [6].

[68] *Ng Ka Ling (No 1)* (n 43) [77].

[69] Interpretation by the Standing Committee of the National People's Congress of Articles 22(4) and 24(2)(3) of the Basic Law of the Hong Kong Special Administrative Region of the People's Republic of China (Adopted at the Tenth Session of the Standing Committee of the Ninth National People's Congress on 26 June 1999).

[70] *Gurung Kesh Bahadur v Director of Immigration* (2002) 5 HKCFAR 480, [24].

[71] *HKSAR v Ng Kung Siu* (1999) 2 HKCFAR 442.

proportionality test to closely examine whether the limited restriction by such prohibition on the guaranteed right to freedom of expression is proportionate to the aims sought to be achieved.[72] Although at the end the CFA upheld the constitutionality of the National Flag Ordinance, it was on the basis that protection of the national flag and the regional flag from desecration, having regard to their unique symbolism, would play an important part in the attainment of these goals of national unity and territorial integrity when Hong Kong was at the early stage of the new order following resumption of the exercise of sovereignty by the PRC.[73] In giving his concurrent judgment, Justice Bokhary opined that the limited restrictions on freedom of expression imposed under the National Flag Ordinance:

> lie just within the outer limits of constitutionality. Beneath the national and regional flags and emblems, all persons in Hong Kong are – and can be confident that they will remain – equally free under our law to express their views on all matters whether political or non-political: saying what they like, how they like.[74]

In short, for around two decades since the handover, the Hong Kong judiciary has positioned itself carefully in its exercise of constitutional review power.[75] As later discussion shows, this stands in sharp contrast with the judicial stance in the NSL era in which the Hong Kong courts have essentially abstained from carrying out any meaningful constitutional review.

2.2. Common Law with Chinese Characteristics

So far, we have traced the development of the common law in Hong Kong from the early colonial period with its dark roots in stringent law-and-order to the transitional period of handover in which the libertarian aspects of common law have been reinforced by the local judiciary based on its understanding of the constitutional guarantees under the Basic Law and the HKBORO.[76] Without the constitutional gloss, the common law is a vulnerable instrument to protect human rights, especially freedom of the press. Yet when the common law continues to evolve under the unprecedented social experiment of 'one country two systems', a new set of challenges arises. While the common law system in Hong Kong is

---

[72] PJ Yap, 'Freedom of Expression' in Chan and Lim (n 30)738–39.
[73] *Ng Kung Siu* (n 71) [61].
[74] ibid [98].
[75] The final and overriding power of the NPCSC has also been demonstrated on five notable occasions. H Zhu, 'Beijing's "Rule of Law" Strategy for Governing Hong Kong: Legalisation without Democratisation?' (2019) *China Perspectives* 23; J Chan, 'Reconciliation of the NPCSC's Power of Interpretation of the Basic Law with the Common Law System in HK' (2020) 50 *Hong Kong Law Journal* 675.
[76] Ip (n 17).

intended to be kept apart from the socialist civil law system,[77] the line between them is getting blurred as the years go by.

Under the leadership of President Xi Jinping, there was a significant development in the understanding and operation of the 'one country two systems' policy in Hong Kong in light of a new holistic approach to national security adopted in 2014.[78] The holistic view of national security is a concept with Chinese characteristics, aiming to build an all-embracing national security system which encompasses all major fields including political, homeland, military, economic, cultural, social, science and technology, information, ecological, resource and nuclear security.[79] In other words, dissenting voices and ideologies which differ from the socialist ideology must now be seen through the prism of national security.

The HKSAR is obliged to follow the new agenda on national security under the National Security Law passed in 2015. It is not a coincidence that the White Paper of One Country Two Systems of 2014 was issued by the State Council earlier in June 2014,[80] which is the first official document since the 1997 handover to set out Beijing's authority over the territory. According to the heavyweight pro-establishment figure and former Legislative Council president Jasper Tsang, the White Paper was a 'turning point' in China's policy towards the city, as the concept of the central government exercising 'comprehensive jurisdiction' and 'supervisory power' over Hong Kong was first officially stated.[81] This may be contrasted with Article 22 of the Basic Law which specifies that no department of the Central People's Government may interfere in the affairs which the HKSAR administers on its own in accordance with the Basic Law. The White Paper states that 'many wrong views are currently rife in Hong Kong' with regard to the 'one country two systems' principle and some residents are 'confused or lopsided in their understanding' of the principle.[82] The White Paper stresses that the most important thing to do in upholding the 'one country' principle is to maintain China's sovereignty, security and development interests, and loving the country is the basic principle for Hong Kong's administrators, which expressly include judges of the courts at different levels and other judicial personnel.

---

[77] *ML v YJ* (2010) 13 HKCFAR 794, [114] (Litton NPJ): 'The separation of Hong Kong's legal system from that of the Mainland, as entrenched in art 2 of the Basic Law, is fundamental to the concept of "one country, two systems", as referred to in the Preamble to the Basic Law.'

[78] 'Xi Jinping: Adhere to the Holistic View of National Security and Take the Road of National Security with Chinese Characteristics' (in Chinese) (*CPC News*, 16 April 2014), http://cpc.people.com.cn/n/2014/0416/c64094-24900492.html.

[79] ibid. For the English version, see JP Xi, 'A Holistic View of National Security' (*Qiushi* 4 December 2020), http://en.qstheory.cn/2020-12/04/c_607611.htm.

[80] Information Office of the State Council of the PRC (n 14).

[81] K Cheung, 'Ex-LegCo Head: 2014 White Paper Was Turning Point of Beijing Exercising "Overall Jurisdiction" in Hong Kong' *Hong Kong Free Press* (20 November 2017), https://hongkongfp.com/2017/11/20/ex-legco-head-2014-white-paper-turning-point-beijing-exercising-overall-jurisdiction-hong-kong.

[82] Information Office of the State Council of the PRC (n 14).

The critical question remains how Hong Kong can fit into this framework of national security under the 'one country, two systems' model.

2.3. The Uncommon Law in Context – The Era of National Security

Virtually all states have their own laws governing national security. Seemingly it is also fair and reasonable for a state, regardless of whether it is unitary or federal, to have one single NSL to guard its sovereignty and territory. Yet, given the unique situation of Hong Kong under the unprecedented 'one country, two systems' model, Article 23 of the Basic Law requires the HKSAR to:

> enact laws on its own to prohibit any act of treason, secession, sedition, subversion against the Central People's Government, or theft of state secrets, to prohibit foreign political organizations or bodies from conducting political activities in the Region, and to prohibit political organizations or bodies of the Region from establishing ties with foreign political organizations or bodies.

Embedded in the Article is a dual system of national security law,[83] which 'stands at the core of tension and contradiction between the "two systems" in "one country"'.[84] The challenging part is that this controversial provision has used legal concepts under both the common law and the Socialist Party State. Out of the seven prohibited acts, subversion and secession are alien concepts to the common law system.[85] Under PRC law, they used to be classified broadly under the vague, uniquely socialist but omnipotent umbrella of 'counter-revolutionary offence',[86] which are now grouped under the equally sweeping offence of 'acts endangering state security'.[87] The absence of a definitive interpretation on the relevant offences, coupled with an authoritarian attitude on the part of the PRC Government has led to much uncertainty and worry. Before 1997, journalists were particularly

---

[83] F Lin, 'One Country, Two National Security Systems' in C Chan and F De Londras (eds), *China's National Security: Endangering Hong Kong's Rule of Law?* (Oxford, Hart Publishing, 2020) 102.

[84] AHY Chen, 'Hong Kong in China: The Project of "One Country, Two Systems" and the Question of National Security' in Chan and De Londras, ibid 35.

[85] HL Fu and R Cullen, 'National Security Law in Hong Kong: Quo Vadis A Study of Article 23 of the Basic Law of Hong Kong' (2002) 19 *UCLA Pacific Basin Law Journal* 185, 199.

[86] In 1997, the Criminal Law (Criminal Law of the People's Republic of China, adopted at the Second Session of the Fifth National People's Congress on 1 July 1979, and revised at the Fifth Session of the Eighth National People's Congress on 14 March 1997) was amended. It replaced the term 'counter-revolution' with 'crimes endangering state security' under Chapter 1, Part Two. The change, however, does not mean that the scope of what could constitute subversion, sedition or secession was different. It is still a crime to collude with a foreign state and conspire to jeopardise the sovereignty under Art 102, and one who 'organises, plots, or acts to split the country or undermine national unification' commits a crime under Art 103. For further discussion, see W Luo, *The 1997 Criminal Code of the People's Republic of China: With English Translation and Introduction* (Getzville, William S Hein, 1998).

[87] For further discussion on the offence of subversion, sedition and counter-revolution in the Chinese context, see HL Fu, 'Sedition and Political Dissidence: Towards Legitimate Dissent in China?' (1996) *Hong Kong Law Journal* 210.

concerned about the subversion and secession clauses, fearing that any reporting on Tibet, Taiwan and Xinjiang would amount to 'advocating' the 'splitting' of the PRC. Peter Stein describes Article 23 as an 'unnervingly ambiguous section'[88] that contributes to self-censorship in the coverage of political news in the above dangerous zones.

By 2023, 26 years have passed since the establishment of the HKSAR, and the local Government has not yet passed any specific legislation on national security law under Article 23. To some, this 'indefinite postponing' can hardly be justified.[89] The only attempt to pass a local National Security Bill was back in 2003 but the draft bill was fiercely opposed with half a million of people marching on the streets in protest.[90]

However, the earlier fears of the media workers under Article 23 seem to be substantiated under the NSL of 2020, which includes the equivalent offence of 'establishing ties with foreign political organizations or bodies'.[91] In May 2020, the NPC announced that it was going to legislate directly on national security for the HKSAR, a decision made earlier in November 2019 at the fourth plenary session of the Nineteenth Central Committee of the Chinese Communist Party (CCP).[92] This represents a dramatic shift towards a more direct and authoritarian rule on the HKSAR, and a reset of the equilibrium in 'one country two systems', which are in line with the 2014 White Paper and indeed could be understood as a planned move at the right time to implement the concept of the central Government exercising 'comprehensive jurisdiction' and 'supervisory power' over Hong Kong.

First, other than enacting the Basic Law, it was the first time that the NPC made a decision to legislate directly for the HKSAR, authorising the NPCSC to enact a national security law, to be added to Annex III under Article 18 of the Basic Law. Being the supreme organ of state power in the PRC, the NPC's decision is a 'solemn declaration that the content of the decision is of the highest possible legal and political authority' within the Chinese system.[93] Hence, the political and constitutional basis of the NSL was considered to be beyond any legal challenge.[94]

---

[88] P Stein, 'Hong Kong's Press: While Debate Rages About Media Ethics, Self-Censorship Quietly Thrives' (1999) *Nieman Reports* 49, 50.

[89] AHY Chen, 'The National Security Law of the HKSAR: A Contextual and Legal Study' in HL Fu and M Hor (eds), *Hong Kong's National Security Law: Restoration and Transformation* (Hong Kong, Hong Kong University Press, 2022) 20.

[90] E Tong, 'Reviving Article 23 (Part I): The Rise and Fall of Hong Kong's 2003 National Security Bill' *Hong Kong Free Press* (17 February 2018), https://hongkongfp.com/2018/02/17/reviving-article-23-part-i-rise-fall-hong-kongs-2003-national-security-bill.

[91] This is considered as 'collusion with foreign forces to endanger national security' under Arts 29 and 30 of the NSL.

[92] 'Wang Chen Explains the Bill for Decision on Establishing and Improving the Legal System and Enforcement Mechanisms for the HKSAR to Safeguard National Security' (in Chinese) *Xinhua News* (22 May 2020), www.xinhuanet.com/politics/2020-05/22/c_1126019468.htm.

[93] Chen (n 89) 26.

[94] ibid. For discussion on the opposing views, see C Chan, 'Can Hong Kong Remain a Liberal Enclave within China? Analysis of the Hong Kong National Security Law' [2021] *Public Law* 271.

Second, in stark contrast with the process for the drafting and promulgation of the Basic Law (with the set-up of a Consultative Committee consisting entirely of Hong Kong people and a Drafting Committee consisting of both mainland and local people with eminent lawyers and politicians in Hong Kong),[95] the NSL law was passed without any public consultation and without the involvement of local people. The public learnt that the law would be introduced just six weeks before it took effect, and the contents of the bill were kept secret until its eventual enactment.[96] It was considered as an 'imposed constitution'[97] and described as a 'legal blitzkrieg'.[98] Third, the law was drafted in the language and style of the PRC's Soviet-inspired Socialist legal tradition, which is fundamentally different from that adopted in local legislations drafted by common law lawyers. Indeed, there is no official English version of the NSL but only a translation 'for information only', with no legal force.[99] This is at odds with the official bilingual legal system of the HKSAR, a sign suggesting 'new nationalism that could make it more difficult for the law to be subject to international criticism'.[100] All these are so foreign to the Hong Kong common law system. Furthermore, the NSL prevails over any local laws inconsistent with it (Article 62 of the NSL), including any contravening common law principles.[101]

More fundamentally, the NSL was enacted pursuant to the new 'holistic approach to national security'[102] under Xi's leadership, with fundamentally different legal and political dispositions on what constitutes national security, reflecting opposing ideologies between a socialist and a liberal system. The offences created under the NSL are significantly much more intrusive on freedom of expression and association than those under the National Security Bill of the HKSAR in 2003 which, consistent with international law principles,[103] criminalised only conduct which involved the use of force or serious criminal means that seriously endangers national security.[104] The NSL criminalises four types of offences: secession (Articles 20 and 21), subversion (Articles 22 and 23), terrorist activities (Articles 24–27) and collusion with a foreign country or with external elements

---

[95] See 'Some Facts about the Basic Law', www.basiclaw.gov.hk/en/basiclaw/facts.html.

[96] The NPC made the decision to pass the NSL for the HKSAR on 28 May 2020 and the NPCSC enacted the law on 30 June, and the law was gazette in the HKSAR in the same evening and came into force shortly before midnight between 30 June and 1 July 2020. For discussion, Chen (n 65).

[97] Chan (n 94) 274.

[98] Ming-Sung Kuo, 'China's Legal Blitzkrieg in Hong Kong' *The Diplomat* (8 August 2020), https://thediplomat.com/2020/08/chinas-legal-blitzkrieg-in-hong-kong.

[99] See n 10 above.

[100] K Roach, 'Echoes That Build to a Cacophony: Hong Kong's New Security Law Compared to Illiberal Elements of the Security Laws of Liberal Democracies' (University of Toronto, Faculty of Law, 9 January 2021) fn 63, https://papers.ssrn.com/abstract=3763099.

[101] Chan (n 94) 270.

[102] JP Xi, *The Governance of China IV* (Beijing, Foreign Languages Press, 2022) 453 ('To guarantee national security in the new era we must pursue a holistic approach, seize the development').

[103] Principle 2, The Johannesburg Principles on National Security, Freedom of Expression and Access to Information, Freedom of Expression and Access to Information, UN Doc E/CN.4/1996/39 (1996).

[104] National Security (Legislative Provisions) Bill 2003.

to endanger national security (Article 29), violations of which carry a maximum penalty of life imprisonment.[105] These four subject matters overlap with the seven areas under Article 23 of the Basic Law. While the offences of terrorism are covered by the local criminal law,[106] subversion, secession and collusion with foreign forces are drafted in a broad and general manner which may criminalise even entirely peaceful conducts or speeches, and represent distinctly Socialist offences with Chinese characteristics.[107]

It is important to note that the power of interpretation of the NSL is vested with the NPCSC (Article 64), but there is no provision equivalent to Article 158 of the Basic Law which expressly authorises the Hong Kong courts to interpret the NSL on its own in adjudicating cases subject to the final interpretation power of the NSL. This raises a doubt as to whether the Hong Kong courts should adopt the common law principles of interpretation when applying the NSL. After all, the NSL was drafted by mainland law drafters using language common to other national legislations without any known involvement of common law lawyers. There is no legal definition of the term 'national security' under NSL and so there is a strong argument that Hong Kong should follow the novel concept of comprehensive national security adopted under President Xi's leadership and adopt the broad definition of national security under the PRC National Security Law 2015 to cover non-traditional areas of national security such as economic security, cybersecurity, and information security.[108]

In any event, Article 47 expressly takes away the courts' jurisdiction to determine whether an act involves national security or whether the relevant evidence involves state secrets, as it mandates the courts to obtain a certificate from the Chief Executive when such questions arise in the adjudication of a case and the certificate shall be binding on the courts. This moves away from the common law principle that in general it is for the court rather than the executive to interpret what the legislation means and how it should be applied.[109] In practice, an accused

---

[105] NSL, ch 3.

[106] United Nations (Anti-Terrorism) Ordinance (Cap 575).

[107] Arts 102, 103, 106 and 111 of the Criminal Law of the People's Republic of China (n 86). These provisions do not include any requirement for violence or the use of force, and could cover peaceful expression of dissenting opinions. K Loper, 'A Secession Offence in Hong Kong and the "One Country, Two Systems" Dilemma' in HL Fu, CJ Petersen and SNM Young (eds), *National Security and Fundamental Freedoms: Hong Kong's Article 23 under Scrutiny* (Hong Kong, Hong Kong University Press, 2005).

[108] HL Fu, 'China's Imperatives for National Security Legislation' in Chan and De Londras (n 83) 41, 46. The purpose of the holistic approach is to 'securitise the Party State and to govern primarily from the perspective of national security'.

[109] AV Dicey, *Introduction to the Study of The Law of the Constitution*, 8th edn (Carmel, Liberty Fund, 1982) 409: 'Parliament is supreme legislator, but from the moment Parliament has uttered its will as lawgiver, that will becomes subject to the interpretation put upon it by the judges of the land, and the judges, who are influenced by the feelings of magistrates no less than by the general spirit of the common law, are disposed to construe statutory exceptions to common law principles in a mode which would not commend itself either to a body of officials, or to the Houses of Parliament, if the Houses were called upon to interpret their own enactments.'

charged with an offence under the NSL can hardly succeed in arguing that his acts were just an exercise of free speech and did not involve national security, as it is the Chief Executive who has a final say on such a question.

There are various other provisions in the NSL which seek to take away or curtail the jurisdiction of the Hong Kong courts and the common law safeguards associated with criminal trials.[110] Article 60 exempts the Office for Safeguarding National Security of the Central Government and its officers from Hong Kong jurisdiction, and Article 14 excludes decisions of the local National Security Committee from judicial review, so that their acts and conducts done in the name of national security would effectively be immune from any judicial scrutiny. Articles 55 and 56 allow the PRC authorities to assert legal jurisdiction over 'complex', 'serious' or 'difficult cases', meaning that some NSL cases can be tried in mainland China instead of in Hong Kong, notwithstanding that Article 19 of the Basic Law stipulates that the courts of the HKSAR 'shall have jurisdiction over all cases in the Region'.[111] Under Article 44, it is the Chief Executive instead of the judiciary who can determine which judges can hear NSL cases or appeals. The period of appointment for designated NSL judges is only for one year, and there is no procedural safeguard that the appointment will be renewed if the judge makes any ruling unacceptable to the Government. The NSL has also set exceptions to some common law procedural safeguards associated with fair trials such as jury trials (Article 46), open trial (Article 41), and presumption in favour of bail pending trial (Article 42).

In essence, the NSL has materialised the worst fears previously raised by some academics: the triumph of the Chinese system over the common law,[112] the direct application of PRC law on the HKSAR, the creation of national security offences in the territory in a manner unknown to Hong Kong's common law tradition and direct control, and direct rule of the HKSAR by Beijing authorities.[113] One important battleground to test the actual effect of the NSL on the development of Hong Kong's common law is the court room, particularly decisions from the highest court in Hong Kong. It is also in examining the interpretation and implementation of the NSL by the CFA that the vulnerability of the common law is exposed. So far there is only one case which has reached the full bench of five judges in the CFA, which concerned the changing norm for bail application pending trial under Article 42(2) of the NSL. The case concerned Lai Chee Ying, popularly known as Jimmy Lai, a high-profile media mogul, the founder of

---

[110] Chen (n 65); Chan (n 94) 280.

[111] Article 19 provides that the Hong Kong courts have no jurisdiction over 'acts of state such as defence and foreign affairs', but the situations covered by arts 55 and 56 of NSL do not fall within this exception.

[112] Ghai (n 2) 372.

[113] HL Fu, 'The National Security Factor: Putting Article 23 of the Basic Law in Perspective' in S Tsang (ed), *Judicial Independence and the Rule of Law in Hong Kong* (Hong Kong, Hong Kong University Press, 2001) 87; MC Davies, *Making Hong Kong China: The Rollback of Human Rights and the Rule of Law* (New York, Columbia University Press, 2020) 8.

Apple Daily and owner of *Next Media* who is known for his fiercely democratic and anti-CCP stance.

In *HKSAR v Lai Chee Ying*,[114] the CFA was asked to give a correct interpretation on the contested provision of Article 42(2) which stipulates that 'No bail will be granted to a criminal suspect or defendant unless the judge has sufficient grounds for believing that the criminal suspect or defendant will not continue to commit acts endangering national security'.

Prima facie, the provision has seemingly overturned the common law presumption in favour of bail, protected also under section 9(D)(1) of the Criminal Procedure Ordinance (CPO), and Article 5(3) of the BOR, a freedom enjoyed under Article 28 of the Basic Law and Article 9 of the ICCPR. Arguably it is also contradictory to Articles 4 and 5 of the NSL: the former expressly mandates the respect of rights and freedoms, including freedoms of speech and of the press, enjoyed by Hong Kong residents under the Basic Law and the ICCPR, the latter upholds the principle of the rule of law, including the presumption of innocence.

In stark contrast with its unequivocal assertion of constitutional jurisdiction over whether the acts of the NPC or NPCSC are consistent with the Basic Law in *Ng Ka Ling (No 1)* (as mentioned earlier), the CFA was quick to concede (with reference to the clarification judgment in *Ng Ka Ling (No 2)* but not *Ng Ka Ling (No 1)* that the constitutionality of the NSL – any alleged incompatibility between the NSL and the Basic Law or the ICCPR – was beyond the jurisdiction of the court.[115] While the CFA acknowledged that Article 42 must be read as a whole in the context of human rights and freedoms and the rule of law values embodied in Articles 4 and 5 of the NSL, it ruled that Article 42 is a specific exception intended to operate in tandem with other constitutional rights and freedoms.[116] Importantly, the Court made it clear that Article 42 has displaced the statutory and common law presumption in favour of bail,[117] and ruled that from now on a new and considerably more stringent threshold requirement on bail application will be introduced on matters concerning the NSL.[118] In the Court's opinion, the default position and the starting point is 'no bail shall be granted unless the judge has sufficient grounds for believing that the accused "will not continue to commit acts endangering national security"'.[119] The CFA was then adamant in rejecting the lower court's attempt to reconcile Article 42 of the NSL with the pre-existing constitutional human rights regime set in the earlier judgment of *Tong Ying Kit v HKSAR*.[120] In the opinion of the CFA,[121] it was wrong for the lower court

---

[114] *HKSAR v Lai Chee Ying* [2021] HKCFA 3, (2021) 24 HKCFAR 33.
[115] ibid [33]–[37]. For comments, see J Chan, 'Judicial Responses to the National Security Law: HKSAR v Lai Chee Ying' (2021) 51 *Hong Kong Law Journal* 1.
[116] *Lai Chee Ying* (n 114) [42].
[117] ibid [67].
[118] ibid [53].
[119] ibid.
[120] *Tong Ying Kit v HKSAR* [2020] HKCFI 2133.
[121] *Lai Chee Ying* (n 114) [71]–[80].

to interpret Article 42 not as a 'no-bail' provision,[122] to adopt the common law approach in the construction of the NSL,[123] or to construe Article 42 as far as reasonably possible in a manner consistent with the protection of other fundamental rights under the Basic Law and the BOR.[124]

Johannes Chan, in a case commentary, criticised the CFA judgment as disappointing and unsettling.[125] He argued that the CFA has adopted a literal interpretation of Article 42, and accepted too readily that it constituted a specific exception to the general principle of the presumption of innocence and bail protected under the Constitution and the CPO.[126] Furthermore, in his opinion, the stringent standard was contrary to the general purpose of a bail regime, which is to ensure the appearance of the accused to face trial without imposing punishment on him before trial. Most worrying, Chan pointed out it was notoriously difficult to prove negative. In requiring there to be sufficient evidence to substantiate the belief that the accused would *not* commit an offence while on bail, he predicted that the stringent threshold for granting bail would effectively lead to a denial of bail in the large majority of national security cases.

Sadly, Chan's gloomy forecast turned out to be true. More than 70 per cent of bail applications under the NSL had been refused.[127] The success rate for defendants seeking a review of refusal of bail by the High Court was only 17 per cent.[128] The high threshold for being granted bail for those who have been charged under the NSL has created a system of de facto long-term detention without trial. Most have been denied bail and some who were initially granted bail have had it revoked resulting in lengthy pre-trial detention. This is utterly at odds with the common law standard of presumption of bail.

Subsequent to the CFA decision in *Lai Chee Ying*, the Court of Appeal further held in *Tong Ying Kit v Secretary for Justice*[129] that even if there is a right to jury trial in the CFI entrenched in Article 86 of the Basic Law, the decision by the Secretary for Justice to issue a non-jury trial certificate under Article 46(1) of the NSL is not amenable to conventional judicial review challenge. While the Court of Appeal emphasised that the NSL has to be read together with the Basic Law and the Bill of Rights 'to ensure that the defendant's constitutional right to a fair trial as embodied in those provisions is not compromised',[130] it quickly pointed out that

---

[122] *Tong Ying Kit* (n 120) [6] and [48].
[123] ibid [49].
[124] ibid [38].
[125] Chan (n 115).
[126] ibid 9.
[127] The data covered the period between 1 July 2020 and 1 July 2023. L Wong, E Lai, C Yeung and T Kellogg, 'Tracking the Impact of Hong Kong's National Security Law at China File' (*ChinaFile*, 15 August 2023), www.chinafile.com/tracking-impact-of-hong-kongs-national-security-law.
[128] Data was collected between 1 July 2020 and 15 August 2023 from the legal database of Hong Kong Legal Information Institute at https://v2.hklii.hk.
[129] *Tong Ying Kit v Secretary for Justice* [2021] HKCA 912.
[130] ibid [42].

'the provisions in NSL shall prevail over other laws in Hong Kong',[131] and 'even assuming that there is any right to jury trial for prosecution brought by way of indictment, such right had been curtailed by NSL 46'.[132]

3. National Security Law and Freedom of the Press

3.1. Changing Norms of Press Freedom under the NSL

Although Article 4 of the NSL expressly adopts the constitutional provisions under the Basic Law and the ICCPR as applied to Hong Kong which protect the freedoms of speech, of the press and of publication, if one closely analyses other provisions of the NSL, one will find that the freedom of the press has been shaped to fit a pattern that has very little in common with the Liberal concept of a free press under the constitutional common law. For instance, under Article 9, the Government of the HKSAR shall take necessary measures to strengthen supervision and regulation over both the media and the internet. Under Article 10, the HKSAR shall promote national security education through the media and the internet, implying a duty on the said organisations. Under Article 54, the concerned authorities shall take necessary measures to strengthen the management of and services of news agencies of foreign countries.[133]

While the above-mentioned provisions may sound alien to those who are steeped in Hong Kong's common law tradition, they are entirely consistent with the Socialist doctrine of the press where media of mass communication owe a positive duty to support the state and to assist the state in achieving its ends. The state is entirely justified to employ the media for the accomplishment of its objectives. In fact, the first duty of the press is to avoid interference with the objectives of the state.[134] The idea that the press should act as a watchdog or a 'fourth estate' to check on government does not make sense in this context. Given the new holistic approach to national security adopted under President Xi's leadership, it is only natural that the NSL seeks to change the norms of press freedom in Hong Kong.

3.2. Protection of Journalistic Sources

One notable consequence of the changing norm of press freedom concerns the protection of journalistic sources, which is often regarded as one of the basic

---

[131] ibid [81].
[132] ibid [82].
[133] The authorities include the Office for Safeguarding National Security of the Central People's Government in the HKSAR, the Office of the Commissioner of the Ministry of Foreign Affairs in the HKSAR, and the HKSAR Government.
[134] Siebert, Schramm and Peterson (n 13) 28.

conditions for press freedom.[135] Without it, sources may be deterred from assisting the press or speaking to journalists. As discussed above in section 2.1, shortly before the handover, Part XII of IGCO was enacted to afford enhanced status to journalistic material so as to protect journalistic sources being revealed to the authorities. However, under the NSL regime the protection is greatly reduced. Under Articles 43(1) and 43(7) of the NSL, the relevant authorities can search any relevant places (including media organisations) and require a person suspected, on reasonable grounds, of having in possession information or materials relevant to investigation to answer questions and furnish such information. Further, under Schedule 1(1) of the Implementation Rules for Article 43, a magistrate is authorised to issue a warrant for a police officer to search 'specified evidence', which is defined to mean 'anything that is or contains, or that is likely to be or contain, evidence of an offence endangering national security'. If 'specified evidence' can cover journalistic material, then the authorisation procedure under the NSL would deviate from the existing law under the IGCO (sections 84 and 85), which requires law enforcement officers to follow a specific set of meticulous procedures before they can enter premises to search and seize journalistic material, and to apply for a search warrant or production order before a judge of the CFI or District Court.

When two mobile phones belonging to Jimmy Lai were seized in a search of his residence in 2020, in which the content was subject further to a search warrant issued to the police by a magistrate, Lai commenced proceedings and argued that the seized material contained journalistic material, and should be returned to him in *Lai Chee-Ying v Commissioner of Police*.[136] He sought judicial review against the validity of the warrant, arguing that the term 'specified evidence' did not cover journalistic material, and that the magistrate did not have power to issue the said warrant. However, the Court of Appeal ruled that journalistic material is indeed covered by 'specified evidence' so as to serve the legislative purpose of NSL. Despite the fact that IGCO has not been incorporated within the framework of NSL, the Court opined that Schedule 1 operates in tandem with the local laws on search as a coherent whole. In its view, the magistrate will perform the judicial gatekeeping role in exercising his discretion, and will balance freedom of the press and public interest of national security when issuing the warrant. The Court pointed out that since the applicant has not raised the point on whether the magistrate had carried out the balancing test, it was not for the appellant court to examine whether the magistrate had performed the balancing exercise in the case of Lai. What is left unexplored is how to carry out the balancing exercise.

---

[135] *Goodwin v UK* (1996) 22 EHRR 123. In *So Wing Keung v Sing Tao Ltd & Anor* [2005] 2 HKLRD 11, Ma CJHC (as he then was) explained at [36(1)]: 'Journalistic material forms the backbone of the freedom of the press. As a general rule, such material must be given the greatest possible protection from seizure or public exposure; otherwise the press may become inhibited in informing the public of matters it is entitled to know.'

[136] *Lai Chee-Ying v Commissioner of Police* [2022] HKCFI 2688, affirmed [2022] HKCA 1574.

Namely, the Court has not mentioned the required test of proportionality, but only made a vague reference to the value of press freedom and the concerns of national interest.

Also, it is important to note that although Schedule 6 of the Implementation Rules (ie, the Rules on Application for Authorisation to Conduct Interception and Covert Surveillance) expressly refers to journalistic material and gives it the same definition as in the IGCO, there is indeed little protection of journalistic material from interception and covert surveillance by the authorities. A police officer, with the approval of a directorate officer, may make an application to the Chief Executive directly for an authorisation for interception and surveillance.[137] The only requirement under Schedule 6 is that in applying for authorisation the police officer must state 'whether it is likely that any information which may be ... the contents of any journalistic material, will be obtained by conducting the interception',[138] but the Chief Executive (or his delegated officer) may still grant authorisation to intercept journalistic material, and his decision is not subject to any judicial oversight. Additionally, the interception can be conducted covertly without being known by the media concerned.

The NSL regime for covert surveillance and interception is actually based on the old regime of executive authorisation without judicial oversight, which was held by Justice Hartman of the CFI in *Leung Kwok Hung v HKSAR*[139] in 2006 to be inconsistent with Article 30 of the Basic Law which guarantees the right to freely and privately communicate with others. Back then, within six months of the Court's judgment, the HKSAR Government enacted the Interception of Communications and Surveillance Ordinance which in general requires authorisation by a High Court Judge for interception of communications and covert surveillance conducted by law enforcement agencies, plus an additional independent oversight authority by establishing the Office of the Commissioner on Interception of Communications and Surveillance.[140] However, all these protections of judicial and independent oversight are gone under the NSL regime, and it is now entirely up to the Chief Executive (or his designated officer) to decide whether journalistic material can be intercepted. Indeed, if the covert surveillance or interception is done by officers of the Office for Safeguarding National Security of the Central Government stationed in Hong Kong, it is not even subject to any authorisation of the Chief Executive, as their acts are not subject to Hong Kong jurisdiction (Article 60 of NSL). In practical terms, media in Hong Kong now has to operate on the basis that unbeknown to them, journalistic sources may be

---

[137] Implementation Rules for Article 43 of the Law of the People's Republic of China on Safeguarding National Security in the Hong Kong Special Administrative Region, Sch 6(4)(1).

[138] ibid, Sch 6, ss 23(b)(ix) and 24(b)(x).

[139] *Leung Kwok Hung v HKSAR* [2006] HKCFI 123.

[140] Interception of Communications and Surveillance Ordinance (Cap 589); S Hargreaves, 'Past As Prologue: Intercept & Surveillance Rules Under Hong Kong's National Security Law' (2021) 20 *Santa Clara Journal of International Law* 33.

covertly obtained by the authorities in the name of national security without any judicial oversight.

3.3. Freedom to Publish, Self-Censorship and Continued Survival of Media Outlets

The criminal offences of the NSL do not target the media. However, in line with the new holistic approach to national security adopted under President Xi's leadership and the Socialist view on the role of the press, under the NSL regime, the seditious publications offence, which was used for the 'irritating flea-bites of the dissident and the nonconformist',[141] is being revived more than half a century. Since September 2020, the authorities started to prosecute people for publishing or distributing seditious publications in violation of section 10(1)(c) of the Crimes Ordinance.[142]

One of the seditious publication cases which is particularly worthy of attention is the case in *HKSAR v Ng Hau Yi*,[143] which concerned five members of the speech therapist union publishing children's books featuring sheep and wolves, which was believed by the police to be alluding to the protest of the Hong Kong people against the PRC authorities.[144] The defendants were arrested in July 2021 and were charged for 'conspiracy to print, publish, distribute, display and/or reproduce seditious publications' in violation of section 10(1)(c). Being denied bail on national security grounds by the magistrate, one of the defendants sought a review of bail application unsuccessfully before the CFI. She further sought leave to appeal from the CFA, arguing that the lower court should not use the stringent standard of bail review under Article 42 of the NSL to consider her case.[145] However, the three-member Appeal Committee of the CFA considered that it was justified to extend the Article 42 standard to all 'acts' endangering national security,[146] to have a 'complementary application of the laws',[147] concluding that this was consistent with the legislative intention of Article 23 of the Basic Law and the NSL.[148] Writing before the decision of the Appeal Committee, Johannes Chan has already criticised the lower court's approach of applying the NSL bail

---

[141] Siebert, Schramm and Peterson (n 13) 23.

[142] H Wong, 'Hong Kong Supercharges 1938 British Sedition Law to Curb Dissent' (*Bloomberg.com*, 23 August 2022), www.bloomberg.com/news/articles/2022-08-23/hong-kong-supercharges-1938-british-sedition-law-to-curb-dissent.

[143] *HKSAR v Ng Hau Yi Sidney* [2021] HKCFA 42.

[144] C Chau, 'Hong Kong National Security Police Explain Why Children's Picture Books about Sheep Are Seditious' *Hong Kong Free Press* (22 July 2021), https://hongkongfp.com/2021/07/22/hong-kong-national-security-police-explain-why-childrens-picture-books-about-sheep-are-seditious.

[145] *Ng Hau Yi Sidney* (n 143) [6].

[146] ibid [12].

[147] ibid [24].

[148] ibid [19]–[20] and [24].

standard to non-NSL cases in another judgment.[149] He pointed out that this has violated the principle of legality which requires the court to confine Article 42 to NSL charges, and has introduced a draconian regime into the common law system of Hong Kong.

In September 2022, after waiting for than a year, the five defendants were eventually found guilty, and sentenced to 19 months of imprisonment in the District Court.[150] District Judge Kwok ruled that inciting others to violence or to create public disturbance or disorder for the purpose of disturbing constituted authority is not a necessary ingredient for establishing 'seditious intention'.[151] Although he purportedly sought to balance the restriction under the law with the constitutional right of freedom of expression protected under the Basic Law and ICCPR, he quickly concluded that the criminalisation of seditious publication had satisfied the standard of legal certainty, of being rationally connected with a legitimate aim and proving to be necessary for the protection of national security.[152] In his opinion, making sedition an offence is a 'more important tool for protection of national security' because the existence of a nation, its territorial integrity or political independence can be threatened not just by force or threat of force, but by propaganda spreading rumours ... misinformation and disinformation'.[153] Since the maximum term of imprisonment for sedition is two years, the defendants had nearly served their sentence term while on remand.[154]

Given the resurrection of the old colonial law on seditious publication and the Court's extension of the stringent standard for bail application to such cases beyond the offences under the NSL itself in *HKSAR v Ng Hau Yi Sidney*,[155] the freedom to publish in Hong Kong is greatly diminished. The stake may appear too high for publishing any dissenting views against the authorities in view of the breadth of the seditious publications offence under the Crimes Ordinance and though presumed innocent before conviction, anyone charged will lose their liberty immediately before trial because of the stringent threshold for obtaining bail under Article 42(2) of the NSL.

China's intensifying national security advances and sweeping conception of national security interests inevitably results in a shrinking space for the exercise of civil liberties,[156] which has a definite chilling effect on the practice of press freedom in the HKSAR. Within two years of the NSL coming into effect, two

---

[149] Chan (n 115).
[150] *HKSAR v Lai Man-ling and Others* [2022] HKDC 1004.
[151] *HKSAR v Lai Man-ling and Others* [2022] HKDC 981.
[152] ibid [96]–[100].
[153] ibid [102].
[154] Under the sentencing regime in the HKSAR, the convicted will be given a reduction in their sentence of one-third for good conduct while in prison. As a result, a 19-month sentence will be close to 12 months served in prison. *Lai Man-ling* (n 150) [34].
[155] *Ng Hau Yi Sidney* (n 143).
[156] C Chan and F de Londras, 'Introduction: China's National Security in Hong Kong' in Chan and De Londras (n 83) 1.

newspaper outlets (*Apple Daily* and *Stand News*), which were known for their Liberal stance, were forced to close after police raided their offices and arrested their owners and staff, two other independent online media outfits (*Citizen News* and *Mad Dog Daily*) decided to shut down due to the 'need to protect their staff',[157] and an investigative news platform (*Factwire*) also ceased its operation.[158]

By 1 July 2023, about 264 people have been arrested and with about 148 of those charged under the NSL.[159] It was also reported that about 20 media workers and executives have been arrested or detained.[160] At the time of writing, most cases are still awaiting trial with many individuals losing their liberties under pre-trial detention for more than a year, as bail was denied under the stringent threshold test under the NSL.[161] Among the 264 applications for review of bail by defendants before the CFI, four cases involved media owner and workers and all of them were denied bail.[162]

Perhaps the most famous bail application case is the one lodged by Lai Chee Ying in *HKSAR v Lai Chee Ying*,[163] as discussed above in section 2.3. Lai was initially charged with one count of fraud, then with another count of colluding with foreign forces to endanger national security (Article 29(4)), for 'request[ing] a foreign country, an institution, organization or individual outside China to impose sanctions or blockade, or engage in other hostile activities against the HKSAR or the PRC'.[164] While the trial is still pending, Lai has been in custody since February 2021. Lai's application for bail was first rejected by the Magistracy, but granted by Alex Lee, Justice of the CFI, which was later set aside by the CFA and eventually revoked before another NSL designated judge in the CFI.[165]

Although Article 42 of the NSL does not target the media directly, its impact on media workers cannot be underestimated. Sharing a similar fate with Jimmy Lai,

---

[157] Reporters Without Borders, 'RSF Timeline: Two Years of Government Assault on Hong Kong's Press Freedom' (25 March 2022), https://rsf.org/sites/default/files/medias/file/2022/04/Two_years_governement_assault_timeline%20-%20English%20Version_1.pdf.

[158] H Leung, 'Hong Kong Investigative News Platform Factwire Disbands – 4th Outlet to Shutter in under a Year' *Hong Kong Free Press* (10 June 2022), https://hongkongfp.com/2022/06/10/breaking-hong-kong-investigative-news-platform-factwire-disbands.

[159] The data covered the period between 1 July 2020 and 1 July 2023. L Wong, E Lai, C Yeung and T Kellogg (n 127).

[160] H Davidson, 'Hong Kong Democracy and Media Freedom Has "Entered Endgame"' *The Guardian* (10 February 2022), www.theguardian.com/world/2022/feb/10/hong-kong-democracy-and-media-freedom-has-entered-endgame.

[161] L Wong, E Lai, C Yeung and T Kellogg, (n 127). Out of 148 cases charged under the NSL, 104 defendants (70%) had been denied bail.

[162] Data was collected between 1 July 2020 and 15 August 2023 from the legal database of Hong Kong Legal Information Institute at https://v2.hklii.hk. The four applications concerning media owner and workers were *HKSAR v Fung Wai Kong* [2022] HKCFI 1173; *HKSAR v Cheung Kim Hung* [2021] HKCFI 3372; *HKSAR v Wan Yiu Sing Edmund* [2021] HKCFI 1261; and *HKSAR v Lai Chee Ying*; bail initially granted [2020] HKCFI 3161, but set aside by the Court of Final Appeal [2020] HKCFA 45, then finally revoked [2021] HKCFI 448.

[163] *HKSAR v Lai Chee Ying* [2020] HKCFA 45.

[164] ibid [2].

[165] *HKSAR v Lai Chee Ying* [2021] HKCFI 448.

in June 2021, *Apple Daily*'s publisher,[166] its chief editor[167] and its managing editor, along with nine others, were charged with the same offence of 'collusion with a foreign country of with external element to endanger national security' under Article 29(4) of the NSL, and their bail applications were also denied.[168] In another case of *HKSAR v Mo Man Ching Claudia*,[169] a former Legislative Councilor and a veteran journalist was charged with conspiracy to commit subversion contrary to Article 22(3) of the NSL, and has been detained since January 2021. Mo's bail application was denied because of her 'spreading false rumor' and her 'likelihood to continue to commit acts endangering national security'.[170] Evidence relied on by the prosecutor included Mo's interview and WhatsApp conversation with Bloomberg, *The Wall Street Journal* and the BBC expressing her personal opinion on Hong Kong's political situation.[171]

In addition to the above, increasing red lines have been set by the authorities affecting not only journalists but also internet companies. The Government has plans to pass new laws and measures to stamp out 'fake news', 'false information' and 'messages that were destructive to society'.[172] What remains critical is how to define those terms and who the arbiters are. It has been reported that Apple, Google and Facebook have removed apps and pages related to protest and pro-democracy groups.[173] Their fears are not unfounded because under Article 43(4), the relevant service provider is required 'to delete information or provide assistance'. While there has yet to be litigation before court involving internet service providers, it was reported that Hong Kong Broadband Network had blocked an anti-government website in compliance with the NSL.[174]

4. Conclusion

Effective on 30 June 2020, the NSL is gradually, yet definitely, changing the legal landscape of the HKSAR. The common law which is believed to be an

---

[166] *Cheung Kim Hung* (n 162).

[167] K Ho, 'Hong Kong Court Denies Ex-Apple Daily Chief Editor Bail in National Security Case' *Hong Kong Free Press* (13 August 2021), https://hongkongfp.com/2021/08/13/hong-kong-court-denies-ex-apple-daily-chief-editor-bail-in-national-security-case.

[168] *Fung Wai Kong* (n 162).

[169] *HKSAR v Mo Man Ching Claudia* [2021] HKCFI 1435.

[170] ibid [13], [19] and [21].

[171] ibid [14]–[16] and [18].

[172] C Chau, 'Hong Kong Gov't Conducting Legal Study on "Fake News", Says Chief Sec. John Lee' *Hong Kong Free Press* (18 November 2021), https://hongkongfp.com/2021/11/18/hong-kong-govt-conducting-legal-study-on-fake-news-says-chief-sec-john-lee.

[173] A Datt, 'The Impact of the National Security Law on Media and Internet Freedom in Hong Kong' (*Freedom House*, 19 October 2021), https://freedomhouse.org/article/impact-national-security-law-media-and-internet-freedom-hong-kong.

[174] The website blocked is HK Chronicles, a website widely used in the 2019 pro-democracy protests. T Grundy, 'Hong Kong Broadband Network Admits It Blocked Website under National Security Law' *Hong Kong Free Press* (14 January 2021), https://hongkongfp.com/2021/01/14/hong-kong-broadband-network-admits-it-blocked-website-under-national-security-law.

indispensable instrument to Hong Kong's success is undergoing a transformation from a constitutional common law now practised among major common law jurisdictions to an uncommon law with Chinese characteristics. It is shedding its Libertarian spirit and regaining its law-and-order grip. Although the change has so far primarily happened in NSL or related cases, and has yet to spread to the rest of constitutional and administrative law, its precise scope of impact remains to be seen given the all-embracing concept of national security under the new holistic approach.

Despite the widely held assumptions that common law is a blessing from the British Empire to Hong Kong, its preservation hinges much on the self-restraint of the exercise of sovereign power by the Chinese Government.[175] Under the new holistic approach to national security in the PRC, it is the national security legislation enacted by the PRC authorities that has provided a point of convergence between the high-handed rule of the Party State and the oppressive side of common law on the regulation of the press and freedom of expression. Before one can tell how the CFA is going to interpret the broad and vague criminal provisions of the NSL, we have already observed how the CFA has been flexing the procedural muscles of this supreme law.

The presumptions of innocence and of bail, seen as core principles of common law, have become illusory under the CFA's interpretation of Article 42 of the NSL. Although the CFA has made it clear that the grant or refusal of bail does not involve the application of a burden of proof,[176] one can hardly deny the 'operational consequence' of Article 42 is to impose this burden on the defendant to prove the negative, namely they will not continue to commit acts endangering national security. Rather than putting the state to proof, the defendant has been converted into an object, as a witness to establish his own case but can no longer control his tactical interest in the lawsuit.[177] At the same time, in applying a literal interpretation to Article 42, judges have turned from being independent and impartial arbiters to legal technocrats enforcing state policy, and implementing the 'correct decision' of the executive. While stating it is evident that the legislative intention is for the NSL to operate in tandem with the laws of the HKSAR, one has yet to see any attempt from the CFA to seek 'convergence, compatibility and complementarity' with local laws in case of inconsistency.[178]

Instead of a generous approach, a formalistic and literal style of statutory interpretation has been applied. Reversal of cardinal principles affecting fundamental rights, such as the presumption of innocence and bail, is treated as a matter of pure deduction from the legislative intent of the NSL. Protection of journalistic sources is stripped away without careful consideration of the constitutional

---

[175] Chan (n 75).

[176] *Lai Chee Ying* (n 163) [67].

[177] MR Damaška, *The Faces of Justice and State Authority: A Comparative Approach to the Legal Process* (New Haven, Yale University Press, 1986) 127.

[178] *Lai Chee Ying* (n 163) [21].

checks for necessity and proportionality. Rule of Law principles have been reduced to mere rules of law. The present legal debate on national security legislation in Hong Kong has exposed the limits of the common law to develop its public law elements under the Basic Law and the formidable challenge it has to face under a Socialist Party State. What one has witnessed is the unquestioning priority given to NSL provisions by judges. Judicial deference often reflects a deeper attitude of acquiescence of political reality, and an anticipation to reactions of other political actors in the institutional environment.[179]

The 'uncommon' law expresses not only the relations between subjects and subjects, but also their relations to the supreme political power.

---

[179] Ip (n 29) 23.

4

Regulation of Press in India – An Overview of the Legal Framework and Related Concerns

ANNAPPA NAGARATHNA

1. Introduction

India, being the largest democracy in the world, provides legal protection to fundamental freedoms and rights of individuals. Right to freedom of speech and expression is legally recognised as an important right of the citizen under Article 19(1)(a) of the Indian Constitution. Right to freedom of speech and expression is also extended to press and media, thus emphasising upon the need to legally protect this right of the press which is considered as the fourth pillar of democracy. Legal regulatory framework in India hence is based on this constitutional guarantee. Freedom of press, being an important requisite for a democratic legal system, is being guaranteed through the laws of India.

2. Importance of the Freedom of Speech, Expression and Press

The press is a social institution and its functions and character will differ according to the political and economic structure of society.[1] For a democratic country like India, the press is of extreme importance. Freedom of press, according to the First Press Commission, is the 'freedom to hold opinions, to receive and to impart information through the printed word without any interference from any public authority'.[2] The press functions to inform, entertain and educate the public.

---

[1] M Bhaskar, *Press and Working Class Consciousness in Developing Societies: A Case Study of an Indian State – Kerala* (New Delhi, Gian Publishing House, 1989) 7.

[2] ES Venkataramiah, *Freedom of Press: Some Recent Trends* (Delhi, BR Publishing, 1987) 31, quoting from the Press Commission Report at 517.

These functions can be better discharged by the press provided law protects it from unreasonable restrictions imposed by the state and other groups. Freedom of speech, expression and press are rights of extreme importance in a country and they are regarded as essential prerequisites for self-government and democracy.[3] The freedom of press is fundamental to the life of an individual in the democratic polity.[4]

Freedom of the press in a representative democracy with a party government means the right of all political parties to have access to the 'mass media' (that is the press) so that they may appeal to the electorate on the basis of their respective programmes and ideology.[5] Freedom of expression of a citizen on the other hand should consist of various other associated rights including the 'right to receive information from any sources'.[6] Such sources includes press publications as well.

In *Indian Express v Union of India*[7] the Court regarded freedom of press as the 'heart of social and political intercourse the press has now assumed the role of the public educator making formal and non-formal education possible'. In another case, *Indian Express Newspapers v Union of India & Others*,[8] the Supreme Court said that the freedom of press rests on an assumption that 'the widest possible dissemination of information from as many diverse and antagonistic sources as possible is essential to the welfare of the public'. The Court said that the function of the press is to spread news from as many different sources and with as many different facts and colours as possible. The Court also said that a citizen is entirely dependent on the press for the quality, proportion and extent of his news supply.

Freedom of speech and expression which includes freedom of press is crucial for an effective state administration. Through this, the administering state can take into consideration the public's constructive criticisms and thereby plan its actions. This hence can contribute to good governance. The first issue of the *Kesari* newspaper explained the importance of press by stating:

> a newspaper is useful in two ways. Firstly, if the newspapers carry out their duty impartially and dauntlessly, government officials are filled with awe. The purpose that is served, in the night, by lighting the street lamps or by the continuous patrolling of the police, is the purpose that is served by the incessant penmanship of journalists.[9]

It is also interesting to understand the reasons for considering press freedom as important as freedom of speech and expression. According to Acharya Durga Das Basu:

---

[3] ibid 1.
[4] ibid 13.
[5] ADD Basu, *Law of the Press*, 3rd edn (Delhi, Prentice Hall of India, 1996) 12.
[6] ibid 13.
[7] *Indian Express v Union of India* (1985) 1 SCC 641.
[8] *Indian Express Newspapers v Union of India & Others* 1986 AIR 515, 1985 SCR (2) 287.
[9] M Chatterjee, 'Kesari: Tilak's Spirit Lives On' (*Communication Today*, 29 June 2015), https://communicationtoday.net/2015/06/29/kesari-tilaks-spirit-lives-on.

The argument in favour of freedom of the press is the same as that for freedom of speech with a stronger appeal arising from the special features of printed matter, namely, that:

A printed matter records the ideas in a permanent form, which speech cannot;

However larger the audience to a speech may be, a newspaper of book has a larger circulation than spoken works. Even though in modern times, a newspaper has other rivals in the realm of media of expression, such as the radio or the television, the morning daily has still the widest demand in the world and the most potent medium of mass communication.[10]

3. Historical Evolution of the Right

The right to freedom of speech in one way or another has a long history in India. Even during the olden days, most of the kings in India permitted their subjects to exercise these rights as long as they did not go against the interest of the King and the public or to the extent that they were not against other established norms of society. Press freedom too was recognised in some states.

3.1. Ancient and Medieval Period

Even though the right to freedom of speech and press were not explicitly recognised in the ancient Indian legal system, yet these rights were respected in Ancient India. An individual's right to freedom of speech, expression, its other associated rights such as, right to form an opinion, right to choose, right to information, were extensively recognised in the ancient Indian state's laws and practices. Thus, 'freedom of speech' became formally recognised as a fundamental right in India with the passing of the Indian Constitution, yet ancient Indian jurisprudence reveals that these rights were recognised in most of the states.[11]

Since intellectual integrity was given importance, the freedom of expression was recognised. But the right of speech and expression was expected to be exercised for achieving a purpose which was good, such as in the pursuit of truth or for the acquisition of knowledge. People were expected to use the right 'to utter the truth, and to take us closer to the truth'.[12] During Ashoka's reign, the Emperor used newsletters as a way of collecting information about the developments happening in his kingdom.[13] In fact, available information formed the basis of

---

[10] Basu (n 5) 10.

[11] See for details, S Ganesh, 'Ancient Indian Views on Freedom of Expression and Public Discourse', (*Indica*, 15 February 2020), www.indica.today/long-reads/ancient-indian-views-on-freedom-of-expression-and-public-discourse-debates.

[12] ibid.

[13] J Natarajan, *History of Journalism in India* (Delhi, Ministry of Information and Broadcasting, 1997).

discussion by his council of ministers. This system further improved during the Mughal period. During this time, news writers were even obliged to send reports on administration to the headquarters which were used for official purposes. In fact, it is also said that 'for a number of reasons the news writers in the service of East India Company were subject to greater control than those of the Moghul Emperors'.[14]

3.2. Colonial Period

Formal legal regulation of the press began during the colonial rule in India. While on one hand, freedom fighters were using the press as a mode of accumulation of people for the freedom struggle as well as to spread socialism, on the other hand the colonial state imposed regulations upon both freedom of speech as well as upon press freedom as they were against the interests of the ruling state. Freedom fighters in fact used print media as 'one of the weapons against the colonial rulers'.[15] Hence, the state came up with wider censorship strategies.

Kesari, a Marathi newspaper,[16] was founded in 1881 by Bal Gangadhar Tilak, who was one of the prominent leaders of the Indian freedom struggle. Tilak also used this newspaper as a socio-political platform. *Kesari* played a significant role in triggering and driving the socio-political movement in pre-independence times, and also after independence. In fact, *Kesari* acted as Tilak's megaphone for propagating his social and political ideology and countering his opponents.[17] Due to the fact that this newspaper became a mode of spreading consciousness about the need for freedom from colonial rule, it became a basis for strict state regulation. This is emphasised by Mrinal Chatterjee who says:

> Tilak made use of *Kesari* for bringing about political consciousness among the masses for the purpose of the freedom struggle, for giving a new direction to their thinking and for boosting the different agitations and programmes initiated by him. The four-point programme of 'Swaraj, Swadeshi, Boycott and National Education' that Tilak offered to the Congress and to the whole nation, was strongly propagated by *Kesari*. As Tilak took to agitation and confrontation with the British Government, he and along with him *Kesari* had to suffer the rage of the British Rulers. It had to face many court cases. Many times *Kesari* had to furnish sureties and the editors had to suffer imprisonment.[18]

This newspaper often came under legal action and was even held responsible for committing the offence of sedition twice in 1897 and 1908 respectively.[19] Tilak

---

[14] ibid.

[15] D Sethi, *War over Words: Censorship in India – 1930 to 1960* (Cambridge, Cambridge University Press, 2019).

[16] Marathi is a regional language spoken largely in the Maharashtra State of India.

[17] Chatterjee (n 9).

[18] ibid.

[19] ibid.

too was held liable for sedition. Press regulation thus became one of the objectives of state surveillance. According to Devika Sethi, the overwhelming concern of the colonial state with public opinion meant that censorship was carried out not only to proscribe or ban publications but also as a means of exercising surveillance over what was being written and debated in the public sphere.[20] The then Government, in order to supress the Civil Disobedience Movement that began from 1930, imposed various restrictions including by way of enacting the India Press Act, 1931 which aimed at preventing publications that could incite readers to go against the state. The Act stated that it was passed 'to provide against the publication of matter inciting to or encouraging murder or violence.'[21] In 1932 the Government enacted the Foreign Relations Act which was primarily aimed at preventing publication of statements that might cause prejudice to the maintenance of friendly relations between the Majesty's Government and the governments of certain foreign states.[22]

Thus, during colonial rule, freedom of speech and press were hardly legally recognised and respected, it was rather strictly regulated by the state. The Joint Select Committee of the British Parliament, which held similar views to the earlier Indian Statutory Commission headed by Simon, opined that the granting of such rights could 'create a grave risk of declaring many laws unconstitutional and void'. In the case of *Arnold v Emperor*,[23] the Court also refused to attach any privileges to a journalist. However Indian freedom fighters, being influenced by the American Bill of Rights, demanded the recognition and protection of rights and freedoms.[24] Later, while drafting the Indian Constitution, the Constituent Assembly through its resolution declared to recognise freedom of expression.[25] However what followed was constitutional provisions declaring freedom of speech and expression as that which can be subjected to reasonable restrictions. Hence the Constitution Drafting Committee added provisions that assured citizens various fundamental rights, including rights to freedom of speech and expression. It empowered the state to enact laws relating 'to libel, slander, defamation, sedition or any other matter offending against decency or morality or undermining the security of, or tending to overthrow the State'.[26] In fact, during the debates of the Constituent Assembly, the use of terms like 'public order', 'morality', etc as a basis for restricting fundamental freedom was criticised by some members for being vague. Finally, the present Article 19 which guarantees the fundamental right to freedom of speech and expression got added in the form of Article 13 in the final draft of the Constitution.

---

[20] Sethi (n 15).
[21] See www.indiacode.nic.in/repealed-act/repealed_act_documents/A1931-23.pdf.
[22] ibid.
[23] *Arnold v Emperor* AIR 1914 P.C. 116.
[24] Venkataramiah (n 2) 19.
[25] ibid 20, quoting from the *Constituent Assembly Debates, Vol I–IV*.
[26] ibid 23.

3.3. Post-Independence Period

Although freedom fighters had used press freedom as one of the tools to fight against colonial rule, post-independence laws attempted to restrict press freedom to a large extent. It is surprising to see that when India won hard-fought freedom, freedom of the press was not enshrined in the Constitution and no particular legal safeguards were introduced, instead, regulations were introduced, which hindered the free press.[27] Post-independence, the Indian Government enacted various laws imposing restrictions on press freedom including the Press (Objectionable Matter) Act 1951 and the Prevention of Publication of Objectionable Matter Act 1976. The latter was enacted to prevent printing and publication of materials that might incite commission of crimes and other objectionable matter. This Act defined 'objectionable matter' widely by also including under its ambit:

> any words, signs or visible representations which are likely to:
>
> bring into hatred or contempt, or excite disaffection towards the Government established by law in India or in any State thereof and thereby cause or tend to cause public disorder;
>
> promote disharmony or feelings of enmity, hatred or ill-will between different religious, racial, language or regional groups or castes or communities; or
>
> cause fear or alarm to the public or to any section of the public whereby any person may be induced to commit an offence against the State or against the public tranquillity; or
>
> incite any person or any class or community of persons to commit murder, mischief or any other offence; or
>
> which are defamatory of the President of India, the Vice-President of India, the Prime Minister or the Speaker of the House of the People or the Governor of a State; or
>
> which are grossly indecent, or are scurrilous or obscene or intended for blackmail.[28]

The above two laws were later repealed by the Government. The 1976 Act was repealed by the Prevention of Publication of Objectionable Matter (Repeal) Act 1977. It is important to note that this legislature was passed during a state of emergency which was imposed in the country between 1975 and 1977.

With the proclamation of emergency on 25 June 1975, a host of repressive measures and pre-censorship was imposed in India by promulgating an ordinance under Rule 48 of the Defence and Internal Security of India Rules 1971. The influence of the Government on the press can be seen from the fact that during the emergency between 24 June 1975 and 26 January 1976, 208 dailies and 1434 weeklies were closed down. The abolition of the Press Council too during the early

---

[27] M Sharma, 'No Specific Press Freedom, Safeguards: How Indian Journalism Lacks a Free Environment' (*Outlook*, 7 November 2022), www.outlookindia.com/national/no-specific-press-freedom-safeguards-how-indian-journalism-lacks-a-free-environment-news-235239.

[28] See https://lawsisto.com/Read-Central-Act/1647/PREVENTION-OF-PUBLICATION-OF-OBJECTIONABLE-MATTER-ACT-1976.

stages of emergency was a part of the legislative assault on the media.[29] Due to this historical reason, often restrictions imposed through this law have been heavily criticised.

4. Press Freedom versus Press Regulation – Current Legal Framework

Like any other rights, freedom of the press is not an absolute right. Hence, various laws exist which provide for grounds on which press freedom can be restricted and regulated. They include grounds laid down in the Indian Constitution too.

4.1. Indian Constitution under Articles 19(1)(a) and 19(2)

As stated earlier, constituent assembly after a lot of debate proposed to include freedom of speech and expression as a form of fundamental right in the Indian Constitution. The same has been laid down in Article 19(1)(a). The initial version of Article 19(1)(a) which was subject to reasonable restrictions under Article 19(2) laid down wider grounds of restrictions upon freedom, including on the ground of 'libel, slander, defamation, contempt of court or any matter which offended against decency or morality or which undermined the security of or tended to overthrow the state'.[30] Article 19(2) was amended twice in 1951 and 1963 respectively. Judicial interventions through case laws also lead to legal changes in the domain.

Currently the Indian Constitution under Article 19(1)(a) guarantees fundamental freedom of speech and expression by stating: '(1) All citizens shall have the right (a) to freedom of speech and expression'. This right is subject to reasonable restriction imposed under Article 19(2) which states:

> (2) Nothing in sub-clause (a) of clause (1) shall affect the operation of any existing law, or prevent the State from making any law, in so far as such law imposes reasonable restrictions on the exercise of the right conferred by the said sub-clause in the interests of the sovereignty and integrity of India, the security of the State, friendly relations with foreign States, public order, decency or morality, or in relation to contempt of court, defamation or incitement to an offence.

Indian laws including the Constitution do not expressly and specifically recognise freedom of press, yet it is seen as a component of freedom of press. In fact, in the case of *Indian Express v Union of India*,[31] the Court clearly said this by stating that 'the expression "freedom of press" has not been used in Article 19 of

---

[29] Bhaskar (n 1) 71.
[30] Venkataramiah (n 2) 26.
[31] *Indian Express v Union of India* (n 7).

the Constitution but, as declared by this Court, it is included in Article 19(1)(a) which guarantees freedom of speech and expression'. The Court further said that 'Freedom of press means freedom from interference from authority which would have the effect of interference with the content and circulation of newspapers'.[32]

Freedom of press thus is a form of freedom of speech and expression of 'every citizen which includes (i) the right to say what sentiments he pleases before the public or the right to impart information and ideas; (ii) the right to receive information and ideas from others through any lawful medium'.[33] Hence, press freedom like freedom of speech and expression is subjected to restrictions which are 'reasonable' on the following grounds:

- in the interests of the sovereignty and integrity of India;
- the security of the state;
- friendly relations with foreign states;
- public order;
- decency or morality;
- in relation to contempt of court;
- defamation; or
- incitement to an offence.

As mentioned earlier, freedom of press is not a directly recognised right in the Indian Constitution. In the case of *Romesh Thappar v State of Madras*,[34] the Supreme Court of India recognised freedom of press as a component of freedom of speech under Article 19(1)(a). In this case, the Government of Madras had invoked its powers under the Madras Maintenance of Public Order Act 1949, and imposed a ban upon the entry and circulation of an English weekly journal *Cross Roads* in that state. This ban was challenged by Romesh Thappar, the printer, publisher and editor of the weekly, contending it to be contravening his fundamental right to freedom of speech and expression as per Article 19(1)(a) of the Indian Constitution. The Court held that 'there can be no doubt that freedom of speech and expression includes freedom of propagation of ideas, and that freedom is ensured by the freedom of circulation'. The Court held that 'Liberty of circulation is as essential to that freedom as the liberty of publication. Indeed, without circulation the publication would be of little value'.[35] While explaining the scope of 'reasonable restrictions', the Court held that:

> Where a law purports to authorise the imposition of restrictions on a fundamental right in language wide enough to cover restrictions both within and without the limits of constitutionally permissible legislative action affecting such right, it is not

---

[32] ibid.
[33] Basu (n 5) 10.
[34] *Romesh Thappar v State of Madras* AIR 1950 SC 124.
[35] ibid.

possible to uphold it even so far as it may be applied within the constitutional limits, as it is not severable. So long as the possibility of its being applied for purposes not sanctioned by the Constitution cannot be ruled out, it must be held to be wholly unconstitutional and void. In other words, clause (2) of Article 19 having allowed the imposition of restrictions on the freedom of speech and expression only in cases where danger to the State is involved, an enactment, which is capable of being applied to cases where no such danger could arise, cannot be held to be constitutional and valid to any extent.[36]

Hence restrictions to freedom of speech can only be on the grounds provided under Article 19(2).

In *Brij Bhushan Sharma v Delhi*,[37] Brij Bhushan, a journalist, was charged with the offence of sedition for publishing in his newspaper *Swatantra Bharat* an article criticising government policies. Bhushan challenged the constitutional validity of the East Punjab Public Safety Act 1949, under which he was charged, contending it to be violative of freedom of speech and expression. The contention was against section 7(1)(c) of the Act, according to which:

> The Provincial Government or any authority authorised by it in this behalf if satisfied that such action is necessary for the purpose of preventing or combating any activity prejudicial to the public safety or the maintenance of public order may, by order in writing addressed to a printer, publisher or editor require that any matter relating to a particular subject or class of subjects shall before publication be submitted for scrutiny.[38]

The Court in this case, held that the 'imposition of pre-censorship on a journal is a restriction on the liberty of the press which is an essential part of the right to freedom of speech and expression declared by Article 19(1) (a)'.[39] The Court relied upon William Blackstone's commentary, according to which:

> the liberty of the press consists in laying no previous restraint upon publications, and not in freedom from censure for criminal matter when published. Every freeman has an undoubted right to lay what sentiments he pleases before the public; to forbid this, is to destroy the freedom of the press.[40]

The Court finally quashed the impugned order that had imposed a ban on the circulation of the newsletter and thereby upholding the fundamental right to freedom of speech.

In *Express Newsletter v Union of India*,[41] the Supreme Court of India said that:

> This is the concept of the freedom of speech and expression as it obtains in the United States of America and the necessary corollary thereof is that no measure can be enacted which would have the effect of imposing a pre-censorship, curtailing the circulation

---

[36] ibid.
[37] *Brij Bhushan Sharma v Delhi* (1950) SCR 605.
[38] ibid.
[39] ibid.
[40] ibid.
[41] *Express Newsletter v Union of India* 1958 SC 578 (614) [199].

or restricting the choice of employment or unemployment in the editorial force. Such a measure would certainly tend to infringe the freedom of speech and expression and would therefore be liable to be struck down as unconstitutional ....

The Court further said:

It would certainly not be legitimate to subject the press to laws which take away or abridge the freedom of speech and expression or which would curtail circulation and thereby narrow the scope of dissemination of information, or fetter its freedom to choose its means of exercising the right or would undermine its independence by driving it to seek Government aid. Laws which single out the press for laying upon it excessive and prohibitive burdens which would restrict the circulation, impose a penalty on its right to choose the instruments for its exercise or to seek an alternative media, prevent news- papers from being started and ultimately drive the press to seek Government aid in order to survive, would therefore be struck down as unconstitutional.[42]

Thus, through this case the Court indicated that any direct or indirect ways of unreasonably resisting freedom of press would be against the laws. Hence restrictions upon press, if any, must be on the grounds laid down in Article 19(2). The Court clarified this by saying that:

Unless, therefore, a law enacted by the Legislature comes squarely within the provisions of Article 19(2) it would not be saved and would be struck down as unconstitutional on the score of its violating the fundamental right of the petitioners under Article 19(1) (a).[43]

In *Sakal Papers (P) Ltd and Others v Union of India*,[44] the Newspaper (Price and Page) Act of 1956, which allowed the state to regulate the price of newspapers as per the number of pages of the concerned newspaper, was challenged. The Supreme Court held this law as being violative of press freedom under Article 19(1)(a). The Court said that

the right to freedom of speech and expression carries with it the right to publish and circulate one's ideas, opinions and views with complete freedom and by resorting to any available means of publication subject again to such restrictions as could be legitimately imposed under cl. (2) of Article 19.[45]

The Court also recognised the right to free press as that which includes right to circulation, by saying: 'Since circulation of a newspaper is a part of the right of freedom of speech the Act must be regarded as one directed against the freedom of speech'.[46] And since the said interferences by the state could not be justified to have fallen under the grounds provided in Article 19(2), the Court did not permit it to continue. Similarly, in *Bennett Coleman & Co and Others v Union of India &*

---

[42] ibid [207].
[43] ibid [209].
[44] *Sakal Papers (P) Ltd and Others v Union of India* 1962 AIR 305 SC.
[45] ibid.
[46] ibid.

Others,[47] where the state attempted to regulate usage of papers by newspapers by way of rationing and distributing quota of newsprint, the Court declared such regulation as amounting to a breach of Article 19(1)(a).

4.2. Other Fundamental Rights Conferred to the Press

4.2.1. *Right to Freedom of Trade and Business*

It is interesting to note that courts in India have clearly and expressly conferred to the press certain fundamental rights which are otherwise generally conferred upon an individual citizen. Press is not just a medium of expression but also a business. As a business entity it has the right to carry on its commercial activities which is also another fundamental right guaranteed under Article 19(1)(g) of the Indian Constitution. Thus any laws interfering with the right to press can be regarded as unconstitutional.

The Supreme Court, in *Indian Express v Union of India*, said 'Newspaper industry enjoys two of the fundamental rights, namely, the freedom of speech and expression guaranteed under Article 19(1)(a) and the freedom to engage in any profession, occupation, trade, industry or business guaranteed'.[48] It further said:

> while there can be no tax on the right to exercise freedom of expression, tax is leviable on profession, occupation, trade, business and industry. Hence tax is leviable on newspaper industry. But when such tax transgresses into the field of freedom of expression and stifles that freedom, it becomes unconstitutional. As long as it is within reasonable limits and does not impede freedom of expression it will not be contravening the limitations of Article 19(2).

Furthermore, the Court indicated that the state's power to levy taxes on the press must also not be abused:

> While levying a tax on newspaper industry it must be kept in mind that it should not be an over-burden on newspapers which constitute the Fourth Estate of the country. Nor should it single out newspaper industry for harsh treatment. Imposition of a tax like the customs duty on newsprint is an imposition on knowledge and would virtually amount to a burden imposed on a man for being literate and for being conscious of his duty as a citizen to inform himself about the world around him.[49]

4.2.2. *Right to Privacy*

Although earlier judicial decisions of constitutional courts in India had not extended right to privacy to the press, stating that it can only be claimed by individuals, recently the Supreme Court has taken a different stand. While hearing

---

[47] *Bennett Coleman & Co and Others v Union of India & Others* AIR 1973 SC 106.
[48] *Indian Express v Union of India* (n 7) [8].
[49] ibid [11].

a matter involving the use of Pegasus spyware by the Government, the Supreme Court in *Manohar Lal Sharma v Union of India*[50] indicated the need and importance of protecting freedom of privacy in order to further protect freedom of speech and expression in general and of journalists in particular.[51]

4.2.3. *Right to Constitutional Remedies*

Since freedom of press is recognised as a part of freedom of speech and expression guaranteed under Article 19(1)(a), the remedy against its infringement lies in Articles 32 and 226 of the Indian Constitution. According to these articles, constitutional remedies can be sought in case of breach of fundamental rights by approaching the Supreme Court and the state's High Court respectively.

4.2.4. *Other Rights of the Press*

Right to press in itself is a wider term, covering under its ambit various other rights such as right to publish, right to broadcast, right to criticise, right to information, etc. The press also has the right to maintain confidentiality of its sources of information. Although the Press Council of India is empowered under section 15 to collect evidence essential to discharge its duties, law bars the Council from compelling the press to disclose sources of information based on which publications were made. According to section 15(2), the Council cannot 'compel any newspaper, news agency, editor or journalist to disclose the source of any news or information published by that newspaper or received or reported by that news agency, editor or journalist'.

4.3. Not All Fundamental Rights can be Claimed by the Press

It is important to note that apart from the rights guaranteed under Articles 19(1)(a) and 19(1)(g), other fundamental rights guaranteed to a citizen are generally not extended to the press generally – like the right to life, liberty, movement, equality, etc. Court decisions have previously indicated these limits in law. Hence, the press cannot claim freedom to travel as its right. In the case of *Maneka Gandhi v Union of India*,[52] the Court clarified this, stating that 'the right to go abroad on one hand and the right of free speech and expression on the other are made up basically of constituents so different that one cannot be comprehended in the other'.[53]

---

[50] *Manohar Lal Sharma v Union of India* Writ Petition (CRL) No 314 of 2021.
[51] Discussed later in the chapter.
[52] *Maneka Gandhi v Union of India* AIR 1978 SC 597.
[53] ibid (also on MANU/SC/0133/1978 at [45]).

4.4. Restricting Freedom of Press on the Ground of Right to Privacy

In addition to the restrictions imposed under Article 19(2), right to privacy which is guaranteed as being a component of right to life under Article 21 can also be a valid ground to restrict press freedom. Right to life as guaranteed under Article 21 also guarantees right to liberty and privacy. The Indian Supreme Court in the case of *R Rajagopal v State of Tamil Nadu* held:

> the right to privacy is implicit in the right to life and liberty guaranteed to the citizens of this country by Article 21 It is a 'right to be let alone. A citizen has a right to safeguard the privacy of his own, his family, marriage, procreation, motherhood, child-bearing and education among other matters. None can publish anything concerning the above matters without his consent whether truthful or otherwise and whether laudatory or critical. If he does so, he would be violating the right to privacy of the person concerned and would be liable in an action for damages. Position may, however, be different, if a person voluntarily thrusts himself into controversy or voluntarily invites or raises a controversy.[54]

The Court then goes on to justify publications that are unobjectionable by stating that:

> the rule aforesaid is subject to the exception, that any publication concerning the afore-said aspects becomes unobjectionable if such publication is based upon public records including court records. This is for the reason that once a matter becomes a matter of public record, the right to privacy no longer subsists and it becomes a legitimate subject for comment by press and media among others.[55]

The Court further exempts publications made on the matters related to public officials' discharge of duties, by stating:

> In the case of public officials, it is obvious, right to privacy, or for that matter, the remedy of action for damages is simply not available with respect to their acts and conduct relevant to the discharge of their official duties. This is so even where the publication is based upon facts and statements which are not true, unless the official establishes that the publication was made (by the defendant) with reckless disregard for truth. In such a case, it would be enough for the defendant (member of the press or media) to prove that he acted after a reasonable verification of the facts; it is not neces-sary for him to prove that what he has written is true. Of course, where the publication is proved to be false and actuated by malice or personal animosity, the defendant would have no defence and would be liable for damages. It is equally obvious that in matters not relevant to the discharge of his duties, the public official enjoys the same protection as any other citizen.[56]

---

[54] *R Rajagopal v State of Tamil Nadu* 1995 AIR 264 SC [26].
[55] ibid.
[56] ibid [26].

4.5. Free Press, Right to Privacy and Criminal Laws

Indian criminal law to an extent also imposes restrictions upon freedom of speech if such freedom is used to disclose the identity of a victim of sexual abuse. According to section 228A of the Indian Penal Code, printing or publishing 'the name or any matter which may make known the identity of any person against whom an offence under Section 376,[57] Section 376A,[58] 376AB,[59] Section 376B,[60] Section 376C[61] or Section 376D,[62] 376DA,[63] Section 376DB[64] or Section 376E[65] is alleged or found to have been committed' is an offence. Any such publication if made, without the permission of the Court, is made punishable with imprisonment that can extend to two years along with a fine.[66] Parallel to these provisions of the Indian Penal Code, the Criminal Procedure Code also imposes restrictions upon publication of details of a case undergoing inquiry or trial. According to section 327 of the Criminal Procedure Code, an inquiry or trial of rape or an offence under sections 376, 376A 376AB, 376B, 376C, 376D, 376DA, 376DB, 376E of the Indian Penal Code shall be conducted in-camera, and in such case 'it shall not be lawful for any person to print or publish any matter in relation to any such proceedings, except with the previous permission of the Court'. However, the provision also states: 'Provided that the ban on printing or publication of trail proceedings in relation to an offence of rape may be lifted, subject to maintaining confidentiality of name and address of the parties'.[67] Hence to this extent freedom of press is restricted so that the confidentiality of victims of sexual offences are safeguarded and their right to privacy is protected. Right to privacy today is interpreted wide enough to also include the right to be forgotten and right to be let alone.[68] Courts in India have also started restricting press freedom along these lines.[69]

5. Other Laws Regulating Press Freedom

Apart from the aforementioned provisions from the Constitution, there are other laws through which press freedom is regulated. Today's press regulatory framework

---

[57] Indian Penal Code, s 376 imposes punishment for the offence of rape.

[58] Indian Penal Code, s 376A prescribes punishment for rape causing death or resulting in a persistent vegetative state of the victim.

[59] Indian Penal Code, s 376AB deals with the offence.

[60] Indian Penal Code, s 376B imposes punishment for the offence of sexual intercourse by a husband upon his wife during separation.

[61] Indian Penal Code, s 376C deals with the offence of sexual intercourse by a person in authority.

[62] Indian Penal Code, s 376D criminalises gang rape and considers it as an aggravated form of rape.

[63] Indian Penal Code, s 376DA imposes punishment for gang rape on a female under 16 years of age.

[64] Indian Penal Code, s 376DB imposes punishment for gang rape on a female under 12 years of age.

[65] Indian Penal Code, s 376E imposes punishment for repeat offenders.

[66] Indian Penal Code, s 228A(3).

[67] Criminal Procedure Code, s 327.

[68] *Justice KS Puttaswamy v Union of India* (2017) 10 SCC 1.

[69] This aspect is further discussed in the chapter, under section 6, 'Online Versions of Press Publication and Conflicting Concerns'.

in India is to an extent a reflection of the colonial regulatory framework. Hence we have laws that restricts exercise of freedom of press. The following are some of the laws regulating press in India.

5.1. Press and Registration of Books Act 1867

Although this law was enacted prior to the country's independence, this Act continues to apply even today. It provides for the regulation of printing presses and newspapers, for the preservation of copies of books and newspapers printed in India and for the registration of such books and newspapers. It also mandates preservation of copies of every book and newspaper printed in India and for the registration of such books, newspapers and periodicals.[70]

5.2. Press Council Act

The first Press Council Act of 1956 was passed to 'establish a Press Council for the purpose of preserving the freedom of the Press and for maintaining and improving the standards of Newspapers in India'. It was replaced with the Press Council Act of 1978 which was enacted in order to preserve the freedom of the press and to maintain and improve the standards of newspaper and news agencies in India. This Act most importantly lead to the establishment of the Press Council of India which is a quasi-judicial body that adjudicates complaints filed by and against the press.[71] The Council is an autonomous statutory body which is authorised and mandated 'to preserve the freedom of the press and to maintain and improve the standards of newspapers and the news agencies in India'.[72] The Council hence is obliged to perform the following functions:

a)   to help newspapers and news agencies to maintain their independence;

b)   to build up a code of conduct for newspapers, news agencies and journalists in accordance with high professional standards;

c)   to ensure on the part of newspapers, news agencies and journalists, the maintenance of high standards of public taste and foster a due sense of both the rights and responsibilities of citizenship;

d)   to encourage the growth of a sense of responsibility and public service among all those engaged in the profession of journalism;

e)   to keep under review any development likely to restrict the supply and dissemination of news of public interest and importance;

f)   to keep under review cases of assistance received by any newspaper or news agency in India from any foreign source including such cases as are referred to it by the Central Government or are brought to its notice by any individual,

---

[70] As provided in the Act's Introduction.
[71] See for details, www.presscouncil.nic.in.
[72] Press Council Act 1978, s 13(1).

association of persons or any other organisation: Provided that nothing in this clause shall preclude the Central Government from dealing with any case of assistance received by a newspaper or news agency in India from any foreign source in any other manner it thinks fit;

g) to undertake studies of foreign newspapers, including those brought out by any embassy or other representative in India of a foreign State, their circulation and impact. Explanation. For the purposes of this clause, the expression 'foreign State' has the meaning assigned to it in Section 87A of the Code of Civil Procedure 1908 (5 of 1908);

h) to promote a proper functional relationship among all classes of persons engaged in the production or publication of newspapers or in news agencies: Provided that nothing in this clause shall be deemed to confer on the Council any functions in regard to disputes to which the Industrial Disputes Act, 1947 (14 of 1947), applies;

i) to concern itself with developments such as concentration of or other aspects of ownership of newspapers and news agencies which may affect the independence of the Press;

j) to undertake such studies as may be entrusted to the Council and to express its opinion in regard to any matter referred to it by the Central Government;

k) to do such other acts as may be incidental or conducive to the discharge of the above functions.[73]

Thus, the Council is empowered to hear complaints by or against a journalist or an editor, a newspaper or news agency (related to print media). Complaints alleging unnecessary interventions of Government – both Central Government and state may also be filed before the Council, if such interventions affected free functioning of the press or it resulted in infringement of freedom of press/complaints in relation to other related issues such as physical attacks on journalists, or denial of facilities to the press, etc.[74]

5.3. Indian Penal Code

This Code of 1860 is another example of a colonial law continuing to apply even today. The Code criminalises offences such as sedition, defamation, publication, and transmission of obscene and pornographic material, publication of material that might affect law and order, or communal harmony. These crimes are subject to the imposition of imprisonment and fines. These provisions have been even invoked against the press in various cases. However, these provisions must be interpreted on the lines of restrictions imposed under Article 19(2), so that the use of such criminal law provisions do not unnecessarily and unreasonably restrict press freedom.

---

[73] ibid s 13(2).
[74] See for details, www.presscouncil.nic.in/ComplaintsUS13Procedure.aspx#.

5.4. Contempt of Courts Act 1971

This Act classifies contempt into two categories, namely civil and criminal contempt.[75] The Act defines civil contempt as 'wilful disobedience to any judgment, decree, direction, order, writ or other process of a court or wilful breach of an undertaking given to a court'[76] and criminal contempt as:

> publication (whether by words, spoken or written, or by signs, or by visible representations, or otherwise) of any matter or the doing of any other act whatsoever which:
>
> scandalises or tends to scandalise, or lowers or tends to lower the authority of, any court; or
>
> prejudices, or interferes or tends to interfere with, the due course of any judicial proceeding; or
>
> Interferes or tends to interfere with, or obstructs or tends to obstruct, the administration of justice in any other manner. Though courts in India have respected and protected freedom of press but where a press publication comes under any of the above form of 'contempt' act, the concern press can be subjected to liability under the Act.[77]

In *Ashwini Kumar Ghose v Arabinda Bose*,[78] the Court had expressed concern about an article that was published by *The Times of India* newspaper since the article did not just criticise a judgment of the Court but had also attributed motives to the judges. The Court said:

> No objection could have been taken to the article had it merely preached to the Courts of law the sermon of divine detachment. But when it proceeded to attribute improper motives to the Judges, it not only transgressed the limits of fair and 'bona fide' criticism but had a clear tendency to affect the dignity and prestige of this Court. The article in question was thus a gross contempt of Court. It is obvious that if an impression is created in the minds of the public that the Judges in the highest Court in the land act on extraneous considerations in deciding cases, the confidence of the whole community in the administration of justice is bound to be undermined and no greater mischief than that can possibly be imagined. It was for this reason that the rule was issued against the respondents.[79]

However, since the editor, printer and the publisher of the paper in their respective affidavits had stated that they now realise that in the offending article they had exceeded the limits of legitimate criticism, the Court decided to drop the contempt proceedings.

Fair criticism of court decisions or courts administrative actions have usually been exempted from contempt proceedings. In the case of *Debi Prasad Sharma and Others v the King Emperor*,[80] the Court in order to decide if a publication was

---

[75] Contempt of Courts Act 1971, s 2(a).
[76] ibid s 2(b).
[77] ibid s 2(c).
[78] *Ashwini Kumar Ghose v Arabinda Bose* AIR 1953 SC 75.
[79] ibid [2].
[80] *Debi Prasad Sharma and Others v the King Emperor* (1944) 46 BOMLR 11.

contempt or not said: 'test applied by the very strong Board which heard the reference was whether the words complained of were in the circumstances calculated
to obstruct or interfere with the course of justice and the due administration of
the law'. Innocent publications, that is publications on matters in relation to which
a civil or criminal case is pending is also exempt from liability as per section 3
of the Contempt of Court Act. However, if such publication is not innocent, the
same may be legally regulated. There are also many incidences in which courts
have issued interim stay orders against media trial of a pending criminal case.[81]
Breach of such court orders can become a legally valid ground to invoke contempt
proceedings.

5.5. Damages under Civil Law

A person offended due to any newspaper publication can seek compensation by
approaching a civil court. Hence publications amounting to libel, defamation,
and slander, which are recognised as civil wrongs, can be complained against by
approaching a civil court.

5.6. Other Laws

Further, the press, like other citizens, is bound by various general laws such as:

- ordinary forms of taxation;
- application of the general laws relating to industrial relations;
- regulation of conditions of services of the employees;
- laws relating to defamation or contempt of court;
- law of trespass, nuisance, etc, as regards entry by newspaper men into private
  property;
- liability for unfair reporting;
- regulating the commercial activities of the Press, without interfering with its
  freedom of expression.[82]

6. Online Versions of Press Publication and Conflicting Concerns

Although the term 'press' conventionally derives from the conventional printing
press, today the term is used in various senses and contexts thereby also covering other modes of news publication including online publications. Today most

---

[81] Pending criminal cases include pending investigation, inquiry, and trial.
[82] Basu (n 5) 31.

newspapers, newsletters, etc have an online presence. Social media platforms are used by newspaper agencies to promote their news,[83] and such platforms have become a popular source for news. On one hand, they are the platform through which news gets spread through the user's postings and, on the other hand, newspaper agencies also get their e-copies published on it. Such platforms have actually become an extension of a daily newspaper. According to Assocham,[84] 'social media platforms like Facebook, WhatsApp, Instagram and others are rapidly changing the reading and viewing habits of an increasing number of people, mostly youngsters'.[85] This unrestricted platform for being a mode of news dissemination today has raised many concerns, including those relating to right to privacy. In fact these concerns are more serious compared to those that emerged on conventional modes of publication. Publications on digital media has no expiry period and can be accessed from anywhere at any time as it has no geographical limits and is something that cannot be permanently removed from online platforms.

Online publications often raise questions of privacy. In *Justice KS Puttaswamy v Union of India*, the Court said that:

> The impact of the digital age results in information on the internet being permanent. Humans forget, but the internet does not forget and does not let humans forget. Any endeavour to remove information from the internet does not result in its absolute oblit-eration. The foot prints remain. It is thus, said that in the digital world preservation is the norm and forgetting a struggle.[86]

Courts have issued interim orders to remove online content considered to be against a citizen's right to privacy. In *Jorawer Singh Mundy v Union of India and Others*,[87] the Delhi High Court had issued orders for the removal of online content in relation to a previous case in which the petitioner was acquitted for being against his right to privacy and *right to be forgotten*. Online publication of illegal content is also governed through the provisions of other conventional laws such as the Indian Penal Code, as well as through cyber- specific law such as the Information Technology Act 2000. This Act can also be the basis for regulating press in India, especially ones that have an online presence.

---

[83] 'Top Newspapers Use Social Media to Spread News Rather than Engage Audiences' (*University of Jyväskylä*, 1 February 2022), www.jyu.fi/en/current/archive/2022/02/top-newspapers-use-social-media-to-spread-news-rather-than-engage-audiences.

[84] Associated Chambers of Commerce and Industry of India. For details, see www.assocham.org/about-us.php.

[85] 'Paradigm Shift: 80 Per Cent Indians Consume News from Social Media Rather than a Newspaper' *The Economic Times* (23 July 2017), https://economictimes.indiatimes.com/magazines/panache/paradigm-shift-80-per-cent-indians-consume-news-from-social-media-rather-than-a-newspaper/articleshow/59724410.cms?from=mdr.

[86] *Justice KS Puttaswamy* (n 68), quoting R Antani, 'The Resistance of Memory: Could the European Union's Right to Be Forgotten Exist in the United States' (2015) 30(4) *Berkeley Technology Law Journal* 1173.

[87] *Jorawer Singh Mundy v Union of India and Others* WP(C) 3918/2021 & CM Appl. 11767/2021.

Today, one of the major concerns relating to the online publication of news is fake news, news resulting in the offence of defamation, sedition or other illegal acts. Hence certain provisions have been added to the Information Technology Act through which such illegal online content, including that which is published via e-newspaper platforms or social media platforms can be regulated. The Information Technology Act empowers the state and its law enforcement agencies with powers to conduct electronic surveillance and to also block illegal online content.

According to the Information Technology Act, the Government can issue directions for interception or monitoring or decryption of any information through any computer resource. Hence the Government is empowered to conduct e-surveillance or ask for decryption of encrypted information on the grounds of:

> interest of the sovereignty or integrity of India, defence of India, security of the State, friendly relations with foreign States or public order or for preventing incitement to the commission of any cognizable offence relating to above or for investigation of any offence.[88]

Whenever such powers of the Government is alleged to have been misused, the judiciary has come to the rescue of the affected. In *Manohar Lal Sharma v Union of India*,[89] where the state was alleged to have misused Pegasus, a spyware against citizens including journalists, the Court emphasised the importance of freedom of press and its close link to right to privacy. The Court said that:

> It is undeniable that surveillance and the knowledge that one is under the threat of being spied on can affect the way an individual decides to exercise his or her rights. Such a scenario might result in self-censorship. This is of particular concern when it relates to the freedom of the press, which is an important pillar of democracy. Such chilling effect on the freedom of speech is an assault on the vital public watchdog role of the press, which may undermine the ability of the press to provide accurate and reliable information.[90]

The Court also focused on the importance of protecting the confidentiality of sources of journalistic information by saying: 'Protection of journalistic sources is one of the basic conditions for the freedom of the press. Without such protection, sources may be deterred from assisting the press in informing the public on matters of public interest.'[91]

The state under the Information Technology Act is also empowered to regulate abusive online material by way of ordering the removal of such material or by issuing blocking orders. According to its section 69A, the Government is empowered to issue blocking orders thereby blocking public access to any information through any computer resource on the grounds of 'interest of sovereignty

---

[88] Information Technology Act 2000, s 69.
[89] *Manohar Lal Sharma* (n 50).
[90] ibid [39].
[91] ibid [40].

and integrity of India, defence of India, security of the State, friendly relations with foreign States or public order or for preventing incitement to the commission of any cognizable offence relating to above'. In the exercise of this power, the Government has issued blocking orders against multiple online platforms, including some platforms at times alleged to have contained journalistic content.[92]

The Supreme Court in *Anuradha Bhasin v Union of India*,[93] while hearing a petition filed against the Government's internet blocking orders issued in the State of Jammu and Kashmir, held that:

> we declare that the freedom of speech and expression and the freedom to practice any profession or carry on any trade, business or occupation over the medium of internet enjoys constitutional protection under Article 19(1) (a) and Article 19(1) (g). The restriction upon such fundamental rights should be in consonance with the mandate under Article 19(2) and 19(6)[94] of the Constitution, inclusive of the test of proportionality ....

> An order suspending internet services indefinitely is impermissible under the Temporary Suspension of Telecom Services (Public Emergency or Public Service) Rules, 2017. Suspension can be utilized for temporary duration only. Any order suspending internet issued under the Suspension Rules, must adhere to the principle of proportionality and must not extend beyond necessary duration. Any order suspending internet under the Suspension Rules is subject to judicial review based on the parameters set out herein.[95]

Thus, the Court refused to allow internet blocking for an 'indefinite' period thereby insisting on the compliance to 'proportionality' principle while issuing such orders affecting freedom of expression and the right to use the internet. These decisions of the courts are also attempts to balance the concerns of the public interest with freedom of speech and press. On the other hand, it is also pertinent to note that the Supreme Court of India in the case of *Shreya Singhal v Union of India*[96] had upheld the right to freedom of speech and expression of net users, as long as they are within the legal requisites of Article 19(2) of the Indian Constitution.

---

[92] See S Barik, 'IT Min Ordered to Take Down 1,474 Accounts, 175 Tweets: Twitter in Petition' *Indian Express* (8 July 2022), https://indianexpress.com/article/business/social-media-watch-feb-2021-2022-it-min-take-down-accounts-tweets-twitter-8015959.

[93] *Anuradha Bhasin v Union of India* AIR 2020 SC 1308.

[94] According to Article 19(6) of the Indian Constitution: '(6) Nothing in sub clause (g) of the said clause shall affect the operation of any existing law in so far as it imposes, or prevent the State from making any law imposing, in the interests of the general public, reasonable restrictions on the exercise of the right conferred by the said sub clause, and, in particular, nothing in the said sub clause shall affect the operation of any existing law in so far as it relates to, or prevent the State from making any law relating to, (i) the professional or technical qualifications necessary for practising any profession or carrying on any occupation, trade or business, or (ii) the carrying on by the State, or by a corporation owned or controlled by the State, of any trade, business, industry or service, whether to the exclusion, complete or partial, of citizens or otherwise'.

[95] *Anuradha Bhasin* (n 93) [152].

[96] *Shreya Singhal v Union of India* AIR 2015 SC 1523.

7. Contemporary Judicial Interpretations and Other Rights of the Press

As already discussed, in India, the press, like citizens, are vested with the right to freedom of speech and expression as well as freedom of trade. Hence restrictions imposed if any on the press must be reasonable, fair, and just. So is the importance of 'reasonable restrictions' prescribed under Article 19(2) of the Indian Constitution. The press cannot be subjected to unnecessary state interference even through other laws such as criminal laws, the Information Technology Act, or the Press Council of India Act. Recently, Indian courts have interpreted fundamental rights quite widely, taking into consideration the object of law, need of meaningful interpretation laws, as well as by considering the impact of breach of one right upon the other rights of the concerned individual. Such interpretations can be seen especially while interpreting criminal law provisions that were used to target journalists or news reporters.

Indian courts have also recognised journalists' right to free speech by way of granting bail in cases of their arrest made on the basis on their publications. Recently the Supreme Court granted bail to a Kerala journalist Siddique Kappan, who was arrested in October 2020 while he was on his way to report from Uttar Pradesh's Hathras, where an alleged gang rape and murder had been committed.[97] In an earlier case, the Calcutta High Court had made similar observations, while hearing an anticipatory bail application of a TV reporter, Avishek Dutta Roy by saying: 'It is the fundamental right of a press reporter to publish any news, which may not be palatable to the administration'.[98] Hence, the unnecessary invocation of arrest power by the state against journalists is viewed with disfavour, and is regarded as being an infringement of their freedom of speech. Thus, the courts in India have also extended protection to journalists against abuse of legal process, such as illegal arrest and illegal detention.

A similar approach is seen against false or multiple complaints filed against journalists and news reporters by misusing the provisions of criminal laws. In the case of *Arnab Ranjan Goswami v Union of India*,[99] the Court protected Goswami from facing multiple investigations for an alleged programme he had anchored and published on his TV channel, considering it as being in violation of freedom of speech and expression. The Court held:

> But to allow a journalist to be subjected to multiple complaints and to the pursuit of remedies traversing multiple states and jurisdictions when faced with successive FIRs[100] and complaints bearing the same foundation has a stifling effect on the exercise of that

---

[97] 'Supreme Court Grants Bail to Siddique Kappan; Reporter Spent 23 Months in Jail', *The Wire*, 9 September 2022, https://thewire.in/law/supreme-court-grants-bail-to-siddique-kappan.
[98] https://www.livelaw.in/pdf_upload/pdf_upload-379554.pdf.
[99] *Arnab Ranjan Goswami v Union of India* (2020) 14 SCC 12.
[100] First Information Report forms the basis of a police crime investigation.

freedom. This will effectively destroy the freedom of the citizen to know of the affairs of governance in the nation and the right of the journalist to ensure an informed society. Our decisions hold that the right of a journalist under Article 19(1) (a) no higher than the right of the citizen to speak and express. But we must as a society never forget that one cannot exist without the other. Free citizens cannot exist when the news media is chained to adhere to one position.[101]

Hence, the above laws and judicial decisions are an indication of the extent of rights the press has in the country and the grounds and circumstances based on which such rights can be restricted. Despite this, many times journalists' and news reporters' rights are unreasonably resisted for political reasons by ruling states which hinders meaningful enjoyment of press freedom. Judicial scrutiny of such state actions hence becomes an important safeguard for the press.

8. Conclusion

In India, like other democratic countries, the right to freedom of press, even though it has not been recognised as a distinct right, has been regarded as an integral part and component of the right to freedom of speech and expression. The Indian Constitution declares this right as a fundamental right, thereby emphasising the obligation of the state in protecting this right. Hence, laws regulating the press in India cannot be beyond constitutionally imposed 'reasonable restrictions'. However, despite this, at times state action against the press has bought the press under harsh censorship and regulation, thereby raising questions of the legality of such actions. Most of the regulatory frameworks of today to a large extent is a reflection of laws India had before attaining its independence. While some regulatory approaches were a reflection of political will of the state rather than being imposed on the grounds of public interest, such regulations could not survive for long, as they were either repealed or set aside through the court's case laws.

Today the concerns affecting free press is also due to the intersection of conventional modes of press with information technology. However, the basis for imposing restrictions on the press, including its online versions, has to be in conformity with the constitutionally imposed 'reasonable restrictions'. Currently most of the statutory framework of the country tries to balance both the protection of fundamental rights of the citizens including freedom of press along with the state's power to curtail such rights for reasonable purposes. Freedom of press is of immense value to a democratic county like India. 'The liberty of the press remains an Ark of the Covenant. The newspapers give the people the freedom to find out which ideas are correct'.[102] Thus, balancing these above cited conflicting concerns are of extreme importance in a democracy.

---

[101] *Arnab Ranjan Goswami* (n 99) [32].
[102] *Bennett Coleman & Co* (n 47).

5

Israeli Perspectives on Press Freedom and Regulation

TEHILLA SHWARTZ ALTSHULER

1. Introduction: Israel's Press Freedom Paradox

For the past two decades, the Israeli press has been in a state of continuing crisis, composed in fact of four different but related crises that feed into one another.[1] The first is an economic crisis among traditional media outlets (print newspapers and broadcast media) and the undermining of their status by the technology giants. The second is control and concentration of ownership in the Israeli media market, reflected in relations among organisations within the industry in every link and component of the production chain. These connections lead to overlapping interests among media organisations, those covering the news, and those who are being covered, paving the way for them to influence each other. The third is a crisis of professionalism as financial difficulties in news organisations lead to budget cuts, reduce the number of media organisations, degrade the quality of news personnel, and reorder the priorities of journalism. The fourth crisis concerns the relationship between politics and the media, manifested in populist attacks on the media and a debate over the media's loss of public trust.

The root of the matter is that this compound crisis is occurring in a country that suffers inherently from a press freedom paradox. Israel lacks the 'constitutional crutches' that are needed to stabilise the checks and balances between the 'fourth estate' and other branches of the democratic structure, creating doubt about the ability of the Israeli media to serve as a watchdog for democracy. The Israeli media environment appears vibrant, pluralistic and respected for its press freedom despite the lack of robust legal protections.

---

[1] T Shwartz Altshuler and N Feldman, *Toolkit for Contending with the Crisis in the Israeli News Market* (Jerusalem, Israel Democracy Institute, 2021), www.idi.org.il/media/16788/toolkit-for-contending-with-the-crisis-in-the-israeli-news-market.pdf.

In this sense, Israel's media landscape resembles that of other Western media systems in terms of journalistic values and technological sophistication. Furthermore, the number of media voices per capita in Israel is the fourth highest globally.[2]

A deeper look, however, shows that Israeli democracy lacks the constitutional base to ensure the stability of the protection of press freedom. The country's Basic Laws do not specifically address the issue and the Knesset (the Israeli parliament) consistently refuses to correct the lacuna. Admittedly, the Supreme Court has affirmed that freedom of expression is essential to human dignity, implicitly incorporating this value into the Basic Law: Human Dignity and Liberty.[3] Israeli courts have also cited the Declaration of Independence as a source of legal support for press freedom. Nevertheless, weakening the Supreme Court's power, as proposed by the newly installed Government (as of January 2023), threatens to undermine the protection of such rights as are not outlined in the Basic Laws, of which press freedom is one.

In the transition from the British Mandate rule to independence in 1948, several laws that regulated the media industries and the press were left over from the Mandate. Examples are the Press Ordinance of 1933, which requires newspapers to obtain a licence as a precondition for publication, and the Mandatory Defense (Emergency) Regulations of 1945, which authorise the military censor to penalise, shut down or halt the operation of media outlets for national-security reasons. Since then, this legacy has evolved into an innate tension between media control and the liberal perception of free speech even as the structure of the media market has changed dramatically in response to technological advancements.

Several international indexes of press freedom reflect this paradox. Reporters Without Borders ranked Israel 86th among 180 countries in its World Press Freedom Index in 2021.[4] Israel trails far behind the leading Western democracies due to what Reporters Without Borders calls 'noticeable problems' and a 'toxic environment'. Freedom House rated Israel 'partly free' in 2017 and ranked it 64th among 200 countries and territories in its Freedom in the World index that year.[5]

---

[2] A Schejter and M Yemini, 'Media Concentration in Israel' in E Noam (ed), *Who Owns the World's Media? Media Concentration and Ownership Around the World* (Oxford, Oxford University Press, 2016) 942–84, 980.

[3] In 1992, the Knesset approved two Basic Laws: the Basic Law on Human Dignity and Liberty and the Basic Law on Freedom of Occupation. These Basic Laws limited the Knesset's power to infringe on the human rights enumerated therein through legislation. The Supreme Court inferred from the Basic Laws that it can invalidate laws that improperly violate both Basic Laws in what has been termed the Israeli 'constitutional revolution'.

[4] 'Netanyahu Corruption Trial Sheds Light on Meddling in Israeli media' (*Reporters Without Borders*, 5 May 2021), https://rsf.org/en/netanyahu-corruption-trial-sheds-light-meddling-israeli-media.

[5] 'Freedom of the Press 2017' (Freedom House, April 2017) 26, https://freedomhouse.org/sites/default/files/2020-02/FOTP_2017_booklet_FINAL_April28_1.pdf.

2. Freedom of the Press in Israel's Constitutional Theory

2.1. An Unwritten Right

In the state's early years, the Supreme Court defined freedom of the press as an utmost right that constitutes a prerequisite for the realisation of almost all other freedoms. *Kol Ha'am v Minister of the Interior*[6] is generally regarded as the case that enshrined freedom of expression and the press as fundamental rights within the Israeli constitutional framework. Justice Shimon Agranat, the first Chief Justice of the Israeli Supreme Court, recognised freedom of the press as the process of elucidating the truth and noted that to attain this goal, the principle of the right to freedom of expression serves as both a means and an instrument. The Court also noted that the suppression of information from the marketplace of ideas might create a backlash: 'It often happens that the very act of oppression – the actual suspension of the newspaper [titled *Kol Ha'am*, '*Vox Populi*'] in which the matters objected to have been published – endows them with an exaggerated value in the eyes of the public.'[7]

This position was reiterated in the Supreme Court's ruling 50 years later in the affair surrounding *Jenin, Jenin*, a movie that purported to document an Israel Defense Forces operation in the Jenin refugee camp, and attributed war crimes to its soldiers. Although the film was found to have made false representations and the Council for the Review of Films and Plays decided to prohibit its screening in Israeli cinemas, the Supreme Court ruled that 'the Council has no monopoly on the truth' and that both libel suits and free arguments are excellent ways to challenge the claims raised in the movie.[8]

However, the heavy weight given to the value of freedom of the press is far from self-evident.[9] The State of Israel does not have a constitution or even an ordinary law that guarantees freedom of expression or the press. Like many democratic rights and values, this freedom exists only thanks to a creative ruling by the Israeli Supreme Court. As mentioned above, the activist ruling was born in the *Kol Ha'am* affair in 1953, in which the Minister of the Interior ordered the closure of two newspapers, one in Hebrew and one in Arabic, that belonged to the Israeli

---

[6] *Kol Ha'am Ltd v Minister of the Interior* HCJ 73/53, 16 October 1953, English translation at https://versa.cardozo.yu.edu/opinions/kol-haam-co-ltd-v-minister-interior.

[7] ibid F(4)(b).

[8] *Bakri v Israel Film Council* HCJ 316/03, 11 November 2003, English translation at https://versa.cardozo.yu.edu/opinions/bakri-v-israel-film-council. In November 2022, the Supreme Court rejected Bakri's appeal against his charge for defamation, and left intact the amount of compensation that Mohammad Bakri was obligated to pay to IDF reserve soldier Nissim Magnaji. See C Maanit and J Houri, 'The Supreme Court Rejected Bakri's Appeal Against his Charge for Defamation in the Movie *Jenin, Jenin*' (*Ha'aretz*, 23 November 2022), www.haaretz.co.il/news/law/2022-11-23/ty-article/.premium/00000184-a4ec-d7bb-a3d6-f6fe4a090000 (in Hebrew).

[9] *Kol Ha'am* (n 6).

Communist movement, claiming that they expressed dangerously strong criticism of the Israeli Government. The Court, headed by Chief Justice Agranat, revoked the closure orders on the basis of the existence of freedom of the press in Israel as a legal principle that the Government must respect.[10]

To overcome the difficulty of a lack of statutes or constitutional clauses guaranteeing this freedom, the Supreme Court gave a paragraph in the Declaration of the Independence of the State of Israel, which asserts that the state is democratic by nature, binding legal effect. Although the Declaration does not explicitly use the phrases 'democracy' or 'freedom of expression and the press', the Court took the bold step of holding that no such explicit statement is necessary.

By so ruling, Chief Justice Agranat turned the Declaration of Independence into a surrogate constitution. Nevertheless, it was only a surrogate and not an actual constitution. Therefore, it did not empower the Court to invalidate laws that infringe on freedom of expression. The novelty of the ruling, however, lies in its provision of a narrow interpretation of these laws. The Mandatory law in the *Kol Ha'am* case (section 19(2) of the Press Ordinance) stated that the Minister of the Interior may close the newspaper if, in his opinion, the content published in it 'may' (likely) harm public peace or public order. Justice Agranat held that the word 'may' should be interpreted as 'probable', meaning that only a high, almost inevitable, probability can justify the infringement of freedom of expression and the press.

Throughout the years, the Court has repeatedly criticised these powers, and interpreted them narrowly. Only in 2017, however, did the Knesset repeal the Press Ordinance after a protracted struggle led by the Association for Civil Rights in Israel (ACRI).[11] Nevertheless, the political metaphor of 'proximity to certainty' has become the cornerstone of constitutional theory regarding freedom of expression in Israel, print media, political speech, electronic media, film and the internet.[12] It is reminiscent of the US Supreme Court's 'clear and present danger' test, which expresses the notion that freedom of speech enjoys preference over other democratic values. It should be noted that not all Supreme Court justices over the years have fully shared the notion of an inherent priority of the right to press freedom over other rights and values. For example, the fifth Chief Justice, Moshe Landau, recommended 'horizontal demarcation of rights of equal status, without favoring a right at the expense of other rights'.[13]

---

[10] ibid.

[11] See M Negbi, 'We Got Rid of the Sphinx' (*The Seventh Eye*, 16 June 2016), www.the7eye.org.il/207453 (in Hebrew). Also note that Chapter 94 of the Mandatory Defense (Emergency) Regulations of 1945 was cancelled with the update of the Israeli Anti-Terror Act 1996.

[12] See M Negbi and A Weinberg, *Freedom of the Journalist and Freedom of the Press: Media Law and Ethics* (Ra'anana, The Open University Press, 2020) chapter 1 (in Hebrew).

[13] *Ha'aretz Daily Newspaper Ltd and Others v The Israel Electric Corporation Ltd* CA 723/74, 24 February 1977, English translation at https://versa.cardozo.yu.edu/sites/default/files/upload/opinions/Ha%27aretz%20Daily%20Newspaper%20v.%20Israel%20Electric%20Corporation.pdf; and the appeal: *Israel Electric Corp. v Ha'aretz* CFH 9/77, 27 August 1978, English translation at https://versa.cardozo.yu.edu/opinions/israel-electric-corp-v-haaretz.

2.2. The Constitutional Revolution

As previously mentioned, in 1992 the Knesset approved two 'Basic Laws', one of which is the Basic Law: Human Dignity and Liberty. In subsequent decades, the Supreme Court used these Basic Laws to instigate a 'constitutional revolution' in Israel by inferring from these statutes that it had the power to invalidate laws that properly violated them.[14] These Basic Laws, however, do not explicitly mention the rights to freedom of the press, expression and information. Courts have used this omission to demonstrate the weakness of the right to freedom of the press relative to rights explicitly enshrined in the Basic Laws. For example, when journalists' right to freedom of expression clashed with the right of a newspaper publisher to dictate what would be published in the newspaper that they owned, the Court allowed the right of the publisher to prevail, in part because their property rights are included in the Basic Law whereas freedom of the press is not.[15]

Chief Justice Aharon Barak expressed a dissenting opinion in this matter, stating that freedom of expression is part of the Basic Law: Human Dignity and Liberty even if not explicitly mentioned in it because it is integral to the right to dignity enshrined in section 2 of the Basic Law.[16] For years, there was no consensus among Supreme Court justices on this question. In 2015, however, all nine members of the panel agreed that freedom of expression is a constitutional right. The case revolved around the Boycott Law,[17] which allows compensation to be claimed from those who call for a boycott of the state of Israel. In their decision, the justices accepted the claim that freedom of expression protects public calls for boycotts and were later divided over whether the infringement of the right was justified.

This judicial determination established freedom of expression as a constitutional right within the current constitutional framework. This, however, does not ensure the upholding of press freedom at the level of implementation because the Basic Law: Human Dignity and Liberty itself grants immunity to laws that contradict it provided they were enacted before it, that is, before 1992. As many of the laws that restrict press freedom date back to the British Mandate or the state's early decades, the courts cannot invalidate them.

2.3. Racist Speech

Whether all forms of expression are entitled to equal protection under Israeli law has also been the focus of controversy. In 1985, Israeli society had to deal with the

---

[14] *United Mizrahi Bank v Migdal Cooperative Village* CA 6821/93, 9 November 1995, English translation at https://versa.cardozo.yu.edu/opinions/united-mizrahi-bank-v-migdal-cooperative-village.
[15] Negbi and Weinberg (n 12).
[16] A Barak, 'The Right for Dignity as a Constitutional Right' (1994) 41 *Haprklit* 271 (in Hebrew).
[17] The Prevention of Harm to the State of Israel through the Boycott Law, 5771-2011.

extent of the right of Meir Kahane, a Knesset member who headed a racist Jewish supremacy movement, to enjoy exposure in the public media.[18] The Supreme Court overturned a decision by the board of directors of the Israel Broadcasting Authority to prohibit Kahane from being invited to participate in current-affairs programmes.[19]

Chief Justice Aharon Barak stated that 'Indeed, racism is fundamentally false, but the truth will come to light only by the free confrontation of ideas and opinions'.[20] The Knesset did not adopt this concept and, in 1986, prohibited publications that contained incitement to racism or Holocaust denial in Israel, but qualified the ban by determining that no prosecution would be undertaken without the Attorney General's approval.[21] Just as it recognised the freedom of racist expression, so did the Supreme Court acknowledge the freedom of pornographic expression. The Court unanimously rejected a petition from feminist groups to ban the broadcast of the Playboy channel on multi-channel television, and upheld the decision of the relevant regulator to settle for a 'code-based access' approach.

The assassination of Prime Minister Yitzhak Rabin in 1992 and the incitement that preceded it triggered a legal and ethical controversy over whether the press should platform instigators and their incitement. Four days after the assassination, the Attorney General wrote to all media outlets in the country, warning them not to interview inciters or quote them directly. This was strongly resisted by the journalistic community, the President of the Press Council even challenging the Attorney General's very authority to give instructions to private media outlets. Does freedom of the press also apply to commercial advertising? Again the Supreme Court responded in the affirmative, stating that rude advertisements can be broadcast even though their audience is captive. Nevertheless, the Court held that the protection afforded to freedom of commercial expression is weaker than that granted to freedom of political expression.[22]

2.4. Unequal Speech Rights

Do all those who express themselves enjoy equal protection? Some laws in Israel imply the opposite. For example, the National Civil Service Law (2014) prohibits senior civil servants from criticising their ministries' policies at a press conference, in an interview with a journalist, in a speech or in a book. All civil servants of

---

[18] I Galnoor and D Blander, 'The Media in Israel – Do They Weaken or Strengthen Democracy?' in I Galnoor and D Blander, *The Handbook of Israel's Political System* (Cambridge, Cambridge University Press, 2018) ch 13.

[19] *Kahane v The Israel Broadcasting Authority* HCJ 339/85, P.D. 41(2)1, 1997 (in Hebrew).

[20] ibid.

[21] The Prohibition of Holocaust Denial Law 1986.

[22] *Kidum Initiatives and Publishing Ltd v The Israel Broadcasting Authority* HCJ 606/93, P.D. 48(2)1, 1994.

any rank are enjoined against criticising the Government and its ministries in an insulting or offensive manner in any media interview, broadcast or book. Violation of the prohibition is a disciplinary offence that may result in dismissal and deprivation of a pension. These penalties have resulted in several court cases.

Moreover, the rules are applied unequally between Hebrew and Arabic speakers. For example, the Supreme Court continued to allow the Government to use the purportedly restricted powers emanating from the British Mandate Press Ordinance and other press-restrictive legislation against Israeli-Arab journalists and media outlets. Thus, the courts have upheld the suspension of the publication of newspapers in several cases[23] and decisions to deny licences to newspapers meant to be published in Arabic.[24] Another example is the requirement laid down by the Government Press Office (GPO) for journalists operating in Israel to have proper accreditation to attend official press conferences, access government buildings, and cross Israeli military checkpoints. Hundreds of foreign journalists are generally accredited. However, the GPO has occasionally refused to provide press cards –especially to Palestinians – on national-security grounds, thus blocking the affected reporters from entering Israel.[25]

Since those who wish to engage in news reporting would find it challenging to do so without a GPO press card, the Court ruled that the GPO may set conditions but must be 'reasonable', especially for Palestinians living in the Occupied Territories. Over the years, the GPO has tried to revoke press cards on the grounds of certain coverage, especially in the context of events in the Occupied Territories. Despite this, the Court reiterated its ruling that refusal to issue official documents on such a basis, as in the case of press cards for Al Jazeera journalists in Israel, should be downscaled.[26]

2.5. Freedom of Information

The right to freedom of the press and the right to freedom of information are related and interdependent. Thus, Chief Justice Meir Shamgar ruled that '[w]ithout sources of information, journalism is like a seasonal stream whose sources have dried up, and the freedom to publish it – becomes meaningless'.[27] In Israel, however, the two rights are differentiated in their constitutional status. The right to freedom of information is enshrined in the Freedom of Information Law,

---

[23] See, eg, HCJ 644/ 81, regarding the Arabic newspaper *Al Fajar*.

[24] See, eg, HCJ 322/ 81.

[25] See GPO's official website: www.gov.il/en/departments/government-press-office/govil-landing-page.

[26] *Saif v Government Press Office* HCJ 5627/02 and HCJ 8813/02, 25 April 2004, English translation at https://versa.cardozo.yu.edu/opinions/saif-v-government-press-office.

[27] *Citrin v Disciplinary Court of the Bar Association in the District of Tel Aviv* MP 298/86 7 April 1987, English translation at https://versa.cardozo.yu.edu/opinions/citrin-v-disciplinary-court-bar-association-district-tel-aviv.

5758-1998, which went into effect in 1999 and created a revolution of transparency in the workings of public authorities. The novelty of the law is that it allows every citizen to request information from a public authority without having to give a reason for the request. This revolution, however, is partial because the law exempts government authorities from providing information wherever disclosure may harm national security, violate another citizen's privacy, interfere with the proper functioning of the public authority or reveal trade secrets. In addition, it is explicitly noted in the statute (Article 14) that it does not apply to any security agencies.[28]

Since the law was enacted, the Supreme Court has ruled numerous times in ways that strengthen government obligations to provide information, including internal protocols such as recommendations from the Attorney General regarding the prosecution of Benjamin Netanyahu and his wife on charges of receiving favours. In particular, the courts held that freedom of information requests from journalists should be treated with particular importance because the activities of journalists and media outlets are a guarantee for the existence of a free and functioning society.[29] Journalists and activist groups have used Freedom of Information Act (FOIA) requests to obtain newsworthy pieces of information.[30] The importance of freedom of information was further reinforced when the Supreme Court ordered Prime Minister Netanyahu to document the dates of talks that he had held with the editor of the newspaper *Israel Hayom* (*Israel Today*) pursuant to a FOIA request filed by the investigative journalist Raviv Drucker.[31]

3. The Israeli News-Media Market

3.1. Overview

Motti Nieger has proposed a three-phase history of the Israeli media, each phase several decades long and focusing on certain media technologies and platforms:

- the state-owned media and the unified Socialist era (1948–1977), constructed around partisan newspapers and state-owned public television channels and radio stations;

---

[28] Y Arbel and T Shwartz Altshuler, *Information Wants to Be Free: Implementing the Freedom of Information Act in Israel* (Jerusalem, Israel Democracy Institute, 2008), www.idi.org.il/media/3506/pp_74.pdf.

[29] *State of Israel, Courts Administration v The Marker – Ha'aretz Newspaper Ltd* AAA 3908/11, 22 September 2014, English translation at https://versa.cardozo.yu.edu/opinions/state-israel-courts-administration-v-themarker-%E2%80%93-haaretz-newspaper-ltd.

[30] See, eg, *Ha'aretz v Ministry of Foreign Affairs* AAA 2975/15, 6 June 2016, English translation at https://versa.cardozo.yu.edu/opinions/haaretz-v-ministry-foreign-affairs.

[31] R Hovel, 'Is Netanyahu the De Facto Editor of Adelson's Newspaper? Court Rules PM Must Divulge Phone Records with Adelson' *Ha'aretz*, 8 August 2017, www.haaretz.com/israel-news/2017-08-08/ty-article/netanyahu-must-reveal-timing-of-calls-with-adelson-top-court-rules/0000017f-e662-df5f-a17f-fffe523f0000.

- the segmented and competitive commercial era (1970–2010), built upon private newspapers and commercial television channels and radio stations;
- the polarised multichannel digital era (2000–present), based on the introduction of broadband internet connection and various digital outlets that it supports, such as news sites, social media and smartphone applications.[32]

Israelis are active news consumers. Mainstream Hebrew newspapers serve an estimated 1.5 million daily readers out of a population of less than 10 million. The pluralistic makeup of Israeli society is reflected in the press landscape, which includes more than a dozen daily newspapers and a wide range of weeklies and news websites serving readers from various religious, ethnic and linguistic groups. The major newspapers are privately owned and some freely criticise government policies and aggressively pursue cases of official corruption. Nonetheless, the press market in Israel appeals to a limited consumer readership due to the smallness of the state and the Hebrew-speaking market, and is very centralised.[33]

The leading privately owned TV channel, Keshet 12, and Israel's public radio station, Reshet Bet, hold an important place in the media landscape. Television news is dominated by two leading players: News 12 (Keshet Broadcasting News Company) and News 13 (the news company of the merged channel Reshet-10). The daily *Yedioth Ahronoth* and the freebie *Israel Hayom* are the leading print-media competitors, while the daily newspaper *Haaretz* exerts much influence on decision-makers despite its small readership. Israel also has Arabic- and Russian-language media outlets and an openly partisan press catering to ultra-Orthodox Jews.[34]

New players have entered the market and became central in it. *Israel Hayom* was founded to compete with *Yedioth Ahronoth*, a 'declared legal monopoly' in the daily-newspaper market. The online news website market offers a broader range of competitors. Ynet is the most widely read news website; generally, the dominant players are related to print or television content bodies (Ynet from *Yedioth Ahronoth* and Mako from Keshet Broadcasting). Business newspapers have also emerged.

Recent decades have seen a significant decline in the prominence of the state-run Israel Broadcasting Authority (IBA)[35] in the television market due to competition from private television and radio outlets, political interference in IBA programming, and poor management. The IBA was closed in 2017 and replaced by a new national public radio and television service, the Israeli Public Broadcasting

---

[32] M Neiger, 'Israel's Media Landscape: Democratic Practice, Constrained Environment' in PR Kumaraswamy (ed), *The Palgrave International Handbook of Israel* (Singapore, Palgrave Macmillan, 2023) 1–19.

[33] AM Schejter, 'How the People of the Book Became the People of the Media: The Israeli Media Landscape' in G Ben-Porat et al (eds), *Routledge Handbook on Contemporary Israel* (London, Routledge, 2022).

[34] Shwartz Altshuler and Feldman (n 1).

[35] T Liebes, 'Performing a Dream and its Dissolution: A Social History of Broadcasting in Israel' in J Curran and M Park (eds), *De-Westernizing Media Studies* (London, Routledge, 2000) 271–87.

Corporation (IPBC), Kan (Here), with an annual public budget of $240 million. Unlike its predecessor, the IPBC is gaining popularity among Israelis, less for its journalistic work than for its original content and digital orientation.[36]

Israelis are rapid adopters of new media technologies and most subscribe to cable, satellite or over-the-top television services. International streaming services such as Netflix have snared a significant market share as complementary services.[37] The penetration of establishmentarian social networks (Facebook, Twitter, Instagram, TikTok and WhatsApp) is very high in Israel[38] and, in a survey I conducted in 2019, I found that Israelis make intensive use of social networks as a source of news.[39] Another survey from 2021 reinforces these findings.[40]

3.2. Israeli Media Economics

The Israeli advertising market is tiny in relation to gross domestic product (GDP) and is steadily shrinking. In recent years, advertising expenditure relative to GDP has been only 0.32 per cent, slightly more than half the level in countries such as France and Germany. In the United States and the United Kingdom, the expenditure rate is more than one per cent, three times higher than in Israel. Moreover, in Israel, despite an increase in private consumption, large advertisers have hardly increased their advertising spending during the past decade.[41]

Since the advertising pie has not grown significantly in the last decade and although commercial television and print journalism continue to maintain a significant share, digital outlets are gradually taking a bite out of them. In 2019, the share of digital advertising surpassed that of television – 38 per cent of the advertising pie, an increase of about 13 per cent over the previous year. Digital advertising nearly tripled from 2010 to 2019. Some 62 per cent of all digital advertising budgets are directed to Facebook and Google. Google's revenue in Israel from advertising alone is estimated at $170 million annually. In the end, most private media entities in Israel suffer from losses or meager profit margins.

The use of branded content and unmarked 'native advertising' – paid material that blends into the surrounding content – is an increasingly important revenue

---

[36] O Klein Shagrir, 'Digital First! Reinventing Israeli PSB and Manufacturing Legitimacy Online' (2019) 8(16) *VIEW Journal of European Television History and Culture* 74–87.

[37] M Wayne, 'Global Streaming Platforms and National Pay-Television Markets: A Case Study of Netflix and Multi-Channel Providers in Israel' (2019) 23(1) *The Communication Review* 29–45.

[38] 'Teens, Parents, and Screens in Israel: A Survey of Uses and Gaps (Summer 2022)' (*Israel Internet Association*, 2022), www.isoc.org.il/sts-data/screentime_2022 (in Hebrew); 'The Extent of Use of Social Media and other Online Platforms by the Israeli Public (Summer 2021)' (*Israel Internet Association*, 2021), www.isoc.org.il/sts-data/2021 (in Hebrew).

[39] T Shwartz Altshuler, *Public Trust in the Media and Social Networks, Special Survey* (Jerusalem, Israel Democracy Institute, 2019), www.idi.org.il/media/13354/public-confidence-in-the-media-and-social-networks-in-israel.pdf (in Hebrew).

[40] Bezeq Annual Internet Report 2021, www.bezeq.co.il/internetandphone/internetreport (in Hebrew).

[41] Shwartz Altshuler and Feldman (n 1).

source for major media outlets in Israel. The most-viewed news website, Ynet, is also the site that hosts the most native advertising. Private companies and government ministries pay millions of Shekels to websites, newspapers and commercial television channels to get their messages out, the paid nature of their content often obscured even though, under existing law, branded content is forbidden absent full disclosure. Class-action suits have sharpened the obligation to mark branded content as such in all media, including social networks.[42] Also, branded content is forbidden in commercial television news programmes due to the belief that it may undermine the public's trust in the media and its ability to serve as a free and open platform for opinions. The prohibition, however, is not always enforced.[43]

The technological and economic changes in the past two decades have led to structural changes in the Israeli news-media map. As the news-media industry's diversity of voices increases, all its categories are suffering an economic crisis. The broadcasting channels, all owned by Israeli and foreign capitalists, are having difficulty generating profits in a crowded market with complicated regulations and are forced to operate at heavy losses to shareholders. News websites that provided free content and attained high exposure have found it challenging to generate profitability from advertising only and have erected paywalls (*Ha'aretz* and *The Marker*, Ynet Plus, *Globes*, and Mako for Keshet subscribers).

4. Press and Media Regulation

4.1. Press Regulation

The Press Ordinance (1933), which required newspapers to obtain a licence as a precondition for publication and empowered the Minister of the Interior to close newspapers for reasons of public order, is a striking example of Israel's anti-democratic inheritance from the British Mandate.[44] While the *Kol Ha'am* ruling severely restrained the Government's power to shut down a newspaper, governments in Israel have used their powers to deny licences. In an investigative report published in *Ha'aretz* in 2016, it was found that 62 such requests were denied for various reasons in the previous decade alone.[45] As mentioned above, legislation repealing the Press Ordinance passed in 2017.

---

[42] O Persiko, 'An Achievement to Combat Misleading the Public on Social Media' (*The Seventh Eye*, 18 December 2022), www.the7eye.org.il/473375 (in Hebrew).

[43] T Chessler and T Shwartz Altshuler, *Regulation of Branded Content in Israeli Media* (Jerusalem, Israel Democracy Institute, 2014), www.idi.org.il/media/3941/regulating_branded_content.pdf (in Hebrew).

[44] A Schejter, 'The End of the Post-Colonial Era: The Transformation in Israeli Media Law on the State's 70th anniversary' (2022) 67 *Publizistik* 109–26.

[45] D Dolev, 'Interior Ministry Has a Stranglehold on the Publication of Newspapers in Israel' *Ha'aretz* (16 January 2016), www.haaretz.com/israel-news/2016-01-16/ty-article/.premium/newspaper-still-subject-to-state-licensing/0000017f-e376-d7b2-a77f-e3778da90000.

4.2. Broadcasting Regulation

Broadcasting regulation in Israel aims to impose not only prohibitions but also positive obligations. The American 'Fairness Doctrine', abandoned in the United States decades ago, is still binding in Israel, and its purpose is to ensure that the information transmitted in the broadcast media is essentially balanced and reflects all opinions in Israeli society.[46] Three regulatory bodies have been established to oversee both public and commercial broadcasting. It is their responsibility to ensure that frequencies and broadcasting channels are entrusted to hands committed to the public interest, that broadcasters are investing in original Israeli productions, and that they are financially stable.

4.3. Public Broadcasting Regulation

When the IPBC was established in 2016 to replace the IBA, the television levy that had traditionally been the means of financing public broadcasting in Israel was abolished. Since then, the economic survival of public broadcasting has been entirely dependent on the state budget and, to prevent abuse of this dependency, barriers between the Government and the IPBC have been erected. Thus, the IPBC is governed by a public council appointed by a retired judge under a series of criteria established by law. Even so, the fact that the corporation is funded solely from the state budget has made it a hostage of politicians; in recent years, politicians on the right side of the political map in particular have expressed the need to limit the Corporation's budgets or make the Corporation even more subordinate to the political echelon.[47]

4.4. Commercial Television Regulation

The Second Authority for Television and Radio was founded as the regulatory overseer of commercial broadcasting in order to ensure that the diverse licensed media companies will serve the public welfare. Although the authority is an independent extra-governmental regulator, the Government continues to exert de facto control over it via its ability to appoint its board of directors and by taking frequent legislative initiatives. Since the 1990s, it has been mandatory by regulation to entrust all television channels' news and current-affairs programmes to a separate dedicated company that the broadcasting licensees fund in its entirely.

---

[46] *Hamifkad Haleumi v Attorney General* HCJ 10203/03, 20 August 2008, English translation at
https://versa.cardozo.yu.edu/opinions/hamifkad-haleumi-v-attorney-general.
[47] B Ravid, 'Miri Regev: Why Set Up New Broadcasting Corporation if We Don't Control It?' *Ha'aretz*
(31 July 2016), www.haaretz.com/israel-news/2016-07-31/ty-article/miri-regev-why-set-up-new-broadcasting-corporation-if-we-dont-control-it/0000017f-efe0-d223-a97f-effd6b9b0000.

The licensees, however, hold only a 60 per cent controlling stake in the news company; the remainder is held by the public via the Second Authority, which has a veto power over the appointment of the company's editor-in-chief.

The strict separation of news broadcasting from the licensees was critically damaged in 2018 with the rush enactment of an amendment to the Israeli Commercial Broadcasting Law that relaxed the conditions for licensing of small television stations and exempted them from having to establish a separate news company. The legislation was intended directly to ease the restrictions for Channel 20, a television channel that clearly and openly supports Netanyahu and therefore faced regulatory sanctions on the grounds of not being fair and balanced.

4.5. Multichannel Television Regulation

Multichannel television platforms in Israel are not allowed to establish their own news channels and are required by law to air the broadcasters' news programmes. The Telecommunications Law was amended in 1986 to form the Cable Broadcasting Council, which soon afterwards began to award cable franchises. When satellite television was introduced in the 'noughties', the Council's authority was extended to satellite platforms as well. The Council is a unit of the Ministry of Communication; it answers to the Minister and their policy.[48]

As the Telecommunications Law and the Second Authority Law were overhauled in response to the advent of broadband internet and direct-to-home satellite, and the pending expiration of the first round of radio and television broadcasting licences, cross-ownership rules were tightened to ban cross-ownership of newspapers, cable and broadcast television.

In the past 25 years, voices have been heard about the need to unite the two regulatory authorities in order to avoid unnecessary redundancy, but this has yet to occur.

4.6. Over-the-Top and Streaming Regulation

The need to decide how to regulate the online equivalents of television channels and new players who transmit commercial television broadcasts via streaming on the internet infrastructure has yet to be addressed. At the end of 2022, a bill proposed by the Ministry of Communications would apply various levels of supervision to the entire audio-visual market including broadcasting, multichannel cable and satellite television, and television over the internet, but it has not matured into legislation.[49]

---

[48] A Schejter and N Tirosh, 'Audiovisual Regulation Transition in Israel: A View from Within' (2016) 7(1) *International Journal of Digital Television* 39–63.
[49] ibid.

4.7. Regulation of Concentration in the Media Market

Concern about media concentration and ownership surfaced when Israeli media and telecommunication providers transitioned from a primarily public sector to a mostly private market. Over the years, the Supreme Court has been concerned that in a reality of control of the media market by a small group of stakeholders, the marketplace of ideas will accommodate only a limited range of opinions, making it justifiable for the state to take remedial action.[50]

Many entities in Israel's media field are interconnected. These connections occur at each stage of the production chain and on all content platforms – print, broadcast, and online – and are not confined to a single media type.[51] Structural ties and vertical and horizontal business collaborations create overlapping interests between media entities and between journalists and the subjects of their coverage. These affinities open the door to mutual influence between them and affect the free flow and quality of information.[52]

Current Israeli antitrust law makes no special provisions for dealing with media or news-content providers. The general antitrust laws are not sufficiently sensitive to the unique features of concentration of ownership in the news-content market. They focus on traditional criteria of price and quantity without addressing declines in product quality in the democratic context of the marketplace of ideas. They also ignore the motivation of competitors in this marketplace not only to maximise profits but also to amass power in order to influence the public discourse. Therefore, most merger applications in the media market are approved, usually on the justification that one of the mergees is a 'failing company' that would not survive without the merger.[53]

5.   Press and Politics

5.1. The Israeli Media between Politics and Capital

The past two decades in the Israeli media market have also been characterised by control by wealthy individuals whose primary business activity is not in media: Eliezer Fishman in *Globes* and *Yedioth Ahronoth*; Yitzhak Tshuva and the Wertheim family in Keshet; Ron Lauder, Yossi Mayan and Arnon Milchan in Channel 10; Len Blavatnik in the merged channel Reshet-13; Sheldon Adelson

---

[50] *Israel Journalist Union v The Prime Minister* HCJ 2996/17, 2 January 2019.

[51] Schejter and Yemini (n 2).

[52] A Wiener and T Shwartz Altshuler, *Concentration of Ownership in the News Content Market* (Jerusalem, The Israel Democracy Institute, 2020), www.idi.org.il/media/14030/concentration-of-ownership-in-the-news-content-market.pdf (in Hebrew).

[53] 'Q&A about the Merger of Channel 10 and Channel 13' (Israel Antitrust Authority), https://cdn.the7eye.org.il/uploads/2018/08/reshet10-QA.pdf (in Hebrew).

in *Israel Hayom*; Shaul Elovitch in the Walla website; and Nochi Dankner in the *Ma'ariv* newspaper are cases in point.

There is sometimes an intimate connection between those controlling the media and decision-makers at the highest levels. The connections are manifested in influencing political coverage and leveraging media control for advantages in other markets. Examples are common: the editor-in-chief of *Israel Hayom* used to have frequent telephone conversations with Prime Minister Netanyahu; Netanyahu's relationship with Elovitch, owner of the Walla website, led to an indictment against both on charges of bribery; Milchan was pressured by Netanyahu to acquire control of Reshet, and promote a merger with Keshet, as revealed in the 'Case 1000' investigations;[54] the owner of Reshet-13, Blavatnik, admitted in testimony to the police that Netanyahu had pressured him to acquire control of the channel from Ilan Shiloah, who owned the channel's shares and is considered a fierce opponent of Netanyahu; and attempts were made to appoint a chair for News 10 per political loyalty[55] and to appoint board members in regulatory authorities according to this key.[56] Fishman at *Globes* and Dankner at *Ma'ariv*[57] used their media outlets as instruments of influence to promote business and personal interests, knowingly leading to biased, incomplete, and sometimes false coverage[58] and degrading journalists' work and journalistic ethics. Eventually, each had to sell his controlling stake in the newspaper due to heavy losses in other arenas of activity. Dankner served a 16-month prison sentence in 2018–2020 for running stocks; Fishman was declared bankrupt in 2017.

The most striking example of capital, media and government interrelations in Israel is that of the late billionaire Sheldon Adelson. Adelson, ranked 17th on the *Forbes* list of the wealthiest Americans in 2019, was a political supporter of the Israeli militant Right and US President Donald Trump. He founded the freebie *Israel Hayom* in 2007 in order to give blatant support to Netanyahu, which he did at least until the latter lost the premiership in 2021. *Ha'aretz* reported that *Israel Hayom* lost more than $200 million in its first seven years of publication,[59]

[54] A Kaplan Sommer, 'Netanyahu on Trial: Everything You Need to Know' *Ha'aretz* (15 May 2020), www.haaretz.com/israel-news/2020-05-15/ty-article/.premium/netanyahu-trial-corruption-news-israel/0000017f-e70e-da9b-a1ff-ef6f1a2d0000.

[55] G Weitz, 'The Man the Prime Minister Pushed for Channel 10 Wants to Harm His News Company' *Ha'aretz* (12 June 2020), www.haaretz.co.il/news/law/2020-06-12/ty-article/.highlight/0000017f-e6c4-d97e-a37f-f7e552410000 (in Hebrew).

[56] A Bein-Leibowitz, 'Comptroller's Report: The Excessive Influence of the Ministry of Communications on the Second Authority and the Cable and Satellite Council: The Political Pressures Outside' *Globes* (4 May 2020), www.globes.co.il/news/article.aspx?did=1001327313 (in Hebrew).

[57] O Persico and G Margalit, 'The Pirit of Globes' (*The Seventh Eye*, 24 January 2017), www.the7eye.org.il/232643 (in Hebrew).

[58] O Persico, 'At Nochi's Request' (*The Seventh Eye*, 4 February 2015) www.the7eye.org.il/145729 (in Hebrew).

[59] U Blau, 'Adelson's Pro-Netanyahu Free Daily Newspaper Lost $190 million in Seven Years' *Ha'aretz* (9 January 2017), www.haaretz.com/israel-news/2017-01-09/ty-article/adelsons-pro-netanyahu-daily-lost-millions/0000017f-ef49-d0f7-a9ff-efcd81580000.

but proved to be a worthwhile political investment as a consequence of Netanyahu's successful election campaigns.[60]

The growing popularity of *Israel Hayom* destabilised the Israeli media landscape, mainly because the publisher of *Yedioth Ahronoth* saw it as a direct threat to his newspaper's viability. In response, *Yedioth Ahronoth* adopted a critical editorial policy toward Prime Minister Netanyahu and pressured Knesset members to pass legislation that would force Adelson to sell *Israel Hayom* instead of handing it out for free. While the bill did not pass, the votes of coalition members to support it were one of the main reasons Netanyahu called for early elections in 2015, which he eventually won.

In 2019, Prime Minister Netanyahu and Arnon Mozes, the publisher of the Yedioth Ahronoth Group, were indicted for fraud and breach of trust (Netanyahu) and attempted bribery (Mozes). Mozes allegedly offered Netanyahu a change for the better in coverage of Netanyahu and his family by the media under his control, and a change for the worse in the coverage of his political opponents, in exchange for which Netanyahu would use his influence to advance legislation and take other measures to impose other restrictions on *Israel Hayom*.[61]

5.2. Media and Politics in Israel: A Toxic Relationship

Between 2000 and 2022, relations between politicians and news media in Israel deteriorated, mainly around the figure of Prime Minister Netanyahu. In its review for 2022, Reporters Without Borders wrote the following:

> Journalists are exposed to open hostility from members of the government. Smear campaigns have been waged against media outlets and journalists by politicians with the help of their party and supporters, exposing their targets to harassment and anonymous messages and forcing them to seek personal protection.[62]

Politicians, as well as their parties and supporters, have indeed engaged in several smear campaigns against the media. The journalists in question needed protective measures due to harassment or threats. Many Israeli journalists have harsh and historical fixations about Netanyahu and have been increasingly open about them over the years. On the other hand, Netanyahu is seriously preoccupied with his

---

[60] G Grossman, Y Margalit and T Mitts, 'Media Ownership as Political Investment: The Case of *Israel Hayom*' (*Projects at Harvard*, 30 January 2020), https://projects.iq.harvard.edu/files/pegroup/files/grossman_et_al_4.21.pdf; M Dahan and M Bentham, 'The Ripple Effects of a Partisan, Free Newspaper: Israel Hayom as Disruptive Media Actor' (2017) 17(1) *Studies in Communication Sciences* 99–106.

[61] R Wootliff and TOI, 'Netanyahu to Stand Trial for Bribery, Fraud and Breach of Trust, Pending Hearing' *Times of Israel* (28 February 2019), www.timesofisrael.com/netanyahu-to-stand-trial-for-bribery-and-breach-of-trust-pending-hearing; 'Netanyahu Trial: Editor "Told to Drop Negative Stories about Israel PM"' (*BBC World*, 5 May 2021), www.bbc.com/news/world-middle-east-56606223.

[62] 'Netanyahu Corruption Trial' (n 4).

relations with the media, reflected in his direct attacks and his attempts to intervene in multiple segments of the press market.[63]

Moreover, Netanyahu may have even wanted to change the public's perception of the Israeli media as objective, impartial and agenda-free by instilling the alternative perception of opinions expressed as plainly belonging to the owner of the media outlet rather than to the outlet itself. As the years passed, Netanyahu's intervention in the media market intensified,[64] culminating in his decision to keep the communications portfolio in his own hands, and drafting a clause in the coalition agreement after the 2015 elections that prohibited support for legislation on media matters without his consent.

It was discovered later that Netanyahu had been speaking daily with the owners and editors of *Israel Hayom*, and had intervened, directly or through his agents, in the establishment of public broadcasting, television commercials and appointments for the Israeli Defense Forces radio station and the Knesset Channel. The revelations in the indictments regarding involvement in print and digital media indicate the degree and depth of this involvement, extending not only to the content but to the entire life cycle of the media. The purpose was not necessarily to shut down the media but to signal that their existence depended on the Prime Minister.[65]

6. The Crisis of Journalistic Professionalism and Public Trust

The economic changes and the surrender to political pressures have undermined journalistic professionalism, and steadily degraded workforce quality and willingness to invest in journalistic investigations that require time and resources, as well as financial backing in the event of libel suits. They have also led to the growing incidence in the Israeli media of biased 'docu-activism' rather than classical journalism. In this sense, aside from the blessing of having so many voices representing the cultural and political diversity of the Israeli public arena, the myriad channels that have flourished are also abetting the polarisation of Israeli society.

---

[63] Shwartz Altshuler and Feldman (n 1); see also Z Beauchamp, 'To Understand What the Trump Investigation Might do to America, Look at Israel' (*Vox*, 19 August 2022), www.vox.com/policy-and-politics/23301390/trump-investigation-mar-a-lago-search-netanyahu.

[64] N Tucker, 'How Bibi Strove to Become Israel's King of Ratings' *Ha'aretz* (12 November 2019), www.haaretz.com/israel-news/2019-11-12/ty-article/.premium-how-bibi-strove-to-become-israels-king-of-ratings/0000017f-f268-d497-a1ff-f2e8e9530000.

[65] A Pfeffer, 'Netanyahu Dreamed of an Israeli Fox News. This Is What He Got Instead' *Ha'aretz* (5 December 2021), www.haaretz.com/israel-news/2021-12-05/ty-article/netanyahu-wanted-an-israeli-fox-news-this-is-what-he-got-instead/0000017f-f88f-d47e-a37f-f9bffd3c0000; A Pfeffer, 'Adelson's Paper Is No Longer Backing Netanyahu. Who Will It Champion Next? *Ha'aretz* (1 February 2022), www.haaretz.com/israel-news/2022-02-01/ty-article/.premium/israel-hayom-is-no-longer-netanyahus-paper-who-will-it-champion-next/0000017f-f4ac-d5bd-a17f-f6be28f30000.

Shuki Taussig, Editor in Chief of the media watchdog website The Seventh Eye, has identified three deeply troubling characteristics of Israeli media practice. First, a few star journalists are enslaved by their sources and receive too much media attention. Second, the priorities in coverage disserve the public interest. Reporters and commentators who cover political and military topics as if they were horse races are given first billing in media news sections and leave environment, health, education and welfare in second place. In addition, journalists are forced to subordinate their professional ethos to external interests:

> Most people who come to the meat grinder of studios and press offices arrive with a sense of mission. But too often, in too many media outlets, they are forced to sell their conscience and adapt themselves to their superiors' changing whims and the needs of the owners and the politicians and businessmen whom their owners wish to serve.[66]

In addition to the above, problematic journalistic practices have multiplied, such as 'clickbait' and yellowing of headlines, receiving funds in exchange for favourable press coverage, and over-focusing on media criticism of other channels instead of creating new and independent journalistic content.

Even the positive processes of diversity in the Israeli media market are sometimes unhelpful in strengthening the journalistic ethos. In October 2020, the well-known, right-wing journalist Kalman Libeskind wrote:

> For years, we wanted the general media to include journalists who grew up in different habitats in order to diversify and enrich it. To some extent, it has happened. There are now more 'other' faces in the media than in the past. However, in addition to these, 'media wildcats' have emerged – people who, for the most part, have never written a news item, never collected information, never rummaged through a yellowing archive, never spoken to a source, and never cross-referenced a story … people without journalistic understanding, people without journalistic ethics, people without respect for journalistic values.[67]

By participating in social networks, journalists are able to abandon their commitment to institutional journalistic ethics, and publish information that has not been reviewed, reveal their political opinions and positions, and get involved in online fights – degrading the public's trust in them.

Politicians' attacks on the media in search of political support, coupled with the decline in journalistic professionalism, have translated into deterioration of the public's trust in the press and the media in 2012–2022.[68] Thus, the Israel Democracy Index for 2022, capturing changes in public trust in institutions, finds the media at the bottom of the pecking order in public and other governmental

---

[66] S Tausig, 'What is independent journalism' (*The Seventh Eye*, 6 February 2019), www.the7eye.org.il/318600 (in Hebrew).

[67] K Libeskind, 'The Dangerous Flowerbed: On the Wild Crops That Grew on the Margins of the Right-Wing Press' *Ma'ariv* (25 September 2020) (in Hebrew).

[68] A Panievsky, 'The Strategic Bias: How Journalists Respond to Antimedia Populism' (2020) 27(4) *The International Journal of Press/Politics*.

institutions.[69] One way of coping with the decline in journalistic professionalism and public trust in the media is to strengthen the commitment to journalistic ethics. Journalistic ethics in Israel are enshrined in the Code of Ethics of the Press, the implementation of which is governed by the Israeli Press and Media Council, a voluntary body established in 1963, comprised of representatives of publishers, journalists and the public, and funded by the media outlets themselves. The Council has an ethics tribunal that considers itself authorised to hear ethical complaints even against non-members of the Council. In practice, however, the tribunal's decisions regarding such journalists are not perceived by media owners as well as journalists as having importance. Although the Code of Ethics purports to obligate media owners to follow its rules and even to ensure the fulfillment of the conditions for ethical journalistic work, there is currently no legal ability to enforce this on the owners of media outlets.

In 2021, the Journalists' Union, the body that represents the majority of Israeli journalists, withdrew its membership from the Press Council. Therefore, as of 2022, the Council does not represent active journalists. In addition, the Yedioth Ahronoth Group, one of the country's largest media groups, withdrew from the Council about a decade ago. Several media outlets have developed and adopted unique codes of ethics to which they adhere, such as the code of ethics of the IPBC[70] and the codes that are part of the broadcast media regulations. Ultimately, the Press Council is not a significant body in terms of the ability to implement or enforce journalistic ethics in Israel. In the late 1990s, a public committee proposed to enshrine the status of the Council in special legislation. Its recommendations were never implemented.[71] In 2012, the Supreme Court gave a significant boost to the status of ethical standards by ruling that media outlets can be protected from defamation lawsuits if they publish inaccurate information but act honestly and with adherence to journalistic ethics and the rules of 'careful and responsible journalism'.[72]

7. Journalistic Privileges

7.1. Confidentiality of Journalistic Sources

Article 117 of the Penal Code prohibits public servants from revealing information that they are exposed to in the course of their duties – a broad injunction that

---

[69] T Herman et al, *The Israeli Democracy Index for 2021* (Jerusalem, Israel Democracy Institute, 2022), https://en.idi.org.il/media/18096/the-israeli-democracy-index-2021.pdf.

[70] T Shwartz Altshuler, *The IPBC 'Kan' Code of Ethics*, https://kanweb.blob.core.windows.net/download/files/%D7%A7%D7%95%D7%93%20%D7%94%D7%90%D7%AA%D7%99%D7%A7%D7%94%20%D7%A9%D7%9C%20%D7%AA%D7%90%D7%92%D7%99%D7%93%20%D7%94%D7%A9%D7%99%D7%93%D7%95%D7%A8.pdf (in Hebrew).

[71] Y Karniel, 'For the Benefit of the Media and the Public: Reinventing the Press Council' *Globes* (16 December 2020), www.globes.co.il/news/article.aspx?did=1001353401.

[72] *Anonymous v Orbach* CFH 2121/12, 18 September 2014, English translation at https://versa.cardozo.yu.edu/opinions/anonymous-v-orbach.

exposes those who provide information to journalists to the risk of prosecution. A major factor that may mitigate the deterrent effect of this ban is the confidentiality of journalistic sources. Indeed, according to the Code of Ethics of the Press and Media Council, journalists will not disclose information provided to them under the condition that it remains confidential. However, journalistic privilege is not enshrined in legislation as is, for example, doctor–patient and lawyer–client privilege. Nevertheless, in 1987 the Supreme Court recognised the existence of a confidentiality that permits a journalist not to disclose his or her sources of information except at the discretion of the Court, which determines whether the information in question is relevant, substantive, and necessary for the case being heard.[73]

In 2012, the Supreme Court ruled that journalistic privilege extends not only to the confidential source itself but also to information that may reveal the identity of the source. The Court also directed the Knesset to codify the relationship of journalist and source in legislation. Meanwhile, the courts continued to uphold journalists' rights. For example, a court ruled in 2015 that a journalist employed by Keshet Channel 12 need not surrender to police raw footage from an interview with a woman accused of tax evasion and running a prostitution ring.[74] Nevertheless, authorities have continued to conduct investigations and surveillance with the aim of uncovering journalists' sources. In addition, it has been established that if a newspaper or journalist is derelict in the duty to protect a source, the source may demand compensation from them.[75] This was stated in a civil suit brought by the former soldier Anat Kamm against *Ha'aretz* and its reporter Uri Blau in 2013, after Blau's identification of Kamm as the source of leaked classified military documents led to her arrest, conviction and incarceration.[76]

Wiretapping by investigative law-enforcement authorities against journalists is a severe violation of freedom of the press and journalistic confidentiality. The Wiretapping Law, 5739-1979, and the Criminal Procedure Law (Powers of Enforcement – Communication Data), 5768-2007, allow the police to receive telecom metadata from Israeli phone and cellular companies for investigative purposes, in disregard of the confidentiality of journalistic sources. In 2017, the police admitted that they had transcribed conversations between sources and journalists and claimed that they did so because journalistic confidentiality in Israel is relative. In the same case the Public Broadcasting Corporation petitioned

---

[73] *Citrin* (n 27).

[74] *State v Makor Rishon Hameuhad (Hatzofe) Ltd* LCrimA 761/12, 29 November 2021, English translation at https://versa.cardozo.yu.edu/opinions/state-v-makor-rishon-hameuhad-hatzofe-ltd. See also N Hasson, 'Israeli Police Seek to Use Press Photos Against anti-Netanyahu Protesters' *Ha'aretz* (15 September 2020), www.haaretz.com/israel-news/2020-09-15/ty-article/.premium/israeli-police-seek-to-use-press-photos-against-anti-netanyahu-protesters/0000017f-e147-d7b2-a77f-e3470a210000.

[75] *Glatt berkowitz v Kra* CA 9705/11, 21 October 2014; *Ha'aretz Publishing v Kamm* CA 1442/19, 13 January 2020; O Persiko, 'An End to Anat Kamm's Lawsuit Against Ha'aretz' (*The Seventh Eye*, 13 January 2020), www.the7eye.org.il/357370 (in Hebrew).

[76] T Shwartz Altshuler and S Yaroslavski-Karni, *Regulating the Confidentiality of Journalistic Sources in Israel* (Jerusalem, Israel Democracy Institute, 2015), www.idi.org.il/media/3410/confidentiality_of_journalistic_sources.pdf.

a district court with an unusual request to impose a gag order on the contents of wiretapped conversations between a journalist of the channel and a famous singer, Margalit Sanaani, relating to a criminal attempt to harm the singer.[77]

During the Covid-19 pandemic, the Israeli Government decided to use the capabilities of its Israel Security Agency (ISA or Shin Bet) for contact tracing based on phone location data. Irrespective of the profound violation of human rights inherent in this process, which was unmatched in any Western country during the pandemic, the Supreme Court accepted the demand of the Journalists' Union to exclude journalists from the mass surveillance so as not to compromise journalistic confidentiality.[78]

In 2022, the ACRI petitioned the Supreme Court to strike down a section of the Shin Bet Law, the statute that regulates the activities of this largely secret service that is not subject to public scrutiny. The section in question requires all communications companies in Israel to provide the service with information about every call or message that takes place through them. The ISA has been storing them in a database called 'The Tool' for about 20 years. The Tool was the instrument used during the pandemic, which is how it became known to the public. As the petition was litigated, ACRI argued that holders of confidentiality, primarily journalists, should be excluded from the law. Data stored in The Tool, ACRI contended, can give the ISA the ability to know where a journalist was, with whom he spoke, how long the conversation lasted, and more. That is, by researching media data the ISA can discover the journalistic sources of a particular piece of information even if the journalist and the source did not talk on the phone but only met carrying phones. The ISA claimed that it had indeed used The Tool to monitor journalists' activities not only in security investigations, but this was done only a few times. As a result, the Journalists' Union sought to join the proceedings as an amicus of the Court, and at the time of writing, the petition is pending.[79]

In the spring of 2022, Israelis received the explosive allegation that the police had illegally spied on dozens of them using NSO Group Pegasus surveillance technology. The charge led to a process of updating current legislation to set boundaries for police use of such technologies. The Journalists' Union demanded an exemption for journalists from surveillance by law enforcement entities.[80]

---

[77] Eli Senyor, 'Police Admits: We Listened and Transcribed Conversations with Journalists' *YNET*, 5 February 2019, https://www.ynet.co.il/articles/0,7340,L-5458565,00.html (in Hebrew).

[78] https://www.itonaim.org.il/%D7%A2%D7%99%D7%AA%D7%95%D7%A0%D7%90% D7%99%D7%9D-%D7%99%D7%95%D7%97%D7%A8%D7%92%D7%95-%D7%9E%D7 %90%D7%99%D7%9B%D7%95%D7%A0%D7%99-%D7%A9%D7%91%D7%94%D7%9B- %D7%A2%D7%9B%D7%A9%D7%99%D7%95-%D7%9E%D7%A2/ (in Hebrew).

[79] C Maanit, 'Israel Seeks to Shield Shin Bet High-tech Spying: The Justice Ministry Is Drafting an Amendment to Give the Agency Legal Basis for What It Does Anyway' *Ha'aretz* (4 February 2022), www.haaretz.com/israel-news/2022-02-04/ty-article/.premium/israel-seeks-to-legitimize-shin-bet-high-tech-spying/0000017f-def1-d3a5-af7f-feff96a40000.

[80] N Zeveloff, 'Israeli Journalists Call for Spyware Exemption after Israel Denies Illegal Pegasus Use' (*Columbia Journalism Review*, 28 March 2022), https://cpj.org/2022/03/israeli-journalists-call-for-spyware-exemption-after-israel-denies-illegal-pegasus-use.

7.2. Defamation and the Israeli Press

The Defamation Law, 5725-1965, makes it very easy to file libel suits in Israel and causes most of the ensuing discussion to focus on the protections outlined in the law. The law establishes primary defences that journalists and media outlets may use. The first is 'truth and public interest', meaning that the publication is provably accurate and in the public interest. The second is 'responsible press', which means that even if the publication cannot be proved accurate, it is probably the product of careful and responsible journalistic work.[81] Over the years, the courts have greatly expanded these defences to protect the freedom of the press and the ability to practice investigative journalism. This major expansion of the media's immunity from libel suits has attracted public criticism on the grounds that the media abuse this immunity and journalists do not check facts or seek a response from those they have maligned. By amending the Defamation Law, the Knesset took a modest and limited remedial step. It required media outlets that publish information that may harm a person's good name to update this information if an official decision is published, purging the person's name if he or she so requests.[82]

The Code of Ethics of the Press Council establishes a set of duties aimed at avoiding unnecessary harm to people's good name. Among them are the obligations to be accurate with the facts, to request a response, to correct mistakes, and to clarify when the coverage is factual and when it is opinion. According to section 8B of the Code, those significantly harmed by errors or material inaccuracies will be given a fair opportunity to respond. The response will be published as soon as possible and with due prominence. Section 9B requires that the person whose name or dignity may be harmed by information published must be contacted and receive a response within a reasonable time before publication, depending on the circumstances. A response will be provided relatively as part of the posting or within a reasonable time after it has been posted. In 2021, the Council's ethics tribunal even ruled that journalists cannot avoid the responsibility of being accurate in facts even when they publish opinion pieces. With the massive increase in the use of the internet and social networks, the courts are clearly inclined to take a less forgiving approach and set a higher bar for compensation in libel suits regarding online publications. In 2016, the journalist Igal Sarna reported on his personal Facebook page an alleged quarrel between Prime Minister Netanyahu and his wife. The Netanyahus sued Sarna, and the lawsuit was accepted and approved in two appellate courts. *Yedioth Ahronoth*, Sarna's employer, was not sued because the journalist posted the content on his personal Facebook page.[83]

---

[81] *Orbach* (n 72).
[82] Negbi and Weinberg (n 12) ch 7.
[83] R Hovel, 'Journalist Who Wrote Netanyahu Was Kicked Out of Car by Wife to Pay $32,500 in Damages' *Ha'aretz* (11 June 2017), www.haaretz.com/israel-news/2017-06-11/ty-article/journalist-who-wrote-netanyahu-was-kicked-out-of-car-by-wife-to-pay-32-500-in-damages/0000017f-df87-d3ff-a7ff-ffa7e1a90000.

Israel has no clear legal doctrine that strikes the proper balance between the right to a good name and the right to freedom of expression in the context of strategic lawsuits against public participation (SLAPPs) in general, and those in the digital world in particular. The courts have recognised the characteristics of SLAPPs and the essential nature of free public discourse – in the context of the balance between freedom of expression and the right to a good name – in shaping public opinion on matters of substantial public interest. However, they have refrained from adopting an anti-SLAPP legal doctrine and, on several occasions, have urged legislators to amend the Defamation Law so that they may contend with the chilling effect of these lawsuits.[84] Until the desired legislation is enacted, the tools that the law currently offers, ie, the protections provided by the Defamation Law and the procedural tools of the Civil Procedure Regulations for summary strike-out or dismissal due to abuse of process, are available to defendants in SLAPPs. The protections in the Defamation Law, however, do little to counter the chilling effect of SLAPPs because the defendant does not achieve a true victory even if he or she ultimately wins the case.

7.3. Public Interest and Privacy Invasion by the Media

In Israel, the right to privacy is protected by section 7 of the Basic Law: Human Dignity and Liberty and by the Protection of Privacy Law, 5741–1981. The Protection of Privacy Law states that violating a person's privacy is forbidden without his consent. Said consent, however, may be implicit, adduced from a person's behaviour, and not necessarily explicit verbal consent. Court hearings that are usually open to the public are also closed when it comes to private matters, such as hearings in family court or matters related to minors and victims of sexual offences. The tension between press coverage and privacy protection has accompanied the public discourse in Israel for many years. Under the Protection of Privacy Law, details that violate a person's privacy may be published if they are in the 'public interest'. According to the courts, this concept excludes 'details intended to satisfy gossipers' needs', but includes matters necessary for a functioning democratic public discourse, provided journalists act in good faith and out of professional duty.[85]

In general, the courts have prioritised the public's right to know and freedom of the press over the right to privacy and provided a broad interpretation of the notion of 'public interest' in cases such as the media's right to reveal details of public figures' private lives, such as an extramarital affair or the discovery of a severe

---

[84] R Aridor Hershkowitz and T Shwartz Altshuler, *SLAPP: Characteristics, Dangers and Ways of Contending with Them* (Jerusalem, Israel Democracy Institute, 2022), www.idi.org.il/media/17839/slapps-characteristics-dangers-and-ways-of-contending-with-them.pdf (in Hebrew).
[85] M Birnhack, 'Constitutional Privacy in Israeli Law' (Tel Aviv University, 17 April 2022), https://papers.ssrn.com/sol3/papers.cfm?abstract_id=4082324.

illness.[86] At the same time, public criticism has been levelled over the years against the media for abusing press freedom and violating privacy unnecessarily. Since Israel has suffered severe terrorist blows, most of the criticism revolves around yellow coverage of terrorist attacks, the publication of victims' names before families are notified, and infiltration of hospitals and cemeteries. Additional contexts of abusive coverage, such as pressuring families of victims of sexual crimes to be interviewed, have been alleged. Therefore, the Israeli media moves among different poles: covering events professionally, ensuring the privacy of citizens who are 'heroes against their will' and their families, competing in the communications market and fearing that competitors will 'scoop' them, and a civil obligation not to serve as pawns in the hands of terror organisations and terrorists.

The Press Council's Code of Ethics has been amended several times in reference to the issue of privacy in covering terrorist attacks and casualties. In fact, it is an undulating movement whereby the media trespass reasonable boundaries; receive public, legal and ethical criticism; limit the invasion of privacy for a certain time, and then go back to trespassing boundaries.

7.4. Journalists' Rights versus Media Owners' Rights

While Israeli courts have played a decisive role in protecting press freedom in its classic form, they have been oblivious to the need to protect the freedom of journalists vis-a-vis the interests that control the media outlets that employ them. The President of the National Labor Court ruled that a journalist must humbly accept the employer's regulations not only regarding work arrangements and tasks but also concerning what the employer will or will not publish.[87] The grave potential consequences of the current legal situation in this regard became clear in the criminal cases surrounding Prime Minister Netanyahu's relations with the publisher of the newspaper *Yedioth Ahronoth*, Arnon Mozes ('File 2000'), and with the owner of the Walla! news portal, Shaul Elovitch ('File 4000'). In both cases, indictments were filed against the media owners, alleging that they had acted to change and distort coverage in their own media in order to serve their financial interests. Following the revelations in the 2000 case, an application for a class-action suit was introduced against *Yedioth Ahronoth*, alleging the infringement of journalistic freedom in the newspaper.

In November 2015, an Israeli Arab journalist sued his former employer for wrongful dismissal after the outlet, a local newspaper, fired him late in Operation Protective Edge, the conflict between Israel and the Gaza-based Hamas militant group in the summer of 2014. The journalist claimed he had been fired because of

---

[86] Negbi and Weinberg (n 12) ch 9.
[87] Y Yoaz, 'National Labor Court Loses Its Biggest Champion of Workers' Rights Today' *Ha'aretz* (6 October 2006), www.haaretz.com/2006-10-04/ty-article/national-labor-court-loses-its-biggest-champion-of-workers-rights-today/0000017f-f165-df98-a5ff-f3ed31e10000.

his political views. The Journalists' Union joined the lawsuit. At roughly this time, two other journalists brought wrongful-dismissal suits against *Israel Hayom* after they were terminated in the wake of a leaked speech given by the paper's editor in chief. The dismissals followed a comprehensive inquiry by management after the leak, including polygraph testing of employees.

One of the proposals that has emerged over the years to protect the freedom of journalists has been to view private mass media as 'bi-material' entities, private-sector bodies that are subject to some of the obligations that administrative law imposes on government authorities, such as fairness, reasonableness and equality. This proposal, however, has been shelved due to fears of over-involvement of the courts in the work of the media.

8. Restrictions on Journalistic Work about Israel

8.1. Military Censorship and Gag Orders

Censorship of information that may endanger a country's security during times of emergency or war is customary in democracies and is considered a derivative of the right to life, for which limiting press freedom is justified and even essential. At the same time, military-censorship and gag-order regulations in Israel are problematic. The formal guidelines for applying military censorship are provided by the British Mandatory Defense (Emergency) Regulations (1945), which empower the military censor to penalise, shut down, or halt the printing of a newspaper for national-security reasons. In practice, however, the censor's role is quite limited and under strict judicial oversight.[88] Moreover, the formal arrangement is softened by a 1996 informal censorship agreement between the media and the Israel Defense Forces.[89]

Notwithstanding the problematic nature of the existing regulations, the media outlets and the security establishment have cooperated in perpetuating them. In this sense, both sides prefer undemocratic and vague rules that are loosely enforced and thus easier to live with to the establishment of an unknown new arrangement that could be advantageous to everyone involved.[90]

---

[88] *Schnitzer v Chief Military Censor* HCJ 680/88, 10 January 1989, English translation at https://versa. cardozo.yu.edu/opinions/schnitzer-v-chief-military-censor.

[89] T Shwartz Altshuler and G Lurie, *Censorship and State Secrets in the Digital Age* (Jerusalem, Israel Democracy Institute Publishing, 2016), www.idi.org.il/media/3422/%D7%A6%D7%A0%D7%96%D7 %95%D7%A8%D7%94-%D7%95%D7%A1%D7%95%D7%93%D7%95%D7%AA-%D7%91%D7%99 %D7%98%D7%97%D7%95%D7%A0%D7%99%D7%99%D7%9D.pdf (in Hebrew).

[90] H Nossek and Y Limor, 'The Israeli Paradox: The Military Censorship as a Protector of the Freedom of the Press' in S Maret (ed), *Government Secrecy. Research in Social Problems and Public Policy*, Vol 19 (Bingley, Emerald, 2011) 103–30, www.emerald.com/insight/content/doi/10.1108/ S0196-1152%282011%290000019011/full/html.

An alternative channel that security authorities have employed in recent years – petitioning the court to issue gag orders – exists despite there being no proper legal basis for this practice.[91] In late 2015, for example, a sweeping gag order was imposed on information pertaining to the investigation of an alleged act of terrorism by Jewish perpetrators, in which three members of a Palestinian family in the West Bank village of Duma were killed.

In addition to gag orders and military censorship, which constitute prior restraint, the criminal code includes provisions that address the discovery of valuable security secrets, which are unjustly termed 'severe espionage offenses'. These provisions amount to post-facto penalties because they are invoked after the information in question has been published. The provisions do not establish a coherent hierarchy of severity that distinguishes among different types of information (for example, between highly sensitive information and information that does not involve serious damage when disclosed), types of informants (for example, among security services employees, soldiers or journalists), and types of publications (for example, between the source that initially disclosed the information and someone who shared it on social media).

Journalists often evade the restrictions by leaking a story to a foreign outlet and then republishing it as being of 'foreign origin', and bloggers outside Israel publish concrete information that is barred from publication inside the country. Some claim that it is impractical to enforce military censorship in view of changes in the media world that allow security secrets to be revealed digitally (on the internet, social media, etc). However, the military censor has shown a growing interest in tracking information posted online as well, especially on social media. He has made it clear to online news sites that they must submit material for prior review just like the traditional press, and even sent personal messages to Israeli citizens whose Facebook accounts deal with security matters, warning them that they must submit materials for review before publishing them on social media.

8.2. Violence against Journalists

Deliberate violence against or harassment of journalists is relatively rare in Israel. The principal targets have traditionally been Arab journalists – both foreign and local, often in and around Jerusalem – though many incidents have also stemmed from private or commercial conflicts (such as within the ultra-Orthodox and Israeli Arabic-language media sectors) and police harassment of journalists who report from demonstrations concerning social and economic matters.

---

[91] N Landau, *The State vs the Press: The Rise of Gag Orders in Israel* (Reuters Institute for the Study of Journalism, 2016), https://reutersinstitute.politics.ox.ac.uk/sites/default/files/research/files/The%2520 State%2520vs%2520The%2520Press%2520-%2520The%2520Rise%2520of%2520Gag%2520Orders%2 520in%2520Israel.pdf.

In May 2015, on the holiday marking the unification of Jerusalem under Israeli control, the Israeli police used extraordinary means – including physical removal and containment – to prevent reporters from covering the day's traditional demonstrations and the way they handled violent clashes in the Old City. According to the Journalists' Union, between 2020 and 2022 there were 27 cases of police violence against journalists, 16 Jewish and 11 Arab.[92] The incidents took place at ultra-Orthodox demonstrations, political demonstrations, in east Jerusalem, on the Temple Mount, and during Operation Guardian of the Walls in May 2021, among other locations. Some of the journalists attacked were well-known, such as Moshe Nussbaum of News 12, who was attacked after trying to comment on violence against demonstrators; *Ha'aretz* reporter Gidi Weitz, who was handcuffed and taken to a police station in December 2021 on the false charge of interfering with police in the performance of their duties; and *Ha'aretz* photographer Tomer Applebaum, who was brutally attacked by police as they dispersed a demonstration on Tel Aviv's Rabin Square in April 2020. In August 2022, AFP photographer Ahmed Garbely, who had come to document the visit of a far-right Knesset member to the Temple Mount, was violently beaten. That month, the heads of the Journalists' Union wrote to the Attorney General complaining that no indictments or complaints had been filed against police in the vast majority of cases of violence against journalists.

8.3. Movement Restrictions on Journalists

Due to ongoing conflicts with Palestinian groups and neighbouring countries, journalists in Israel often face travel restrictions. A long-standing law forbidding Israeli citizens from traveling to 'enemy states' such as Lebanon and Syria without permission from the Interior Ministry has, on occasion, been applied to journalists. Press-freedom organisations have condemned the selective application of the law and the potential effects of such travel restrictions on the diversity of news available to the Israeli public. Although Israeli journalists are generally barred from entering the Palestinian territories without explicit military approval, in practice the military frequently ignores the presence of these journalists there. It does bar Israeli reporters from visiting the Gaza Strip. Arab journalists in Israel encounter more difficulties in their work than do their Jewish counterparts; furthermore, Arab media coverage of criminal activity is sometimes restricted by the very gangs that commit it.

In 2017, the Press Council approached the police, accusing them of evicting journalists and photojournalists from coverage areas and confining them to restricted areas. The ACRI, the Journalists' Union and the Foreign Journalists Association petitioned the Court to establish a procedure for police conduct

---

[92] ID Cohen, 'Journalists Union to the State Attorney: DIP is Not Performing its Duties' Ha'aretz (9 August 2022), www.haaretz.co.il/gallery/media/2022-08-09/ty-article/00000182-823e-dafe-affe-dbbef0900000 (in Hebrew).

vis-a-vis journalists. Such a procedure was published in late 2018, allowing police to prevent journalists and photographers from accessing the scene of an event if there is a concern of harm to human life, obstruction of an investigation or violation of privacy. However, the police chief at the scene of the event must consider alternatives that would mitigate the infringement of freedom of the press, including the allocation of a police force to escort journalists to the scene.[93]

In April 2022, a Palestinian terrorist carried out a shooting attack in the heart of Tel Aviv, murdering three civilians and wounding many others. He fled the scene on foot and was killed only the next morning. From the moment the initial news of the attack was received, the television networks and news websites switched to an open studio that dealt with the incident and reported directly from the field. As a consequence, journalists at the scene chased the security forces as the latter pursued the terrorist. The detailed live coverage was severely criticised. The claim was that the absence of self-censorship in the broadcasts led to the exposure of the identity of fighters in elite units, their methods of operation and their weapons. During the broadcasts, misinformation and sometimes disinformation were transmitted, fomenting panic among the public. In a very unusual move, the spokespersons for the Israel Police, the Israel Defense Forces (IDF), and the ISA sent an open letter to all media outlets countrywide, claiming that some of their number had turned the pursuit of the terrorist into a reality show.[94]

On a different note, in October 2022, as part of the preparations for the 25th Knesset elections, the left-wing Meretz party informed Channel 14, a channel that vigorously supports Netanyahu, that it would not allow the channel to broadcast from the party's headquarters on election day. The Court accepted the petition that Channel 14 submitted in response, ruling that 'blocking the media's path from attending an event of considerable public nature, when it is aimed at a specific journalistic body and to it only, is equivalent to damaging the "hard core" of freedom of the press'.[95]

9. Freedom of the Press in the Digital Age

All the general laws that apply to written publications, relating to matters such as defamation and privacy, also apply to online forums. The Knesset Elections Law

---

[93] O Persiko, 'Reason for Restriction: Special. After Delays, the Police Published its Updated Procedure for Addressing Journalists in the Field' (*The Seventh Eye*, 16 October 2018), www.the7eye. org.il/306528 (in Hebrew).

[94] S Fried, 'Thousands of Complaints and a Scathing Letter: The Controversy Surrounding Coverage of the Attack in Dizengoff Reached the Knesset' (*Makor Rishon*, 14 April 2022), www.makorrishon. co.il/news/476387/ (in Hebrew).

[95] *Jewish Israeli Channel Ltd v Meretz – The Left of Israel headed by Zehava Galon* HCJ 22/7232 (in Hebrew); Y Freidson, 'Court Orders Meretz to Let Channel 14 Broadcast From Party HQ on Election Night' *Ha'aretz*, (1 November 2022), www.haaretz.com/israel-news/elections/2022-11-01/ty-article/.premium/court-orders-meretz-to-let-channel-14-broadcast-from-party-hq-on-election-night/00000184-2fdf-db86-a394-afff05bc0000.

(Propaganda Methods), the main statute that regulates campaign advertising in Israel, was passed in 1959. This law prohibits the broadcasting of 'election propaganda' on television and radio for 60 days before Election Day unless it is shown in state-authorised slots allocated to each of the parties for campaign advertising. These prohibitions are difficult to enforce and generally no longer appropriate for our times. Candidates, political parties and other non-party actors publish freely on digital platforms, exert growing influence on the electorate and are not subject to any legal strictures.[96]

As for the liability of social media for harmful content published on their platforms, in the eyes of the Israeli courts such platforms are not 'media', and therefore do not have the kind of editorial responsibility that applies to media. Conceptually, then, the courts regard the platforms as 'safe harbours', ie immune from liability as long as they are not informed of illegal content and are not charged a 'notice and takedown'.[97] Following the enactment of the Digital Services Act of the European Union, several public committees published recommendations relating to the need to create a wider framework of responsibility for social media platforms. None of these recommendations, however, has matured to legislation.

Between 2017 and 2021, the Government proposed a so-called 'Facebook Bill' several times. According to the bill, the Ministry of Justice would be allowed to ask for a court order to remove any content from news sites and social media platforms if said content may constitute an offence under the Penal Code and if it may harm the security of a person, national security or the state economy. The bill drew significant opposition based on its breadth – the fact that it would relate to any criminal offence, including the kind that restricts expression in the Penal Code, and might cause severe and disproportionate infringement of the right to press freedom by creating the possibility of presenting news websites with a removal order.[98]

10. Summary and a Glimpse Toward the Future

Although the right to press freedom in Israel is safeguarded by a constitutional framework that operates primarily through the courts, vast controls over the

---

[96] T Shwartz Altshuler and G Lurie, *Digital Campaign Advertising and the Threat to Elections* (Jerusalem, Israel Democracy, 2020), www.idi.org.il/media/15554/digital-propaganda-and-the-threat-of-elections.pdf (in Hebrew).

[97] T Zieve, 'Threading a Needle on Social Media Reforms in Israel' (*Jewish Insider*, 3 November 2021), https://jewishinsider.com/2021/11/social-media-internet-yoaz-hendel-israel-u-s-hate-speech-regulation.

[98] M Kremnitzer, 'The Bill on Social Media Incitement Is a Danger to Freedom of Expression' *Haaretz* (30 December 2021), www.haaretz.com/israel-news/2021-12-30/ty-article/.premium/the-bill-on-social-media-incitement-is-a-danger-to-freedom-of-expression/0000017f-e313-d7b2-a77f-e317f2400000; T Shwartz Altshuler, 'Censorship, Democracy and the "Facebook Bill"' *Jerusalem Post* (28 November 2017), www.jpost.com/opinion/censorship-democracy-and-the-facebook-bill-515450.

news-media ecosystem remain in place. These controls are more sophisticated than they were in the early days of the country, derived from legal and economic processes, and reflect a corrupt relationship between the media and politics. It seems, however, that other processes have matured that will impact the news industry in the coming years: new possibilities of media financing such as micro-payments and not-for-profit journalism, technological developments such as generative AI that will enhance the journalistic process and the matching of content to consumers, increased regulation and taxation of the digital giants and reimbursement of the traditional media industry for content presented on plat-forms. Greater public trust will strengthen the status of the media, in part through an understanding of the limitations of social networks in providing a reliable picture of the world but perhaps also due to future court decisions in Cases 2000 and 4000, which may construct a new normative framework for relations among capital, government and the press.

Given all these processes, Israel is facing an urgent challenge to create sustain-able models of activity for the news industry that will offer news organisations long-term stability and protection from corruption both on the part of capitalists and politicians and by other interested parties. To accomplish this, Israeli citizens will have to imagine a new three-way contract among the state, the producers of journalistic content and the public. Such a contract should promote the creation and dissemination of content and information, ensure a high-quality news prod-uct, contend with the major players in the market, and incentivise investments in innovative formats and techniques for processing information and making it accessible to the public. Most importantly, the reform in the news market would achieve its objective only with a change in the journalistic ethos. Such a change requires cultural and political will; even economic models will not suffice. We have to clarify for ourselves what proper journalism is, what is considered a professional journalistic work process, how the journalistic ethos can be bolstered, and how a diverse news market should function.

6

Freedom versus Regulation:
An Evolving Free Press in South Korea

AHRAN PARK AND KYU HO YOUM

1. Introduction

South Korea was the embodiment of permacrisis in the 1960s through to the mid-1980s due to its persistent authoritarian politics. It was often dubbed an 'impossible country' until June of 1987,[1] when Korea was brought to 'the threshold of a remarkable political achievement: the passage ... from backwardness and authoritarianism to prosperity and democratic rule'.[2]

Fast-forward to the early 2020s: Korea – along with two other Asian countries, Japan and Taiwan – is counted among the 35 'liberal democracies'. More remarkably, Korea outranks the United States in the V-Dem global democracy list of nearly 180 countries. Furthermore, it is notable that Korea is in the top 10 per cent of the Liberal Democracy Index, while the United States is conspicuously missing.[3] 'Following the efforts towards democratizations by the June [1987] Democracy Movement during the late 1980s', V-Dem noted, 'the country [South Korea] experienced great improvements in all three aspects of liberal democracy [ie, equality before the law and individual liberty, judicial constraints on the executive branch, and legislative constraints on the executive branch]'.[4] By all accounts, Korea is now viewed as a functioning constitutional democracy. The rule *of* law, not the rule *by* law, is the guiding light for Korea's governing process, as singularly showcased by the Constitutional Court of Korea's globally touted role in ushering in democratic politics in recent decades.[5]

---

[1] See generally, D Tudor, *Korea: The Impossible Country* (Tokyo, Tuttle, 2012).
[2] 'Breakthrough in Seoul' Editorial, *The New York Times* (30 June 1987) 30.
[3] 'Democracy Reports' (*V-Dem Institute*, March 2022), www.v-dem.net/publications/democracy-reports.
[4] F Andersson and V Mechkova, 'Country Brief: South Korea' (*V-Dem Institute*, June 2016), www.v-dem.net/country_reports.html.
[5] KH Youm et al, 'Korea' in *Media, Advertising, Entertainment Law Throughout the World* (Egan, Thomson Reuters, forthcoming).

It is no wonder that Korea's ongoing experience with freedom of expression is attracting international attention; it is not an object of fleeting curiosity for Korea-oriented scholars but a worthy case of a free speech laboratory.[6] Neither law academics nor law practitioners overlook Korea, the world's most wired and media-saturated nation, when reflecting on what they might consider in balancing free speech with conflicting interests.[7] And it is fascinating to consider the question of whether Korea has emerged as more of an exporter than an importer of free speech jurisprudence, as suggested by a 2014 essay on the US influence on Korean law:

> Korean law is now less limited to Korea. Korea's selectively creative adoption of foreign laws has received attention abroad .... The impact of Korea on foreign law will undoubtedly grow, particularly in the areas of international regulation, FOI [freedom of information] and copyright.[8]

Regardless, although freedom of speech and the press in Korea has been guaranteed as a right under the Constitution – through several amendments since 1948, when its first democratic republic was established – free speech and free press were recognised more often in the books than in reality, especially until the late 1980s. Given that press law existed in Korea primarily as the dictatorial leaders' tool against the news media most of the time, there was little or no in-depth discussion of constitutional practice or theory prior to Korea's emergence as a Liberal democracy in the 2000s–2020s. As a case in point, the book *Press Law in South Korea* devotes not one single chapter to press freedom and responsibility from a theoretical perspective.[9]

This chapter aims to correct that omission by examining press law and regulation in democratic South Korea in the past three decades. We approach our topic by imagining the future while at the same time remembering the past. This is all the more fitting because Korea is one of the most fast-changing and dynamic sociopolitical and econo-cultural powerhouses in the past 20 years, as encapsulated by the Korean Wave as a global phenomenon.[10] This chapter begins with an overview of press freedom as a constitutional right in Korea. Next it examines

---

[6] See, eg, D Keats Citron, *The Fight for Privacy: Protecting Dignity, Identity, and Love in the Digital Age* (New York, WW Norton, 2022); DJ Solove, *The Future of Reputation: Gossip, Rumor, and Privacy on the Internet* (New Haven, Yale University Press, 2007), on 'dog poop girl' in Korea.

[7] E Kim and J Lee, 'South Korea: Relatively Healthy, Still Trying Hard to Adapt to Digitalisation' in J Trappel and T Tomaz (eds), *The Media for Democracy Monitor 2021: How Leading News Media Survive Digital Transformation* (Nordicom, University of Gothenburg, 2021) 393.

[8] KH Youm, 'Free Speech Jurisprudence in South Korea: Legal Transplants from the United States' in *The Global Implications of Korean Law* (Sejoing-si, Korea Legislation Research Institute, 2014) 154.

[9] KH Youm, *Press Law in South Korea* (Ames, Iowa State University Press, 1996).

[10] See generally, Y Kim, '*Hallyu*: Korean Wave Media Culture in a Digital Age' in DY Jin and N Kwak (eds), *Communication, Digital Media, and Popular Culture in Korea: Contemporary Research and Future Prospects* (Lanham, Lexington Books, 2018) 423–42.

theories of press freedom[11] that have marked Korean press law and regulation (including what makes press freedom stand apart from freedom of speech).[12] Then it includes a critical analysis of press regulations (including statutory, administrative, self-regulatory and indirect laws), followed by an overview of what kinds of protections exist for journalists in terms of the journalists' privilege, defamation, citizens' right to erasure, and freedom of information (FOI). Finally, this chapter examines how the intersection of press regulation and the new technologies pose regulatory and non-regulatory challenges.

2. Press Freedom as a Constitutional Right

Throughout its history,[13] the Constitution of Korea has stipulated freedom of expression. But the freedom of expression clause of the Constitution was revised to varying degrees throughout the eight times that the Constitution has been amended. Sometimes freedom of expression was qualified, depending on whether 'except as specified by law' was part of the constitutional text.[14] And although licensing or censorship of speech or the press was disallowed as a rule, prior screening of motion pictures and dramatic plays was occasionally allowed 'for the maintenance of public morality and social ethics'.[15]

In practice, Koreans experienced freedom of the press, as a right or as a privilege, for the first time during the US military Government's rule in 1945–1948. But their free press experience was fraught with more challenges than the American rulers anticipated, and this was not surprising. Journalism scholar Jae-kyoung Lee in Seoul opined: 'the South Korean media have lacked such an institutional foundation. Simply put, the idea of the free press in South Korea was nothing more than a superficial imposition of a foreign idea which completely lacks indigenous institutional support'.[16]

---

[11] Press freedom in our study centres on the relationship of the press with the Government, so our attention to 'journalistic' freedom as an internal aspect of press freedom is less than substantial, although we touch on it when relevant. For a discussion of 'newsroom democracy' see Kim and Lee (n 7) 400–401.

[12] In our chapter, 'press' and 'media' are deliberately differentiated in that 'press' refers to the print mode of mass communication, while 'media' refers to the non-print, ie electronic mode of mass communication. The press–media distinction will be clarified when the terms are used in a sentence or paragraph.

[13] For an informative synopsis of Korean constitutional history, see 'Constitutional History of the Republic of Korea' (*ConstitutionNet*, April 2018), https://constitutionnet.org/country/republic-korea.

[14] K Yang, *Constitutional Law Lecture* (Seoul, Bopmunsa, 2014) 521 (in Korean).

[15] Constitution of Korea, art 18(1), amended in 1962.

[16] J Lee, A Crisis of the South Korean Media: The Rise of Civil Society and Democratic Transition 6 (1993) (paper presented at the Association for Education in Journalism and Mass Communication in Kansas City), quoted in Youm (n 9) 37.

In the 1960s, however, a court ruling proved the institutional support of at least one provincial district court judge. In an Anti-Communist Act case in 1967, Judge Pyong-chae Han stated that press freedom cannot be restricted merely on the grounds that anti-Communism happened to be the national policy of Korea. He reasoned:

> *Freedom of the press* is most important for survival of a *political democracy*. Only press freedom can ensure an *ideal national consensus* for us. It can also protect civil rights from being *infringed upon by the government*. It contributes to our playing a creative role in our overall national development through its *criticism and factual reporting*. Indeed, press freedom is a *life-and-death issue* for our democracy (emphasis of 'life-and-death issue' retained; other emphases added).[17]

Here 'press' refers to a newspaper as an institutional speaker. The case left no room for doubt as to the importance of press freedom, especially given the history of the case as the first of its kind (national security versus news reporting), the logic of the court opinion (connecting the press to 'political democracy') and the designation of the media's structural role (the press as the fourth branch to check the three-branch Government).

This case, though, was a notable exception at the time in terms of implementing press freedom in practice. It was not until Koreans firmly placed democratic politics in position in 1987 that press freedom became powerfully ensconced in practice. The new law and order for mass media in Korea is laid out by the current Constitution, as amended in 1987, the 'year of the constitutional miracle'.[18] The 1987 Constitution considerably expanded individual rights. One of the most notable improvements in Koreans' civil rights was in the realm of freedom of expression.[19] In particular, freedom of the press is enumerated in Article 21 of the Constitution. Article 21(1) states that 'every citizen has the freedom of speech and the press', and Article 21(2) prohibits the press and publications from being licensed or censored. The constitutional clause on freedom of speech and the press applies the same way regardless of what medium of communication is involved. In other words, the phrase 'speech and the press' in the Constitution is not limited to oral and print media: production and manufacturing of disks and videos and movies, for example, are also protected as long as they are used as a means of communication to express thoughts.

---

[17] Taegu District Court, 65 Ko 8762, 18 October 1967 (quoted in Youm (n 9) 159).

[18] T Kim and SD Lee, 'Republic of Korea (South Korea): The Influence of US Constitutional Law Doctrines in Korea' in *Constitutional Systems in Late Twentieth Century Asia* (Seattle, University of Washington Press, 1992) 322. For an insightful look into the constitutional revolution in Korea of 1987, see JM West and EJ Baker, 'The 1987 Constitutional Reforms in South Korea: Electoral Processes and Judicial Independence' in W Shaw (ed), *Human Rights in Korea: Historical and Policy Perspectives* (Cambridge, Harvard Council on East Asian Studies, 1991) 221–52.

[19] Kim and Lee (n 7) 322. The media law reforms following the constitutional amendment in 1987 are discussed in depth in KH Youm, 'South Korea: Press Laws in Transition' (1991) 22 *Columbia Human Rights Law Review* 401–35.

The Free Speech and Free Press Clause of the Korean Constitution is less than clear in some aspects. But it is clear that freedom of the press is not absolute. For example, the press is forbidden to infringe on 'the honor or rights of others, public morals, or social ethics' (Article 21(4)). Furthermore, although the standards of both news services and broadcast facilities are subject to statutory requirements necessary to 'ensure the functions of newspapers' under law (Article 21(3)), freedom of the air, which is read into 'the press' under the Constitution,[20] is 'far more strictly regulated'. This is especially the case with the entry, content and cross-ownership of broadcasting than freedom of newspapers because of the technological and economic scarcity and social impact of broadcasting.[21]

3. Theories of Press Freedom

Why does freedom of expression as a whole and freedom of the press specifically exist as a *fundamental* right – yes, more than a *constitutional* right – for Koreans? This 'why' question is intertwined with the underlying purpose of freedom of expression as a human right proclaimed by the Universal Declaration of Human Rights. Considering the axiomatic proposition that democracy will not survive without free speech and free press, Korea since its post-Second World War founding has invariably included freedom of expression as a basic right in its Constitution. It is not entirely clear, however, whether the framers of the Korean Constitution pondered, like the framers of the US Constitution did in the 1780s–1790s,[22] *why* freedom of expression should be among the citizens' enumerated rights, *what* they intended to read into the right, and *how* the right should be implemented.[23] In fact, it was not until Koreans firmly placed democratic politics in place in 1987 that a few Korean jurists and scholars theorised about freedom of the press in earnest; after all, they felt little need to do so when freedom of expression was viewed by Korean leaders as an expendable luxury only for those in 'advanced' countries in the West.

3.1. Marketplace of Ideas, Right to Know and Watchdog Role

Theories expounded on press freedom in Korea have covered the typical press freedom topics: marketplace of ideas, right to know and watchdog role. Judge

---

[20] Supreme Court, 2015Du48474, 21 November 2019.

[21] J Moon, 'Freedom of Expression and Its Limitations' in *Media and the Law* (Seoul, Communication Books, 2017) 5 (in Korean).

[22] See AR Amar, *The Bill of Rights: Creation and Reconstruction* (New Haven, Yale University Press, 1998).

[23] For a concise framing of the First Amendment theory on free speech, see RA Smolla, *Smolla and Nimmer on Freedom of Speech* (Egan, Thomson Reuters, 2022) § 2:3, which is exceedingly helpful when approaching the free speech theory from the why, what, and how perspectives.

Han's extraordinary free press ruling[24] highlights that he was keenly aware of the 'marketplace of ideas' theory,[25] ensuring that ideas are allowed to compete with each other for acceptance in an open process, and of the 'democratic self-governance process'[26] theory that permits citizens to debate politics and governance without interference. This seminal free press case epitomises the 'public discourse theory' on media freedom.[27] Much later, but in a similar vein, noting that democratic politics is unthinkable without free expression and exchange of ideas, Korean constitutional law scholar Jae-wan Moon wrote that 'a country with no guarantee of freedom of expression cannot be labeled a democratic nation in its strict sense'.[28] Moreover, freedom of institutional media speech takes on an instrumental value because it contributes to the citizens' formation of diverse public opinions as a public duty and their role as a watchdog over those in power.[29]

Korean courts after Judge Han have endeavoured to answer why freedom of the press should be treated as a fundamental right for Koreans. The Constitutional Court has defined freedom of speech and the press as 'a means of self-actualisation through which an individual forms his or her personality' and 'a means of self-governing that makes citizens participate in political decision-making'.[30] Furthermore, the Court stated that media reporting helps arouse the public's interest in democracy and encourages the citizen's active participation in politics.

Freedom of the press, as interpreted by Judge Han, meant a negative freedom – that is, absence of governmental restraint. With the advent of the information age, freedom of the press is now expanded far enough to include the 'right to know' as 'freedom of information that encompasses the Government's positive help in facilitating the media organisations' active collection, processing and distribution of information'.[31] Therefore, press freedom and the people's right to know are essential because 'securing an open space for the free exchange of ideas and opinions' and 'disseminating information through the media' are the critical components of a democratic system.[32]

---

[24] See n 17 above.

[25] JS Mill, *On Liberty* (London, John W Parker and Son, 1859) 31–99.

[26] The influential free speech theory under the First Amendment, which posits that 'democratic self-government' justifies freedom of speech as a constitutional right in America, has its genesis in A Meiklejohn, *Free Speech and Its Relationship to Self-Government* (Clark, Lawbook Exchange, 1948). For the most perceptive analysis of the Meiklejohnian theory, see Smolla (n 23) para 2:28, 2–27 to 32–34.

[27] J Oster, *Media Freedom as a Fundamental Right* (Cambridge, Cambridge University Press, 2015) 28–44. 'Public discourse', according to Oster, is 'an open, free and argumentative communicative process aimed at reaching understanding and forming public opinion on matters of public concern', ibid 29.

[28] J Moon (n 21) 4.

[29] Y Park, *Freedom of the Press* (Seoul, Pakyoungsa, 2013) 104–105 (in Korean).

[30] Constitutional Court, 97Heonma265, 24 June 1999.

[31] ibid.

[32] Park (n 29).

Meanwhile, the 'checking value' of freedom of the press,[33] to which Judge Han alluded in his Anti-Communist Act opinion, derives from the press's watchdog role in a democracy: monitoring the Government and public officials to ensure that democratic politics functions properly. In the early 1990s, the Constitutional Court had called attention to the checking value of the right to know in holding the Government responsible to the people, linking the right to know to democratic society because it promotes individual and social values such as self-fulfillment, the search for truth, participation in political decision-making and a balance between stability and change.[34]

As a vigilant watchdog, the press must actively and critically report on powerful entities. Not surprisingly, those who have been the subject of critical reporting have frequently challenged news media by suing reporters for defamation and other related claims. Notably, however, Korean courts have considered the press's surveillance function in weighing the right of a free press against social and individual interests:

> The significance of press freedom is not limited to delivery of information and the realisation of the right to know. One of the essential functions of the press is to monitor the Government and public officials. Only when the media functions properly as a watchdog for society, democracy is able to function properly. Thus, critical press reporting on the Government and public officials should be encouraged, even though such reporting may be viewed as defamatory to the public figures. If the public figures file defamation lawsuits against the press, such lawsuits will have a serious chilling effect on the press and journalists. As a result, the public figures will achieve their intended purpose – silencing the press.[35]

3.2. Court Interpretations

In its early years, the Constitutional Court of Korea, sounding like the US Supreme Court on the 'preferred position' of the First Amendment,[36] held that freedom of the press is entitled to greater protection than other constitutional rights. In 1990, the Constitutional Court stated, albeit not in a press freedom context, that the 'natural demand evolving from the *preferred position* of freedom of expression' leads to restrictions on the broad application of the National Security Act (emphasis added).[37] One year later, the Korean Court found that '[b]ecause freedom of the press serves as the very foundation of the survival and development of

---

[33] The 'checking value' of free speech means 'the value that free speech, *a free press*, and free assembly can serve in checking the abuse of power by public officials'. V Blasi, 'The Checking Value in First Amendment' (1977) 2 *American Bar Foundation Research Journal* 527 (emphasis added).

[34] Constitutional Court, 89Honka104, 2 February 1992.

[35] Seoul High Court, 2014Nu5912, 10 February 2015.

[36] See *Thomas v Collins* 323 US 516, 529–50 (1945).

[37] Constitutional Court, 89Honma113, 2 April 1990.

a democratic country, modern constitutional law is characterised by the *preferred position* it especially holds' (emphasis added).[38] But it was in no way obvious at the time what would constitute the 'preferred position'[39] of free press, and how it would emerge through court cases.[40]

3.3. Press Freedom as Distinct from Speech Freedom

Freedom of the press is arguably a 'derivative' of freedom of speech, but the origin of *the press* and the Government's response (in England) are revelatory conceptually. That is, press freedom could not be more different from speech freedom.[41] Thus, few discerning free speech commentators will quibble about the irrefutable role of an institutional press in democracy. In particular, freedom of the press in Korea is akin to freedom of speech as a passive concept in the sense of no governmental interference. But freedom of the press has an active value in the national law and order in that it requires the press to carry on a 'public duty' of facilitating the formation of public opinion. Therefore, the state should respect freedom of the press when confronting challenges in order to systematically secure the freedom.[42]

Articles 21(1) and 21(2) on freedom of speech and the press of the Korean Constitution are textually modelled after the First Amendment to the US Constitution.[43] But there has been little judicial or scholarly discussion of freedom of the press as distinct from freedom of speech in Korea – in contrast with the controversy over the Free Press Clause of the First Amendment.[44] The leading media law expert in Korea, Yongsang Park, former Chairman of the Press Arbitration Commission, maintained that the Korean Constitution only provides freedom of speech and the press 'horizontally', and that the scope and substance and legal character of press freedom is 'unclear'.[45] He added: 'Should an opportunity arise for discussion of a constitutional revision, there shall be a task ready to systematise the Free Speech and Press Clause'.[46]

---

[38] Constitutional Court, 89Honma165, 16 September 1991.

[39] For a detailed analysis of the 'preferred position' of freedom of speech and the press in American law, see HW Stonecipher, 'Safeguarding Speech and Press Guarantees: Preferred Position Postulate Reexamined' in BF Chamberlin and CJ Brown (eds), *The First Amendment Reconsidered: New Perspectives on the Meaning of Freedom of Speech and Press* (New York, Longman, 1982) 89–128.

[40] Yang (n 14) 524.

[41] A Reed Amar, *The Words That Made Us: America's Constitutional Conversation, 1760–1840* (New York, Basic Books, 2021) 442.

[42] Y Park, *Freedom of the Press* (Seoul, Pakyongsa, 2013) 103–105 (in Korean).

[43] Y Park, *Freedom of Expression* (Seoul, Hyonamsa, 2002) 49, 71 (in Korean).

[44] See S Potter, 'Or of the Press' (1975) 26 *Hastings Law Journal* 631–37.

[45] Park (n 42).

[46] Park (n 43) 55.

4. Statutory, Administrative, Self-Regulatory and Indirect Press Regulation

Press regulation in Korea has four components: statutory, administrative, self-regulatory and indirect ones.

4.1. Statutory and Administrative Law

In Korea as a civil law system, statutory and administrative law is made up of statutes enacted by the National Assembly and of rules and regulations made and enforced by administrative agencies. Some laws and regulations more directly affect the press than others. The major statutes for the media industry include the Act on Promotion of Newspapers Etc. (Newspaper Promotion Act), the Broadcasting Act, the Act on Arbitration and Remedies for Damage Caused by Press Reports (Press Arbitration Act), the Act on the Promotion of News Communications and the Act on Promotion of Periodicals, Including Magazines. The Newspaper Promotion Act, the Broadcasting Act, and the Press Arbitration Act constitute the core of the Korean media legislation because they bear pervasively on the print and electronic media industry. Designed to guarantee the freedom and independence of the print and broadcast media, they serve as a structural mechanism to ensure and enhance the media's responsibilities to society and individuals.

Korea has a unique registration system for newspapers, internet newspapers, internet news services, news agencies, magazines and other periodicals. The Newspaper Promotion Act requires anyone planning to publish a newspaper, an online newspaper, or an online news service to register the name of the newspaper, the type and frequency of publication, the publisher's name and address, and other details with the mayor or governor. The registration system was designed to ensure that the press fulfilled its social responsibilities, but as the number of internet media has exploded, it is now being used instead to figure out the numbers of the registered press companies. Article 12 of the Newspaper Promotion Act states that the mayor or governor must submit matters of newspaper registration to the Ministry of Culture, Sports and Tourism on a quarterly basis. A person who intends to publish a magazine must also register the necessary matters with the mayor or governor under the Periodical Promotion Act, which is similar to the Newspaper Promotion Act. There were 24,766 registered newspapers, internet news services, and other periodicals as of December 2022: 14,427 newspapers, 291 internet news service, 54 news agencies and 9,994 periodicals.[47]

---

[47] Newspapers etc. Registration Statistics, Ministry of Culture, Sports and Tourism (in Korean), https://pds.mcst.go.kr/main/regstatus/selectRegStatusDetail.do.

The Press Arbitration Act 2005 is in a class by itself among press statutes of the world. The law, which applies only to news reports in print and broadcasting and on the internet, provides for the right of an individual to request a correction of inaccurate factual news and to reply to factual assertions in a news story if the individual has been damaged by the allegations (Articles 14 and 16). The statute also stipulates a right to demand a follow-up story to a previous report about a suspect in criminal proceedings if the suspect has been acquitted of criminal charges (Article 17). As a special type of media legislation, the Press Arbitration Act is 'an effective remedial system' that facilitates the balancing of freedom of the press against an individual's right to reputation (Article 1).

The right of reply was challenged as a violation of the 'essential aspect' of freedom of the press under the Constitution. But the Constitutional Court rejected the challenge:

> In order to counter the effect of the offending news article, the right of reply guarantees the injured party an opportunity for defense through the same news organisation .... [T]he right of reply requirement can contribute to the discovery of truth and formation of correct public opinion. Readers often depend on information provided by the news media and cannot make a sound judgment until they hear the opposing arguments of the other parties.[48]

The Press Arbitration Act does not prevent the claimants for correction or reply to a news report from pursuing appropriate litigation (separately or simultaneously with other measures): the claim for corrections or replies under the Press Arbitration Act may be taken to a special three-judge media panel of the Seoul District Court. If the claim is accepted – and, in fact, the law requires Korean courts to prioritise defamation or related lawsuits involving news media over other lawsuits[49] – the court order for the correction or reply must be obeyed, although the order may be appealed to the Seoul High Court.

What if the original court order is successfully challenged on appeal but the challenged story has already been corrected or replied to as judicially mandated? Article 28(3) of the Press Arbitration Act states:

> In cases falling under Paragraph (2) [If it becomes apparent that all or part of a request for a report on a corrected statement, etc., should have been dismissed as a result of a hearing on the objection procedures relating to correction, etc., requests], any judgment to accept such request shall be revoked, it shall be declared that the details of a judgment for revocation may be reported upon request of the relevant press organisation, etc. If it has already carried out its duty to report a corrected statement or contradictory statement or to make a further report, then it shall be ordered, upon such request, that the other party should pay such organisation, etc., the expenses incurred in making a

---

[48] Constitutional Court, 89Honma165, 16 September 1991. For a comparison of the right of reply in press law globally, see KH Youm, 'The Right of Reply and Freedom of the Press: An International and Comparative Perspective' (2008) 76 *George Washington Law Review* 1017–64.

[49] Press Arbitration Act, Art 29.

report on the corrected statement or contradictory statement or a further report which has already been made and incurred in making a report on the judgment for revocation and such ordinary fees for carrying or broadcasting as are deemed appropriate. In such cases, the amount of such payments shall not exceed the fees for the relevant carrying or ordinary broadcast advertising costs.

Litigation is not the only option for claimants. When press reports violate the personal rights of others, the victim may request relief from the Press Arbitration Commission rather than filing a lawsuit. The Press Arbitration Commission is an independent government agency tasked with resolving disputes over news articles. Once a claim from a petitioner is received, an arbitral tribunal conducts conciliation or arbitration.

The Press Arbitration Commission provides four types of remedies for a petitioner. First, a petitioner who suffers harm as a result of a partially or entirely false report may file a correction request with the publisher (Article 14). The petitioner must prove that the original report contains false facts, while the press must prove that the report is true. Second, a petitioner can request that the news organisation publish a reply to a previous article (Article 16). The contradictory reply is not required to prove the falsity of the original report. Third, a petitioner can request a follow-up story when the petitioner is proven to be innocent or not guilty. The petition for the follow-up story must be filed within three months after the criminal case against the petitioner was resolved (Article 17). Finally, a petitioner may request press organisations to reimburse for monetary damages for violations of personal rights such as reputation and privacy (Article 30).

4.2. Self-Regulatory Laws

In addition to statutory and administrative laws, there is a self-regulatory aspect to regulation of free press. The Korea Press Ethics Commission is a self-regulatory body established by the media. The Commission was founded in 1961 by the Korea News Editors Association. The Korea Press Ethics Commission oversees the newspaper ethics code relating to press freedom and responsibility, and establishes the code of ethics for reporting suicide, the rules for reporting disaster and the rules for reporting general election opinion polls.[50] But Korean media commenters noted that:

> Codes of ethics exist both at the national and the firm levels. [However,] [n]ewsroom practice does not always match what is laid out on paper .... Although these [press complaint] instruments are in place for ethical journalistic practices, they are not always observed, and oftentimes [are] overlooked in practice.[51]

---

[50] In Korean, www.ikpec.or.kr.
[51] Kim and Lee (n 7) 412, 413.

4.3. Indirect Media Laws

Finally, in addition to the aforementioned laws directly applicable to the press, indirect laws affect the Korean media as regulations of general applicability. When the news media publish defamatory articles or invade the right of privacy, for example, the Civil Act or Criminal Act may kick in. Besides, although not used as frequently as in the past, the National Security Act can be invoked against media publications when they touch on national security issues. This is more often the case with alternative news media. Finally, from an access-to-government-records perspective, the Official Information Disclosure Act is more pertinent to the media's freedom of information than other statutes.

5. Press Protections … or Not

Does the Press Clause carve out journalists in print and broadcast media for special treatment due to their real and imagined particular work of gathering, processing and disseminating news of public interest to a wider segment of society? Not as extensively as might be assumed.

5.1. Journalists' Privilege

Consider the question of whether professional journalists should be in a similar position to doctors and lawyers when they are ordered to cooperate with criminal investigations. That is, can they refuse the law enforcement authorities' request to share what they have learned through news reporting? Korean reporters, whether for print or broadcast media or citizen journalism, are not accorded a 'journalists' privilege' to protect confidential sources, and no Korean court has yet ruled on shield law issues within a journalistic context. The Criminal Procedure Act and the Civil Procedure Act require citizens in general to testify in court.[52] A witness who fails to obey a summons for no good reason may be arrested.[53] Exceptions include practicing lawyers, doctors and a select group of other licensed professionals, who may object to the seizure of materials related to another person's secrets. Because journalists are not covered by this exemption, however, they cannot challenge the seizure of materials in their possession.[54]

---

[52] Criminal Procedure Act, Art 136; Civil Procedure Act, Art 303. For a discussion of the Civil Procedure Act, see S Lee and KH Youm, 'Korea' in CJ Glasser, Jr (ed), *International Libel and Privacy Handbook: A Global Reference for Journalists, Publishers, Webmasters, and Lawyer* (New York, LexisNexis, 2022), KOR-15 to KORE-16.

[53] Criminal Procedure Act, Art 152.

[54] ibid Art 12.

Interestingly, during the authoritarian rule in 1980–1987, the now-repealed Basic Press Act provided for the journalist's privilege. But it was never invoked by Korean journalists. When Korea moved forward to a more democratic press system in the late 1980s, commentators suggested that a new shield law with fewer exemptions should be introduced as a statutory right for investigative journalists to better serve the Korean public.[55] This suggestion was not embraced.

5.2. Defamation

Defamation is a crime or a tort (civil wrong) in Korea. The Criminal Act states that 'anyone who defames another by publicly alleging facts shall be punished by imprisonment for not more than two years, or by a fine not exceeding five million Won' (Article 307(1)). It also stipulates that 'a person who defames others by publicly alleging false facts shall be punished by imprisonment for not more than five years, suspension of qualifications for not more than ten years, or a fine not exceeding ten million Won' (Article 307(2)). The news media are more severely punished for defamation than are individuals because of their far-reaching potential to inflict reputational damage when information, whether true or false, is published by 'newspapers, magazines, radio or other publications' with 'intent to defame another' (Article 309(1)). But defamation is justified when the alleged facts are true and primarily for the public interest (Article 310). Truthful facts are such expression that 'the significant component of the material accords with the objective facts' – and even exaggerated expression or expression containing a minor deviation from the truth is acceptable.

In a libel case involving a *Korea Forum* article, the Supreme Court of Korea reasoned that since 'breathing space' must exist for freedom of the press, truth should be factored in when considering the overall purpose of the challenged article.[56] Even if the expression does not exactly correspond to the truth, the Court held, it is not necessarily actionable defamation. The Court concluded that there is no illegality when a speaker or a publisher incorrectly believes the information to be true, as long as there is a 'substantial reason' for such misunderstanding.

The American 'actual malice' principle of *New York Times v Sullivan* – ie, knowledge of falsity or reckless disregard for the truth – is not recognised in Korea. But the Supreme Court of Korea has pointed out that defamation laws have historically been abused to 'limit and suppress public criticism of those in power',[57] and the judicial approach to expanding press freedom against defamation lawsuits by public officials is considerably informed by the so-called *Sullivan* doctrine of the US Supreme Court. To be sure, it is not identical. But it is close in spirit. For

---

[55] KH Youm and MB Salwen, 'A Free Press in South Korea: Temporary Phenomenon or Permanent Fixture?' (1990) 30 *Asian Survey* 325.
[56] Supreme Court, 2000Da37524, 22 January 2002.
[57] ibid.

a good illustration, look at the 2003 Korean Supreme Court case that strengthened press freedom.[58] In this public official defamation case, the Court held that '[m]atters related to policy making or government performance should be subject to public monitoring and criticism'.[59] To adequately protect the press as a watchdog, the Supreme Court remarked, media reports should not be easily punished for defamation of a public official if the reporting was not a reputational attack that was 'malicious' or that lacked 'considerable probability'.[60]

In a challenge by the KBS (Korea Broadcasting System) to administrative sanctions, the Seoul High Court, while referencing *Sullivan*, emphasised the importance of guaranteeing freedom of the press:

> Safeguarding public debate is an essential, political obligation of our Government under the liberal democracy guaranteed by our constitution, as suggested by the *Sullivan* decision of the United States. Even if the debate includes violent, poignant and sometimes offensively sharp attacks on the Government or public officials, such debate should never be stifled and should be allowed to spread as widely and vigorously as possible. For an investigative reporting program focusing on a matter of social significance, the need for press freedom becomes even more pressing. This demonstrates the superiority of a liberal democratic political system that allows for diverse and free public debate. In the current global village, where the world communicates across national borders through technological advancement, an open political system and the guarantee of press freedom are the best measures for national security.[61]

The Government, the Seoul High Court continued, should be extremely cautious in exercising its power to punish media reporting unless the contents are false or misleading.

But a number of defamation lawsuits continue to be filed against the press by public figures. According to the 2021 Press Judgment Report, 117 libel lawsuits were brought against the media. While 48 cases were filed by private figures, 69 cases were filed by public figures (23 politicians, 13 professionals, eight public officials, five journalists, two celebrities and 18 others).[62] Thus, libel litigation by public figures remains an occupational hazard for the press in Korea.

5.3. Citizens' Right to Erasure

Requests to delete or block news articles are novel issues for the Korean press in a changing media environment. In the internet age, news articles can be easily retrieved and redistributed via web portals, SNS and other digital outlets. Thus,

---

[58] Supreme Court, 2002Da62494, 22 July 2003.
[59] ibid.
[60] ibid.
[61] Seoul High Court, 2014Nu5912, 10 February 2015.
[62] 2021 Press Judgment Report, (Public Arbitration Commission), www.pac.or.kr/kor/pages/?p=201&magazine_new=M01&cate=MA05&nPage=1&idx=1068&m=view&f=&s=.

there is an obvious need to delete or block online news articles that violate individuals' reputation or privacy for no justifiable reason. The Supreme Court of Korea has accepted the right to erasure of news articles for protection of personal rights. In 2013, the Court, for the first time, recognised the right of an individual to delete news stories for protection against interference with his or her 'moral right'.[63] In demanding deletion of news stories to regain one's right to reputation, the claimant must assert a claim that meets the following conditions: (1) the news content is false or unrelated to the public interest; and (2) the article seriously and significantly infringes on the reputation of others.

After a news agency published an online article that 'a naval officer molested a foreign woman', for instance, the officer claimed that the story contained false information and asked for the article's removal as part of his libel suit. In the news story, the officer was identified by his family name and age. Although the article concerned the public's right to know and was of interest to the public, the Seoul High Court concluded that the reporter failed to look further into other facts in verifying the serious allegations against the military officer. The media defendant was ordered to pay 20 million Won in damages, in addition to erasing the defamatory article.[64]

However, deletion of news should not be available as the tempting first option against suing the press. Indeed, the Seoul District Court held that deleting articles should not be utilised as an easy method to employ.[65] The Court cautioned emphatically that 'erasing news stories fundamentally prevents the existence of specific expressions, thereby limiting freedom of expression'.[66] The Court denied the deletion request on the grounds that the defamatory article complained of was published in the public interest and that correction of the article could have a similar impact on the plaintiff's recovery of reputation as deletion would.

Courts generally believe that because media reports have historical value in reflecting the social situation at the time of writing, judging the value of a news article solely on the basis of the current time and deciding to remove it arbitrarily should be avoided. This is truly the judicial acceptance of what the noted American journalism historian David Sloan has aptly called 'present-mindedness'.[67] If the factual allegations contain obvious false information or violate others' rights by misrepresenting their true context, however, the press should more actively consider editing or deleting its contents in *digital* circumstances (as opposed to circumstances involving other types of media, where other options exist).

---

[63] Supreme Court, 2010Da60950, 28 March 2013.
[64] Seoul High Court, 2018Na2007953, 20 December 2018.
[65] Seoul Central District Court, 2016Gahap547119, 11 January 2017.
[66] ibid.
[67] D Sloan, *I Remember: A Memoir, 1947–2022* (Northport, Regimen Books, 2022) 207. ('Judging the past by the present is an error that's familiar to trained historians. It is known as present-mindedness.') For an insightful elaboration on present-mindedness, see JD Startt and WD Sloan, *Historical Methods in Mass Communication*, 4th edn (Northport, Vision Press, 2019) 56–58.

5.4. Freedom of Information: On Both Sides of the Press Wall

Access to government records is a statutory right in Korea. When the National Assembly passed the Act on Information Disclosure by Public Agencies in 1996, it was the Korean version of the Freedom of Information Act (FOIA) of the United States. From a freedom of the press perspective, access to information as an affirmative right to know for journalists is considered crucial to the 'enabling environment' for free and independent media. The media, without laws on public access to government agency records and meetings, are usually hindered from functioning as an active, informative channel of communication for the public. Overall, Korean journalists have 'fairly high' informational freedom for their reporting. According to Eun-mee Kim and Jae-woo Lee, the authors of an informative study of the Korean media, the Korean FOI law has 'drastically' expanded informational availability, which may explain the 'relative satisfaction' of Korean journalists with the news reporting process.[68]

On the flip side, broadcasting media, *both* public and private, are subject to disclosure of information under the Broadcasting Act.[69] The access-to-information requirement of the Broadcasting Act applies to all the broadcasting stations except Korean Broadcasting System (KBS), a government-invested corporation and Educational Broadcasting System (EBS), which was established under the Korean Educational Broadcasting System Act. KBS and EBS as public institutions are subject to the Official Information Disclosure Act. An FOI request to KBS raised a freedom of the press issue.[70] A supporter of Woo-Suk Hwang, a disgraced biomedical scientist who fabricated stem cell research in Seoul, requested a temporary tape for an edition of KBS TV's *Tracking 60 Minutes*. KBS did not respond to the FOI request for the tape for 20 days, which amounted to KBS's denial of the request.[71] One of the key issues in the case was whether the release of the requested tape would violate KBS's freedom of the press under the Constitution and the Broadcasting Act. The Seoul High Court ruled that it would not.

On appeal, the Supreme Court of Korea disagreed. The Supreme Court held that the 'unlimited mandatory disclosure' of the information about the planning, organisation and production of a broadcasting programme would discourage broadcasting activities.[72] This would hurt the broadcasting company's management and business interests and further affect the broadcaster's 'freedom and

---

[68] Kim and Lee (n 7) 419.
[69] See Broadcasting Act (2020), Art 90(5).
[70] Seoul High Court, 2007Nu24731, 2 July 2008.
[71] Official Information Disclosure Act, Art 11(5) states: 'In the event that any public institution does not decide on whether or not to disclose information within 20 days from the date on which a request is made for disclosing such information, such public institution shall be deemed to have decided not to disclose the information.'
[72] Supreme Court, 2008Du13101, 23 December 2010.

independence of broadcasting'. The Court stated that KBS's refusal of the information in question fell within the trade secret exemption under the Official Information Disclosure Act and protected its own 'legitimate interest'.[73]

6.   Press Freedom and Platform Regulation: Converging Challenges

The internet has transformed human communication and dramatically altered how people read and watch news. According to Digital News Report 2021, of the Reuters Journalism Institute at Oxford University, Korea is the number one country among 46 countries surveyed about using news through search engines and news-gathering services, but relatively few Koreans access news by directly visiting the page.[74] In other words, many Korean media users access news through online news services such as web portals rather than visiting media companies' websites or news apps. In Korea, news consumption has been fixed through portals, particularly two major portals, *Naver* and *Daum*,[75] although recently YouTube and social media have been on the rise for news consumption.

6.1. Fake News

As the use of news via various digital platforms grows, so do societal concerns about its side effects. The occurrence and spread of so-called fake news are common issues. Since former US President Donald Trump fuelled the fake news controversy starting with his 2016 election, fake news has become a social problem in South Korea as well.[76] Concerns about fake news or disinformation remain, but finding a solution is difficult because determining the authenticity of a specific expression is fundamentally problematic. Furthermore, it takes time, and, in many cases, authenticity is not clear even after time has passed. During the Covid-19 pandemic, the general public was unable to judge the authenticity of medical or scientific information, such as viruses and vaccines. Who should have the authority to determine authenticity has also been a point of contention.

There is a growing demand for media platforms to be regulated in order to respond to disinformation. To force the digital platform to uphold its social responsibility, dozens of bills to regulate fake news were introduced in the National Assembly in 2017–2022, but they were not passed due to the ambiguity of the term 'fake news' and overregulation of platforms.

---

[73] ibid.
[74] 'Digital News Report 2021' (*Reuters Institute for the Study of Journalism*), https://reutersinstitute. politics.ox.ac.uk/digital-news-report/2021.
[75] Kim and Lee (n 7) 394.
[76] 'Digital News Report' (n 74).

6.2. Regulation

In Korea, arguably the world's most wired nation, the Government, over the years, has paid keen attention to the crucial role of telecommunication – and regulation of that telecommunication – in its drive to make the country an industrial powerhouse. Among the major telecommunication statutes that govern online communication are the Information and Communications Network Act (ICNA), the Framework Act on Intelligent Informatisation, the Telecommunications Business Act, and the Protection of Communications Secrets Act. The pillar of the regulatory structure for online service is the ICNA. As other telecommunication statutes do, this law is intended to improve the quality of citizens' lives and to enhance public welfare by facilitating the use of information and communication networks, safeguarding personal information of those using information and communication services, and creating an environment in which people can use the networks 'in a healthier and safer way' (Article 1).

Internet service providers, such as portals, are governed by the ICNA. The statute states that the victim of defamation or invasion of privacy or other personal rights may request the internet service provider that managed the harmful contents to delete the contents or publish a rebuttable statement by presenting explanatory materials (Article 44(2)(1)). When receiving a request for deletion or rebuttal of harmful contents, the internet service provider should delete the content or implement temporary blocking regarding the content. Temporary blocking, which was implemented when the ICNA was amended in 2007 (Article 44(3)), is a novel process to protect personal rights on the internet. The previous law simply required internet service providers to delete harmful information or post rebuttals at the request of the victim. But such deletion or rebuttal without more was insufficient to prevent the spread of damage through the internet.

Indeed, temporary measures proved effective in preventing the spread of damage, but several flaws in their effectiveness have been identified. If the information publisher objects and requests reposting, it is unclear what action the operator should take. Moreover, the action to be taken after the 30-day interim measure is left to the operator's discretion, leaving the follow-up procedure unclear. Another criticism is that the temporary measures violate online freedom of expression by excessively restricting access to online contents. In 2020, however, the Constitutional Court upheld the temporary measures under the ICNA.[77] Considering the rapid dissemination of defamatory or private information on the internet, it remains all but impossible to recover from the damage through ex post damages or criminal punishment. Hence, the Court determined that the temporary measures met the requirement for balancing free speech with personal rights, as access to information is restricted for a relatively short period of less than 30 days.

---

[77] Constitutional Court, 2016Hunma275, 26 November 2020.

6.3. Court Rulings

At present, portals do not fall under the umbrella of the media because they are not 'press'. The Press Arbitration Act defines 'press' as 'broadcasting, newspapers, periodicals including any magazines, news communications or online newspapers' (Article 2(1)). But portals are considered to have a function similar to that of the press.

The Seoul High Court has ruled on a portal operator's liability for posting a defamatory false news article on its main webpage.[78] Emphasising the press's usual three key functions – reporting, editing and distribution – the Court zeroed in on the portal's functions. The Court found that: (1) the portal's 'distribution' function of information outperforms that of the existing news media; (2) the portal's function of 'selecting news articles and placing them in the main news section' is no different from the news media's 'editing' function; and (3) the portal has a 'reporting' function when it receives and disposes of stories from other media outlets.[79]

To the Seoul High Court, the portal was more than just a 'conduit' for news articles: it also functioned as the 'press' with full coverage, editing and distribution capabilities of newsworthy stories. Thus, if a portal website places a defamatory news story of a media company in its main news section, the portal must compensate for the reputational damage of the person mentioned because the portal bears liability as a co-illegitimate actor with the press organisation.[80] This case is unique in that the portal was ruled to be analogous to the press. One year later, the Supreme Court of Korea issued a seminal decision on portals' liability for defamation.[81] After a woman committed suicide because of a one-sided breakup, rumours and news articles about her and her ex spread online quickly. Many internet users, who were outraged at the man for kicking the woman, tracked him down and made threatening phone calls. The man sued *Daum*, *Naver* and other major portals, arguing that the portals helped distribute defamatory postings and news articles.[82]

The Supreme Court's decision of 2009 highlights two key points. First, when the internet service provider such as the web portal collects, selects and publishes news articles, it does more than just provide a search-and-access function; the portal recognises the content of specific defamatory articles and *actively* distributes them. Consequently, portals that selectively post articles, like the press organisations that publish original articles, are liable for reputational damage stemming from the distribution of the defamatory articles. In other words, the internet service provider that exercises editorial control over the article is liable for the same damage that the publisher causes.

---

[78] Seoul High Court, 2006Na92006, 16 January 2008.
[79] ibid.
[80] ibid.
[81] Supreme Court, 2008Da53812, 15 April 2009.
[82] ibid.

Second, the Supreme Court was divided on portals' responsibility for handling the request of deletion from victims. If and when the internet service providers provide online space with risks but at the same time receive economic benefits from the information distribution, the majority of the Court held, internet service providers should take responsibility for appropriate risk management as creators and managers of the risk sources. Therefore, the internet service providers should comply with a request for deletion or blocking of harmful contents. Furthermore, the internet service providers should be liable even when the victim did not request deletion or blocking: (1) if they specifically recognised or could recognise the existence of the harmful posting; and (2) if it would have been technically and economically feasible to manage and control the harmful posting.[83] But in a separate opinion, three justices argued that an internet service provider's liability for defamation should be limited to cases in which the victim requested that harmful content be deleted and such deletion was technically and economically feasible.

7. Summary and Conclusion

Press freedom is no longer rhetorical hyperbole for Koreans. It is a real thing, and Koreans have experienced it for the past 35 years. The path to press freedom has been long and originally torturous. Although the constitutional guarantee of freedom of expression was in place from the birth of the Korean Constitution, freedom of the press was rarely in action until 1987, when Korea became a democratic country. The theoretical beginnings of free press also did not occur until the mid-1980s, when freedom of the press was considered by jurists especially. While there was little precedential reference to invoke in Korean law, freedom of the Korean press was anchored to the classic rationales for its value: discovery of truth, self-governing process, self-realisation, and more.

Along with freedom of press came responsibility, which was enforced via a number of regulations, including statutory, administrative, self-regulatory and indirect. Different types of media – print, broadcasting and online – in Korea are treated differently due to their distinctive structure and impact, which is very much like in other countries. The most notable law of Korea directly affecting the print and non-print media is the Press Arbitration Act. It provides for the right of correction and reply for an individual who feels injured by news reporting. The statute even requires publication or broadcasting of a follow-up story for a criminal suspect who has been exonerated. Equally important, the law helps facilitate public access to the news media, albeit in a limited way. Relatedly, the Press Arbitration Commission is an important agency in equalising the playing field for Korean news media, the news-consuming public and those in the news.

---

[83] ibid.

Regulation in Korea is more skeptically reviewed by an independent judiciary. The Constitutional Court of Korea represents an institutional sensitivity to the value of press freedom as an integral part of Korea's thriving democracy. The liberalising interpretation of defamation law is a case in point when public officials or public figures sue the news media. But in other areas, protections for journalists are arguably not as strong. For example, there is no journalist's privilege. This deserves systemic attention from Korean press organisations because protection of news sources is universally recognised as a right by court decision or statute – and, perhaps more widely, as a journalistic aspiration. Furthermore, citizens have the right to erasure; and although FOI laws work to the advantage of journalists who are seen as having a 'right to know', citizens can use FOI laws 'against' the news media.

Online communication is challenging the press and the Government as well. Liability for defamation and invasion of privacy is increasingly less addressable under the outmoded pre-internet standard. The deletion of news information as a way to neutralise defamatory, false news is a new development with profound implications for Korean press law. Although some aspects of online communication, like portals, are not technically considered 'the press' under Korean law, they are nevertheless treated as such. Such issues are taking on more urgency in Korea's fast-changing media ecosystem. Like any country balancing press freedom and the many issues associated with it, Korea has experienced growing pains. In terms of self-regulation, for example, there is a gap between what is on the books and what takes place in practice. Meanwhile, journalistic freedom, separate from press freedom as an institutional concept, is of limited relevance to the everyday life of Korean journalists as a cause of overriding concern.

But in terms of those issues with which Korea is still struggling, Korea is not alone. A number of nuanced media law and regulation issues[84] are not necessarily limited to Korean media. At the moment, for example, the Court of Justice of the European Union is reviewing how the right to be forgotten will be processed when the right to be forgotten complaint directly affects news media archives.[85] Clearly, Korea is part of the vanguard of countries addressing free press challenges in order to create an optimal free press environment. Of course, overall, Korea has a commendable free press environment. Korea's V-Dem and Liberal Democracy Index rankings illustrate its remarkable place on a global scale. Korea has become a model of free press, and its system in some ways even rivals that of the United States. While Korea still has some work to do, that type of improvement is simply part and parcel of the role and responsibility of a world leader in democracy.

---

[84] See P Lambert, *The Right to Be Forgotten*, 2nd edn (London, Bloomsbury Professional, 2022) 445–57.
[85] D Voorhoof, '*Hurbain v Belgium* Before the Grand Chamber' (*Legal Human Academy*, 30 March 2022), http://legalhumanacademy.org/hurbain-v-belgium-before-the-grand-chamber.

PART II

Africa

7

Transforming Information and Communication Technologies from Infrastructures of Freedom to Architectures of Political Repression: The Case of Internet Shutdowns in Egypt and Cameroon

LYOMBE EKO

1. Introduction

Political systems assign specific ideological functions to the media in general, and journalism, in particular. Journalism is a multi-cultural field. Despite its multiple forms, journalism plays 'functionally equivalent'[1] roles in different polit-ico-cultural systems.[2] That is to say, despite their different iterations and cultures, the media have a specific role to play in each society. Their stock-in-trade is usually information, education and entertainment, as defined and practised under specific politico-cultural systems. Journalistic cultural fields therefore reflect diverse governmentalities or logics of governance with respect to individual freedom, representative government, the protection of civil liberties[3] and different geographies of freedom of expression of around the world.[4] In other words, governments have 'different solutions to solve similar problems'.[5]

---

[1] cf R Michaels, 'The Functional Method of Comparative Law' in M Reimann and R Zimmermann (eds), The Oxford Handbook of Comparative Law (Oxford, Oxford University Press, 2006) 339–82.

[2] P Bourdieu, 'L'emprise du journalisme' (1994) 101(1) Actes de la recherches en sciences sociales 3–9.

[3] M Foucault, Dits et écrits (Paris, Gallimard, 1994) Vol 3, 655–721.

[4] L Eko, 'Legal Contexts in Reporting Scandal in the United States, the United Kingdom, and Russia' in H Tumber and S Waisbord (eds), The Routledge Companion to Media and Scandal (London, Routledge, 2019) 193–201.

[5] Michaels (n 1) 351.

Journalists in Africa are confronted with multiple legal and ethical issues on a daily basis. One of the most evident of these problems is the tension between the human right of freedom of expression and journalistic responsibility. The excessive governmentality of authoritarian regimes with respect to the right of freedom of speech and of the press can be contrasted with systems of regulated self-regulation in liberal democracies. These systems of government are based on the notion that the government is not an end in and of itself. Western countries traditionally assign a watchdog role to the media. In these societies, the media are expected to investigate and denounce human rights violations, corruption, conflicts of interest, institutional, corporate and individual exploitation and predation. They do this through a process that Pierre Bourdieu calls 'eclectic neutrality'.[6]

The media are neutral on some issues and fervent partisans in others. In many democratic countries, there are professional organisations or governmental institutions that regulate the media and moderate their excesses, under regimes of regulated self-regulation.[7] In these countries, the excesses of the press have shone the spotlight on the harms a legally free and unfettered press can cause to democracy if it is not moored in ethics. There is therefore an emphasis on watching the watchdog, not muzzling it.[8] After all, the law commands, but the most ethics can do is recommend.

In some parts of the world, particularly in Africa, journalism has social responsibility, development and even ideological and propaganda roles. In these jurisdictions, journalism and the media are conceptualised as instruments of national popular mobilisation, economic and social development controlled by the state. Under these regimes, journalists are not viewed as watchdogs of society, whose job is to denounce corruption and malfeasance. State media and journalists are often expected to play the role of political panegyrists whose laudatory, editorial journalism is aimed at protecting the status quo, maintaining neo-patrimonial authoritarian regimes in power.[9] However, in the post-Cold War era, new forms of journalism emerged to challenge the informational monopolies of the state media in sub-Saharan Africa. Satirical journalism grounded in traditional African humouristic parody and satire emerged in multiple French-speaking African countries,[10] while a subversive, anti-authoritarian 'guerilla' or 'defiant' journalism emerged in Nigeria, Cameroon, the Ivory Coast and other countries.[11] Guerilla

---

[6] Bourdieu (n 2) 6.

[7] W Schultz and T Held, *Regulated Self-Regulation as a Form of Modern Government* (Luton, University of Luton Press, 2004) 3–21.

[8] Eko (n 4).

[9] F Fukuyama, *Political Order and Political Decay: From the Industrial Revolution to the Globalization of Democracy* (New York, Farrar, Strauss & Giroux, 2014) 285–98.

[10] L Eko, 'It is a Political Jungle Out There: How Four African Newspaper Cartoons Dehumanized and "Deterritorialized" African Political Leaders in the Post-Cold War Era' (2007) 69(3) *International Communication Gazette* 219–38; E Watremez, 'The Satirical Press in Francophone Africa: Naughty Boys and Little Sneakes' (1992) 21(10) *Index on Censorship* 34–36; A Mbembe, *On the Postcolony* (Berkeley, University of California Press, 2001) 142–72.

[11] D Olorunyomi, 'Defiant Publishing in Nigeria' (1996) 10(4) *Media Studies Journal* 65–74, 65; L Eko, 'Press Freedom in Africa' in DH Johnston (ed), *Encyclopaedia of International Media and*

journalists gathered their 'news', composed their publications in underground newsrooms, and printed their newspapers in surreptitious presses, to thwart governmental censors and police seizures of desk-top publishing equipment.

Nevertheless, even journalists who ply their trade in oppressive, censorious environments are not free of ethical challenges and journalistic malpractice. Issues of journalistic malpractice involving receiving payment for positive stories, rumour-mongering, publication of unverified information, invasion of privacy, defamation, manipulation of photographs and visual images and so on, dog the independent media and citizen journalists who practice a journalism of subsistence. Nevertheless, in Africa North and South of the Sahara, the fundamental tension is between the right of freedom of the press and authoritarian governmental censorship and persecution of the defiant, independent private press for political and ethical reasons.

2. Deterritorialisation and Internet Shutdowns

The diffusion of the internet to Africa in the late 1990s, the connection of African telecommunication systems to the innovative network of computer networks provided the African independent press new online publication platforms for material that was often censored in physical space.[12] In these early days of the internet, the United States, the birthplace of the internet, was preaching a laissez-faire approach to cyberspace, which was viewed as a market-based democratising and liberalising force. As the internet diffused to all parts of the continent, African computer scientists and engineers 'reinvented' it by adapting it to different languages and scripts. While the deterritorialisation of journalism from real space to virtual space represented an escape from the long arm of authoritarian censors, this reality did not last long. The telecommunications infrastructures that interconnect African information and communication technology networks to the networks of the rest of the world are owned by governments or para-statal corporations. This effectively made governments the gatekeepers and regulators of the gateways to the internet for their respective national territories. They used this structural power to control and regulate the internet and its content in times of political disputes, strife and crises.

One of the most paradoxical trends in online communication on the African continent is the proliferation of the highly censorious practice of internet shutdowns. Indeed, the most effective methods of internet control and censorship on the African continent has been the strategic, partial or complete shutdown of the

---

Communications (Cambridge, Academic Press, 2003) Vol 2, 95–116; C Monga, *The Anthropology of Anger: Civil Society and Democracy in Africa* (Boulder, Lynne Rienner, 1996) 110–11.

[12] L Eko, 'The Art of Satirical Deterritorialization: Shifting Cartoons from Real Space to Cyberspace in Sub-Saharan Africa' (2015) 77(3) *International Communication Gazette* 248–66.

internet in times of political instability and unrest. The goal is to prevent members of the civil society from using the internet and its networked social media platforms like Facebook, WhatsApp, Twitter, Instagram and YouTube to organise anti-government protests. On 19 February 2011, *The Daily Nation*, a newspaper in Nairobi, Kenya, published a cartoon in which the former Prime Minster of Ethiopia, Meles Zenawi, was shown shouting orders to armed Ethiopian officers: 'I want this Facebook, Twitter arrested!'.[13] Ethiopia is not the only African country that has problems with the internet and its associated social media platforms. On 30 December 2017, the Minister of Posts, Telecommunications and New Information and Communication Technologies of the Democratic Republic of Congo, Emery Ndjovu, wrote an official memorandum to Africell DRC, the Congolese subsidiary of the transnational information technology and cellular telephone company Africell, ordering it to terminate all its SMS and internet services in the national territory of Congo with immediate effect, for unspecified reasons of 'state security'. The Minister invited the chief executive officer of Africell to attend a meeting at his office on New Year's Day 2018 to discuss the modalities of an 'eventual' lifting of the ban.[14]

The cartoon of the Ethiopian Prime Minister and the abrupt and internet shutdown order imposed on Africell RDC succinctly and pithily summarise the attitude of many African countries and their leaders with respect to the internet and its associated networked social media platforms. Since 2011, the governments of Algeria, Cameroon, Congo-Brazzaville, the Democratic Republic of Congo, Gambia, Egypt, Ethiopia, Eritrea, Gabon, Ivory Coast, Kenya, Libya, Togo, Sudan, Tunisia, Zimbabwe and others have, at one time or the other, resorted to selective, targeted or complete internet and mobile telephone shutdowns as a means of stifling popular political dissent. The goal of these anti-communication activities has generally been to prevent opposition parties, political opponents, separatist groups, civil society information activists and cyber hacktivists from using mobile telephones, the internet and its associated networked social media platforms – and especially SMS text-messaging – to organise political rallies and anti-government demonstrations. This development amounts to widespread transformation of the infrastructures and instrumentalities of information and communication technology into components of authoritarian architectures of repression.

3. Aim of this Study

The wave of targeted, censorious internet interference, selective 'disconnectivity' and outright shutdowns across Africa in the name of national security and other governmental interests less than 20 years after the United Nations Millennium

---

[13] ibid.

[14] 'DR Congo Government cuts Internet Ahead of Anti-Kabila Protest' (*AfricaNews*, 31 December 2017), www.africanews.com/2017/12/31/dr-congo-government-cuts-internet-ahead-of-anti-kabila-protest.

Development Goals, and the subsequent enthusiasm over internet connectivity, is a historic, international counter-communication phenomenon that is significant and worthy of academic study. It is especially so given that telecommunications and internet policies are ensconced in, and mirror, specific governmentalities or national conceptualisations of political governance.[15] Since information and communication technologies are what Michel Foucault called a 'capacity–communication–power' nexus, they are crucial in the maintenance of specific political regimes. Selective internet disconnectivity actions taken by specific regimes to disrupt communication are therefore barometers of the level of democracy and respect for freedom of expression in specific political dispensations. This subject is also significant because selective internet disconnectivity or shutdowns are incompatible with the human right of freedom of expression set forth in Article 19 of the Universal Declaration of Human Rights 1948, which provides: 'Everyone has the right to freedom of opinion and expression; this right includes freedom to hold opinions without interference and to seek, receive and impart information and ideas through any media and regardless of frontiers.'

The aim of this chapter is to explore, describe, analyse and explain the phenomenon of internet shutdowns in Africa, using as a comparative case study the internet disconnectivity or shutdowns in Egypt and Cameroon. Though many African countries have shut down the internet in times of political crisis, the internet disconnectivity of Egypt (North Africa) and Cameroon (Sub-Sahara Africa) are distinctive in that they were the first and longest-lasting internet shutdowns in the world, respectively. This chapter focuses on this counter-intuitive, disfunctional disconnectivity of Egypt and Cameroon. Deliberate governmental internet disconnectivity for political and national security reasons undermines computer security, defined as confidentiality, integrity and availability of the visible and invisible aspects of the internet. This consists of infrastructures, platforms, databases, networks and the like, that have become crucial to the very existence of the information society.[16] Disconnectivity or shutdowns undermine the certainty, security, stability and reliability of online communication in specific countries. It is not compatible with the type of open, predictable, global, electronic commerce system promoted by the United Nations and the United States when the internet was opened up to commercial and cultural activity in the early 1990s. The study was carried out within the framework of the diffusion of innovation perspective, which holds that each innovation diffuses from a centre of innovation is like a drop of water in a pool, and ripples or diffuses to its periphery. In the process, the innovation is 'reinvented' and redeployed to suit the realities of the new politico-cultural spaces to which it diffused.[17]

---

[15] Foucault (n 3).

[16] CP Pfleeger and SL Pfleeger, *Security in Computing*, 3rd edn (New York, Pearson, 2002) 314–23.

[17] G Tarde, *Les lois de l'imitation* (Paris, Felix Alcan, 1890); B Ryan and N Gross, 'The Diffusion of Hybrid Seed Corn in Two Iowa Communities' (1943) 8 *Rural Sociology* 15–24; E Rogers, *Diffusion of Innovations*, 4th edn (New York, Free Press, 1995) 10–22; J Kinnunen, 'Gabriel Tarde as a Founding Father of Innovation Diffusion Research' (1996) 39(4) *Acta Sociologica* 431–42.

The premise of this chapter is that the internet, an innovation of innovations diffused to Africa, was reinvented politically, culturally and even linguistically. African languages and scripts like Amharic were digitised and standardised to work on computers anywhere in the world. More than that, the infrastructures and software were modified to suit specific political and cultural contexts – in short, information and communication technologies were instrumentalised and deployed in the context of political power struggles and unequal power dynamics between the state and fledgling independent media.[18] Censorious policies essentially transformed the internet and information and communication technologies into components of governmental architectures of repression which served the political and ideological interests of the ruling elite, for purposes of maintaining the status quo. Internet shutdowns are described and explained in terms of disconnectivity, a neurobiological term that explains the mechanistic process of 'abnormal functional integration of brain processes' caused by 'aberrant wiring' of neurons, as well as other biological issues.[19] Information and communication technology nodes and networks mimic the human brain and its neurobiological networks. In the case of internet disconnectivity or shutdowns, governments deliberately tamper with the information and communication technology networks for political reasons.

4. From Internet Connectivity to Internet Disconnectivity

This censorious wave of internet 'counter-connectivity' – or 'disconnectivity', to borrow a concept from neurobiology – is paradoxical because in the 1990s, the major priority of the international community and virtually all African governments was 'internet connectivity'.[20] Western and African researchers and policy-makers spoke of the existence of a 'digital divide,' a perceived global, structural and informational duality and inequality, a chasm between 'information rich' countries that had access to information and communication technologies (the connected) and the 'information poor' that did not have access to these technologies (the unconnected).[21] The digital divide was perceived as an international security issue. Writing in the *Boston Globe*, Hiawatha Bray declared that 'Africa is ground zero in the effort to solve one of the world's most serious emerging

---

[18] Foucault (n 3).

[19] K E Stephan, KJ Friston and CD Frith, 'Dysconnection in Schizophrenia: From Abnormal Synaptic Plasticity to Failures of Self-monitoring' (2009) 35(3) *Schizophrenia Bulletin* 509–27.

[20] L Eko, 'Internet Law and Regulation' in W Donsbach (ed), *Concise Encyclopedia of Communication* (Boston, Wiley–Blackwell, 2015) 288–90.

[21] P Norris, *Digital Divide: Civic Engagement, Information Poverty, and the Internet Worldwide* (Cambridge, Cambridge University Press, 2001) 3–68; G Nulens et al, *The Digital Divide in Developing Countries: Towards an Information Society in Africa* (Brussels, Vreije Universiteit Brussel, 2001) 130–60.

problems: bridging the digital divide between the developed and the developing worlds'.[22]

Since the 1990s, conceptualisation and diffusion of the internet in Africa has been dominated by the discourse of development communication. The United Nations Development Programme, the United Nations Educational, Scientific and Cultural Organization, the International Monetary Fund (IMF), the World Bank and the rest of the global aid industry recommended that African countries connect their telecommunications infrastructure to the internet, and include information and communication technologies in their economic development programmes and policies. The then Secretary-General of the United Nations, Kofi Annan, declared that by connecting to the internet, African countries would 'leap-frog' or bypass certain painful stages and processes of development, become part of the global economy, and leave behind decades of stagnation, underdevelopment and poverty.[23]

The World Bank embraced this policy, and set out to 'dialogue with national governments to emphasize the importance of taking advantage of the information revolution to accelerate economic development, as well as the need for liberalization, deregulation, privatization, and competition in the telecommunications sector'.[24] The World Bank highlighted the 'liberating effects' of the internet and information and communication technologies.[25] The proposition that the internet and information and communication technologies would be instrumental in the socio-economic and political development of Africa was whole-heartedly embraced by African intellectuals and governments in the 1990s.[26] The belief was that 'strategic use' of information would lead to nation-building and provide a 'climate' for national development. The United Nations Economic Commission for Africa (ECA), the International Telecommunication Union (ITU), the World Bank and other international aid agencies soon launched the African Information Society Initiative (AISI). By 1997, virtually all African countries had been connected to the internet.

The United Nations Millennium Development Goals (2000) specifically called for co-operation between governments and the private sector to 'make available the benefits of new technologies, especially information and communications

[22] H Bray, 'A $1.8b Ring around Africa' *The Boston Globe* (22 July 2001), A25. 8.
[23] M Trombly, 'World Leaders: IT Can Ease Globalization Woes' (2000) 34(37) *Computer World* 14.
[24] IN Kessides, *Reforming Infrastructure, Privatization, Regulation, and Infrastructure* (Washington, World Bank – Oxford University Press, 2004) 29–79, https://documents1.worldbank.org/curated/en/7 09301468779183565/310436360_20050007115940/additional/289850PAPER0reforming0infrastruct ure.pdf.
[25] E Baranshamaje et al, *Increasing Internet Connectivity in Africa: Issues, Options, and World Bank Group Role* (Addis Ababa, United Nations, 1995) 3–16.
[26] L Eko, *New Media, Old Regimes: Case Studies in Comparative Communication Law and Policy* (Lanham, Lexington Books, 2012) 355–66; EK Ngwainmbi, 'Africa in the Global Infosupermarket: Perspectives and Prospects' (2000) 30(4) *Journal of Black Studies* 534–52; B Pearson, 'Africa Telecom Meet Seeks Renaissance' (*Variety*, 5 May 1998), https://variety.com/1998/biz/news/africa-telecom-meet-seeks-renaissance-1117470433.

technologies'[27] to peoples in the developing worlds. This involved boosting access to telephones and cellular telephony, increasing personal computer use and specifically boosting internet connectivity in developing countries. In Africa, this meant connecting all parts of the continent to the internet and mobile telephony as a means of giving African peoples, who are structurally on the margins of the global information and communication technologies networks,[28] access to vast rivers of data, information and knowledge that were part of the information societies of North America, Europe and parts of Asia. Information and communication technologies were thus conceptualised as instruments of development and freedom in countries and regions dominated by authoritarian regimes.[29] The international community was mobilised under the auspices of the United Nations, the World Bank and the IMF to support international governmental, non-governmental and corporate solutions to the continent's perceived internet connectivity problems.

5. Background: Internet Connectivity in Africa

The contemporary situation of massive internet and social media use in Africa is very different from the reality that obtained just a few years ago. Telecommunications were traditionally regulated as common carriers of person-to-person communication lines, while information technology and computers were hardly regulated. The mass media were regulated as 'one-to-many' communication channels. The 'one' who controlled the mass media and did most of the communicating was the government, while the 'many' were the so-called masses at whom mass governmental-mediated messages were directed. The convergence of the mass media, information technology and telecommunications changed the fundamental basis of communication, and posed complex public policy problems that had a profound impact on societies around the continent. The importance of the internet as an instrument of development was impressed upon African leaders, as a group, by international, bi-lateral and multilateral aid and development agencies. In 1990, the ITU convened the African Regional Telecommunication Development Conference in Harare, Zimbabwe. This conference set up an African Telecommunications Policy Study Group which produced an 'African Green Paper' that set out the orientations and policy outlines for future telecommunications development on the African continent. These

---

[27] See www.un.org/millenniumgoals/2008highlevel/pdf/newsroom/MDG%20Overview%20FINAL. pdf.
[28] L Eko, 'Life in the Margins of Globalization: Media Liberalization, Commercialization and Hegemony in Africa' in L Artz and Y Kamalimpour (eds), The *Media Globe: Trends in International Mass Media* (Albany, SUNY, 2006) 1–20.
[29] S Kalathil and T Boas, *Open Networks, Closed Regimes: The Impact of the Internet on Authoritarian Rule* (Washington, Carnegie Endowment for International Peace, 2003) 13–103; L Eko, 'Putting African Accents in United Nations Internet for Development Policies' (2013) 10(3) *Journal of Information technology and Politics* 341–56; Eko (n 26) 355–77; Eko (n 28) 1–20; Ngwainmbi (n 26).

included the creation of an enabling environment for telecommunications, privatisation of the telecommunications sector, as well as the establishment of policy, legal and regulatory frameworks in the sector.

The kick-off to Africa's official venture into the internet was the African Regional Symposium on Telematics for Development which was held in Addis Ababa, Ethiopia, in 1995. The meeting was held under the auspices of the ECA and the ITU. At this meeting, representatives from 38 African countries, building on past telecommunication policy initiatives undertaken under the ambit of the ITU, notably, the Harare Telecommunication Development Conference, recommended that African countries connect their telecommunications infrastructure to the internet, and include information technology in their development policies and plans. The African Green Paper which was produced by the Policy Study Group set up by the Harare Conference, was adopted in 1996 at the next African Regional Telecommunication Development Conference that was held in Abidjan, Ivory Coast.[30]

6. Perceived Need for Internet Connectivity in Africa: The Developmentalist Aspiration

Adoption of the internet in Africa did not follow the traditional process of adoption of innovation advanced by Everett Rogers and others.[31] Indeed, the traditional, five-stage adoption process: awareness, interest, evaluation, trial and adoption are not applicable to internet adoption in Africa. Under pressure from international finance institutions, namely, the World Bank and the IMF, as well as aid agencies, African governments seemed to have simply gone from awareness to adoption. International leaders called on African governments to connect their respective countries to the internet, and so leapfrog or skip years ahead in the development process. By connecting to the internet, these poor countries were told that they would be able to bypass expensive information and telecommunications technologies. It was envisaged that by being connected to the internet, African countries would have increased access to information (markets, news, weather, health, and so on) and have greater access to educational materials, online journals, books, courses, and so on. The proposition that the internet could be instrumental in the socio-economic and political development of Africa has been whole-heartedly embraced by the international community and most African intellectuals.[32]

Indeed, the 'technological leapfrogging' metaphor emerged from the diffusion of innovation perspective. Diffusion of innovation theory holds that countries on the political and economic periphery of the world usually join innovations at

---

[30] See AF-RTDC-96, www.itu.int/pub/D-TDC-AF.
[31] Rogers (n 17) 161.
[32] Ngwainmbi (n 26) 536.

a late stage. These countries learn from the experiences of the innovation and sub-innovation centres, and 'leapfrog' decades of evaluation, experimentation and testing of specific innovations.[33] These countries on the fringes of the global economy can be described as late adopters that manifest an accelerated diffusion rate over a short span of time, and arrive at an approximate stage in technological innovation as the innovation and sub-innovation centres. This seems to have been the reasoning behind international efforts to encourage African countries to connect to the internet and thereby leapfrog or bypass decades of expensive communication technology. Internet diffusion and connectivity in Africa thus emerged from an international developmentalist agenda.

7. Africa and the ITU World Summits on the Information Society

The ITU spearheaded a veritable technological and policy deterritorialisation, the emergence of a global information society with the organisation of the World Summit on the Information Society (WSIS) in Geneva (2003) and Tunis (2005).[34] The technologically-driven deterritorialisation of society to a global informa-tion society was set forth in the Declaration of Principles that emerged from the Geneva phase of the WSIS. In the Declaration, the representatives of the peoples of the world at that meeting expressed a 'common desire and commitment to build a people-centred, inclusive and development-oriented Information Society, where everyone can create, access, utilize and share information and knowledge'.

> Information and Communication Technologies (ICTs) have an immense impact on virtually all aspects of our lives. The rapid progress of these technologies opens completely new opportunities to attain higher levels of development. The capacity of these technologies to reduce many traditional obstacles, especially those of time and distance, for the first time in history makes it possible to use the potential of these tech-nologies for the benefit of millions of people in all corners of the world.[35]

Mindful of the fact that the global information society and its African variant, the AISI, that was being spearheaded by the ECA, the ITU and the Organization for African Unity (renamed the African Union) could not function without freedom of expression within and across national and regional borders, the WSIS stressed freedom of information, communication and interconnectivity in real space and

---

[33] A Grübler, 'Time for a Change: On the Patterns of Diffusion of Innovation' (1996) 125(3) *Daedalus* 19–43.

[34] International Telecommunication Union, 2005, World Summit on the Information Society, 1–12, www.itu.int/net/wsis/documents/doc_multi.asp?lang=en&id=2267|0.

[35] Document WSIS-03/GENEVA/DOC/4-E, *Declaration of Principles Building the Information Society: A Global Challenge in the New Millennium* (12 December 2003), para A.1, www.itu.int/net/wsis/docs/geneva/official/dop.html.

cyberspace. Principle 4 of the Declaration of Principles emphasised that communication was one of the cornerstones of the Information Society:

> We reaffirm, as an essential foundation of the Information Society, and as outlined in Article 19 of the Universal Declaration of Human Rights, that everyone has the right to freedom of opinion and expression; that this right includes freedom to hold opinions without interference and to seek, receive and impart information and ideas through any media and regardless of frontiers. Communication is a fundamental social process, a basic human need and the foundation of all social organization. It is central to the Information Society. Everyone, everywhere should have the opportunity to participate and no one should be excluded from the benefits the Information Society offers.[36]

Freedom of expression does not seem to have survived the internet diffusion reinvention and localisation in Africa. Government after government sought to ostensibly protect the public interest in online communication by outlawing fake news, safeguarding national security, combating terrorism, secessionism, tribalism, hate speech, and protecting public morality. These censorious actions essentially eviscerated the right of freedom of expression across the continent. The wave of internet disconnectivity, disruptions and manipulations that have taken place in Africa since 2010 run counter to the ethos and principles of the WSIS: internet connectivity, universal access to telephone communications, knowledge and information.

In the diffusion of innovation perspective, the world is in a perpetual state of innovation and change, and this change requires the penetration of inventions. These inventions diffuse or spread from a centre of innovation to other areas through a process of imitation.[37] Furthermore, innovations are often modified or re-invented in the course of the diffusion process, such that they fit each existing culture or environment they come into contact with.[38] The internet is one of the fastest diffusing innovations in the history of communication. The diffusion of the internet around the world has not followed the normal curve of adoption.

8. Instrumentalisation of Information and Communication Technologies in Africa

National telecommunications infrastructures have traditionally been symbols of national sovereignty and power. The founding documents of the International Telegraph Union, the predecessor of the ITU, emphasise the pre-eminent and predominant role of nation-states in the regulation of telecommunications infrastructures and networks. That regulatory logic has been deterritorialised from

---

[36] ibid para A.8.

[37] Tarde (n 17) H Earl Pemberton, 'The Curve of Cultural Diffusion Rate' (1936) 1(4) *American Sociological Review* 547–56; Rogers (n 17).

[38] Ryan and Gross (n 17); Rogers (n 17); J Kinnunen, 'Gabriel Tarde as a Founding Father of Innovation Diffusion Research' (1996) 39(4) *Acta Sociologica* 431–42.

physical space to the internet and entrenched in information and communication technologies in most African countries. Cyberspace is a global system of assemblages of information and communication technologies and infrastructures that are in a 'capacity–communication–power' nexus.[39] Foucault's assertion is a very apt description of the situation in Africa.

Foucault conceptualised telecommunications technologies and the mass media as instrumentalities of power and power dynamics that are marked by certain 'instrumental modalities or instrumentalisation'.[40] This construct refers to the re-signification or re-conceptualisation, deployment or utilisation of the instrumentalities of communication for purposes of getting the upper hand in the life-and-death political power struggles between authoritarian neo-patrimonial states and their opponents.[41] Foucault further suggests that in these contexts of unequal power dynamics, instrumentalisation is essentially 'weaponisation' of communication.[42] It includes the use of 'complex control mechanisms', that regulate the performance of communication infrastructure through a process of 'load-shaping'. In the language of cyberspace, that refers to the increase or reduction of bandwidth for purposes of control. Instrumentalisation also includes systems of surveillance, and the power to open or shut down communications infrastructure for political purposes, through implicit or explicit rules and regulations. This is because the act of communication is essentially an exercise in the 'transformation of reality, of the other', and as such, it is an expression of relations of power. Therefore, to communicate is to 'act on the other'.[43] Foucault also suggests these characteristics of relations of power demonstrate that power has been 'progressively "governmentalised", elaborated, rationalised and centralised in the form of, or under the protection of state institutions'.[44]

8.1. Research Questions and Method

In this chapter, we explore how the governments of Egypt and Cameroon instrumentalised the internet, mobile telephony and cyberspace as part of their architectures of repression. The following research question emerged from the literature: How did Egypt and Cameroon change from countries that actively promoted internet connectivity in the late 1990s to countries that actively engaged in internet disconnectivity less than 20 years later? How did Egypt and Cameroon instrumentalise the internet and mobile telephony in the context of political crises in both countries? In order to answer the research questions, a politico-cultural and

---

[39] Foucault (n 3) 123–24.
[40] ibid 241.
[41] Fukuyama (n 9) 283–91.
[42] Foucault (n 3) 655–721.
[43] ibid 233–41.
[44] ibid 241.

policy analysis of the two jurisdictions under study was carried out. Regulation of the infrastructural resources (networks), and content of information and communication technologies in the two countries was also carried out. I also examined the national policies of the two countries in matters of freedom of expression.

In order to determine the nature of the internet regulatory regimes of the two countries under study, I carried out what Pierre Legrand called 'hermeneutic interventions'[45] or interpretations of the laws, regulations and regulated representations of the two countries in the domain of telecommunications. The aim of this analysis was to establish the politico-cultural contexts and the power dynamics that triggered instrumentalisation of mobile telephony, the internet and social media platforms in both countries. Since this study was concerned with telecommunications and internet policy, I carried out a textual analysis of the telecommunications laws and policies of Egypt and Cameroon to determine the role of government in regulating the infrastructures of both countries. I also analysed the official regulatory orders and pronouncements, with respect to internet shutdowns. This included internal memoranda and circular letters.

8.2. Results – From Internet Connectivity to Internet Disconnectivity in Egypt and Cameroon

The first research question was concerned with how the governments of Hosni Mubarak of Egypt and Paul Biya of Cameroon evolved from administrations that actively promoted internet connectivity and access in the late 1990s to countries that actively engaged in internet disconnectivity less than 20 years later. The answer to this counter-intuitive transformation is found in the rapid diffusion of information and communication technologies, especially mobile telephony, mobile internet and social media platforms on the continent. These technologies led to the emergence of information activists, enabled the growth of civil society groups, and facilitated the creation of online spaces of political opposition and resistance that were beyond the control of authoritarian regimes that had, for decades, enjoyed absolute control over the traditional media – newspapers, radio and television. In other words, the liberating power of information and communication technologies made authoritarian governments suspicious of them.

In the early days of the internet, the late 1990s, some African governments showed signs of fear of the new assemblage of technologies that were creating a new freedom space in Africa. Since national telecommunication administrators in Egypt, Cameroon and virtually all other African countries were internet service providers and domain name service administrators, they tended to provide direct access to the internet only to embassies and non-governmental organisations

---

[45] P Legrand, 'The Same and the Different' in P Legrand and R Munday (eds), *Comparative Legal Studies: Traditions and Transitions* (Cambridge, Cambridge University Press, 2003) 240–311, 253.

within their national territories. However, after a wave of privatisation of African telecommunication services under the IMF and World Bank structural adjustment programmes, these governments lost their monopolies as internet access providers.

Electronic mail forums were Africa's first forums of free expression. All types of groupings ranging from the PanAfrican News Agency to insurgents and rebel groups quickly went online. Africa's rebel groups became 'cyberrebels' who used the internet to tell the world their side of the story. No matter where they were physically located, rebels maintained webpages hosted in sympathetic African countries and used these pages to distribute information, raise funds and recruit new members. Furthermore, technologies like internet mirror sites, email message attachments, and re-mailing from generic servers around the world, rendered government controls ineffective. These groups could also call or send email messages to newsrooms around the world. Rebels in Sierra Leone, Liberia, Senegal, Democratic Republic of Congo, Congo-Brazzaville, Angola, Sudan, Ethiopia, Algeria, and the Muslim Brotherhood in Egypt, Igbo (Biafran) separatists in Nigeria, and Anglophone separatists in Cameroon, all made extensive use of the internet to get their message across, raise funds around the world, and recruit members.

9. The Cellular Phone Boom

The diffusion of relatively cheap, easy to use cellular phones put communication at the fingertips of millions, and broke government monopolies of information for good. One of the consequences of improving telecommunications infrastructures on the continent was a cell phone boom that transformed communications on the continent.[46] From 2000 to 2010, there was a 2,300 per cent growth in internet connectivity in Africa. By 2021, connectivity growth had surpassed 10,000 per cent.[47] During that period, the use of mobile telephony in African countries grew more rapidly than in any other region of the world. In terms of sheer volume, by 2010, the number of mobile connections in Africa had surpassed those of Western Europe.[48] Sebastiana Etzo and Guy Collender,[49] as well as Pádraig Carmody,[50] describe the political, economic, social and cultural impact of mobile telephony on the African continent as revolutionary because of its use in personal monetary

---

[46] M de Bruijn, F Nyamnjoh and I Brinkman (eds), *Mobile Phones: The New Talking Drums of Everyday Africa* (Langaa, African Studies Center, 2009) 11.

[47] Internet World Stats, 2022, www.internetworldstats.com/stats1.htm.

[48] J May and E Adera, 'The ICT/Poverty Nexus' (2011) 48(3) *United Nations Chronicle* 30–33.

[49] S Etzo and G Collender, 'The Mobile Phone "Revolution" in Africa: Rhetoric or Reality?' (2010) 109(437) *African Affairs* 659.

[50] P Carmody, 'A Knowledge Economy or an Information Society in Africa? Thintegration and the Mobile Phone Revolution' (2013) 19(1) *Information Technology for Development* 24.

transactions, trade in commodities, monitoring of elections, public health communication and social communication. The availability of cheap Chinese and Korean mass-produced, stripped-down camera phones that provide internet access and enable users to make phone calls, send text messages, take pictures and share them with individuals, or participate in virtual groups via free mobile platforms like Google's WhatsApp and Telegram, changed the communicational power dynamics on the African continent. Governments that for decades enjoyed monopolies over communication via official government radio and television stations, broadcasting only official government information and discourse in a one-way, top-down fashion, lost their communicational exclusivity as cell phones diffused to all parts of the continent. For many African newspapers, the internet and social media platforms provided outlets where journalists, cartoonists, caricaturists and comic strip artists, who had a brush with the law, or had either been banned, censored or had their work seized, could 'deterritorialise' and present their work online.[51]

Mobile phones were 'reinvented' and re-contextualised to fit the continent's culture of 'orality'.[52] The advent of relatively cheap Android phones, as well as the decision of the International Phonetic Association and the Dallas-based Summer Institute of Linguistics to create new phonetic keyboards with hundreds of characters corresponding with African languages led to the popularisation of 'free' global social media platforms like Facebook, Wikipedia, Twitter, WhatsApp, Instagram and Telegram. These platforms moved the internet beyond the control of governments, and delivered rivers of information directly to users in English, French, Arabic, Swahili, Amharic, Yoruba and virtually all the hundreds of languages on the African continent. Furthermore, mobile telephony and media platforms have created an unprecedented situation where sensitive government documents that demonstrate corruption and abuse of power are leaked and posted on social networking sites.

To complicate matters for dictatorial regimes across the continent, the internet, social media and mobile telephony became catalysts for change. Information activists within a number of countries used the mobile telephones and social media to organise and coordinate strikes, boycotts and massive anti-government demonstrations in physical space.[53] In the face of global discontinuities and uncertainties engendered by globalisation and revolutionary developments in information and communication technologies, most African countries tried to apply old censorious rules to the new, global media environment. In the next section, I describe and explain how the contextually different political cultures and telecommunications governance regimes of Egypt and Cameroon provided similar authoritarian solutions to the identical problem of popular demands for change.

---

[51] Eko (n 12) 248.
[52] L Kibora, 'L'Appropriation du SMS par une "société de l'oralité"' in de Bruijn, Nyamnjoh and Brinkman (n 46) 110–24, 111.
[53] L Eko, *New Media, Old Authoritarian Regimes: Instrumentalization of the Internet and the Social Media in the 'Arab Spring' in North Africa* (Lanham, Lexington Books, 2012) 129–59.

10. Regulation of Information Technology Infrastructures in Egypt

The Arab Spring in North Africa (from 2010 to 2011) and the subsequent over-throw of authoritarian governments in Algeria and Sudan in 2019, demonstrated the power media activism and the use of mobile internet applications for politi-cal organising and resistance. Egypt has been described as a 'semi-authoritarian and patrimonial [or] neopatrimonial country power framework in which private and state interests are inseparably intertwined'.[54] Under structural adjustment and privatisation agreements signed between Egypt, the IMF and the World Bank, the Egyptian government launched a series of tightly controlled privatisation exercises in the telecommunications sector. The government used the privatisation process to extend its hegemony in the area of information and network technologies and cellular telephony. In order to expand their reach as broadly as possible, global information and communication technology companies sign joint venture or part-nership agreements, memoranda of understanding or other bilateral instruments of cooperation with nation-states or their telecommunications administrations or regulators.

For more than half a century, Egypt did not have a private press. President Gamal Abdel Nasser nationalised the mass media in 1960, and brought them under direct government control. Nasser's successors, Anwar Sadat and Hosni Mubarak, both military officers, continued the direct governmental control of the mass media. The press laws in Egypt divided the profession into national (government-controlled) and opposition (party) journalism. It was against the law to 'defame' the president and his family, and to criticise government officials and institutions. Most of the press laws were selectively applied to opposition party newspapers. To make matters worse for the press, Islamic militants killed journalists who were not sympathetic to their cause from time to time.

The National Telecommunications Regulatory Authority regulated the govern-ment-owned telecommunications networks and backbones in Egypt. Under Article 60 of the Telecommunication Regulation Law 2003, a government-owned company, Telecom Egypt was granted

> the exclusive right to establish, operate and exploit international transmission networks between Egypt and any other country through international gateways via submarine and terrestrial cables, microwave links and satellites for fixed services and provides telephone, fax, telex and telegraph services over such networks.

The result was that the Egyptian government controlled the border gateway proto-col routes that connected Egypt to the rest of the world. This policy of governmental control of the infrastructures of telecommunication was a continuation of more

---

[54] Z Hafez, 'The Culture of Rent, Factionalism, and Corruption: A Political Economy of Rent in the Arab World' (2009) 2 *Contemporary Arab Affairs* 458–80.

than 50 years of government nationalisation of the instrumentalities of the media and telecommunications in Egypt. This monopoly power essentially ensured that the government of Egypt owned, controlled and regulated all the telecommunications networks and internet gateways to and from the Egyptian national territory.

Additionally, all telecommunications operators were required by law to provide, at their own expense, hardware and software that would interface with governmental telecommunications apparatuses, in order to 'enable the Armed Forces, and National Security Entities [the Presidency, the Ministry of Interior and the National Security Authority] to exercise their powers within the law'. This essentially meant that, under Article 64 of Telecommunication Regulation Law 2003, all telecommunications operators in Egypt were required to ensure that governmental agencies could have access to their systems and networks whenever they wanted to. Article 65 was a broad provision that gave the Egyptian authorities the power to set up a national telecommunications emergency plan:

> The TRA shall, in cooperation with the Armed Forces and the State concerned entities, prepare a prior plan for the operation of Telecommunication Networks to be implemented during natural and environmental disasters and periods of general mobilization … and any other cases related to National Security. Such plan shall be updated periodically in order to secure Defense and National Security. The Operators and telecommunications Service Providers shall commit themselves to implement such plan.

While this may not be unusual, the fact that Egypt had been under emergency rule since the assassination of President Anwar Sadat in 1981, gave the government extraordinary powers to control the telecommunications networks and the telecommunications service providers of the country in emergency situations – which was all the time.

11. Information and Communication Technologies as Architectures of Repression in Cameroon

In Cameroon, the telecommunications infrastructure is a part of a highly repressive system that has no freedom of speech or expression. Journalists and ordinary citizens are arrested and imprisoned without trial if the authorities find objectionable social media content in their telephones, in the course of random checks. The main instrument of repression is the 2014 Law on Repression of Terrorism.[55] This law had been passed in response to the Islamist Boko Haram terrorist activities in Nigeria and North Cameroon. The vague, over-broad and highly elastic Cameroon anti-terrorism law, which provides that the death penalty could be imposed on citizens who, either as individuals or in a group, carry out, abet or

---

[55] Amnesty International, Country Report: Cameroon, 2017/2018 (2018), www.amnesty.org/en/countries/africa/cameroon/report-cameroon.

sponsor terrorism, is routinely used to arrest and imprison journalists, activists and political opponents of the Biya regime. The law also criminalises 'incitement to rebellion', and 'creating a general uprising in the country'. Cameroon opposition parties and journalists, as well as international human rights organisations, have condemned the law as an instrument of repression, and suppression of dissent and criticism of the excesses and corruption of the government.[56] Indeed, journalists have been arrested, tried and convicted in the Yaoundé Military Tribunal for 'publishing false news', 'complicity with and non-denunciation of terrorist acts', 'non-denunciation of information and sources' and other vague charges brought by military prosecutors.[57] Furthermore, the National Communication Council of Cameroon (NCC), is an 'autonomous' media regulator created by presidential decree in 1991 ostensibly to serve as the ethical watchdog that promotes the professionalisation of media is a tool of media repression. Its other roles include promotion of governmental ideologies of national unity, peace and culture. The NCC's main task is extra-judicial content regulation. It is empowered to issue warnings, extra-judicial temporary suspension of journalists for unethical activities, and permanent interdictions against 'unprofessional' (read anti-government) media organisations and journalists. Over the years, the NCC has become a censorious agency that powerful members of the government and the ruling elite routinely use to suppress newspapers, intimidate and ban journalists, and silence independent media owners. Interestingly, the NCC has no enforcement mechanism at its disposal so journalists and media outlets close to the regime can ignore its decisions with immunity.

12. Instrumentalisation of the Internet and Information Technologies: Internet Disconnectivity in Egypt and Cameroon

The second research question was concerned with how Egypt and Cameroon instrumentalised the internet and mobile telephony in the context of political crises in both countries. Egypt was the first country in the world to deliberately shut down its mobile telephone networks and disconnect itself from the internet in a desperate but vain attempt to halt a popular, social media-driven revolution. On 28 January 2011, in an act of utter desperation, the beleaguered government of former Egyptian President Hosni Mubarak ordered the four internet service providers and cell phone companies in the country of 80 million people – Link

---

[56] C Johnson, 'Cameroon: New Law on Repression of Terrorism Passed' (*Global Legal Monitor*, 18 December 2014), www.loc.gov/item/global-legal-monitor/2014-12-18/cameroon-new-law-on-repression-of-terrorism-passed/.

[57] Amnesty International, 'Cameroon: A Turn for the Worse: Violence and Human Rights Violations in Anglophone Cameroon' Index Number: AFR 17/8481/2018 (12 June 2018), www.amnesty.org/en/documents/afr17/8481/2018/en.

Egypt, Vodafone/Raya, Telecom Egypt, Etisalat Misr – to shut down their services. Before the mobile phone companies literally pulled the plug on their services, the Egyptian government ordered them to send messages – and these were drafted by government officials – to all their customers warning them not to participate in any illegal anti-government demonstrations. A few hours later, Egypt suffered a massive electronic communication blackout as the internet service providers turned off the border gateway protocol routes that connected Egypt to the rest of the internet.[58]

The internet blackout lasted five whole days. This desperate act, which was unprecedented in the annals of internet history, was aimed at shutting down the social media – Facebook, Twitter, Wikipedia, Myspace and text messaging – which the Egyptian government considered the motor of the youth-led popular uprising that had paralysed the country, and brought the government to the verge of collapse. In a statement on its London-based website, British-owned mobile phone operator, Vodafone, which had a heavy presence in Egypt, stated that:

> Under the emergency powers provisions of the Telecoms Act, the Egyptian authorities can instruct the mobile networks of Mobinil, Etisalat and Vodafone to send messages to the people of Egypt. They have used this since the start of the protests. These messages are not scripted by any of the mobile network operators, and we do not have the ability to respond to the authorities on their content.
>
> Vodafone Group has protested to the authorities that the current situation regarding these messages is unacceptable. We have made clear that all messages should be transparent and clearly attributable to the originator.[59]

After a global hue and cry, Vodafone issued a statement to the effect that: 'We would like to make it clear that the authorities in Egypt have the technical capability to close our network, and if they had done so it would have taken much longer to restore services to our customers.'[60] The Egyptian government had the technical capability to switch off all telecommunications services in the country because it controlled all the networks and internet gateways. The provision of the Egyptian Telecommunications Act may have paved the way for the Mubarak regime to institute a five-day internet blackout at the height of the power struggles that ultimately resulted in the collapse of his regime.

According to Al-Ahram Online, the online edition of the Egyptian government-owned newspaper, *Al-Ahram*, an Egyptian administrative court ruled that the five-day internet and mobile telephony blackout (from 28 January to 2 February 2011) was not the spontaneous act of a desperate, crumbling regime. The court held that the strategy of shutting down the internet and the mobile telephone

---

[58] J Cowle, 'Egypt Leaves the Internet' (*CounterCurrents.org*, 28 January 2011), www.countercurrents.org/cowie280111.htm.

[59] 'Vodafone Group PLC – Response on Issues Relating to Mobile Network Operations in Egypt' (*Vodafone*, 22 February 2011), https://media.business-humanrights.org/media/documents/files/media/documents/vodafone-statement-re-egypt-22-feb-2011.pdf.

[60] ibid.

networks was a long-standing policy posture. The administrative court held that the government had carried out experiments on shutting down all or parts of the internet in the country as early as 2008, and that the last experiment had been carried out in October 2010, just three months before the Egyptian Revolution. The court ruled that after internal disturbances in 2008, the Egyptian government had compelled internet service providers and mobile phone companies, under its emergency powers, to participate in its network withdrawal experiment that involved cutting off the internet in entire cities or governorates (provinces), blocking specific websites, extracting the identification and passwords of information activists, slowing down web-traffic, and ensuring that telecommunication companies could quickly respond to governmental directives to shut down parts or all of their services in times of national emergency.[61] The court's findings clearly demonstrate that the Egyptian government had transformed the telecommunications infrastructures of the country into a component of its architecture of repression. The government was the gateway of the telecommunications infrastructure and the internet within its national territory.

13. Instrumentalisation of Information and Communication Technologies in Cameroon

On 17 January 2017, David Nkoto Emane, Director General of Camtel, the Cameroon government-owned telecommunications network operator, internet services provider, controller and operator of the country's satellite communications and border gateway protocols, wrote confidential letter No 006/DG to Minette Libom Li Likeng, the Cameroon Minister of Posts and Telecommunications. The subject matter of the letter, which was leaked and posted on social media platforms, was 'suspension of internet services to certain sensitive regions'. The letter stated that:

> Further to your high instructions, Camtel has taken all measures necessary to implement the suspension. Nevertheless, it appears that some Internet service operators did not follow your instructions to the letter. As soon as I was informed, I personally formed a team on Camtel sites in Yaoundé, Douala, Kribi, and Limbe [where the gateways to the SAT-3/WASC and other international sub-marine fiber-optic cable systems are located] to carry out your instructions in a coercive manner.[62]

The Camtel Director General told the Minister that this targeted internet shutdown showed the need for the government to monitor internet service at the submarine fibre optic cable landing points, border gateways and satellite stations. The Director added that this partial internet shutdown demonstrated the necessity of

---

[61] S El-Wardani, 'Egypt's Connections Blackout was Planned since April 2008' (*Ahram Online*, 30 May 2011), http://english.ahram.org.eg/NewsContentPrint/1/0/13282/Egypt/0/Egypts-connections-blackout-was-planned-since-Apri.aspx.
[62] D Nkoto Emane, Confidential Letter No. 006/DG to Mrs Minette Libom Li Likeng, Cameroon Minister of Posts and Telecommunications (2017).

'acquiring the modern tools to guarantee our [cyber]sovereignty'.[63] Essentially, the partial internet shutdown in question was a reference to the government's telecommunications blockade of the Northwest and Southwest regions that had revolted against the authoritarian, Francophone government of President Paul Biya who had been in power for 40 years. The telecommunications blockade of the English-speaking regions demonstrated the necessity of creating some kind of national 'kill switch' that would enable the government to shut down all or parts of the internet in Cameroon as the need arose.

That confidential Cameroon government correspondence was evidence that the government had decided to sever all internet and mobile phone communication in the English-speaking region of the country, a region with a population of eight million people. This was part of the affirmative decision of the government to violently suppress non-violent demonstrations by English-speaking lawyers, teachers, students and members of civil society groups, who were asking for political and cultural change. These political demands by unarmed civilians in the Anglophone regions were met with brutal repression, targeted killings, arrests, imprisonment, beatings and torture by the Cameroon armed forces, led by the feared and brutal, Israeli, French and American trained and armed Rapid Intervention Brigade (known by its French acronym BIR), as well as the army, the gendarmerie and the police. In addition to creating and training the BIR and the Presidential Guard to resemble Israeli Special Forces, Israeli 'technical advisers', former military officers approved by the Israeli government, were based at the Cameroon President's office, where they set up and managed telecommunications surveillance for the Biya regime.[64]

The Anglophone uprising was quickly transformed into a social media-driven revolt led by Anglo-Cameroonians in the diaspora – particularly the United States, the United Kingdom, Canada and South Africa. Others in Nigeria, Belgium, Germany and the Scandinavian countries joined the fray. Despite the internet blackout in English-speaking Southern Cameroon, activists and ordinary citizens succeeded in taking cell phone pictures and videos of the atrocities and human rights violations committed by the military, travelling to towns in the Francophone part of Cameroon and posting these images on social media platforms. This created an unprecedented global Anglo-Cameroon virtual community that could be called upon to hold demonstrations in Western countries.

It was in order to silence dissent on the internet, and to prevent Anglophone activists from using social media platforms and mobile telephony to organise further demonstrations, or post images of BIR, military, gendarmerie and police brutality to the world, that Minette Libom Li Likeng, Minister of Posts and Telecommunications, ordered the government-owned telecommunications company, Camtel, to cut-off the internet and mobile telephony in the two English-speaking regions.

---

[63] D Nkoto Emane, Suspension du service internet dans certaines régions sensibles. Letter No 006/DG (2017).

[64] Amnesty International, 'Cameroon: Anglophone Regions "Gripped by Deadly Violence" – New Report' (11 June 2018), www.amnesty.org.uk/press-releases/cameroon-anglophone-regions-gripped-deadly-violence-new-report.

This censorious action essentially froze the 'Silicon Mountain', the information and communications technology start-up community of the University town of Buea, which was known internationally and had been featured on CNN International. When members of that internet start-up community set up a makeshift internet 'refugee camp' on the banks of the Mungo river, the geographical border between the English and French-speaking regions Cameroon, where internet and mobile telephone signals were available, Cameroon law enforcement officials moved in and demolished the camp. That first censorious internet blackout, which lasted 95 days and turned out to be the longest, governmental, anti-communication act of the internet age, was quickly noticed around the world. Global internet activists launched a #BringBackOurInternet campaign. No less a personality than Edward Snowden, the former American information technology intelligence contractor who revealed American overnment surveillance and data collection programmes, and was living in exile in Russia, joined the campaign. He criticised the Cameroon government on Twitter, saying: 'This is the future of repression. If we do not fight it there, it will happen here. #KeepItOn #BringBackOurInternet.'[65]

The Cameroon government reacted negatively to this campaign, seeing it as an attempt to 'destabilise' the country. It ordered the cell phone companies to send the following SMS texts to all cell phone account holders in the country:

> Dear Subscriber, do not be an accomplice to disinformation and destabilization of our country via the social media .... You face 20 years imprisonment if you are the author of false declarations or slanderous accusations MINPOSTEL (Ministry of Posts and Telecommunications).

The censorious actions of the Cameroon government with respect to the internet in the English-speaking regions of Cameroon ironically occurred after the UN General Assembly had endorsed a UN Human Rights Council resolution that recognised access to the internet as a human right, and condemned, '*unequivocally* measures to intentionally prevent or disrupt access to or dissemination of information online in violation of international human rights law and calls on all States to refrain from and cease such measures'.[66]

14. Discussion and Conclusion

While the European Union, the United States, the United Kingdom and China are grappling with the excesses of the so-called 'Big Tech' information and communication technology companies and their interactive online platforms, Facebook, X (formerly known as Twitter), Instagram, Sina Weibo, Tencent QQ, and so on, in many authoritarian African countries, the problem is still the classic situation

---

[65] D Searcey and F Essomba, 'African Nations Increasingly Silence Internet to Stem Protests' *The New York Times* (10 February 2017).

[66] UN Human Rights Council, *The Promotion, Protection and Enjoyment of Human Rights on the Internet*, A/HRC/32/L.20 (27 June 2016).

of government control and censorship of the media. Journalistic malpractice and unethical activity on the part of journalists abound. However, media malpractices and unethical behaviours pale in comparison to the suffocating cloud of silence, the climate of fear that many countries unleash on journalists and the media from time to time. As this analysis of the situation in Egypt and Cameroon demonstrates, since 2010, many African countries have resorted to the drastic act of shutting down the internet and mobile telephone networks countrywide, or in specific regions, at the slightest hint of popular discontent. The main conclusion is that in Egypt and Cameroon, the internet does not do things to authoritarian governments, authoritarian governments do things to, and with, the internet in the name of cybersovereignty. Egypt and Cameroon are essentially gateway regulators of the internet that grant or deny access to the internet in the name of national security or some other government interest.

The government or a governmental entity controls and regulates the cyberinfrastructures – the telecommunications infrastructures, networks, border gateway protocols and nodes that connect specific countries to the rest of the world.[67] Furthermore, the government also regulates and controls the rivers of data and information that flow through the infrastructures of the internet. Gateway regulatory regimes use firewalls, content filtering, proxy servers and other means to shield the country from unwanted external internet content.[68] Governments across Africa have resorted to internet shutdowns as a means to stifle dissent and prevent cyberactivists from using social media and mobile telephony to organise anti-government demonstrations. Internet shutdowns are extreme acts of anti-communication that are strikingly at variance with the very logic of the internet.

Shutting the internet down was the most widely reported act of communicational instrumentalisation of the Arab Spring and sub-Sahara Africa. In effect, it was widely known that the main reason for creation of the decentralised, redundant network of networks that became the internet was to ensure the survivability of the United States' military command and control networks even during 'worst case attacks' in the event of a thermonuclear conflict between the United States and the Soviet Union.[69] The internet was therefore touted as a robust indestructible invention that routed its rivers of information around obstructions and infrastructural outages. It turns out the internet is not dictator-proof. It is vulnerable to deliberate, governmental disconnectivity. Egypt and Cameroon instrumentalised their telecommunications networks as part of their respective architectures of repression in the struggles that pitted their autocratic regimes against civil society informational activists.

---

[67] L Eko, 'Many Spiders, One World Wide Web: Towards a Typology of Internet Regulation' (2001) 6 *Communication Law and Policy* 448–60, 476; N Choucri and DD Clark, 'Who Controls Cyberspace?' (2013) 69(5) *Bulletin of the Atomic Scientists* 21–31.

[68] L Eko, A Kumar and Q Yao, 'To Google or Not to Google: The Google Digital Books Initiative and the Exceptionalist Intellectual Property Law Regimes of the United States and France' (2012) 15(7) *Journal of Internet Law* 12–30; Choucri and Clark (n 67) 23; Kalathil and Boas (n 29) 57.

[69] P Baran, 'On Distributed Communication Networks' (1964) 12(1) *IEEE Transactions on Communication Systems* 1–9, 2.

8

Free Expression of the Traditional Media in South Africa and the Constraints Imposed by Law

JOHN CAMPBELL AND SUHAIL MOHAMMED

1. Introduction

There is not much statutory or regulatory restriction on free speech for the South African print media, apart from a constitutional prohibition on hate speech (given effect by an act of Parliament) together with statutory protection of data. The broadcast media, however, is subject to a stricter (but far from oppressive) regulatory regime than is the print media. So the main constraint on both today is therefore what, in South Africa, is called the common law. But this is not the English common law, rather Roman-Dutch law that was received into South Africa by way of early Dutch colonial conquest and preserved by the British Empire after it permanently took the Cape in 1806 during the Napoleonic wars.

Roman and Roman-Dutch law protect personality rights by way of the *actio injuriarum*, an action that dates back roughly 2,000 years in Roman law as a general remedy for aggressions on the person (*corpus*), dignity (*dignitas*) and reputation (*fama*). The basic feature of Roman law of *injuria* is that it is a system of general principles, rather than of discrete wrongs developed in isolation from each other (as in English common law). In other words, application of the general principles yield the answers for complaints as diverse as unlawful imprisonment, malicious prosecution, defamation, insult and breach of privacy. It is defined as the *wrongful* and *intentional* impairment of these rights.[1] The terms 'wrongful' and 'intentional' are important limits on the action and, as will appear below, play an important role in moderating the potential of defamation and privacy, in particular, to restrict free speech. It is not the full bouquet of infringements of dignity that is the focus of this chapter, because most either do not, or very seldom, arise in the context of the traditional media. This chapter, therefore, is confined to defamation and privacy plus the statutory and regulatory inhibitions mentioned above.

---

[1] *Hofmeyr v Minister of Justice* 1993 (3) SA 131 (AD) 154.

Roman law, of course, did not recognise any right to free speech. While South African law in the pre-constitutional era did, this was tepid, lacked conviction and, as will appear in the following section, ineffective not only against the legislative onslaught of the apartheid Government, but also in failing to prevent the courts of those days tilting the Roman-Dutch common law against free expression by imposing strict liability on the media for defamation.[2] This was a significant step backwards for free speech in Roman-Dutch law, and was only reversed in the constitutional era.

2. The Constitution

The starting point in modern South African law, for the purpose of understanding how regulatory and legislative restrictions and the Roman-Dutch common law work, is the constitutional protection of the rights of dignity, privacy and freedom of expression set out in the Constitution:

10. Human dignity

Everyone has inherent dignity and the right to have their dignity respected and protected.

…

14. Privacy

Everyone has the right to privacy, which includes the right not to have—

(a)   their person or home searched;
(b)   their property searched;
(c)   their possessions seized; or
(d)   the privacy of their communications infringed.

…

16. Freedom of expression

(1)   Everyone has the right to freedom of expression, which includes-

    (a)   freedom of the press and other media;
    (b)   freedom to receive and impart information and ideas;
    (c)   freedom of artistic creativity; and
    (d)   academic freedom and freedom of scientific research.

(2)   The right in subsection (1) does not extend to-

    (a)   propaganda for war;
    (b)   incitement of imminent violence; or
    (c)   advocacy of hatred that is based on race, ethnicity, gender or religion, and that constitutes incitement to cause harm.

---

[2] *Pakendorf v De Flamingh* 1982 (3) SA 146 (AD) 157 E–157 F; dealt with in more detail below.

It can immediately be seen that section 16(1) of the Constitution confers broad protections for freedom of expression. In particular, everyone has it (with specific mention of 'press and other media') and it protects the receipt of information, as well as its expression. This reinforces the protection because any inhibition will need to be tested not merely against the speaker's (whether media or not) rights but also against the *listener's* rights.

There is no legal significance in the fact that privacy is expressly recognised and mentioned in section 14 of the Constitution but reputation is not. The *actio injuriarum* remains the modern remedy available to vindicate the constitutional rights to reputation and privacy that are both subsumed, in constitutional-era South African Law, into the foundational right to dignity. When courts decide cases under the *actio injuriarum* there is a balance, that lawyers in the United Kingdom (UK) would recognise, between the rights to dignity (that is defamation and privacy) on the one hand, and free speech on the other.

The right to dignity, it should be acknowledged, also protects individuals from insult. But this hardly ever arises in the context of media reports save, perhaps, regarding satire and cartoons. *Laugh It Off Promotions CC v South African Breweries International* was a trademark dispute concerning satirical T-shirts that parodied the Carling Black Label trademark by changing the words in the label to include phrases suggesting the exploitation of the black labour force. The Constitutional Court accepted that parody was a relevant factor in the determination of the dispute and reversed the original judgments that had interdicted further sale of the T-shirts.[3] The same approach is likely to inform defamation actions, where appropriate.

The guarantee of freedom of expression in the Constitution does not merely temper the rights to dignity but it also operates to an almost unlimited extent beyond this. For instance, it recognises the profession of journalism, and protects its practitioners. Thus an application by the South African National Editors Forum on behalf of journalists who sought protection from a political party aggrieved by their criticism, resulted in an order interdicting that political party from intimidating, harassing or threatening the journalists, and also restricting the political party's use of social media to those effects. The rationale was the journalists' right to carry out their professional duties in the media as guaranteed by the constitutional right to free expression;[4] the right to freedom of expression also does not tolerate legislative attempts to restrict access to information that it is in the public interest to publish. Section 41(6) of the National Prosecuting Authority Act 1998 prohibited publication of information in a closed bribery inquiry involving a Cabinet Minister, but the High Court held that this was an unjustified limitation on the right to freedom of expression guaranteed by Section 16 of the Constitution;[5] nor

---

[3] *Laugh It Off Promotions CC v South African Breweries International* [2005] ZACC 7 [64] and [66].
[4] *South African National Editors Forum v Black Land First* [2017] ZAGPJHC 179.
[5] *The Mail & The Guardian Ltd v Maharaj* [2016] ZAGPPHC 613.

will the right to freedom of expression permit legal professional privilege to clog the flow of information discovered by journalists.

A memorandum concerning the legal implications of South African Airways' (SAA) withdrawal from a continuing agreement to purchase an aircraft due to financial difficulties in the absence of a government bailout, prepared by in-house counsel, was leaked. Publication of this memorandum gave rise to significant public scrutiny of SAA's financial viability and its mismanagement of public funds. On appeal, the High Court in Johannesburg found that SAA's attorney-client privilege was not absolute and could not be invoked to suppress the dissemination of information in the public interest.[6] Given the perfectly rational judicial reluctance in South Africa and other comparable jurisdictions to attenuate legal professional privilege (the privilege pertaining between clients and their legal advisors however named – in South Africa it is called attorney-client privilege), this latter case illustrates the power of section 16 of the Constitution in demolishing seemingly impregnable common law obstacles to the disclosure of information of public importance.

Perhaps the most important such court intervention regarding the practice of journalism, is the protection of the identities of sources who often, and for very good reasons, insist on anonymity. Even in the pre-constitutional era there was one decision excusing a journalist from being compelled to testify as to the identity of a source.[7] Although no general privilege against disclosing journalists' sources was found, the Court in this case, *S v Cornelissen*, weighed up the public advantages in having the source disclosed, and the public prejudice to the flow of information that the testimony would result. But in the constitutional era, protection of sources has been hardened. The Constitutional Court, building on the work of Tsoka J in the Johannesburg High Court in the *Bosasa Operations (Pty) Ltd v Basson* case, and on the protection of free expression in section 16 of the Constitution, has to a considerable degree reinforced that protection in these terms:

> I agree that keeping the identity of journalists' sources confidential is protected by the rights to freedom of expression and the media. This court has acknowledged the constitutional importance of the media in our democratic society, and has confirmed that '[t]he Constitution thus asserts and protects the media in the performance of their obligations to the broader society, principally through the provisions of section 16. It follows that the confidentiality of journalists' sources, which is crucial for the performance by the media of their obligations, is protected by section 16(1)(a). Like the High Court, I place reliance on Tsoka J who held as much in *Bosasa*. Relying on local and foreign authority, he put it thus:
>
> '[I]t is apparent that journalists, subject to certain limitations, are not expected to reveal the identity of their sources. If indeed freedom of press is fundamental and *sine qua non* for democracy, it is essential that in carrying out this public duty for the public

---

[6] *South African Airways v BDFM Publishers* 2016 (2) SA 561 (GJ).
[7] *S v Cornelissen; Cornelissen v Zeelie NO* 1994 (2) SACR 41 (W).

good, the identity of their sources should not be revealed, particularly, when the information so revealed would not have been publicly known. This essential and critical role of the media, which is more pronounced in our nascent democracy founded on openness, where corruption has become cancerous, needs to be fostered rather than denuded.'[8]

3. Regulatory and Statutory Constraints on the Media

3.1. Rules, Codes and Statutory Bodies

The South African print media is largely self-regulated through the Press Council of South Africa. The Press Ombudsman, established by media organisations and print media owners, is the adjudicative arm of the Press Council where disputes arise between members of the public and media organisations. It enforces a code which, briefly, provides for duties to report news truthfully, accurately, fairly and in a balanced manner, and to avoid discrimination on the basis of race, gender, sex, pregnancy, marital status, ethnic or social origin, colour, sexual orientation, age, disability, religion, conscience, belief, culture, language and birth or other status, and not to make any prejudicial or pejorative reference to such status unless strictly relevant to the matter reported and if in the public interest. Almost all newspapers and magazines in South Africa subscribe to the Press Code. The Press Code contains guidelines relating to comment, headlines, posters, pictures and captions, confidential sources and the coverage of violence. Sanctions for breach of the Press Code include a reprimand or correction, but there is no power to impose fines, damages or to suspend or expel a member from the Press Council.

The broadcast media, however, is required to be licensed and is subject to statutory regulation in the form of the Code of Conduct of one or other of two bodies created by statute – the Broadcasting Complaints Commission of South Africa (BCCSA) and the Independent Communications Authority of South Africa (ICASA). They have identical codes of conduct that require broadcasters to report the news truthfully, present it fairly and in the correct context without intentionally or negligently departing from the facts and with no distortion, exaggeration, misrepresentation or omission. Further, to state where verification of facts has not been made and, if necessary, to rectify anything that is afterwards discovered to have been incorrect. Both statutory bodies have wider powers of sanction

---

[8] *AmaBhungane Centre for Investigative Journalism NPC and Another v Minister of Justice and Correctional Services and Others; Minister of Police v AmaBhungane Centre for Investigative Journalism NPC and Others* 2021 (3) SA 246 (CC) [115]; *Bosasa Operations (Pty) Ltd v Basson* 2013 (2) SA 570 (GSJ) [38].

than the Press Ombudsman, including the power to impose fines. An example of BCCSA regulation in practice occurred regarding what is known in some quarters as 'fake news'. A television station was found to have violated the BCCSA Code by featuring an interview with a famous COVID-19 conspiracy theorist. Objections from the public were registered and the BCCSA found that the broadcast involved the balance between free expression and the need to protect citizens from misinformation. The television station was ordered to broadcast an apology and to pay a fine.[9]

On the other hand, the broadcast media has won significant expansions for coverage of court proceedings and Parliament by way of the application of the Free Expression guarantee in the Constitution. In *Van Breda*,[10] the Supreme Court of Appeal was confronted with a ban on the recording of criminal proceedings against a high profile defendant, and found that courts were entitled to determine, on a case-by-case basis, the nature and scope of audio-visual broadcasting of court proceedings. In this case, the SCA held that such broadcasting was an incident of the right to free expression guaranteed by section 16 of the Constitution, protecting the right of the press to disseminate information as well as that of the public to receive it; and when a controversy arose as to whether Parliament was entitled to enact rules prohibiting live television broadcasting of incidents of disorder in a parliamentary session, the Supreme Court of Appeal held that these restrictions violated the right to an open parliament and were therefore unconstitutional and unlawful.[11]

The Digital Media and Marketing Association is an independent non-statutory association for members of the digital industry and its code is roughly the same as the other codes. If there is any difference between the print media's self-regulation and regulation of the broadcast media, it is this: The broadcast media is held to a higher standard of objectivity than the print media but, given the power and immediacy of images as against reading an article in a newspaper, this does not seem unreasonable and has not successfully been challenged in South Africa under section 16 of the Constitution.

3.2. Legislation

The only significant statutory constraint on freedom of expression is found in sections 10 and 12 of the Promotion of Equality and Prevention of Unfair Discrimination Act 2000 that prohibit (and confine the ambit of) hate speech. This is speech defined in section 10(1), read with the definition in section 1 of that Act, as speech based on race, gender, sex, pregnancy, marital status, ethnic

---

[9] *Media Monitoring Africa v eNCA Channel 403* (2020) BCCSA (Case No 09/2020).
[10] *Van Breda v Media 24 Ltd* 2017 (2) SACR 491 (SCA).
[11] *Primedia Broadcasting v Speaker of the National Assembly* 2017 (1) SA 572 (SCA).

or social origin, colour, sexual orientation, age, disability, religion, conscience, belief, culture, language and birth or any other ground where discrimination causes or perpetuates systemic disadvantage, undermines human dignity or adversely affects the equal enjoyment of a person's rights and freedoms in a serious manner that is comparable to discrimination on one of the aforesaid grounds. Those sections attracted the recent attention of the Constitutional Court which has ameliorated them so that only publication of expression which meets a new standard for hate speech,[12] more stringent than in the clauses enacted by Parliament, will be prohibited, subject to the section 12 exception which allows for *bona fide*, fair and accurate reporting in the public interest, provided that such expression does not offend the categories of speech specifically excluded from protection by section 16(2) of the Constitution (being propaganda for war, incitement of imminent violence, advocacy of hatred that is based on race, ethnicity, gender or religion and that constitutes incitement to cause harm).

Then there is the Protection of Personal Information Act 2013, which expands freedom of expression because the statutory prohibition on the processing of personal information, excludes information processed solely for the purpose of journalistic or artistic expression to the extent that such an exclusion is necessary to reconcile, as a matter of public interest, the right to privacy with the right to freedom of expression. The Children's Act 2008, in common with many other countries, requires that all proceedings in a children's court will be closed to everyone other than an individual performing professional court duties and almost inevitably results in the exclusion of journalists. So there is very little statutory interference with media freedom of expression in South Africa. The prohibition on hate speech has, in the main, different targets and will in all likelihood be far more of an issue in social media circles and low circulation publications to like-minded people. At any rate, given South Africa's history of racist speech, a prohibition on hate speech is widely supported and is here to stay.

3.3. Reasons for Light Regulation

In order to understand the relative weakness of statutory and regulatory inhibitions imposed on the media in South Africa today, one needs to appreciate the position before the fall of apartheid and the transition to constitutional democracy in 1994. Before 1994, and under the apartheid Government, there was an extensive system of statutory censorship of the South African media. In these years section 6 of the Internal Security Act 1950, for example, empowered the Government to prohibit any publication calculated to further the objects of communism, or which conveyed information calculated to endanger the state or

---

[12] *Qwelane v South African Human Rights Commission and Another* [2021] ZACC 22; *SAHRC on behalf of South African Jewish Board of Deputies v Masuku and Another* [2022] ZACC 5.

the maintenance of public order and, from 1960, these prohibitions were extended to the objects of the African National Congress and the Pan-Africanist Congress, and their members. The ban applied not only to publications that furthered the objects of these organisations, but also to objects that were 'similar'[13] (which could be almost anything).

There were other statutory constraints such as the Prisons Act, which made it an offence to publish false information about the experiences of a prisoner or the administration of a prison without reasonable steps to verify the truth of the information (with the onus on the accused) and the Defence Act which prohibited the publication of the movements of the Defence Force with the result that the invasion of Angola in 1975/6 only became public after the event.[14] There was also a constant threat of censorship and, in order to escape censorship by the Publications Control Board[15] that had been created in 1963 and amid pressure from the Government, the South African Newspaper Press Union (an association of newspaper proprietors) drew up a code of conduct to govern newspaper reporting.

The political implications of the code of conduct were revealed by Clause 3(d) which stated that 'while the Press retains its traditional right of criticism, comment should take cognisance of the complex racial problems of South Africa, the general good, and the safety of the country and its peoples'. The South African Society of Journalists refused to subscribe to this code because it had been adopted without their consent and it undermined the freedom of the press. In 1974, when the 1963 censorship legislation was replaced by the Publications Act 1974, the press was again excluded from the ambit of censorship, but only on the basis that a newly constituted Press Council was empowered to impose steep fines on newspapers infringing the code of conduct and on the basis of a new clause which read:

> insofar as both news and comments are concerned, it is further accepted that the standards applying to South African publications exact from them due care and responsibility concerning matters which can have the effect of stirring up feelings of hostility between the different racial, ethnic or religious or cultural groups in South Africa, which can affect the safety and defence of the country and its peoples.[16]

Then came the 1980s' states of emergency (as a matter of law, each state of emergency was confined to a period of 12 months, but was then renewed). It would be a tedious (and, for us, dispiriting) exercise to analyse those regulations in full. We think it more convenient to quote an extract from a book written by one of the editors of the small liberal weekly newspaper, *The Weekly Mail*, on the consequences to it of the 1987 emergency regulations:

> But the bulk of the regulations were aimed at the press. Reporters and photographers were not allowed into 'unrest areas', which barred them from almost all townships.

---

[13] J Dugard, *Human Rights and the South African Legal Order* (Princeton, Princeton University Press, 1978) 157–58 and 165.
[14] ibid 182–83.
[15] Created by the Publications and Entertainments Act 1963.
[16] Dugard (n 13) 184–85.

They could not report on 'police action' in curbing unrest, nor could they name detainees. The most damning clause created a new offence called the 'subversive statement': any spoken or written remark which might arouse in the mind of some member of the public a desire to commit an anti-social act, like staying away from school, or not paying rent.

There was nothing strange about the blanket ban on the press. As long as the press could not report, the police could go about their brutal work with impunity. No cameras would see guns fire on demonstrators or squatters. No reports would name those in detention, which meant that if some detainees went missing, no-one would ever know. The government had learned some useful lessons in the past year. As long as foreign television screens showed scenes of South African police baton-charging black squatters, the public pressure for tougher sanctions was bound to remain high. If foreign television viewers could not watch unrest in South Africa, they would find something else to watch instead, and pressure for sanctions would abate.[17]

The light regulation of the media in South Africa today, therefore, is primarily the result of a general revulsion against the excesses of censorship in the apartheid years, resulting in the Freedom of Expression clause in the Constitution (set out above) which precludes any statutory restrictions on the media today, apart from that on hate speech. Another reason for the generally light regulation of the media, we should probably add, is that protections for privacy were always present in Roman-Dutch law, with no constitutional override as in the United States of America, and so the media in South Africa never invaded private lives in the same way as in some other countries that did not recognise a right to privacy. That brings us to the only real constraint on freedom of expression in South Africa – the Roman-Dutch common law.

4. The *Actio Injuriarum* (Defamation)

4.1. Introduction

The overriding right is dignity which incorporates the right to good name and reputation.[18] Both that right and the right to freedom of expression, can only be attenuated where 'necessary'. Where these rights clash, as they must do in a defamation action, a plaintiff's rights to dignity and reputation are to be recognised and protected by an appropriate limit on the defendant's rights of free speech.[19] This often involves 'the application of a general criterion of

---

[17] I Manoim (ed), *'You Have Been Warned': The First Ten Years of The Mail & The Guardian* (New York, Viking, 1996).

[18] *Holomisa v Argus Newspapers Ltd* 1996 (2) SA 588 (W), 606 E – 606 F, approved in *National Media Ltd v Bogoshi* 1998 (4) SA 1195 (SCA), 1216 H–1217 D.

[19] *Midi Television t/a E-tv v Director of Publications* 2007 (5) SA 540 (SCA) 544 [9]; *Khumalo and Others v Holomisa* 2002 (5) SA 401 (CC) [25] and [27].

reasonableness based on considerations of fairness, morality, policy and the court's perceptions of the legal convictions of the community'.[20]

In fact, this vague statement is a wholly inadequate description of what is a fastidious and intricate technical balance. The process starts by weighing the scales heavily in favour of dignity and reputation, and against free speech. This is because once defamatory publication 'of and concerning' the plaintiff is proved, a series of presumptions is triggered: of wrongfulness (which means that the onus is on the defendant to prove the defences of truth and public benefit, fair comment, privileged occasion and reasonable publication), of fault (which is intention or negligence, as the case may be) and damages (although the precise measure remains a matter for evidence and argument).[21] But the technical rules for pleading and trial are not easy and can operate as traps for the unwary, redressing, to some degree, the imbalances created by the presumptions.

4.2. The Elements of the Action

4.2.1. Title to Sue

The first requirement is that any proposed plaintiff must be permitted to sue. This is really only relevant in that the Government, or government entities, are precluded from suing for defamation (although individuals in government may do so). The reason for prohibiting the Government from suing for defamation is that:

> It would involve a serious interference with the free expression of opinion hitherto enjoyed in this country if the wealth of the state, derived from the state's subjects, could be used to launch against those subjects actions for defamation because they have, falsely and unfairly it may be, criticised or condemned the management of the country.[22]

It remains only to note that juristic persons (including both trading and non-trading corporations) may sue for defamation,[23] although the relief they are entitled to is a more complicated matter and is dealt with below.

4.2.2. Jurisdiction

The courts in defamation cases have accepted that the residence of the defendant within the court's jurisdiction is sufficient to establish jurisdiction

---

[20] *Bogoshi* (n 18) 1204 D – 1204 E; *Hardaker v Phillips* 2005 (4) SA 515 (SCA), 525 B.

[21] *Mackay v Phillip* (1830) 1 Menz. 455, 463; *Marais v Richard and Another* 1981 (1) SA 1157 (AD), 1166 G – 1166 H; *National Media Ltd and Others v Bogoshi* 1998 (4) SA 1196 (SCA), 1202 G; *Hardaker* (n 20) 524 F–524 H.

[22] *Die Spoorbond v SAR* 1946 AD 999, 1012.

[23] *Dhlomo NO v Natal Newspapers (Pty) Ltd and Another* 1989 (1) SA 945 (AD), 952 E – 953 D, 954 A – 954 E; *Caxton v Reeva Forman (Pty) Ltd* 1990 (3) SA 547 (AD), 561.

regardless of where publication occurred: In the early case of *Mackay v Philip*[24] the defendant excepted to the particulars of claim on the basis that the Court did not have jurisdiction to try the matter because there had been no proof of publication in the Cape. However, the Chief Justice of the Cape Colony dismissed the exception and based the jurisdiction of the Court on the residence of the plaintiff and the defendant;[25] and in *Tsichlas v Touch Line Media (Pty) Ltd*,[26] the Court found that a principal place of business and presence in the jurisdiction of the Court was 'sufficient to provide [the] court with jurisdiction' in respect of the defendant company.[27]

4.2.3. Publication

Publication is, as in all comparable jurisdictions, required. This, in South Africa, means comprehensible publication. So if a statement that is defamatory of someone is made to someone else in a language that the latter does not understand, or is made only to a person who is deaf and not in a position to lipread, there is no publication.[28] And re-publication of defamatory allegations already in the public domain, constitutes a further publication and therefore a fresh *injuria*.[29]

In South Africa, a plaintiff is required to plead the name of the publishees who it proposes to call to prove publication.[30] Although where publication is in a newspaper, magazine or book, South African courts, like UK courts, hold this to be to the 'world at large' where publication can be inferred and particular acts of publication do not have to be pleaded.[31] It is doubtful whether this presumption applies to electronic communications and South African courts are likely to follow other Commonwealth courts in finding that there must be proof that some person has accessed the relevant site and read the material complained of[32] because this is a matter of fact.[33] It is insufficient to merely allege that the defamatory matter

---

[24] *Mackay v Philip* 1830 Menz 455. See also *Rogaly v General Imports (Pty) Ltd* 1948 (1) SA 1216 (C).

[25] See, for a discussion of the case, JM Burchell, *The Law of Defamation in South Africa* (Cape Town, Juta, 1985) 80.

[26] *Tsichlas and Another v Touch Line Media (Pty) Ltd* 2004 (2) SA 112 (W).

[27] ibid 119 H.

[28] *Sutter v Brown* 1926 AD 155, 164.

[29] *African Life Assurance Society Ltd v Robinson & Co Ltd* 1938 NPD 277, 302.

[30] *Benson v Simpson and Robinson* 1917 WLD 126, 133; *Pillay v Naidoo* 1916 WLD 151, 153.

[31] *African Life Assurance Society Ltd v Robinson & Co Ltd and Central News Agency* 1938 NPD 272, 296–97; *Clear Channel Independent (Pty) Ltd v Ad-Outpost (Pty) Ltd* 2007 JDR 1305 (W).

[32] *Godfrey v Demon Internet* [2001] QB 201 (QBD) [33]; *Al Amoudie v Brisard* [2006] EWHC 1062 (QB) [1], [31]–[33] and [37]; *Dow Jones & Co Inc v Yousef-Abdul Latif Jameel* [2005] EWCA Civ 75 [17]; *Applause Stores Productions Ltd v Raphael* [2008] EWHC 1781 (QB) [70]; *Carrie v Tolkien* [2009] All ER (D) 96 [17]; *Lonzim Plc v Sprague* [2009] EWHC 2838 (QB) [19]; *Kaschke v Osler* [2010] EWHC 1075 (QB) [30]; *Crookes v Newton* 2009 BCCA 392; 96 BLCR (4th) 315 [41]–[44].

[33] *Baturina v Times Newspapers Ltd* [2010] EWHC 696 (QB) [38], this point unaffected on appeal [2011] EWCA Civ 308; *Trumm v Norman* [2008] EWCH 116 (QB) [33]–[35]; *Brady v Norman* [2008] EWHC 2481 (QB) [23]–[26]; *ZAM v CFW* [2013] EWHC 662 [108].

was posted on the internet and was accessible in the jurisdiction of the court.[34] This means that plaintiffs complaining of social media publications are in a far less advantageous position than if they were complaining of a newspaper or television publication, and this is likely to discourage litigation in respect of social media publications.

4.2.4. Meaning

Meaning is the first factual issue to be determined in any defamation case because it is the meaning of the allegedly defamatory text that determines what must be proved in order to sustain a defence.[35] Where there is more than one meaning or sting pleaded, each sting is a discrete cause of action that must be justified; and what must be justified is the pleaded sting and not the actual words used.[36] The principles governing the establishment of the meaning of an allegedly defamatory statement are as follows:

- In the normal course, the meaning of an article is for the judge to determine. It is determined by the meaning which an ordinary, reasonable reader would attribute to the words in the context of the document as a whole, and Colman J has warned against bringing to bear a 'supercritical' approach, a 'morbid or suspicious mind' or an 'abnormally sensitive' outlook.[37]

- The meaning of the words alleged to be defamatory is a matter of construction, and not of evidence. Evidence is both unnecessary and inadmissible.[38]

- The concept of a reasonable reader excludes a person who is prepared to give a meaning to words that cannot reasonably be attributed to them.[39]

- English decisions, in this particular area, reflect precisely the same approach as that taken by courts in South Africa and the general approach can seldom have been more comprehensively set out than in *Jeynes v News Magazines Ltd* as follows:

    (1) The governing principle is reasonableness.
    (2) The hypothetical reasonable reader is not naïve but he is not unduly suspicious. He can read between the lines. He can read in an implication more readily than

---

[34] *Creative Resins International Ltd v Glassam Europe Ltd* [2006] All ER (D) 178 [23]; *Nationwide News Ltd v University of Newlands* [2005] NZCA 317, 28–29 [48]–[49]; *Budu v British Broadcasting Corporation* [2010] EWHC 616 (QB) [31]–[43].

[35] *Independent Newspapers Holdings Ltd & Others v Suliman* [2004] 3 All SA 137 (SCA) [19].

[36] *Times Media Ltd & Others v Niselow and Another* [2005] 1 All SA 567 (SCA) [22]–[29]; *Modiri v Minister of Safety and Security and Others* [2012] 1 All SA 154 (SCA) [13] and [18]; *HT Group (Pty) Ltd v Hazelhurst and Another* [2003] All SA 262 (C) [12]–[14].

[37] *Channing v SA Financial Gazette Ltd & Others* 1966 (3) SA 470 (W), 474 A – 474 C; *Sutter* (n 28) 163 and 168; *HRH King Zwelithini of KwaZulu v Mervis & Another* 1978 (2) SA 521 (T), 526 H – 527 A; *Times Media* (n 36).

[38] *Geyser en Ander v Pont* 1968 (4) SA 67 (W), 70 A – 70 B; *Johnson v Beckett and Another* 1992 (1) SA 762 (AD), 773 B – 773 D.

[39] *Demmers v Wyllie* 1980 (1) SA 835 (AD).

a lawyer and may indulge in a certain amount of loose thinking but he must be treated as being a man who is not avid for scandal and someone who does not, and should not, select one bad meaning where other non-defamatory meanings are available.

(3) Over-elaborate analysis is best avoided.

(4) The intention of the publisher is irrelevant.

(5) The article must be read as a whole and any 'bane and antidote' taken together.

(6) The hypothetical reader is taken to be representative of those who would read the publication in question.

(7) In delimiting the range of permissible defamatory meanings, the court should rule out any meaning which, 'can only emerge as the product of some strained, or forced, or utterly unreasonable interpretation ...'

(8) It follows that it is not enough to say that by some person or another the words 'might' be understood in a defamatory sense.[40]

- Where a judge is required to determine the meaning of text, the correct approach is to ask himself what overall impression the text has made on him, and *then* to check that against the detailed textual arguments put forward by the parties.[41] In other words it is:

    particularly important where, as here, a judge is providing written reasons for his conclusion as to the meaning to be attributed to the words sued on, that he should not fall into the trap of conducting an over-elaborate analysis of the various passages relied on by the respective protagonists. The parties are entitled to a reasoned judgment but that does not mean that the court should overlook the fact that it is ultimately a question of the meaning which would be put on the [text] by the ordinary reasonable reader. Such hypothetical reader is assumed not to be a lawyer.[42]

- And it is important to emphasise that the exercise is not to ascertain the sense in which the words were understood by the recipients of the information, but in what sense they would be reasonably understood.[43]

- This is why words are normally construed in their natural and ordinary meaning, ie the meaning in which reasonable people of ordinary intelligence, with the ordinary persons' general knowledge and experience of world events, would be likely to understand them.[44]

- The onus is on the plaintiffs to prove, on a balance of probabilities, the defamatory meaning they contend for.[45] What follows relates to the requirements for pleading meaning in defamation cases, and if this appears to be a technically delicate exercise, then the reason is that this is one way of restraining the chilling effect that the law of defamation has on free speech.

---

[40] *Jeynes v News Magazines Ltd* [2008] EWCA Civ 130 [14].
[41] *Armstrong v Times Newspapers* [2006] EWHC 1614 (QBD) [31].
[42] *Charman v Orion Publishing Group Ltd* [2005] EWHC 2187 (QBD) [11].
[43] *Rudd v De Vos* [1892] 2 CTR 383, 384; *Johnson v Rand Daily Mails* 1928 AD 190, 195–96 and 204.
[44] *Demmers* (n 39) 842 B – 842 H.
[45] ibid 842 H – 843 E.

- Apart from the shortest and most straightforward of defamatory allegations, meaning is pleaded in one of two ways:

  - by alleging a genuine secondary meaning or innuendo, described by Schreiner JA 'as an unusual meaning which could only be attributed to the words by a hearer having knowledge of special circumstances';[46]
  - by characterising the aforesaid specific meanings pleaded as quasi-innuendos or stings; or, in different terminology, by paraphrasing or elaborating the allegedly defamatory matter without going beyond its ordinary meaning.[47]

- Reliance on a genuine innuendo or secondary meaning must be supported by pleading the special circumstances that might justify a departure from the ordinary meaning of the language.[48]

- Regarding quasi-innuendos or stings, the exercise of interpretation is based only on the impression produced by a perusal of the published statement, and not on extraneous facts.[49]

- Clear and accurate pleading of the meaning of a defamatory text becomes all the more important when the textual possibilities of an allegedly defamatory text are not clearly demarcated. In particular, a defamatory allegation may actually impute some or other unlawful or immoral conduct; or it may impute that a person is merely suspected of some or other unlawful or immoral conduct; or it may merely impute that there are grounds for investigating whether someone participated in some or other unlawful or immoral conduct. These three different levels of meaning, recognised in many countries with a comparable law of defamation, are now adopted by the South African courts.[50]

- These different layers of meaning must be carefully distinguished because the available defences require different facts for each different level of meaning. As regards a defence of truth and public benefit, for example, the first layer would require proof of the actual unlawful or immoral conduct; the second layer would require merely proof of facts that reasonably give rise to a suspicion; but, the third layer requires merely proof of reasonable grounds for an

---

[46] *National Union of Distributive Workers v Cleghorn & Harris* 1946 AD 984, 997; *Ngcobo v Shembe & Others* 1983 (4) SA 66 (D), 69 F.

[47] *Demmers v Wyllie and Others* 1978 (4) SA 619 (D), 622 D – 622 E; *De Villiers v Schutte* 2001 (3) SA 834 (C), 839 F.

[48] *Die Middelandse Nasionale Pers v Stahl*, 1917 AD 630, 637; *National Union of Distributive Workers* (n 46) 989, 993 and 996.

[49] *Sachs v Werkerspers Uitgewers Maatskappy Bpk* 1952 (2) SA 261 (W), 271 A – 273 B; *Conrad v Behnson* 1960 (4) SA 760 (SWA), 763 B; *Gayre v SAAN Ltd* 1963 (3) SA 376 (T), 378 H – 379 A; *Marais v Steyn and Another* 1975 (3) SA 479 (T), 486 B – 486 C; *HRH King Zwelithini* (n 37) 524 D – 524 H and 529 F; *Demmers* (n 47) 6232 F – 6232 H; *Demmers* (n 39), 845 H; *Sindane v Van der Merwe and Others* 2000 (3) SA 494 (W), 500 E (this decision was upset by the Supreme Court of Appeal – 2002 (2) SA 32 (SCA) – but on a different point); *De Villiers* (n 47) 839 E.

[50] *Independent Newspapers Holdings Ltd & Others* (n 35) [24], [30]–[33], [37] and [77]; *Times Media* (n 36), [18]–[21]; *The Citizen 1978 (Pty) Ltd and Others v McBride and Others* [2011] ZACC 11 [125]–[128].

investigation. This is illustrated in *The Citizen v McBride*[51] where the plaintiff's plea that the articles meant that he had been involved in arms dealing was rejected because they meant only that he may have been so involved. As the plaintiff did not plead this latter meaning, there was nothing for the defendant to justify in this regard.

- Finally, where a meaning is pleaded as a sting, it is the sting that is to be justi-fied, not necessarily every factual allegation upon which the sting is based.[52] Plaintiffs are restricted to the meanings pleaded.[53] The effect of this, of course, is that every sting amounts to a cause of action because each may attract different defences based upon different facts.[54]

These rules have the potential to make defamation litigation a minefield. Exaggerating the defamatory nature of the allegation is a self-defeating exercise because if the pleaded stings or innuendos are not sustained, the defendant has nothing to justify and wins the case. It is important to stress that these require-ments of pleadings are not mindless technicalities – they are a crucial component of the balancing exercise between protecting reputation on the one hand, and free expression on the other hand.

4.2.5. 'Of and Concerning'

A plaintiff in a defamation action must allege and prove that the defamatory matter was published of and concerning that person. It must refer to, or concern, that person.[55] Roman-Dutch law does not require that the plaintiff be actually named. In *Bane v Colvin*, the Court held that 'it is not necessary that the name of a plaintiff should be specifically mentioned before he, as an individual, could sue'.[56] However in that matter the plaintiff bore precisely the same name as the company that was the subject of the article and it is also required, as noted by Tindall JA in *Young v Kemsley*,[57] that the reasonable reader must know that the plaintiff is the unnamed person referred to.[58] This fact, then, needs to be pleaded and proved.[59] Illustrating this issue, is the matter of *Roos v Stent and Pretoria Printing Works*,[60] where the plaintiff director had asked the Court to hold that the remarks (made of a company's board while not mentioning him by name) were especially applicable

---

[51] *The Citizen v McBride* 2010 (4) SA 148 (SCA), 158 E.

[52] *Modiri* (n 36) [13] and [18].

[53] *Demmers* (n 39), 845 H; *Sindane* (n 49) 500 E (this decision was upset by the Supreme Court of Appeal – 2002 (2) SA 32 (SCA) – but on a different point); *De Villiers* (n 47) 839 E; *The Citizen* (n 51).

[54] *Times Media* (n 36) is a good example of this principle in practice.

[55] *A Neumann CC v Beauty Without Cruelty International* 1986 (4) SA 675 (C), 679.

[56] *Bane v Colvin* 1959 (1) SA 863 (C), 867.

[57] *Young v Kemsley* 1940 AD 258, 273.

[58] *Visse v Wallach's Printing and Publishing Co Ltd* 1946 (1) TPD 441, 448; *Geyser en Ander v Pont* 1968 (4) SA 67 (AD), 71 C and 71 F – 71 G; *A Neumann CC* (n 55) 680 C.

[59] *Sachs* (n 49) 265 A – 265 E; *Geyser en Ander* (n 58); *A Neumann CC* (n 55) 685 I – 686 E.

[60] *Roos v Stent and Pretoria Printing Works* 1909 TS 988, 1009.

to him as a director who had recently resigned. The Judge, while agreeing that the remarks were especially applicable to him, went on to find that the question was what a person reading the article at the time that it was published would understand it to mean; and found no evidence that the general public had any means to acquire this knowledge.

4.2.6. Relief

Damages, as set out above, are now presumed. A plaintiff who is a human being need not plead details regarding quantification of general damages for sentimental loss or particulars of reputation, standing in the community or character.[61] Here, again, the two competing constitutional rights – dignity and free speech – collide. An affront to dignity must be compensated but, as asserted by the Supreme Court of Appeal, 'too high an award of damages may act as an unjustifiable deterrent to the exercise of freedom of expression and may inappropriately inhibit the exercise of that right'.[62] Roman-Dutch law does not permit punitive damages. Damages must be sufficient only to vindicate reputation and assuage wounded feelings (also called a *solatium*).[63]

The Constitutional Court has very recently held that juristic persons do not have an unqualified right to an award of general damages in respect of harm to reputation because they have no right to dignity and no feelings to hurt, making damages for hurt feelings unnecessary. But the Constitutional Court also held that a juristic entity does have a common law right to its good name and reputation, protected by the constitutional right to Equality, and enforceable by way of an award for general damages only where, in the court's discretion, the defamatory statements published are not characterised as 'public discourse in public interest debates'.[64]

However, damages cannot be claimed for actual patrimonial (that is, economic) loss.[65] The main reason is that an action for defamation, in Roman-Dutch law, offers the plaintiff advantages not present in other actions for economic loss, being the suite of presumptions already referred to. So an action for defamation would not require a plaintiff to prove falsity, for example, while in an action for malicious falsehood the plaintiff would bear the onus of pleading and proving falsity. The right to dignity (in the form of reputation) justifies the plaintiff's advantages in a defamation action, but not in an action for pure economic loss.[66] These limitations on damages are another critical element in the balancing exercise between

---

[61] *Simmonds v White* 1980 (1) SA 755 (C), 758.
[62] *Mogale and Others v Seima* [2005] ZASCA 101 [9].
[63] ibid [11].
[64] *Reddell and Others v Mineral Sands Resources (Pty) Ltd and Others* [2022] ZACC 38 [150].
[65] *Media24 Ltd v SA Taxi Securitisation (Pty) Ltd* [2011] ZASCA 117.
[66] See also, J Campbell, 'An Anomaly: Special Damages for Libel' (2011) 3(2) *Journal of Media Studies* 193–97.

reputation and free expression. In South Africa, a successful defamation plaintiff will almost always be out of pocket after the trial because, unlike in the UK, successful South African plaintiffs seldom recover much more than a third of their costs and the cautious approach to the quantum of damages means that the short-fall is often not made up. This is manifestly a disincentive to sue.

A defamed party (including a juristic person) is also entitled to an interdict (an injunction in English law) prohibiting further publication of the defamatory statements.[67] While there is no absolute bar on an interdict prior to publication or trial, the courts have set the bar very high:

> A court 'must be satisfied that the matter complained of is libellous; that no defence, e.g., that the statement is true and for the public benefit, could be successfully set up in an action on the libel; nothing has occurred, e.g., consent to publication, to deprive the plaintiff of … [the] remedy. If there be any doubt upon any of these points then the interdict should be refused and the case is one to be decided at the trial.[68]

In practice, this means that a:

> plausible claim by a respondent that, with the advantage of discovery and being able to subpoena witnesses and documents, they will be able at trial to produce evidence to sustain their defence, will ordinarily suffice to establish the requisite foundation for the defences raised.[69]

4.3. Defences

There are many defences to the *actio injuriarum* negativing both wrongfulness and fault that are not dealt with here (both in the context of defamation and in the context of privacy) because they ordinarily do not engage the media. They include necessity, self-defence, obedience to orders, provocation, consent, mistake, jest, intoxication and mental distress. We deal, in what follows, with five defences that are commonly open to media defendants.

4.3.1. Privileged Occasion

In order to succeed in a defence of qualified privilege, a defendant must prove that the statement was published in the discharge of a duty, the exercise of a right or in the furtherance of a legitimate interest. Conventionally the publisher claims a right, duty or interest in conveying the information to the publishee, who has a

---

[67] *Hix Networking Technologies CC v System Publishers (Pty) Ltd* 1997 (1) SA 391 (SCA).

[68] *Roberts v The Critic Ltd and Others* 1919 WLD 26, 28–29; *Heilbron v Blignaut* 1931 WLD 167, 168–69; *Buthelezi v Poorter and Others* 1974 (4) SA 831 (W), 836 H – 837 A; *Hix Networking Technologies v System Publishers (Pty) Ltd and Another* 1997 (1) SA 391 (AD), 402 H; *Print Media South Africa and Another v Minister of Home Affairs and Another* 2012 (6) SA 443 (CC) [44].

[69] *NBC Holdings (Pty) Ltd v Akani Retirement Fund Administrators (Pty) Ltd* 2021 ZASCA 136 [30].

corresponding right, duty or interest in receiving it. Such right, duty or interest may be legal, moral or social.[70] This is judged objectively. Did the circumstances, in the eyes of a reasonable person, create a duty, right or interest which entitled the defendants to speak as they did? This question is answered by reference to public policy. Does public policy justify publication?[71] It is important to note that what is privileged is the *occasion*, not the mere information or words.[72] In order to come within this defence, a defendant must allege and prove that the statement complained of was germane to the occasion.[73] Privilege can be defeated if the defendants were actuated by malice, meaning that they had no honest belief in the truth of the publication complained of[74] or entertained an improper motive.[75]

4.3.2. Truth and Public Benefit

Superficially, this defence is easy to understand: The defendant must allege and prove the defamatory statement true. But, in practice, this is not so simple because the defendant is not bound by the meanings (including innuendos and stings) pleaded by the plaintiff. If those meanings are unsustainable, the defendant is not called on to defend them. And, in any case, properly pleaded meanings, innuendos and stings are required only to be substantially – not literally – proved true;[76] and 'anything that does not add to the sting need not be justified'.[77] Roman-Dutch law requires, for this defence, not merely truth but also public benefit which 'lies in telling the public of something of which they were ignorant but something which it was in their interest to know'.[78]

4.3.3. Reasonable Publication

A defendant that cannot rely on the truth of the defamatory publication may nevertheless escape liability but pleading and proving that publication was 'reasonable'. The word 'reasonable' shows the origin of this defence in English law, but in Roman-Dutch law it means that the defendant took reasonable steps to verify the correctness of the publication, gave a right of a reply, etc. In other words, in Roman-Dutch law terms, it was not negligent and therefore negates fault as well

---

[70] *Ehmke v Groenewald* 1921 AD 575, 581; *De Vaal v Ziervogel* 1938 AD 112, 121.
[71] *Borgin v De Villiers and Another* 1980 (3) SA 556 (AD), 577 D – 577 G.
[72] *De Waal v Ziervogel* (n 70) 122.
[73] *Joubert v Venter* 1985 (1) SA 654 (AD); *Herselman NO v Botha* 1994 (1) SA 28 (AD) 35.
[74] *Basner v Trigger* 1946 AD 83, 96.
[75] *May v Udwin* 1981 (1) SA 1 (AD); *Naylor v Jansen; Jansen v Naylor* 2006 (3) SA 546 (SCA).
[76] *Johnson* (n 43); *Verwoerd v Paver* 1943 WLD 153; *Times Media* (n 36).
[77] *Yusaf v Bailey* 1964 (4) SA 117 (W) 126.
[78] *Mahomed v Kassim* 1973 (2) SA 1 (RA).

as wrongfulness.[79] This defence, therefore, reverses the imposition of strict liability of the media in defamation cases, referred to in the Introduction. Practically, it means that a false and defamatory publication is not actionable unless also published negligently.

4.3.4. Fair Comment

The statement complained of must have been comment (in other words opinion, not a statement of fact) and fair (which does not imply impartial or balanced). It must be based on facts either generally known or truly stated, and regarding a matter of public interest. As with privilege, it is forfeit if malice is present.[80]

4.3.5. Abuse of Process

There is much disquiet over strategic litigation against public participation (SLAPP) suites in many parts of the world and South Africa is no exception. The Constitutional Court has, for the first time, expressly acknowledged that such suits can be defended where they are an abuse of process.[81] In *Mineral Sands Resources (Pty) Ltd v Reddell*,[82] the plaintiff's mining operations had attracted criticism alleging, amongst other things, environmental vandalism. Such statements were published by several activists including in a series of lectures at the University of Cape Town, in radio interviews, in books, on social media and in television interviews. The activist defendants, on being sued by Mineral Sands, raised a special plea to the effect that the defamation action had been brought for the ulterior purpose of discouraging, censoring, intimidating and silencing them in their public criticisms of the plaintiff and therefore was an abuse of process in violation of the right to freedom of expression entrenched in Section 16 of the Constitution.[83] Upholding the special plea as a species of abuse of process,[84] the Constitutional Court found that in order to sustain such a defence, the defendant would need to prove that the action brought (1) is an abuse of the processes of the court, (2) is not brought to vindicate a right, (3) amounts to the use of court process to achieve an improper end and to cause the defendants financial and/or other prejudice in order to silence them, and (4) violates or is likely to violate, freedom of expression in a material way.[85]

---

[79] *National Media* (n 21); *Hardaker* (n 20).
[80] *Marais* (n 21); *Johnson* (n 38); *Delta Motor Corporation (Pty) Ltd v Van der Merwe* 2004 (6) SA 185 (SCA).
[81] *Mineral Sands Resources (Pty) Ltd and Others v Reddell and Others* [2022] ZACC 37.
[82] ibid [11]–[12].
[83] ibid [13]–[15].
[84] ibid [98].
[85] ibid [96].

5. The *Actio Injuriarum* (Privacy)

5.1. Introduction

The same action protects privacy, also an incident of dignity (albeit specifically recognised in section 14 of the Constitution). This article is concerned, of course, only with public disclosure of private facts and not with physical intrusion into the private sphere because the latter is not conduct typically engaged in by the media.

5.2. What is 'Privacy'?

There is no comprehensive definition of privacy, whether in Roman-Dutch law or anywhere else. Samuel Warren and Louis Brandeis, as far back as 1890, saw it as the right to be let alone.[86] In South Africa, the test is two-fold: A subjective expectation that the information (not merely personal facts, but facts that if disclosed will cause mental distress and injury to anyone of ordinary feelings and intelligence in those circumstances[87]) will be kept private and, so that individual idiosyncrasies do not stretch that net too far, that subjective expectation is also required to be objectively reasonable.[88] The Supreme Court of Appeal, without attempting to define privacy, has illuminated the test by finding that the individual is entitled to determine the limits of the destiny of private facts and to decide when, and under what circumstances, they can be made public; in other words the individual has control over the extent of publication of private facts.[89]

The Constitutional Court has refined this test further. Now the right to privacy operates along a continuum, protecting 'the inner sanctum of a person, such as his/her family life, sexual preference and home environment, which is shielded from erosion by conflicting rights of the community' and it exists 'in the truly personal realm, but as a person moves into communal relations and activities such as business and social interaction, the scope of personal space shrinks accordingly'.[90] This means that the more the activity revealed is a person's inter-relationships with the world, the more attenuated the right to privacy becomes.[91]

---

[86] SD Warren and L Brandeis, 'The Right to Privacy' (1880) 4 *Harvard Law Review* 193, 193; see also *Bool Smuts and Another v Herman Botha* [2022] ZASCA 3 [23].

[87] *National Media Ltd and Another v Jooste* 1996 (3) SA 262 (AD) 270 I; *NM and Others v Smith and Others* 2007 (5) SA 250 (CC) [34] and [137].

[88] *Bernstein and Others v Bester NO and Others* 1996 (4) BCLR 449 (CC) [75]–[76] and [85].

[89] *Jooste* (n 87), 271–72; *Greeff v Protection 4 U* 2012 (6) SA 393 (GNP) 406 and 415–16; *NM* (n 87) 262–63.

[90] *Bernstein v Bester* 1996 (2) SA 751 (CC) [67]; *Mistry v Interim Medical and Dental Council of SA* 1998 (4) SA 1127 (CC) [27]; *National Coalition for Gay and Lesbian Equality v Minister of Justice* 1999 (1) SA 6 (CC) [28]–[32]; *The Investigating Directorate: Serious Economic Offences v Hyundai Motor Distributors (Pty) Ltd* 2001 (1) SA 545 (CC) [15].

[91] *Interim Medical and Dental Council of SA* (n 90) [27]; *The Investigating Directorate* (n 90) [15].

The right is not limited to issues falling within the 'inner sanctum' or 'intimate core' but comes into play whenever persons are able to decide what they wish to disclose to the public and have a reasonable expectation that such a decision will be respected.[92] The protection is greater, and more intense, the closer the invasion is to the intimate and personal sphere.[93] The kinds of information held private, and therefore protected, include HIV-positive status,[94] details of a sexual relationship between a famous person and another,[95] publication of a photograph of a person in an advertisement,[96] tape recordings of confidential conversations,[97] medical records,[98] use of pornography in the home.[99] Disclosure of information acquired in a confidential relationship is also private.[100] Both natural and juristic persons have rights of privacy but, because juristic persons lack personal dignity, their rights are not as extensive.[101]

5.3. Publication

While disclosure to a third party or the public is manifestly sufficient to breach privacy, it is not always necessary. The taking of photographs, and making of photocopies and tape recordings of private moments, information and/or conversations, creates a risk of publication that is sufficient to constitute the *injuria*.[102]

5.4. Fault

For many years, it was thought that a plaintiff suing on a privacy claim under the *actio injuriarum* would be required to show actual intention, as opposed to mere negligence. The Constitutional Court revisited this issue in *NM v Smith*, characterising the issue as 'whether the common law of privacy should be developed to impose liability on those who negligently publish confidential information'.[103] This question resulted in the collision of the plaintiffs' rights to privacy and the

---

[92] *The Investigating Directorate* (n 90) [16]; *Jooste* (n 87) 270–71.

[93] *Bernstein* (n 88) [77]; *Interim Medical and Dental Council of SA* (n 90) [27]; *The Investigating Directorate* (n 90) [15] and [18].

[94] *NM* (n 87).

[95] *Jooste* (n 87); *Mhlongo v Bailey* 1958 (1) SA 370 (W).

[96] *O'Keeffe v Argus Printing and Publishing Co Ltd* 1954 (3) SA 244 (C).

[97] *Motor Industry Fund Administrators (Pty) Ltd v Janit* 1994 (3) SA 56 (W).

[98] *Tshabalala-Msimang v Makhanya* 2008 (6) SA 102 (W).

[99] *Case and Another v Minister of Safety and Security* 1996 (3) SA 617 (CC).

[100] *O v O* 1995 (4) SA 482 (W) (religious advisor – congregant); *Firstrand Bank Ltd v Chaucer Publications (Pty) Ltd* 2008 (2) SA 592 (C) (bank – client); *Swanepoel v Minister van Veiligheid en Sekuriteit* 1999 (4) SA 549 (T) (policeman – informant).

[101] *The Investigating Directorate* (n 90) [17] and [18]; *Universiteit van Pretoria v Tommie Meyer Films (Edms) Bpk* 1979 (1) SA 441 (AD) 455–56.

[102] *La Grange v Schoeman* 1980 (1) SA 885 (E) 895.

[103] *NM* (n 87) [21].

defendants' rights to free expression. The majority held it unnecessary to develop the common law because they found that the defendants had not taken the necessary steps to ascertain whether the plaintiffs had given consent for disclosure of their HIV statuses and were either aware that consent had not been given or, at least, foresaw that possibility and did not guard against it.[104]

There were two interesting minority judgments. O'Regan J favoured following the evolution in defamation law (see above) and would have developed the common law of privacy so as to require a media defendant to demonstrate that publication was not negligent.[105] She found that journalists are entitled to publish information from reliable sources (in this case an academic report) without re-checking everything,[106] and she accordingly would not have found negligence on the defendants' part. Chief Justice Langa disagreed with the majority in their finding that Smith had foreseen that publication would harm the plaintiffs,[107] but held that media defendants, as experts in the business of publishing, should be liable where harm could reasonably have been foreseen[108] – a negligence standard – and that the defendants had been negligent and he therefore concurred in the result.

5.5. Relief

The most effective relief for a threatened disclosure of private information is an interdict prohibiting that disclosure before it happens. This is very different to defamation where interdicts prior to publication mostly tilt the balance too far in favour of the protection of reputation and against free expression. The balance between the right to privacy and free expression is different. A reputation can be repaired by an appropriate award of damages, but privacy, once betrayed, is not capable of repair in the same way. However the *further* publication of private facts can most certainly be interdicted, unlike confidential information which mostly is commercial information that, once published, remains in the public sphere. The difference between that and private information is that publication of private information is an injury to dignity, and each further publication is a further injury to dignity. Those further injuries to dignity can be, and ought to be, interdicted. Nevertheless, there are situations where publication has taken place and that the injury to dignity cannot be forestalled by an interdict. In those situations, a defendant is entitled to damages – not to repair the release of public information, but to assuage feelings of hurt and embarrassment.

---

[104] ibid [64].
[105] ibid [177]–[179].
[106] ibid [187].
[107] ibid [93].
[108] ibid [111].

5.6. Defences

A privacy action can be defended on all usual grounds that the *actio injuriarum* contemplates. First, that the elements of the action are not proved such as where no expectation of privacy in the information actually, or genuinely, existed; or where such expectation is not reasonable. Then there are also the defences excluding wrongfulness and fault. The defamation defences recognised as excluding wrongfulness are not applicable in a privacy application – truth and fair comment would, if recognised, completely undermine the right to privacy because all disclosures of private facts are true, but nevertheless an invasion of privacy. Publication on a privileged occasion is a defence, but subject to the same strict rule in defamation that it must be germane to the occasion and the recipient of the information must have a right, duty or interest in receiving it. A defence of reasonable publication is available because that simply recognises that if the information was published mistakenly and not negligently, or in the belief that the information was not private, the defendant escapes liability on the basis of an absence of intention to invade the plaintiff's privacy. Public interest also constitutes justification, but is probably better seen conceptually as a finding that the published information is not private, because information that it is in the public interest to publish, cannot reasonably be expected to remain private in the first place.

The case of *NM*[109] is an example of the operation of the defences that found its way to the Constitutional Court. The appellants were three HIV-positive women, of deprived circumstances, who had participated in clinical trials for certain drugs. The trials attracted some controversy and Patricia De Lille MP (one of the defendants) investigated the issue and raised her concerns in Parliament. Thereafter, the university that had conducted the trial, commissioned a report that named the three appellants. De Lille was sent a copy of the report, and some years later, Ms Smith wrote a biography of De Lille in which she related the story of De Lille's campaign on behalf of the appellants. Seeing the names of the appellants in the report, Smith included them. The appellants complained of an invasion of their privacy, and sued for damages. A public interest defence was not available because the names of the three women added nothing to the story, with the result that the defendants were restricted to pleading lack of fault. They lost in the Constitutional Court, as set out above, on the basis that the majority found that the defendants had been aware that the plaintiffs had not given consent to be identified, that this had violated their privacy and dignity, and that there was no public interest in their identification.

Another interesting, and unusual, illustration of a defence in action is the decision in *Tshabalala-Msimang v Makhanya*.[110] The respondent was the editor

---

[109] *NM* (n 87).
[110] *Tshabalala-Msimang v Makhanya* [2007] ZAGPHC 161.

of *The Sunday Times* that had reported on the applicant's use of alcohol while in hospital, and had unlawfully acquired copies of her medical records. The applicant was a Cabinet Minister, in fact the Minister of Health, and sought return of the copies of her medical records in *The Sunday Times'* possession and also sought to restrain *The Sunday Times* from further publishing or commenting on those records.[111] The respondents' defence was to justify what otherwise would have been a serious invasion of privacy on the basis of public interest – being that the applicant, as Minister of Health, had authorised a campaign 'against alcohol and substance abuse as one major factor behind many health and social problems in the country', but suffered, herself, from alcohol liver disease caused by many years of excessive drinking before her liver transplant in 2007; that she had not ceased drinking either before or after that transplant and therefore did not qualify for the transplant; that she had been convicted of theft while in political exile in Botswana; that her proposed policies on the HIV/AIDS pandemic in South Africa at that time was, to say the least, controversial; and that she had behaved oppressively to those (including her Deputy Minister of Health) who did not agree with her HIV/AIDS policy.[112]

The Judge noted that even when private information was obtained unlawfully, 'there may well be overriding considerations of public interest which would permit of its publication', and that section 16 of the Constitution provided for a right to receive and impart information although this is always required to be balanced against the right to dignity.[113] Here the finding was that 'the overwhelming public interest points in the direction of informing the public about the contents incorporated in the medical records in relation to the first applicant, albeit that the medical records may have been unlawfully obtained', even though they were required to be returned. No order was made precluding further comment on these issues.[114]

6. Conclusion

Section 16 of the Constitution has proved to be powerfully protective of free speech. The right to the flow of information, often characterised as essential to democracy, has permeated South Africa's Roman-Dutch common law, resulting in the recognition of two new defamation defences – reasonable publication and abuse of process (the pigeon-hole to which anti-SLAPP jurisprudence has been allocated). It has also been invoked to ameliorate legislation, protect journalists in their professional work, open proceedings in Court and Parliament to live

---

[111] ibid [4].
[112] ibid [12].
[113] ibid [34] and [43]–[44].
[114] ibid [56] and [61].

television, override statutory obstruction to the disclosure of official investigations into corruption, to override attorney-client privilege where the public interest demanded this, and to protect the identities of sources. The underlying reason for these protections are to facilitate public participation in a noisy and participatory democracy. An appropriate conclusion to this chapter is the Constitutional Court's description of the reasons for this judicial activity in a judgment given as recently as November 2022:

> One of the more positive features of our nascent democratic order is vibrant, vigilant and vociferous civil society participation in public affairs. In a truly broad based participatory democracy characterised by that kind of public participation, our Constitution's aspirations and values find meaning in the lives of the populace for whose benefit the Constitution was ultimately enacted.[115]

---

[115] *Mineral Sands Resources (Pty) Ltd and Others v Reddell and Others* [2022] ZACC 36 [1].

PART III

The Americas

9

Why is Freedom of the Press Adjunct to Freedom of Expression in Canada?

DAVID MANGAN

1. Introduction

While there are various stresses in a free and democratic society (as section 1 of the Charter[1] identifies Canada), the interaction between freedom of expression[2] and a free press can be challenging. Freedom of expression in Canada (s 2(b) of the Charter) 'ensure[s] that everyone can manifest their thoughts, opinions, beliefs, indeed all expressions of the heart and mind, however unpopular, distasteful or contrary to the mainstream.'[3] This freedom has been contingent upon the individual having access to the information that fosters the formation of these points. The orthodox platform has been print media, with the (relatively) more recent additions of television networks and radio stations. Each of these entities qualify as the press. The platforms for expression and the press ('other media of communication' as set out in s 2(b)) have changed with innovations in information technology in the twenty first century. Section 2(b) also identifies a free press. The question is whether a free press is guaranteed by this provision of the Charter, and if so to what extent.[4] As discussed elsewhere in these volumes, freedom of speech and freedom of the press, though related, are separate concepts.

---

[1] Canadian Charter of Rights and Freedoms, Part I of the Constitution Act, 1982, being Schedule B to the Canada Act 1982, Ch 11.

[2] Freedom of expression contrasts with freedom of speech, the latter being viewed as a more precise concept, see R Martin, *Media Law* (Toronto, Irwin Law, 1997) 4.

[3] *Irwin Toy Ltd v Quebec (Attorney General)* [1989] 1 SCR 927, 968.

[4] Section 2(b) states that 'Everyone has the following fundamental freedoms: freedom of thought, belief, opinion and expression, including freedom of the press and other media of communication.'

While Canadian courts have recognised the contribution of a free press to freedom of expression, appreciation seems to be contingent upon the press's role as a source of information for the public. The press facilitates the individual's freedom of expression; a point seemingly set within the phrasing of section 2(b) of the Charter. Constitutional rights attached to the press, in contrast, have not been as readily recognised by Canadian courts. This separate treatment is the focus of the present contribution.

Canadian scholarship contains much discussion of freedom of expression, but freedom of the press is a less dense reading list.[5] The importance of free speech has been linked to democracy,[6] but the status of the press within this context has not been significantly developed. Political expression deserves constitutional protection 'because it serves individual and societal values in a free and democratic society'; but, it is 'only one form of the great range of expression that is deserving of constitutional protection'.[7] Freedom of expression, which allows 'human agency and identity [to] emerge in discourse',[8] relies significantly upon the free press. And yet, the press's status within the Charter right is a terrain without a clear map. This is in part the dichotomy of a free press in Canada. This collection draws from the print media as a classic example of the concept of a free press grounded in the notion of 'the Fourth Estate'; that is, a function of the press is to act as a 'public watchdog'[9] through the investigation and reporting of abuses of power arising primarily in government.[10] A free press advances knowledge and truth about matters of public interest, thereby strengthening democracy.[11] Canadian courts have been general in statements about the press being free, independent, and associated with the uncovering of truth,[12] and vague on the meaning of a free

---

[5] Canadian writing has also not engaged extensively with the meaning of a free press. See, as one example: 'Freedom of the press must mean that no one outside a newspaper, for example, can set editorial policy for that newspaper'. Martin (n 2) 4.

[6] 'There can be no controversy that such institutions derive their efficacy from the free public discussion of affairs, from criticism and answer and counter-criticism, from attack upon policy and administration and defence counter-attack; from the freest and fullest analysis and examination from every point of view of political proposals'. *Reference re Alberta Statutes* [1938] SCR 100, 133, aff'd [1938] UKPC 46. See also *Retail, Wholesale and Department Store Union, Local 580 v Dolphin Delivery Ltd* [1986] 2 SCR 573, 583–86.

[7] *Ford v Quebec (Attorney General)* [1988] 2 S.C.R. 712, 764. In later cases, the Supreme Court classified expression in a way that there was a form which garnered less protection because it was found to be 'distant from the core of free expression values'. *R v Keegstra* [1990] 3 S.C.R. 687, 772 (where the accused's anti-Semitic comments to students was classified as low-level speech). For further recent discussion on the value of free speech, see C Hutchinson, 'Freedom of Expression: Values and Harms' (2023) 60(3) *Alberta Law Review* 687.

[8] R Moon, *Commissioned Paper: Freedom of Expression*. Background Paper for the Public Order Emergency Commission (September 2022) 2, https://publicorderemergencycommission.ca/files/documents/Policy-Papers/Freedom-of-Expression-Moon.pdf.

[9] *The Observer and The Guardian v the United Kingdom* (1992) 14 EHRR 153 [59].

[10] *Attorney-General v Guardian Newspapers Ltd (No. 2)* [1990] 1 AC 109, 183.

[11] J Charney, *The Illusion of the Free Press* (Oxford, Hart Publishing, 2018) 3.

[12] In Canada, the 'values' of freedom of expression were first discussed in *Ford* (n 7) [56] ff. Despite criticism of the relative lack of critical engagement with these values by the Supreme Court, they have

press itself. The 'synergy'[13] between section 2(b)'s freedom of expression and the concept of the free press within that remains under-developed in Canadian case law.

As the facilitator of individuals' free speech, a free press has been premised upon the presumption of a free, rational individual capable of assessing information autonomously, where this expression actualises personal growth.[14] This idea of the public receiving the product of a free press has been tempered in Canadian law in the course of determining the limitations that may be made to the section 2(b) right by section 1 of the Charter. The various internet-based platforms have arguably fragmented what was more of a centralised source of information.[15] The law assesses the autonomous decision-making of the individual in a more varied and challenging context.[16]

Canadian courts have developed the 'open court doctrine' in which the press is an intermediary between the public and access to matters of important public discourse in a democracy. While these topics have often focused on the conduct of the Government and associated institutions, they also include secondary picketing[17] as well as the 'public's legitimate concern with the integrity of its public service'.[18] As set out in *Ford v Quebec (Attorney General)*,[19] freedom of expression is not limited to political expression. Instead, a 'great range of expression' is recognised. A similarly expansive view of the press has not been expressed by Canadian courts, which refrain from constitutionally recognising the press, particularly its newsgathering activities which inform the public. The restrained treatment is itself instructive. And yet, the reason for this restraint with the press has not been sufficiently discussed. This chapter discusses the tension therein: A press that plays an essential role in the functioning of democracy, but whose standing is treated with notable hesitation.

---

now taken root within the section 2(b) case law: R Elliot, 'The Supreme Court's Understanding of the Democratic Self-Government, Advancement of Truth, and Knowledge and Individual Self-Realization Rationales for Protecting Freedom of Expression: Part I – Taking Stock' (2012) 59 *Supreme Court Law Review* (2nd Series) 436, 511.

[13] J Cameron, 'A Reflection of Section 2(b)'s Quixotic Journey, 1982–2012' (2012) 58(1) *The Supreme Court Law Review: Osgoode's Annual Constitutional Cases Conference* 163, 166.

[14] *Ford* (n 7) 765. In regard to the public being rational, in a case regarding the release of polls around elections, Bastarache J wrote that the 'presumption of this Court should be that the Canadian voter is a rational actor who can learn from experience and make independent judgments about the value of particular sources of electoral information'. *Thomson Newspapers Co v Canada (Attorney General)* [1998] 1 SCR 877 [112].

[15] R Moon, 'Does Freedom of Expression Have a Future?' in E Macfarlane (ed), *Dilemmas of Free Expression* (Toronto, University of Toronto Press, 2022) 23.

[16] 'In the networked public sphere, there is too much information, and people lack effective means to quickly and efficiently verify it, which means that information can be effectively suppressed by creating an even-bigger glut of mashed-up truth and falsehood to foment confusion and distraction'. Z Tufekci, *Twitter and Tear Gas: The Power and Fragility of Networked Protest* (New Haven, Yale University Press, 2017) 230.

[17] *RWDSU v Dolphin Delivery Ltd* [1986] 2 SCR 573.

[18] *Cusson v Quan* 2009 SCC 62 [32].

[19] *Ford* (n 7).

2. A Restrained View of Freedom of the Press

This section outlines the Canadian Supreme Court's recognition of the press's essential role in facilitating freedom of expression in Canadian democracy, without necessarily setting out any autonomous rights in relation to a free press.

2.1. Free Speech as Autonomous from a Free Press

When considering contemporary Canadian press freedom, one may be struck by the tension within modern case law. The press plays a special constitutional role because it facilitates the public's oversight of institutions involved in the governing process, as well as communicating a range of ideas and information to a wide audience.[20] Adjudication of press freedom has not extended to constitutional status for the media. The press's remit is that of informing the public, thereby enabling them to participate within democracy. Newsgathering has not been imbued with similar importance.

Although separation has emerged most clearly within the Charter jurisprudence, the pre-Charter cases set this trajectory. The pre-Charter decisions of the Canadian Supreme Court elaborated on a right of freedom of expression, but the press's role therein is not as developed. The pre-Charter judges wrote of the Constitution[21] as protecting 'freedom of discussion'[22] based upon its Preamble as well as section 129 of the Constitution.[23] This was an individual's 'fundamental right to express freely his untrammeled opinion about government policies and discuss matters of public concern'.[24] The freedom was not unfettered: 'freedom of discussion means ... "freedom governed by law"'.[25] These comments came in the context of Alberta's Accurate News and Information Act. Its purpose was to affect public discussion. In finding the legislation to be *ultra vires*, the Court classified it as giving the Alberta Government of the day 'autocratic powers' that 'could, if arbitrarily wielded, be employed to frustrate in Alberta these rights of the Crown [set out in the Canadian Constitution] and the people of Canada as a whole'.[26] Cannon J wrote in the same decision:

> Freedom of discussion is essential to enlighten public opinion in a democratic State; it cannot be curtailed without affecting the right of the people to be informed through

[20] L Bollinger, *Images of a Free Press* (Chicago, University of Chicago Press, 1991) 20.
[21] British North America Act 1867 (UK), 30 & 31 Victoria, c 3, now the Constitution Act 1867.
[22] *Reference re Alberta Statutes* (n 6). See also the discussion of Rand J in *Saumur v City of Quebec* [1953] 2 SCR 299, and *Switzman v Elbling* [1957] SCR 285.
[23] The phrase in the Preamble, 'with a Constitution similar in Principle to that of the United Kingdom', formed the basis for the protection of 'free discussion'. In *Reference re Alberta Statutes* (n 6) 133, Duff CJC wrote: 'The statute contemplates parliament working under the influence of public opinion and public discussion.' A similar point was later made by Rand J in *Switzman* (n 22) 306.
[24] *Reference Re Alberta Statutes* (n 6) 146.
[25] ibid 133.
[26] ibid 135.

sources independent of government concerning matters of public interest. There must be untrammelled publication of the news and political opinion of the political parties contending for ascendency .... Democracy cannot be maintained without its foundation: free public opinion and free discussion throughout the nation of all matters affecting the State within the limits set by the criminal code and the common law.[27]

In 1957, Rand J (whose opinions on free speech are often referenced), continued the elaboration of this discussion:

Canadian government is in substance the will of the majority expressed directly or indirectly through popular assemblies. This means ultimately government by the free public opinion of an open society, the effectiveness of which, as events have not infrequently demonstrated, is undoubted.

But public opinion, in order to meet such a responsibility, demands the condition of a virtually unobstructed access to and diffusion of ideas. Parliamentary government postulates a capacity in men, acting freely and under self-restraints, to govern themselves; and that advance is best served in the degree achieved of individual liberation from subjective as well as objective shackles.

This constitutional fact is the political expression of the primary condition of social life, thought and its communication by language. Liberty in this is little less vital to man's mind and spirit than breathing is to his physical existence.[28]

With the Charter coming into force (in the mid-1980s), freedom of expression gained explicit recognition of freedom, but within a context of a potential for limitation on all freedoms.[29]

The Charter right is constructed in a suggestive manner. The freedoms are enumerated as thought, belief, opinion, and expression. These four freedoms are said to 'include' freedom of the press. The values protected within the freedom of expression were outlined in 1988 (*Ford*) and have largely stayed within these parameters:

(1) as assuring individual self-fulfilment, (2) as a means of attaining the truth, (3) as a method of securing participation by the members of the society in social, including political, decision-making, and (4) as maintaining the balance between stability and change in society.[30]

These points were 'accepted at face value'.[31] The Charter entrenched freedom of expression:

so as to ensure that everyone can manifest their thoughts, opinions, beliefs, indeed all expressions of the heart and mind, however unpopular, distasteful or contrary to

---

[27] ibid 145–46.

[28] *Switzman* (n 22) 307.

[29] As stated in section 1 of the Charter: 'subject only to such reasonable limits prescribed by law as can be demonstrably justified in a free and democratic society'.

[30] *Ford* (n 7) 765. The Court quoted from TI Emerson, 'Towards a General Theory of the First Amendment' (1963) 72(5) *Yale Law Journal* 877, 878. These were affirmed in the later decision of *Irwin Toy* (n 3) 976. Though, Elliot, in 'The Supreme Court's Understanding' (n 12), has noted the difference in language used for some of these four in *Irwin Toy*.

[31] Elliot (n 12) 445.

the mainstream. Such protection is, in the words of both the Canadian and Quebec Charters, 'fundamental' because in a free, pluralistic and democratic society we prize a diversity of ideas and opinions for their inherent value both to the community and to the individual.[32]

Freedom of expression is to be limited in the exceptional circumstance, where evidence establishes harm, and the limitation can be justified pursuant to section 1 of the Charter.[33] The order of section 2(b) 'indicates that freedom of the press is simply an aspect or implication of freedom of expression'.[34] Freedom of the press is also listed in the same line as 'other media of communication'. In this construction, freedom of expression rests with the individual, and the press facilitates it. A free press may facilitate this freedom, but it may not itself necessarily garner exceptional treatment.

It is left to the Supreme Court of Canada, in particular, to speak to the press's role in a free and democratic society. There have been statements about a free and vigorous press as a support for meaningful debate. Elaborating upon and upholding the open court principle (discussed further below) in the context of excluding the press from a sentencing hearing, Mister Justice La Forest in *Canadian Broadcasting Corporation v New Brunswick (Attorney General)* wrote:

> Debate in the public domain is predicated on an informed public, which is in turn reliant upon a free and vigorous press. The public's entitlement to be informed imposes on the media the responsibility to inform fairly and accurately. This responsibility is especially grave given that the freedom of the press is, and must be, largely unfettered.[35]

He was a lone voice here. Mister Justice La Forest then discussed the open court aspect that permits the press to gather news.[36] A free press derives its role from the necessity of an informed public in a democracy. However, this 'responsibility' also means that the press must be 'largely unfettered'. The public interest function grounding a free press has been criticised for the tension between its societal role and the private for-profit nature of the business of the press.[37] In her dissent to a decision of the Court which upheld a search warrant issued for the premises of the Canadian Broadcasting Corporation, McLachlin J (as she then was) identified the press's 'ability to gather, analyze and disseminate information, independent from any state imposed restrictions on content, form or

[32] *Irwin Toy* (n 3) 968.

[33] J Cameron, 'The Original Conception of Section 1 and its Demise: A Comment on *Irwin Toy v. Attorney General of Quebec*' (1989) 35(1) *McGill Law Journal* 253.

[34] R Moon, *The Constitutional Protection of Freedom of Expression* (Toronto, University of Toronto Press, 2000) 203.

[35] *Canadian Broadcasting Corporation v New Brunswick (Attorney General)* [1996] 3 SCR 480 [23].

[36] He had recognised the newsgathering function of the press in *Canadian Broadcasting Corporation v Lessard* [1991] 3 S.C.R. 421, 429–30: 'freedom of the press not only encompassed the right to report news and other information, but also the right to gather this information'.

[37] See Moon (n 34) 205 ff. He argues that the decline in the number of press outlets means that 'the values of a small group of corporations play a significant role in shaping public debate'. See also his discussion in Moon (n 15) 15–34.

perspective except those justified under Section 1' as a necessity for an 'effective and free press'.[38] Nevertheless, the orthodox approach to the free press remains: 'Important as the constitutional protection of the freedom of the press is, it does not go so far as guaranteeing the press special privileges which ordinary citizens ... would not enjoy.'[39]

Still, with one of the values of freedom of expression being the capacity for individuals to participate in political decision-making,[40] freedom of the press sits somewhat restlessly within the jurisprudence. The contrast between the breadth of the individual's freedom of expression as compared with the paucity of such a clearly wide statement about freedom of the press,[41] despite its integral role in the individual's freedom, stands out. The absence of statements about freedom of the press suggests there is something holding the Supreme Court back from making these comments.

To discuss Canadian courts' approach to the free press requires a short elaboration on the courts' analysis of section 2(b) itself. The approach remains a matter for discussion, particularly when it comes to what expression is protected and how this assessment is being made. In *Irwin Toy Ltd v Quebec (Attorney General)*,[42] the Supreme Court set out a direction for section 2(b) adjudication. Content neutrality is an important facet of the Court's view of speech. This approach arose as a result of the Court concluding that it could not 'exclude human activity from the scope of guaranteed free expression on the basis of the content or meaning being conveyed'.[43] Despite this, these expressive activities could still be limited when analysed under section 1 of the Charter. *Irwin Toy* established a two-step process for the adjudication of freedom of expression. Step one extends *prima facie* protection to any 'activity convey[ing] or attempt[ing] to convey a meaning' because 'it has expressive content'.[44] Therefore activity which does not convey meaning or that does so through a 'violent form of expression'[45] falls outside of the protected sphere of conduct. Step two involves a determination of 'whether the purpose or effect of the government action in issue was to restrict freedom of expression ... either by directly restricting the content of expression or by restricting a form of expression tied to its content'.[46] If this

---

[38] *Canadian Broadcasting Corporation v Lessard* (n 36) 451.

[39] ibid 436.

[40] 'It is difficult to imagine a guaranteed right more important to a democratic society than freedom of expression. Indeed a democracy cannot exist without that freedom to express new ideas and to put forward opinions about the functioning of public institutions. The concept of free and uninhibited speech permeates all truly democratic.' *Edmonton Journal v Alberta (Attorney General)* [1989] 2 SCR 1326, 1336.

[41] 'We live in a free country where people have as much right to express outrageous and ridiculous opinions as moderate ones'. *WIC Radio Ltd v Simpson* 2008 SCC 40 [4].

[42] *Irwin Toy* (n 3).

[43] ibid 969.

[44] ibid.

[45] ibid 978.

[46] ibid.

arises, then the purpose affects the expression guaranteed protection. But, if the aim is to 'control the physical consequences of particular conduct', then the purpose does not affect the protected freedom.[47] The analysis can become somewhat distorted with the unfortunate by-product of undermining its clarity:

> In this way and, perhaps inadvertently, *Irwin Toy* diminished the *Ford* values because it enabled courts to make a summary finding of breach and shift the analysis to s.1. That approach lowered the claimant's burden under s.2(b) but dispensed with the guarantee's values, effectively relegating them to irrelevance at that stage of the analysis. Paradoxically, then, *Irwin Toy*'s generous interpretation of expression undermined s.2(b), because its *prima facie* standard of breach rendered analysis of the nature and severity of the violation unnecessary.[48]

Soon after *Irwin Toy*, the contextual approach (where the merits of the expression were assessed) emerged as the dominant means of determining the matter. With the criticism that the phrasing creates a 'foregone conclusion that disagreeable expression would fail the standard',[49] this led to Dickson J's statement that the expression in question 'contribute[d] little to the aspirations of Canadians or Canada in either the question for truth, the promotion of individual self-development or the protection and fostering of a vibrant democracy where the participation of all individuals is accepted and encouraged'.[50] The justification of limiting this expression, then, became a matter of distance from the touchstone of the values set out in *Ford*: 'The further that expression is from the core values of this right the greater will be the ability to justify the state's restrictive action.'[51] This measurement was not limited simply to 'disagreeable expression' as it later included limits on third-party spending in elections,[52] and the embargo on the release of election results.[53] Has the analysis remained focused on content neutrality, and protection of a range of expression? One critique is that it has not, and that it has instead 'transparently and unapologetically invited the Court to pass judgment on the content of expression'.[54]

The press freedom is inserted into this, as one author called it, 'quixotic journey'.[55] *R v Denis*,[56] a decision about confidentiality of sources, summarises the situation. The majority identified the media as having a 'unique' role: 'By investigating, questioning, criticizing and publishing important information,

---

[47] ibid.
[48] J Cameron, 'Resetting the Foundations: Renewing Freedom of Expression Under Section 2(b) of the Charter' in B Bird and D Ross (eds), *Forgotten Foundations of the Canadian Constitution* (Toronto, Lexis Nexis, 2022) 128 (references omitted).
[49] Cameron (n 13) 166, 174.
[50] *Irwin Toy* (n 3) 766.
[51] *R v Lucas* [1998] 1 SCR 439 [34].
[52] *Harper v Canada (Attorney General)* 2004 SCC 33.
[53] *R v Bryan* 2007 SCC 12.
[54] Cameron (n 13) 172.
[55] ibid 166.
[56] *R v Denis* 2019 SCC 44.

the media contribute to the existence and maintenance of a free and democratic society.' The press ensure a 'free flow of information'[57] which additionally aids in addressing 'a democratic deficit in the transparency and accountability' of institutions.[58] Still, the Court reiterated that freedom of expression 'includes freedom of the press',[59] thereby refraining from recognising it as a distinct right in itself. The open court principle, discussed next, offers one example of the hesitation identified within the Supreme Court's statements on a free press.

2.2. The Open Court Principle and Newsgathering

The Supreme Court of Canada established the principle of openness in court proceedings in *Nova Scotia (Attorney General) v MacIntryre*[60] where Lamer J (as he then was) set out four 'broad policy considerations': respect for the individual's privacy, protection of the administration of justice, effecting the will of Parliament, and 'a strong public policy in favour of "openness" and respect of judicial acts'.[61] These comments were made within the context of criminal search warrants and information, but they remain of more general pertinence. With regards to the individual's privacy, the consideration is a simple one: 'covertness is the exception and openness the rule'.[62] This basis for restricting openness can only arise where the need to protect social values is 'of superordinate importance'.[63] Open justice in this context has been described as 'an amalgam of free expression and press interests'.[64]

As the concept of open courts developed, there were points at which it seemed that freedom of expression was given particular emphasis. In *RWDSU v Dolphin Delivery Ltd*,[65] the Court wrote of freedom of expression as 'one of the fundamental concepts that has formed the basis for the historical development of the political, social and education institutions of western society'. The freedom of expression was also said to 'protect listeners as well as speakers'.[66] This was interpreted as describing the public's right to have access to information relating to

[57] ibid [45].
[58] This statement originated in *R v National Post* 2010 SCC 16 [55], a case about journalists' confidential sources, but was cited in *Denis* (n 56) [45].
[59] *Denis* (n 56) [46].
[60] *Nova Scotia (Attorney General) v MacIntryre* [1982] 1 SCR 175.
[61] ibid [53].
[62] ibid [59].
[63] ibid [63].
[64] Cameron (n 13) 166.
[65] *RWDSU* (n 17) 583.
[66] *Ford* (n 7) 767. This remark was made within the context of commercial expression.

public institutions. The press holds a 'fundamentally important role' in providing this access[67] because the general public relies upon the press to inform them

> about court proceedings – the nature of the evidence that was called, the arguments presented, the comments made by the trial judge – in order to know not only what rights they may have, but how their problems might be dealt with in court.[68]

In *Edmonton Journal v Alberta (Attorney General)*, the Supreme Court wrote of freedom of expression as uniquely important to a democratic society.[69]

Openness of the courts allows the public to scrutinise and criticise their operation. By 1996, openness had become 'one of the hallmarks of a democratic society'[70] and was 'inextricably tied to' section 2(b) of the Charter,[71] in part due to the facilitative function of permitting the public to discuss and form opinions of courts.[72] The open court principle, and the media's role in this openness, additionally has a function in public confidence in courts and the administration of justice. Making the link between open courts and freedom of expression, the Supreme Court wrote:

> The right to freedom of expression is just as fundamental in our society as the open court principle. It fosters democratic discourse, truth finding and self-fulfilment. Freedom of the press has always been an embodiment of freedom of expression. It is also the main vehicle for informing the public about court proceedings. In this sense, freedom of the press is essential to the open court principle.[73]

The absence of further elaboration or commentary is notable because a free press is integral to the open court principle. In assessing when the open court principle may be outweighed, the *Dagenais/Mentuck* test sets out the parameters for a court when a publication ban should be ordered:

(a)   such an order is necessary in order to prevent a serious risk to the proper administration of justice because reasonably alternative measures will not prevent the risk; and
(b)   the salutary effects of the publication ban outweigh the deleterious effects on the rights and interests of the parties and the public, including the effects on the right to free expression, the right of the accused to a fair and public trial, and the efficacy of the administration of justice.[74]

The Court has developed the serious risk aspect of this test so that privacy may be an exception to the open court principle where an individual's dignity is the matter at serious risk.

[67] *Edmonton Journal v Alberta (Attorney General)* [1989] 2 SCR 1326, 1339.
[68] ibid 1339–40.
[69] ibid 1336.
[70] As stated by La Forest J in *New Brunswick* (n 35) [22].
[71] ibid [23].
[72] ibid [24].
[73] *Canadian Broadcasting Corp v Canada (Attorney General)* 2011 SCC 2 [2].
[74] *R v Mentuck* 2001 SCC 76 [32] which developed from *Dagenais v Canadian Broadcasting Corp* [1994] 3 SCR 835; Cameron (n 48) 147, described this test as 'highly protective' of s 2(b).

In *M.E.H. v Williams*,[75] the Ontario Court of Appeal wrote that a serious risk to the public interest other than that affecting the proper administration of justice can be part of this first stage analysis. Purely personal interests, however, will not suffice: 'the personal concerns of a litigant, including concerns about the very real emotional distress and embarrassment that can be occasioned to litigants when justice is done in public, will not, standing alone, satisfy the necessity branch of the test'.[76]

The Supreme Court of Canada in *Sherman Estate v Donovan*[77] has found that privacy can be a basis for an exception to the open court principle where an individual's 'human dignity is shown to be at serious risk'.[78] The decision, then, provided the Court with the opportunity to 'decide whether privacy can amount to a public interest in the open court jurisprudence and, if so, whether openness puts privacy at serious risk here so as to justify the kind of orders sought by the appellants'.[79] In discussing how the open court principle could be limited by privacy (when it is a matter of public concern), Kasirer J reminded that both concepts are not beyond limitation: the 'right of privacy is not absolute; the open court principle is not without exceptions'.[80] The dissemination of personal information (information of a 'highly sensitive character'[81]) may, in certain situations, constitute 'an affront to a person's dignity'.[82] This form of dignity 'is a related but narrower concern than privacy generally; it transcends the interests of the individual and, like other important public interests, is a matter that concerns the society at large'. The 'affront to dignity' would be on a scale that 'society as a whole has a stake in protecting'.[83] To avail of this exception, the applicant must establish facts that such a dignity dimension of their privacy is at serious risk, and that the information in the court file

> is sufficiently sensitive such that it can be said to strike at the biological core of the individual and, in the broader circumstances, that there is a serious risk that, without an exceptional order, the affected individual will suffer an affront to their dignity.[84]

The possibility for privacy to form a public interest basis against the open court principle may be a point to monitor moving forward. In an abstract manner, the interest of an individual or small group outweighing those of the public can elicit negative attention. Still, the discussion in *Sherman Estate* suggests that the strong public policy favouring openness remains in place, and that a high threshold would need to be met in order to displace it.

---

[75] *M.E.H. v Williams* 2012 ONCA 35.
[76] ibid [25].
[77] *Sherman Estate v Donovan* 2021 SCC 25.
[78] ibid [7].
[79] ibid [6].
[80] ibid [31].
[81] ibid [33].
[82] ibid [7].
[83] ibid [33].
[84] ibid [35].

Does the open court principle not fit with the work of the free press in news-gathering? Indeed, newsgathering may be the core function of the press.[85] It is at least a primary means by which it informs the general public so that individuals may participate in the democratic process. In 2019, the Supreme Court wrote that freedom of the press 'encompasses the ability of the media to gather information, maintain confidential relationships with journalistic sources and produce and publish news without fear of obstacles to their activities'.[86]

For matters arising after October 2017, there is the Journalistic Sources Protection Act.[87] This legislation responded to revelations in 2016 that Quebec police had been surveilling journalists for years.[88] The Act sets out protections for confidentiality of a journalistic source as well as a framework for applications for search warrants, production orders and other orders related to the work of a journalist. The present discussion does not delve into the intricacies of these matters.[89]

With facts arising prior to the coming into force of this Act, *R v Vice Media* was a decision about a production order from the Royal Canadian Mounted Police to Vice Media to produce screen shots of the messages exchanged with the source.[90] These exchanges could have implicated the source in terrorism offences. Vice Media had published three stories based on the exchanges between one of its journalists and a source (a Canadian suspected of having joined a terrorist organisation based in Syria). The majority upheld the production order because 'the state's interest in investigating and prosecuting the alleged crimes outweighs the appellants' right to privacy in gathering and disseminating the news'.[91] It was only the dissent (a five to four decision) that took a further step:

> I see no reason to continue to avoid giving distinct constitutional content to the words 'freedom of the press' in s.2(b) .... A strong, independent and responsible press ensures that the public's opinions about its democratic choices are based on accurate and reliable information. This is not a democratic luxury – there can be no democracy without it.[92]

---

[85] Cameron (n 13) 165.

[86] *Denis* (n 56) [46].

[87] S.C. 2017, ch 22.

[88] *Denis* (n 56) [67].

[89] On these, see, eg, *R v National Post* 2010 SCC 16 and *Globe and Mail v Canada (Attorney General)* 2010 SCC 41. For discussion see J Cameron, 'Of Scandals, Sources and Secrets: Investigative Reporting, *National Post* and *Globe and Mail*' (2011) 54 *Supreme Court Law Review* (2nd Series) 233.

[90] *R v Vice Media* 2018 SCC 53. This decision has elicited much commentary. See, eg, BOliphant, 'Does Independent Protection for Freedom of the Press Make a Difference? The Case of *Vice Media v Canada (Attorney General)*' in D Newman, D Ross, B Bird and SE Mix-Ross (eds), *The Forgotten Fundamental Freedoms of the Charter* (Toronto, Lexis Nexis, 2020).

[91] *Vice Media* (n 90) [5]. The Court also noted that the disclosure of information would not reveal a confidential source, nor any 'off the record' or 'not for attribution' communications.

[92] ibid [110].

The media had '*independent* rights'.[93] Here the dissent identified the media's newsgathering as grounding rights: 'its right to gather and disseminate information for the public benefit without undue interference'.[94]

2.3. Libel and the Press

Freedom of the press has also contended with the private law tort of defamation (specifically libel). Defamation in Canada has not been viewed with uniform praise. It was criticised as being at a 'low level' in 1979,[95] and later for setting an '*extremely minimal*' threshold for a *prima facie* claim; leading to the following indictment of Canadian defamation law: 'The cases indicate that virtually all critical comment ... which portrays a person in an uncomplimentary light will be considered to be defamatory'.[96] The potential chilling effect of this threshold as currently calibrated remains a concern. Canadian libel largely follows the common framework of the *prima facie* claim and its defences. The Canadian libel claim requires the plaintiff to establish before the Court:

> (1) that the impugned words were defamatory, in the sense that they would tend to lower the plaintiff's reputation in the eyes of a reasonable person; (2) that the words in fact referred to the plaintiff; and (3) that the words were published, meaning that they were communicated to at least one person other than the plaintiff.[97]

As in other common law jurisdictions, free speech and protection of reputation are the parameters for libel adjudication. Mister Justice Cory, in *Hill v Church of Scientology of Toronto*,[98] attempted to elaborate upon the importance of reputation within the Charter. This can be a challenge because there is no explicit protection for reputation in the Charter, whereas there is for freedom of speech. He characterised a good reputation as 'closely related to the innate worthiness and dignity of the individual', warranting protection equal to freedom of expression.[99] For Cory J, the fundamental importance of the right to an individual remains central to a democracy. This importance can be found, as one

---

[93] ibid [109].

[94] ibid [112]. Here there are echoes of La Forest J in *New Brunswick* (n 35) [24]: 'freedom of the press not only encompassed the right to report news and other information, but also the right to gather this information'.

[95] As noted by Dickson J (as he then was) in *Cherneskey v Armadale Publishers Ltd* [1979] 1 SCR 1067, 1095.

[96] L Klar and C Jeffries, *Tort Law*, 6th edn (Toronto, Carswell, 2019) 904. This remark has been in successive editions of this textbook. The authors continued: 'The cases indicate that virtually all critical comment ... which portrays a person in an uncomplimentary light will be considered to be defamatory.'

[97] *Grant v Torstar* 2009 SCC 61 [28].

[98] *Hill v Church of Scientology of Toronto* [1995] 2 SCR 1130.

[99] ibid [107].

example, in a person's good reputation 'which enhances an individual's sense of worth and value'.[100] On the relation, in defamation adjudication, to the place of reputation, Cory J concluded:

> Although it is not specifically mentioned in the Charter, the good reputation of the individual represents and reflects the innate dignity of the individual, a concept which underlies all the Charter rights. It follows that the protection of the good reputation of an individual is of fundamental importance to our democratic society.[101]

The Court has remained vague regarding the further details pertaining to the significance of reputation in the libel balancing exercise.

The recognition of a Charter right to free speech with common law recognition of the value of protection of reputation also points to a conceptual problem. It may be difficult to give equal weight to two interests when one is explicitly stated in the Constitution and the other is read into it. The Canadian Supreme Court has read protection of reputation into the Charter because it is not explicitly identified. The Supreme Court of Canada established that Charter principles remained applicable to the common law: 'Charter values, framed in general terms, should be weighed against the principles which underlie the common law. The Charter values will then provide the guidelines for any modification to the common law which the court feels is necessary.'[102]

The establishment of the responsible communication on matters of public interest defence, by the Canadian Supreme Court in *Grant v Torstar*,[103] was the by-product of the Court's assessment of existing defences to protect media as wanting. The non-exhaustive criteria in *Grant* for this defence[104] gives rise to foreseeable, concerned commentary.[105] Foremost, there is a strong possibility of lower courts employing the criteria exhaustively (despite the Supreme Court's final point being 'any other relevant circumstances'). Explaining why it created this new defence, the Court canvassed existing defences at the time. Justification applied only when proof showed the statement to be substantially true. Meeting this threshold some years later, when the matter reached the Court, tilted the balance against journalists:

> The practical result of the gap between responsible verification and the ability to prove truth in a court of law on some date far in the future, is that the defence of justification is often of little utility to journalists and those who publish their stories.[106]

---

[100] ibid [108].

[101] ibid [120].

[102] ibid [97]. The matter was also addressed in *WIC Radio* (n 41) [2]: 'This is a private law case that is not governed directly by the Charter. Yet it was common ground in the argument before us that the evolution of the common law is to be informed and guided by Charter values.'

[103] *Grant* (n 97).

[104] ibid [126].

[105] It may be that this is currently arising: H Young, "Anyone ... in any Medium"? The Scope of Canada's Responsible Communication Defense' in AT Kenyon (ed), *Comparative Defamation and Privacy Law* (Cambridge, Cambridge University Press, 2016) 17.

[106] *Grant* (n 97) [33].

Moreover, qualified privilege, in Canadian law to that point, had taken a strict view of the duty-interest special relationship which largely had not included news media. The defence applies where the following criteria are met:

A. The publication is on a matter of public interest, and
B. The publisher was diligent in trying to verify the allegation, having regard to:
    a) the seriousness of the allegation;
    b) the public importance of the matter;
    c) the urgency of the matter;
    d) the status and reliability of the source;
    e) whether the plaintiff's side of the story was sought and accurately reported;
    f) whether the inclusion of the defamatory statement was justifiable;
    g) whether the defamatory statement's public interest lay in the fact that it was made rather than its truth ('reportage'); and
    h) any other relevant circumstances.[107]

Chief Justice McLachlin set out a broad understanding of what the Court intended with public interest:

> To be of public interest, the subject matter 'must be shown to be one inviting public attention, or about which the public has some substantial concern because it affects the welfare of citizens, or one to which considerable public notoriety or controversy has attached'.... The case law on fair comment 'is replete with successful fair comment defences on matters ranging from politics to restaurant and book reviews'.... Public interest may be a function of the prominence of the person referred to in the communication, but mere curiosity or prurient interest is not enough. Some segment of the public must have a genuine stake in knowing about the matter published .... The public has a genuine stake in knowing about many matters, ranging from science and the arts to the environment, religion, and morality. The democratic interest in such wide-ranging public debate must be reflected in the jurisprudence.[108]

The Court elaborated extensively on its reason for establishing this new defence. It classified as 'notional'[109] the possibility of setting the matter within the duty-interest concept of qualified privilege when applied to journalists and the world at large. Two overarching factors compelled the Court to take this step, principle and jurisprudence. Regarding the former, the Court evaluated then-current Canadian law as 'inconsistent' with the principle of freedom of expression as established in the Charter due to its chilling effect. Jurisprudence largely[110] referred to other

---

[107] ibid [126].
[108] ibid [105]–[106].
[109] ibid [93].
[110] The Court referenced the Ontario Court of Appeal's decision in *Quan v Cusson* 2007 ONCA 771, overturned 2009 SCC 62, which identified the trend in other common law jurisdictions.

Commonwealth common law jurisdictions having some similar form of defence in place.[111]

Preceding the recognition of a new defence in *Grant*, the Supreme Court in 2008 revised its analysis of the defence of fair comment. As set out in *WIC Radio Ltd v Simpson*,[112] fair comment protects opinions including 'deduction, inference, conclusion, criticism, judgment, remark or observation which is generally incapable of proof'.[113] Canadian statutes, such as Ontario's Libel and Slander Act,[114] had outlined it. The provision permits some scope for media to make statements without being held to the truth of each one:

> a defence of fair comment shall not fail by reason only that the truth of every allegation of fact is not proved if the expression of opinion is fair comment having regard to such of the facts alleged or referred to in the words complained of as are proved.

Similarly, the defendant need not have held the opinion expressed so long as 'a person could honestly hold the opinion'. The Supreme Court in *WIC Radio* expanded the scope of this defence by amending an aspect of the test (noted in full below) to include opinions that 'anyone could honestly have expressed', as opposed to only opinions by 'fair-minded' people. A defendant applying for protection from this defence must establish the following:

> (a) the comment must be on a matter of public interest; (b) the comment must be based on fact; (c) the comment, though it can include inferences of fact, must be recognisable as comment; (d) the comment must satisfy the following objective test: could any person honestly express that opinion on the proved facts?; and (e) even though the comment satisfies the objective test the defence can be defeated if the plaintiff proves that the defendant was actuated by express malice.[115]

Together, these defences offer some support for a free press. Clearly the defence of responsible publication in the public interest is aimed directly at protecting the press. It may be suggested that the revised fair comment defence also implicates the free press insofar as the scope for protection of published opinions has expanded. Nevertheless, the trajectory remains set within the right of the individual, and how the press can facilitate this.

The so-called anti-SLAPP (strategic lawsuits against public participation) legislation extends the emphasis on the individual's freedom of expression set out in the aforementioned cases on freedom of expression. Taking the changes to the Province of Ontario's Courts of Justice Act,[116] passed as the Protection

---

[111] The Court cited the following decisions as examples: *Reynolds v Times Newspapers Ltd* [2001] 2 AC 12; *Lange v Australian Broadcasting Corp.* (1997), 145 ALR 96; *Lange v Atkinson* [1998] 3 NZLR 424; *National Media Ltd v Bogoshi* 1998 (4) SA 1196 (SCA).
[112] *WIC Radio* (n 41).
[113] *Ross v New Brunswick Teachers' Assn.* 2001 NBCA 62 [56] and cited in *WIC Radio* (n 41) [26].
[114] R.S.O 1990, c.L.12, ss 23–24.
[115] *Grant* (n 97) [31].
[116] S.O. 1990, c. C-43.

of Public Participation Act, 2015,[117] suggests some movement along these lines. This also raises the troubling question of what constitutes a free press. It may be that anti-SLAPP has been developed with the individual in mind. However, the notion of the citizen journalist poses some definitional challenges.[118] It has a more direct effect on those who use information technology to speak on matters of public interest. Sections 137.1 to 137.5 give legislative force to a concern for speech in the public interest.[119] These provisions permit defendants in certain libel proceedings arising 'from an expression made by the person that relates to a matter of public interest' to seek an order from a court to dismiss the action.[120] The public interest forming the object of this legislation carries the same meaning as the public interest identified by the Supreme Court of Canada in *Grant*.[121] The anti-SLAPP provisions fall short of a detailed examination of the merits of the statements. Instead, they set out 'a judicial screening or triage device designed to eliminate certain claims at an early stage of the litigation process'.[122]

3. A More Direct Treatment

The above discussion demonstrates a consistent line from the Supreme Court of Canada: Freedom of expression is protected, but what a free press entails remains vague. There are two points that should be addressed: attending to the concept of the free press within section 2(b) of the Charter; and reconsidering the libel framework, specifically the question of what is defamatory.

An effort has been made above to demonstrate that the Supreme Court of Canada has stopped short of recognising free press as an autonomous concept with the Charter protection of freedom of expression. In addition to those remarks, some sense of urgency is reinforced. Recognising that the public needs access to the newsgathering efforts of the press imbues this activity with some level of importance to the functioning of democracy. Refraining from recognising that

---

[117] S.O. 2015, c. 23.

[118] On citizen journalists, see P Coe, 'Press Regulation in the United Kingdom in a Changed Media Ecosystem' in P Wragg and A Koltay (eds), *Global Perspectives on Press Regulation* (Vol 1) (Oxford, Hart Publishing, 2023) ch 10. In the Canadian context, Richard Moon has offered the following: 'It may also be the case that freedom of the press rights, while formally available to anyone who gathers and disseminates news, can only be made by organizations and individuals that adhere to the professional standards that are traditionally, although not invariably, followed by mainstream media, such as checking sources and correcting errors. The requirement of due diligence in reporting is not always met by citizen journalists or smaller partisan news sites, either because they lack the necessary resources to fact check or because accuracy is not their primary concern.' Moon (n 8) 33–34.

[119] The purposes of the provisions are stated in s 137.1.

[120] Sections 137.1(3) and 137.1(4) outline the parameters for an order or a refusal to make an order to dismiss.

[121] See *Grant* (n 97) [105]. This point was made in relation to the anti-SLAPP legislation under consideration here in *1704604 Ontario Ltd v Pointes Protection Association* 2018 ONCA 685.

[122] ibid [73].

newsgathering, in this context, does not warrant recognition of any autonomous right or privilege requires further discussion.[123] This means that there must be an elaboration of what a free press entails, and if this does not involve an autonomous constitutional right (rather than one that is derivative of the individual's freedom of expression), then a dialogue regarding why the Court will not take this step is necessary.

A step that does not require the Court to discuss the contents of a free press, the Court should refine its approach at common law to the classification of a defamatory comment.[124] Through the increasing reliance on the libel defences to recalibrate the tort, attention has been diverted from the *prima facie* claim.[125] In particular, the tripartite claim contains the means by which to augment protection of speech without necessarily drawing exclusively upon the defences.

The now classic statement regarding the measurement of a defamatory remark comes from Lord Atkin in *Sim v Stretch*,[126] when he restated the assessment in the now familiar form: 'would the words tend to lower the plaintiff in the estimation of right-thinking members of society generally?' Citing *Sim*, the Supreme Court of Canada referred to this test as 'an objective standard, that of the right-thinking person'.[127]

The gap in the libel defences to protect responsible press publications necessitated the Supreme Court's recognition of a new defence in *Grant*.[128] The Canadian Supreme Court's establishment of this defence of responsible publication on matters of public interest typified how the widening breadth of protection of freedom of expression has largely been effected through the libel defences. In the twenty-first century, the defences have been imbued with increasing importance as the tools for preserving a widening scope for freedom of expression.[129] This, it is contended, has led to an unsatisfactory state which undermines the clarity of the protection of freedom of expression by suggesting that free speech must be 'saved' by the defences in libel. Better delineating the parameters for what constitutes a defamatory remark can, without resort to discussions about the constitutional right(s) of a free press, extend the scope for the work of a free press.

There has been little engagement in Canadian case law with a refocusing of adjudication within the *prima facie* claim. A rare example has been Lebel

---

[123] As well as a theoretical approach according to Cameron (n 13) 178 ff.
[124] This could also be done in conjunction with reconsideration of s 2(b) such as that argued in Cameron (n 48).
[125] D Mangan, 'Perplexing Platforms for Tort' (2019) *Supreme Court Law Review* (2nd Series) 177.
[126] *Sim v Stretch* [1936] 2 All ER 1237, 1240. This decision remains a reference point in Canadian tort textbooks regarding the analysis of defamatory content. See, eg, R Solomon, M McInnes, E Chamberlain and S Pitel, *Cases and Materials on the Law of Torts*, 10th edn (Toronto, Carswell, 2019) 1152.
[127] *Bou Malhab v Diffusion Metromedia CMR Inc.* 2011 SCC 9 [35].
[128] *Grant* (n 97) [2].
[129] D Mangan, 'Situating Canadian Defamation and Privacy Law in Comparative Context' in A Koltay and P Wragg (eds), *Research Handbook on Comparative Privacy and Defamation Law* (Cheltenham, Edward Elgar, 2020).

J's minority opinion in *WIC Radio*. He focused upon opinions which would be inferences or value judgements based upon facts in the public domain. Mister Justice Lebel relied upon the following statement regarding opinion from a regularly-cited Canadian source on defamation:

> If the expression of opinion by the defendant on facts which are true are reasonably understood by those to whom they are published as opinions, and nothing else, they say nothing derogatory about the plaintiff which does not already inhere in the facts that have been recited.[130]

Two components stand out as essential in Lebel's opinion. First, the context of the statement should establish the opinion as one derived from facts in the public domain. Second, there is a threshold consideration: 'before a prima facie case can be made out, there must be a realistic threat that the statement, in its full context, would reduce a reasonable person's opinion of the plaintiff'.[131] Here, Lebel J enters into an area which would be discussed in the UK a few years later.

Libel remains actionable *per se*. And yet, the English courts in *Jameel (Yousef) v Dow Jones & Co Inc*[132] and in *Thornton v Telegraph Media Group Ltd*[133] asserted the existence of a threshold in Lord Atkin's outline in *Sim*. This paved the way for section 1 of the Defamation Act 2013.[134] As identified by Lebel J, determining whether a statement constitutes a defamatory remark implicitly contains a threshold assessment of the impugned words. The contention here is that this point – what constitutes a defamatory remark – must be further developed within Canadian case law.

4. The Canadian Supreme Court and Freedom of the Press

In his concluding chapter in Volume 1 of this collection,[135] Wragg critically dissects the often-used characterisation of the freedom of the press as a positive and even noble force. Drawing from English examples, he contends that this depiction of the press is not invariably accurate. Other contributors to Volume 1 have identified the press's 'duty … to impart … information and ideas on all

---

[130] R Brown, *Defamation Law: A Primer*, 2nd edn (Toronto, Carswell, 2013) 185.
[131] *WIC Radio* (n 41) [78].
[132] *Jameel (Yousef) v Dow Jones & Co Inc* [2005] QB 946.
[133] *Thornton v Telegraph Media Group Ltd* [2010] EWHC 1414.
[134] The issue before the courts in *Lachaux v Independent Print Ltd* [2019] UKSC 27 centred on the drafting of the UK Defamation Act 2013. The Court ruled: 'This shows, very clearly to my mind, that it not only raises the threshold of seriousness above that envisaged in *Jameel (Yousef)* and *Thornton*, but requires its application to be determined by reference to the actual facts about its impact and not just to the meaning of the words.' ibid [12].
[135] P Wragg, 'Conclusion: European Visions of a Free and Regulated Press' in Wragg and Koltay (n 118) ch 12.

matters of public interest'.[136] Polish press's duty to provide 'reliable' information draws attention to a more precise concept within the discussion of freedom of the press. However, as Wragg notes, reliability can become a difficult concept to legally justify when it is used to adjudicate polemical expression (and not simply matters of reputation).

The impression derived from the Supreme Court of Canada is a wary admission of the press's role, including its importance in a functioning democracy. This chapter has argued for the Court's elaboration of the freedom of the press. A significant discussion is to be had on the question of whether freedom of the press is an equivalent right to freedom of speech, or whether it is something other than equivalent.[137] Nevertheless, the fact of the Canadian Supreme Court's hesitant treatment of an autonomous freedom of the press remains noteworthy. Wragg's argument of distinguishing between press malpractice and press freedom[138] may provide some path for the Court's explication, if it focuses on accountability (though making good of wrongs when it comes to the concept of speech has been a challenging endeavour in democracies) and is embedded within a framework of duties and interests (familiar in defamation law)[139] or duties and responsibilities.[140]

---

[136] J Oster, 'The Press Freedom Jurisprudence of the European Court of Human Rights' in ibid ch 11. See also J Kulesza, 'Freedom of the Press and Press Regulation in Poland' in ibid, ch 7.

[137] For a discussion of freedom of the press as a superior or equivalent right to freedom of speech see, P Wragg, *A Free and Regulated Press* (Hart Publishing, 2021) 24–31.

[138] See ibid, Part III.

[139] Though there may be some overlap with codes of practice such as that in Belgian Raad voor de Journalistiek (December 2016).

[140] Pietro Dunn and Oreste Pollicino use this framework in 'Freedom of the Press in Italy' in Wragg and Koltay (118).

10

Media Regulation in Chile: Authority and Liberty Compounded*

JOHN CHARNEY

1. Introduction

Two influential narratives have contributed to shaping media regulation throughout Chilean republican history. The first recognises that media freedom is a basic freedom and a central instrument of democratic government. However, it also sees the free press as a potential threat to other cherished values such as reputation, public morals or national security. This narrative has famously influenced the treatment of the press by the Constitution and the law throughout history. Recognised as a fundamental right since the very first constitutional experiments, freedom of the press has also been intensely and severely regulated to prevent abuses that may harm reputations, incite public disorder or affect national security. Even if international organisations have repeatedly adverted to the problems attendant to the criminalisation of speech, this is an institutional factor which is hardly subjected to academic debate and completely absent in the political discourse in Chile.

The second narrative is related to the way the media is organised to fulfil its public remit. In contrast to the first narrative, there has been strong debate about this one, especially since the return to democracy in 1990. The debate divides those who think that structural pluralism and content diversity can only be achieved if the role of the state is reduced to safeguarding a competitive media landscape. On the other side of the debate are those who argue that complete liberalisation of media markets achieve nothing but highly concentrated markets controlled by the economic elite. These positions have clashed in Chile's institutions many times over the last 30 years. Through legislation the Parliament has tried to strengthen the role of the state in promoting media pluralism and content diversity with little success due to constitutional restrictions. That constitution, enacted during

* This contribution forms part of Fondecyt Research Project No 11181088 whose main researcher is the author.

Augusto Pinochet's dictatorship, promotes the liberalisation of media markets and is guarded by a Constitutional Court that has been generally resistant to any form of interference in the structure of the media. Most recently these positions faced off in a failed constitutional process that tried to amend the Constitution's regulation of media freedom, among many other aspects.

The conflation of both narratives in Chilean media regulation gives form to an ambiguous system that combines an authoritarian approach to the limits of the free press with a liberal approach to structural media regulation. This ambiguity will appear throughout this chapter's overview of Chilean media regulation. The most significant normative sources of media regulation, from the Constitution to special statutory regulation, will receive special attention. Constitutional, judicial and administrative case law are also analysed where necessary and relevant. Even if the focus lies on regulation, this chapter will examine the two aforementioned central narratives to understand the core justifications of different regulatory options, the institutional factors that have favoured some decisions over others and the difficulties encountered in a system that is extremely sensitive to technical and political developments.

This chapter consists of five sections apart from this introduction. Section two provides a general approach of the history and theory of media freedom in Chile. Section three looks at the free press as a fundamental right and explores its function in the constitutional system. Sections four and five examine general media regulation contained in the Press Act 2001 and specific regulation of television and radio broadcasting. Finally, section six looks at 'new' technologies and the problems of insufficient and out-dated regulation.

2. Theory of Press Freedom

Since the early beginnings of the Republic, there has been an ambiguous approach towards the free press. Hailed by some as a necessary prerequisite for the intellectual progress of society and the cornerstone of democracy, it has also been seen at times as a threat to political cohesion and an instrument of moral corruption.[1] Banned during the colonial period, the press was only introduced in Chile at the beginning of the nineteenth century by the Junta de Gobierno, the first governing body erected after Napoleon invaded Spain in 1808 and the traditional structure of the Spanish empire collapsed.[2] Efforts were made by the Junta to bring to Santiago a printing press from Argentina not only to publish provisions of the Government but also to align public opinion with the principles

---

[1] For discussions of the free press during the early period of the Chilean republic, see AM Stuven and G Cid, *Debates republicanos en Chile* (Santiago, Universidad Diego Portales, 2013) 34–70.
[2] S Collier, *Ideas y política de la independencia chilena 1808–1833* (Santiago, Fondo de Cultura Económica, 2012) 78.

of the new government.[3] At this early stage, apologists in Chile echoed many of the arguments introduced abroad to defend the freedom of the press. In a tone reminiscent of some passages of John Milton's *Areopagitica*, Camilo Henriquez, editor of the first newspaper in Chile, *La Aurora*, claimed that:

> Never, therefore, is lost what the friends of humanity write. The great mass of lights scattered in both worlds, the cries of the wise shall not be ineffectual. Let useful truths be spread; their seeds are immortal; the time will come when they sprout.[4]

Defences of the free press mounted shortly thereafter, by the time the provisional Constitution of 1818 was being drafted, also take a cue from Milton's argument. Among them was the claim – made by Milton and later reproduced by John Stuart Mill in his *On Liberty* – that the presumption of infallibility, held by governments to censor the expression of ideas that they consider false, prevents the discovery of truth and intellectual progress of society.[5]

The period saw defences other than those based on the epistemic contribution of the free press. The political benefits of a free press have also been considered thoroughly since the beginning of the Republic. In fact, the nascent Republic required a cohesive public opinion, informed of the political principles that inspired the revolution and aligned with the republican tenets that shaped the workings of the new government.[6] An additional political function of the free press clearly identified from the beginning of the Republic was control against despotic government.[7] Thus, the press was seen in this period as an instrument of social cohesion, which, backed by the principles of autonomous government, would be able to dismantle the colonial authoritarian heritage.[8]

If some of these epistemic and political defences were persuasively articulated, they carry with them some inconsistencies or tensions that express an historical anxiety about the consequences of unrestrained public discourse. From an epistemic point of view, the problem was that a society in which only a few had received formal education could only achieve intellectual progress if guided by the ideas of the most cultivated minds of their time.[9] From a political perspective,

---

[3] R Silva Castro, *Prensa y periodismo en Chile (1812–1956)* (Santiago, Ediciones Universidad de Chile, 1958) 8.

[4] C Henríquez, 'De la influencia de los escritos luminosos sobre la suerte de la humanidad' *La Aurora de Chile* (7 May 1812).

[5] J García del Río, 'De la libertad de imprenta' *El Sol de Chile* (3 July 1818).

[6] This is the way the drafter of the Constitution of 1823, Juan Egaña, saw the function of public opinion; see Stuven and Cid (n 1) 355.

[7] See García del Río (n 5).

[8] See C Rivera, 'Prensa y política. El poder de la construcción de la realidad. Chile, Siglos XIX y XX' in I Jaksic and JL Ossa (eds), *Historia política de Chile, 1810–2010* (Santiago, Fondo de Cultura Económica, 2017) I, 213.

[9] This problem, clearly identified by C Henríquez, 'De la opinión pública' *La Aurora de Chile* (30 July 1812), was also identified by JS Mill, 'The Spirit of the Age' in AP Robson and JM Robson (eds), *Newspaper Writings: Collected Works of John Stuart Mill* (London, Routledge & Kegan Paul, 1986) Vol XXII, 304.

on the other hand, the purpose of creating a cohesive public opinion lay at odds with the expression of voices that could challenge the central political tenets of the time. So, though the free press was defended as a central value from the very beginning of the Republic, it was also seen as a threat to political stability and to the moral and intellectual progress of society.

The ambivalence towards the value of a free press has been an institutional factor with relevant normative consequences that has prevailed throughout Chilean history. As a matter of fact, this freedom has been guaranteed as a fundamental right since the provisional constitutions drafted during the first decades of the nineteenth century and included in the Constitutions of 1828, 1833, 1925 and 1980. However, broad and severe limits to this freedom have always existed.[10] Of special concern is criminalisation of speech in the form of criminal libel and slander. This is a problem that has not been properly addressed by the political system nor subjected to intense academic scrutiny.[11]

In the last 30 years, the most relevant discussion about media freedom has been about its structure. Although this is not a discussion about the limits of media freedom, it has important implications for the purpose of this chapter. In fact, the way in which the media is structured and organised affects its capacity to fulfil its public remit. As already exposed, the debate divides those who think that the democratic remit of media freedom can only be realised through the liberalisation of media markets and those that argue that state regulation is needed in order to guarantee a plural, diverse media system. These positions have been at the centre of media law regulation and reform and at different times it has separated the approach of Parliament and that of the Constitutional Court. Recently, both positions were confronted in the constitutional process, the outcome of which was the rejection in a referendum of a Constitution that favoured the creation of an integrated system of public media and an active role for the state in the promotion of pluralism and media diversity.[12] Against this proposal, the current constitutional system has promoted an intense liberalisation of media markets. Even though the constitutional proposal was rejected, the discussion about the structure of the media market is likely to continue.

---

[10] For the history of press regulation in Chile, see generally M González Pino and G Martínez Ramírez, *Régimen jurídico de la prensa chilena 1810–1987* (Santiago, Universidad Católica de Chile, 1987); P Ibarra Cifuentes, 'Liberalismo y prensa: Leyes de imprenta en el Chile decimonónico (1812–1872)' (2014) 36 *Revista de Estudios Histórico-Jurídicos* 293.

[11] For some recent discussions, see P Viollier and M Salinas, 'La tipificación de los delitos de injuria y calumnia y su efecto inhibitorio en el ejercicio de la libertad de expresión en Chile' (2019) 15 *Anuario de Derechos Humanos* 41; J Charney, 'La tensión entre la libertad de emitir opinión e informar y la honra de las personas: Importancia y límites de la *exceptio veritatis*' (2016) 29 *Revista de Derecho (Valdivia)* 175.

[12] For an explanation about the causes of the constitutional crisis, see generally, J Charney, P Marshall and E Christodoulidis, 'It Is not 30 Pesos, It Is 30 Years: Reflections on the Chilean Crisis' (2021) 30 *Social and Legal Studies* 627.

3. Constitutional Press Freedom

The current Constitution was enacted in 1980 during Pinochet's regime. Although it has been amended more than 200 times – to the point that some have claimed that it is no longer Pinochet's Constitution – the free speech clause has remained virtually intact.[13] Historically speaking, the free speech clause is an amalgamation of elements that form part of the original version of the Constitution of 1925; the amendments introduced to that constitution in 1970 in order to alleviate the anxieties of a parliament that saw in Salvador Allende's presidential inauguration a threat to the free press; and other provisions incorporated by the Constitution of 1980. This explains why these freedoms, which will be referred here as expressive freedoms, are densely regulated in the Chilean Constitution. In fact, the clause contains three fundamental rights: free speech, free press and the right to information. It also contains a right to reply, the prohibition of state monopoly over the press and the authorisation by the state, universities and other legal entities to operate television broadcasters. Finally, the clause creates a regulator for television broadcasting and a film rating system.

Free speech and free press are separate rights under the terms of the Constitution. The former is defined as the 'freedom to express opinions and to inform, without prior censorship, in any form and by any means, notwithstanding to answer for crimes and abuses committed in the exercise of these freedoms, in accordance with the law'. The Constitution guarantees here freedom of expression and freedom of information. While the former is a manifestation of an individual freedom, which protects any person or legal entity from undue interference with the expression of her ideas and thoughts, freedom of information protects a series of activities involved in the process of informing, including the right to search for information and to disseminate and receive information from third parties.[14] While freedom of expression is a classic negative liberty, freedom of information is something more. On the one hand, it requires non-interference from government in the processes of communication and in the formation of public opinion that takes place in society. But on the other hand, the right to information promotes the existence of a society that is properly informed about matters of public interest.

---

[13] Two amendments have been made to the free speech clause. The first one in 1989 modified the name (and scope) of the media regulator. Originally it had control over television and radio broadcasting. With the amendment its control was reduced only to television. This amendment also abolished a rule which provided that the law shall regulate the public expression of artistic practices. The second amendment was made in 2001 after Chile was found in breach of the American Convention of Human Rights by the Inter-American Court of Human Rights in *Caso 'La última tentación de Cristo' (caso Olmedo Bustos y otros) vs Chile*, Inter-American Court of Human Rights Series C No 73 (5 February 2001), for censoring the film *The Last Temptation of Christ*. The amendment replaced censorship with a rating system for the exhibition and production of films.

[14] See American Convention on Human Rights (entered into force 18 July 1978) 1144 UNTS 123, art 13(1).

If the market is unable to fulfil this purpose, then the state has the duty to intervene. One institutional expression of this is the legal duty of television broadcasters
to broadcast for free campaigns of public interest and electoral broadcast for
presidential and parliamentary elections.

Media freedom, on the other hand, is construed as the right of every person
to 'establish, publish and maintain newspapers, journals and periodicals under
the conditions laid down by law'. The reason why only the written press – and not
television and radio broadcasters – is included in this part of the clause is that
under the original terms of the Constitution a radio and television regulator was
created (although currently it is only a television regulator). Its constitutional
duty was to guarantee the 'correct functioning' of broadcasters, meaning guaranteeing through their programming respect for a series of principles laid down by
law, including democracy, peace and pluralism. The regulator had other, legislative granted regulatory powers. Among its functions it was supposed to grant,
renew, modify and terminate radio and television broadcasting concessions.
Hence, under these rules, radio and television broadcasters were subjected to
constitutional and legal requirements that do not apply to the written press. The
different approach is justified because the former is transmitted over airwaves,
which are a public good. There is a further difference, now between radio and
television. While television concessions could only be given to the state, universities or to legal entities determined by law, no such limitation was imposed on
radio broadcasting. This is the consequence of the constituent's body understanding that television not only had an important educational role, but also the
duty to cultivate national values due to its reach and influence over the public.
Universities and the state were, according to this view, in a better position to
fulfil those ends. Even if in the original version of the Constitution the regulator
was supposed to oversee the functioning of television and radio, a constitutional
amendment in the late 1980s excluded radio broadcasting from its bailiwick.
Currently, as will be analysed in the next section, the regulator only oversees
television broadcasters.

Under the terms of the Constitution, there are two further rules that apply
only to the media (including the written press, radio and television) and not
to individual speakers. The first is a structural rule, which prevents Parliament
from constituting a state monopoly over mass media. This is a much lighter
pluralism rule than the one contained in the 1925 Constitution, which stated
that all relevant opinions shall have the right to use, under fair terms, privately
owned mass media. The second is the right to reply, which even if it is a universal right, it can only be directed against the press. The right to reply, regulated
in detail by law as analysed below, allows any person who has been offended or
unfairly mentioned to obtain a rectification from the media outlet responsible
for the publication.

A few additional notes applicable both to free speech as an individual right and
to media freedom must be added. The first one is about limits. Even if the Chilean
constitutional system has always been generous recognising limits to free speech,

it expressly prohibits prior restraint.[15] Thus, limits to free speech – in the form of abuses or criminal offences – always apply ex post and can only be regulated by law. The American Convention on Human Rights adds that limits are allowed only if they are necessary to protect the rights or reputation of others, national security, public order, health and public morals.[16] The Constitution itself guarantees the rights to reputation, private life and personal data (Article 19 No 4). These rights are not only guaranteed against governmental interference but also against the action of private individuals or legal entities. For in fact, the constitutional system adopts the horizontal effect and allows direct application of the Constitution against private parties. Consequently, it is not uncommon to see collisions between freedom of speech and any of these rights where courts weigh conflicting rights on a case-by-case basis.

In terms of protection, the Constitution contains a number of normative and jurisdictional guarantees designed to protect both, free speech and media freedom. Under the terms of the Constitution any individual or legal person whose expressive rights have been threatened, disturbed or restricted may file a constitutional action against the offender (*recurso de protección*). As said, this action may be directed not only against public bodies but also against any person or private entity that unduly interferes with expressive rights. The clause also contains a number of normative guarantees. First, it establishes that matters related to the speech clause may only be regulated by law. Moreover, in the case of statutes that regulate the television regulator or establishes limits to free speech, the Constitution demands higher quorums for their approval than the ones required for an ordinary law.[17] Second, the Constitution contains the *essential core guarantee*, which prevents Parliament from affecting the essential core of expressive freedoms or making impossible its exercise whenever they are regulated or complemented by legislation. If they do, the Constitutional Court may declare its unconstitutionality.

4. Press Regulation

Introduced in Parliament as a bill in 1993, the Press Act became law in 2001. Providing a general regulatory framework to all media, the Act systematised in one piece of legislation norms applicable to the exercise of the freedom of opinion and information that were previously dispersed across different legal

---

[15] This is true to such an extent that libel proffered through mass media was criminalised in the original version of the Constitution of 1980. Even if this criminal offence was removed from the Constitution in 2005, libel is still criminally sanctioned by law.

[16] American Convention of Human Rights, art 13(2).

[17] While an ordinary law requires the approval of the majority of deputies and senators that participate in the vote, this law requires for its approval 50% plus one of the deputies and senators currently in office.

texts. The Act reaffirms the public function of the free press and, just as all the laws that preceded it, it also establishes limits on the exercise of this freedom and criminalises abusive practices.[18] The Act also includes norms that regulate journalistic practices, recognises rights of journalists such as source protection and journalistic freedom and regulates formal aspects of the administration of media outlets.

Two aspects of the Press Act need to be singled out here. The first is related to the recognition of media pluralism and the right to information. The second, to the duties and limits imposed on the press in the exercise of its functions. In relation to media pluralism and freedom of information, the Act repeats the rules contained in the Constitution about free speech and expands them to confirm a liberty to inform and a right to be informed. It also expands the constitutional freedom to recognise the duty of the state to promote a plural media environment. The way in which these rights and liberties are regulated in the Act express a particular conception of media pluralism that is visible not only in the text of the law but also in what the text omits. A brief description of the discussions that were held about the function and structure of the press during that time and the history of the law itself are useful in understanding this.

During the 1990s, while the Press Act was being discussed in Parliament, it was possible to identify two clear and distinct positions about the function and regulation of the press. There were those that favoured a policy of non-interference, welcomed the liberation of media markets and thought that media pluralism was not compatible with media regulation.[19] On the other side were those who did not trust unregulated media markets' capacity to create a diverse and plural media environment. From this point of view, regulation was required not only to guarantee the freedom of the media to inform but also the right of citizens to receive information from a public sphere capable of reproducing social, political and cultural diversity.[20] These positions were also reflected in parliamentary discussions held during the drafting of the Press Act and even when the Parliament approved provisions designed to guarantee the effective expression of the different visions of society and established explicit limits of control of market power in the media market, these provisions were declared unconstitutional by the Constitutional Court.[21]

---

[18] 'Mensaje de S.E. el Presidente de la República con el que inicia un proyecto de ley sobre las libertades de opinión e información y el ejercicio del periodismo' (*Historia de la Ley N° 19.733*, 8 July 1993), www.bcn.cl.

[19] L Sierra, 'Pluralismo y comunicación social: libertad de expresión y dos conceptos de libertad' (1997) *Revista de Derecho Universidad Austral de Chile* 17.

[20] A Banda Vergara, 'Algunas consideraciones sobre derecho a la información y la ley de prensa' (2002) 13 *Revista de Derecho, Universidad Austral de Chile* 124; P Anguita Ramírez, *El derecho a la información en Chile, Análisis de la ley 19.733 sobre libertades de opinión e información y ejercicio del periodismo (ley de prensa)* (Santiago, Lexis Nexis, 2005) 213–14.

[21] Among the rules declared unconstitutional was one establishing that the state has the obligation to guarantee pluralism by encouraging diverse media and free media competition, ensuring the effective

In terms of medial pluralism, the Press Act – after the decision of the Constitutional Court – endorses a strict liberal approach in which the only relevant regulatory constraints applicable to the structure of media markets are those of competition law. In fact, the Act expresses that pluralism in the media system will favour the expression of social, cultural, political and regional diversity of the country but instead of guaranteeing effective expression of this diversity (as the original draft proposed), it provides the freedom to found, operate and administer media for the purpose of achieving diversity. This is a strict rule of external pluralism that not only assumes that free markets will expand media ownership but also that they will produce content diversity. The system of external pluralism is confirmed by special competition law rules that provide that any changes related to media ownership must be reported to Fiscalía Nacional Económica (FNE) 30 days after they happen. In the case of media that are subject to the system of licensing, such as television and radio broadcasting, these changes need to be reported before their occurrence and must be approved by the FNE. If approval is not granted, then an appeal can be taken to the Tribunal de Defensa de la Libre Competencia (TDLC). In practice, and since the creation of this law, the FNE has only rejected a very limited number of operations.[22] The main reason is that for competition purposes, apart from the rules contained in the Press Act, media are subject to the general rules of competition law and do not receive any special treatment for their public function. These rules have not been able to change what was already in 2001 – the year the Press Act was promulgated – a highly concentrated media market and, in the case of radio broadcasting, highly problematic operations from a competition law perspective have been approved.[23]

A second relevant set of issues regulated by the Press Act are the limits and duties of the press. First, the Act expands a constitutional rule that contains the right to reply whenever a person or a legal entity has been offended or unfairly mentioned by the media. This right is regulated in detail in the Act and applies to the press, radio and television broadcasting. The right to reply must respond specifically to the information that motivates it, and the reply cannot exceed

---

expression of different opinions, as well as the social, cultural and economic variety of the regions. The Court's rationale for declaring this rule unconstitutional was that it not only violated media outlets' editorial freedom but also affected the essential core of the constitutional clause of free speech by attempting prior restraint, which was expressly forbidden in the Constitution. Constitutional Court of Chile, Rol 226-1995, [26]–[31]. Another rule declared unconstitutional by the Court was the one that forbade control of more than 30% of the national print press market, control of more than 15% of the general news market or dominance of two or more different types of media in the same market. According to the Court, these rules violate economic liberty and the right to property, [39]–[53].

[22] P Anguita Ramírez and MJ Labrador Blanes, 'Pluralismo y libre competencia en el mercado de la televisión y radiodifusión: el caso chileno' (2019) 18 *Revista de Comunicación* 29.

[23] Compare G Sunkel and E Geoffroy, *Concentración económica de los medios de comunicación* (Santiago, LOM, 2001) with S Godoy, 'Media Ownership and Concentration in Chile' in EM Noam (ed), *Who Owns the World's Media? Media Concentration and Ownership around the World* (Oxford, Oxford University Press, 2016).

1,000 words or two minutes in the case of radio or television broadcasting. A print publication cannot refuse to publish the reply in full, and must do it on the same or a similar page as the article that caused the reply. In case of radio or television broadcasting, the reply must be aired in the same time frame and share similar features as the one that caused it. As the right to reply is a constitutional right, if the director of the media refuses to publish the reply, or if its publication does not fulfil the legal requirements previously mentioned, the offended may directly approach the Court of Appeal to obtain appropriate relief of its constitutional rights.[24] This right does not include any possible claim of the offended to obtain from the media a public apology.[25]

The Act also regulates criminal and civil offences committed through the media. Among them are hate speech, the disclosure of the identity of minors involved in criminal offences, public affronts to decency, libel and slander. Some attention must be paid to libel and slander because the Press Act modifies the general rules contained in the Criminal Code. Historically, the Chilean system has not only criminalised libel and slander but has also offered poor defences to those accused. Defences against libel were limited to justification, which is available only in cases where libel is directed against a public official and related to her public duties.[26] The Press Act modifies the general rules contained in the Criminal Code to provide wider defences to the media. First, it dismisses as libel the expression of personal opinions based on expert commentary on political, literary, historic, artistic, scientific, technical and sport critique. Second, it expands the cases in which the defence of justification or *exceptio veritatis* may be raised in libel actions to include public interest. Although a similar rule was already contained in the Press Act of 1967, the current Act provides further detail about what should be understood as public interest for the purpose of admitting the defence of justification. According to the Act, public interest issues are those related to the exercise of public functions; those carried out in the exercise of a profession or trade, the knowledge of which is of real public interest; those consisting of activities to which the public has had free access; proceedings that, with the consent of the interested party, have been captured or disseminated by the media; events or manifestations of which the person concerned has left testimony in public records or public archives; and those concerning crimes and misdemeanours.[27]

Even if the Press Act expands the general rules of defences against libel actions contained in the Criminal Code, the system is still very restrictive. In fact, the list of issues that are considered to be in the public interest do not constitute a public

---

[24] Corte Suprema, Rol 765-2007; Corte Suprema, Rol 11.491-2013. In these cases courts have considered a breach of these rules not only against free speech but also against equal treatment.

[25] Corte Suprema, Rol 20.736-2020.

[26] In this justification defence, the proof of truth exempts the defendant from criminal liability. For a comparative analysis, see Charney (n 11) 175–93.

[27] ibid 182–85.

interest defence in its own right. They only constitute a basic requirement for the defence of justification. In other words, only if there is a public interest involved in the libel may defendants be allowed to prove the truth of their expressions and, if successful, protect themselves from liability. If, on the other hand, there is no public interest involved (even if their expressions are true), they will still be liable. The difficulties of proving the truth in defences of justification (because relevant information is usually in the claimant's hands) and the absence of a public interest defence may prevent the development of strong responsible journalism oriented towards issues of public interest.[28] Furthermore and against recommendations from International Human Rights bodies, the Press Act not only keeps libel in the realm of criminal liability but it additionally provides a civil action against defendants in libel cases.[29] It is not difficult to see how these rules express a clear preference for the protection of reputation over the formation of a strong public sphere.

Strong state regulation of the press, manifest in a constitutional right to reply, constitutional protection of the right to reputation, criminal liability for libel and slander and a complaint system managed by the regulator of broadcast television, as will be analysed shortly, may explain the weak culture of self-regulation in Chile. Founded in 1990 by the Mass Media Federation, composed of the three major media associations, including television broadcasting, radio broadcasting and the print press, the Consejo de Ética de los Medios de Comunicación Social (Mass Media Council of Ethics) is an independent self-regulatory body whose members are elected by the Federation and has as its central goal guaranteeing respect for journalistic ethics in the media. The Council issues opinions aimed at orientating journalistic practices in matters such as coverage of catastrophes, economic news, professional secrets, media sources and publication of pictures. It also decides complaints of journalistic ethics violations lodged by individuals or by the Council itself against affiliated members of the Federation. Remedies are limited to naming and shaming through the publication of their decisions or excerpts on the platform of the responsible media organisation. Since its foundation in 1990, the Council has decided less than 300 cases, most of which had no public impact.

5. Press and Media Freedom

There is special regulation in Chile applicable to different media sectors. Broadcast television has a regulatory body overseeing the correct functioning of the system

---

[28] For difficulties related to the proof of truth, see I Loveland, *Political Libels: A Comparative Study* (Oxford, Hart Publishing, 2000) 7–8.
[29] See UNCHR Report of the Special Rapporteur on the Promotion and Protection of the Right to Freedom of Opinion and Expression (2012), para 79; the same principles are contained in the Inter-American Declaration of Principles on Freedom of Expression, Principle 10.

and a public broadcaster established by law, Televisión Nacional de Chile (TVN). This is also true to a much lesser extent of radio broadcasting, which is subject to the Telecommunications Act for the purpose of administrative concessions of airwaves and competition issues. Before looking at television and radio broadcasting regulation in particular, some common rules contained in the Press Act and applicable to all media must be analysed.

Few privileges are given to the media vis-a-vis individual speakers in Chile. One of them, analysed in the previous section, is a broader defence of justification against libel actions when public interest issues are involved. A second, also contained in the Press Act, is not directed to all media but only to those located in provinces. For the purpose of promoting pluralism, the Act contains a rule that establishes that all governmental advertising budget that has a clear regional, provincial or communal identification shall be used mainly and preferably in regional, provincial or communal media. The rule is not only a financial incentive to regional media but it also prevents the practice of buying governmental sympathy through public advertising spending.[30] Finally, the Press Act also provides source protection to editors, directors of media outlets and journalists, including foreign correspondents. Protection is also granted to all those who were present at the time the information was passed to the journalist. Further privileges and duties are found in special media regulation.

5.1. Television Regulation

Television is the most regulated media in Chile. The first Television Act was published in 1970 when only four channels were functioning, three of them belonging to public universities and the other, TVN, a public service broadcaster created in 1969. The Act granted legal concessions for life to the three universities and to TVN, concessions that still remain in force. The Act also created the Consejo Nacional de Televisión (CNTV), a special regulatory agency in charge of enforcing the public remit of television broadcasters. Later, CNTV was given constitutional recognition as an autonomous body by the Constitution of 1980, enacted during the military regime of Pinochet. This system remained until 1989, the last year of the regime, when commercial television was introduced in Chile.[31] The introduction of commercial television broadcasting in 1989 expanded the orbit of control of the CNTV to the new channels created.

The CNTV is regulated by law and is composed of 11 members: its head is appointed directly by the President of the Republic who also appoints the other

---

[30] Public advertisement during 2019 and 2020 was around US$70 million. 'Avisaje y publicidad en la Administración del Estado' (*Consejo para la Transparencia*, 2022), www.consejotransparencia.cl/wp-content/uploads/fiscalizacion_foca/2022/04/Resumen_Avisaje-y-Publicidad_21_04_2022.pdf.

[31] L Sierra, 'Hacia la televisón digital en Chile: Historia y transición' (2006) 103 *Estudios Públicos* 118, 118–19.

10 members with the Senate's approval. The CNTV has several functions and wide control over television broadcasting. First, it has the constitutional duty to enforce the *proper functioning* of television, which the law defines as cultivating:

> permanent respect, through their programming, for democracy, peace, pluralism, regional development, the environment, the family, the spiritual and intellectual forma-tion of children and youth, indigenous peoples, human dignity and its expression in equal rights and treatment between men and women, as well as all the fundamental rights recognised in the Constitution and International Treaties ratified by Chile.

Second, the CNTV has administrative functions. It renews, modifies and even-tually terminates television concessions; it promotes, finances or subsidises cultural, educational programmes or those that contribute to strengthening pluralism and diversity, among others. Although CNTV may not interfere with the editorial freedom of broadcasters, it may establish a quota of up to 40 per cent for Chilean productions broadcasters' programming. Third, the CNTV has normative functions, among which the most relevant is to draft the general rules related to the mandatory transmission of public interest campaigns by television broadcasters.

The CNTV also has a legal duty to enforce pluralism in television, a value that was substantially enhanced in 2014 through a law designed to introduce digital television in Chile (DTV Act). Although pluralism was by that time already posi-tioned as one of the values that television channels should observe as part of the proper functioning rule, the DTV Act introduced several amendments. It first explicitly defined pluralism as respect for 'social, cultural, ethnic, political, reli-gious, gender, sexual orientation and gender identity' diversity. The CNTV must work and design procedures to guarantee due respect of pluralism in news, opin-ion and political debate programmes. The Television Act contains a number of other rules designed to strengthen pluralism. Most noticeable is a structural rule, the only one of its kind in the Chilean media system, that prevents any television concessionary from obtaining more than one concession within the same service zone.[32] There are also rules of internal pluralism referred to the composition of the CNTV: not only the head of the regulator (named by the President of the Republic) but also the other 10 members (named by the President with the approval of the Senate) must reflect the diversity of the Chilean people.

The CNTV has observed a number of procedures to verify if television broadcasters have breached the principle of pluralism.[33] In these cases, courts

---

[32] During the process of drafting the Press Act, the Constitutional Court declared unconstitutional a rule that established limits to market share in the printing press (30%) and in the media market in general (20%), together with a prohibition against cross-media ownership. Constitutional Court of Chile, Rol 226-1995.

[33] In order to enforce the rules contained in the Television Act and the ones produced by the CNTV itself, the regulatory body may sanction violators. Sanctions range from reprimands to terminat-ing licences. The most common sanctions are fines. The Act provides the procedural rules by which sanctions may be applied. It is a summary procedure which can be instigated by any individual if the

have been reluctant to support restrictive interpretations of the rule of political pluralism in political programmes or news and have overruled sanctions applied by the CNTV to broadcasters when they fail to provide, according to the regulator, an accurate portrayal of all the views involved. Such is the case of a broadcaster that was fined by the CNTV for breaching its duty to respect political pluralism as a consequence of an interview of a man convicted of the murder of Jaime Guzmán, a former Senator and close ally of Pinochet, because 'public interest issues of a political nature were raised, without due checks and balances between the participants and without the interviewer refuting, contradicting or relativising the interviewee's statements, which constitutes a breach of the duty to respect pluralism'.[34] Overriding the sanction, the Court of Appeals found that it was no breach of pluralism and hence of the correct functioning of television, if an interviewee is not questioned or countered in his opinion by his interviewer. According to the Court, what must be examined is the operation of the broadcaster in a broader sense. As this same broadcaster had also carried out interviews of military personnel accused of human rights violations, the broadcaster offered a wide range of versions of the events involved, according to the Court.[35]

The CNTV followed this *ratio decidendi* in a case in which the Palestinian community complained that TVN, the state broadcaster, failed in its duty of political pluralism because in a programme of discussion about Israeli military attacks in Gaza, no representative of the Palestinian community was invited to the panel. The CNTV concluded that there was no such breach because political pluralism does not depend on the origin or national belonging of discussants but on the content of the programme itself. The principle of pluralism was met, according to CNTV, because those that participated in the debate not only were qualified professionals, they also evenly represented both positions in the debate. Moreover, the CNTV found that a significant number of Palestinians declined invitations to the programme after representatives of the Palestinian community tried to impose names upon TVN. Given this context any sanction against the broadcaster would have meant a violation of its right to editorial freedom, an undue restriction of its right to define the content of its programmes and the people it invites or interviews.

In relation to religious pluralism the Supreme Court overruled a decision by the CNTV, which had been confirmed by the Court of Appeals, to fine a

---

complaint is against breach of the *proper functioning* of broadcasters, or by the CNTV *ex officio* in any other case. Sanctions consisting of reprimands, fines or suspension of broadcasting can be appealed to the Court of Appeals and those terminating licences can be appealed to the Supreme Court of Justice. However, there is no appeal when the CNTV decides for the broadcaster. Most of the cases that end up in the courts are appeals of fines applied to broadcasters by the CNTV to enforce the *proper functioning* of television (arts 33–40bis).

[34] Consejo Nacional de Televisión, 'Acta de la Sesión Ordinaria del Consejo Nacional de Televisión del día lunes 10 de Mayo de 2021', www.cntv.cl/wp-content/uploads/2021/05/ACTA-10-DE-MAYO-2021_APROBADA.pdf.

[35] Court of Appeals of Chile, Rol 296-2021.

broadcaster for an expression used by a comedian in a parody using language that was considered mockery and public scorn of a sacred Catholic symbol. In its decision, the Supreme Court stated that the limits of free speech have to be analysed in the context in which this freedom is exercised. Considering that the expression was only a game of words used by a comedian in a parody broadcast on a late-night programme, it was incapable of affecting religious freedoms. The purpose of the parody was not to make a mockery of or attack Catholicism, but simply to entertain the public. Rejecting the offensiveness of the expression used and wary of a possible chilling effect if a sanction was applied, the Court ruled that the act did not violate religious pluralism. CNTV also permanently enforces the protection of privacy, especially when the identity of minors is harmfully exposed, reputation can be damaged and against excessive display of violence. In 2021 most of the sanctions applied by CNTV were breaches of fundamental rights (40 per cent) followed by breaches to children's rights (31 per cent).[36]

Finally, it is necessary to add that TVN also forms part of the Chilean broadcasting system and is subject to CNTV's control. TVN is regulated by a law passed in 1992, a few years after the return to democracy, which had as its main goal to guarantee the political autonomy of the broadcaster after almost two decades of control by Pinochet's regime. In order to do that the law made TVN as an autonomous, not-for-profit public enterprise and established that it would be managed by a board of seven directors designated by the President in agreement with the Senate. The President of the board is chosen directly by the President of the Republic. A set of provisions were also established to guarantee its economic independence. Basically, TVN is compelled to secure its own revenues in direct competition with other channels. Even if these rules have secured a broadcaster relatively free from undue political influence, TVN's need to assure its own revenues has severely impeded its public remit. In fact, its dependence on advertisement makes it difficult to create content that does not appeal to mass audiences. That is why its programmatic offering is very similar to private broadcasters'. Even though the law was substantially amended in 2018 to improve the public remit of the broadcaster and to address the challenges of technological innovations, no substantial amendments were made to its governing body and to the way it is financed.

5.2. Radio Regulation

In contrast to television, the Constitution says nothing about radio. In its original wording, however, the Constitution provided for the existence of a National Radio *and* Television Council, which was changed by constitutional amendment in 1989 as a result of successful lobbying by the National Association

---

[36] See www.cntv.cl/2022/08/cntv-fiscalizo-y-resolvio-casi-1-500-casos-durante-2021-y-aplico-58-sanciones.

of Radio Broadcasters of Chile (Asociación Nacional de Radiodifusores de Chile).[37] Its regulation is therefore found at the statutory level in the General Telecommunications Act of 1982, which establishes the procedure for granting, renewing or modifying radio broadcasting concessions. Unlike with newspapers, but similarly to television, only legal entities can hold these concessions. This is because the radio spectrum through which radio waves are transported is a national asset for public use (reiterated in the second article of the Telecommunications Law) and therefore the state is empowered to impose obligations on private individuals regarding its use.

Radio stations have considerably fewer restrictions vis-a-vis television broadcasters. The only material standard of operation to which radio broadcasters must conform was introduced by law in 2015. Emulating a previous amendment of the Television Act, which allowed the CNTV to establish a requirement that up to 40 per cent of television programming consist of domestic productions, a daily quota of 20 per cent domestic music was imposed on all radio stations in order to promote local musical production. From a structural point of view, on the other hand, except from the rules contained in the Press Act, there are no rules designed to prevent the concentration of radio concessions in the hands of a few. The only structural rule applicable to radio broadcasting is the one which prevents corporations with foreign capital equal or greater to 10 per cent from obtaining radio broadcasting concessions in Chile, unless the country where the capital comes from guarantees Chilean corporations equivalent rights and duties. This rule was involved in the analysis of one of the most controversial acquisitions in the recent history of radio broadcasting in Chile in which GLR bought the totality of Ibero Americana Radio Chile shares in 2007. After the acquisition, the dominant actor would control more than 37 per cent of market power in advertisement and more than 30 per cent of FM frequencies available.[38] The Supreme Court confirmed the decision of the TDLC approving the acquisition subject to certain conditions. Those conditions were intended to prevent the threats to competition generated by the acquisition in the radio broadcasting market.[39]

The acquisition of Ibero Americana by GLR shows how pluralism in the Chilean media system is measured according to the economic criteria prevalent in

---

[37] J Contesse Singh (coord.), 'Libertad de expresión: acceso a la información y libertad de comunicación' in *Informe anual sobre derechos humanos en Chile 2010* (Santiago, UDP, 2010) 159. See also S Godoy Etcheverry, 'Televisión digital en Chile: ¿es posible más y mejor TV para los chilenos?' (2009) 4(31) *Temas de la Agenda Pública* 8.

[38] The Comptroller General ordered the relevant administrative body to verify if the rule of reciprocity was fulfilled, which it was. See Contraloría General de la República, Dictamen 1861–2008.

[39] Conditions included the duty to consult the TDLC before the renewal of each radio concession in the future as well as the acquisition of any other concession; extending to two years the prohibition of Ibero Americana from participation in the market; and the duty to waive eight regional radio broadcasting concessions to keep competition conditions in those regions necessary to guarantee media and content diversity. See *GLR Chile Ltda. sobre compra de la totalidad de las acciones de Ibero American Radio Chile S.A.*, TDLC Resolución 27 de Julio de 2007.

Competition Law. The Press Act, as the TDLC expressed, has established that the Competition Law is a proper instrument to achieve or preserve a reasonable level of pluralism and information diversity. Accordingly, the Press Act does not require a different analysis of media mergers and acquisitions than the analysis applied to any other merger or acquisition.[40] A similar perspective guided the Constitutional Court when it declared unconstitutional rules contained in the Press Act that established specific limits of tolerable concentration of media outlets.[41] The problem of this perspective is that it is usually built on the assumption that the Competition Law will stimulate the proliferation of media outlets and content diversity will follow. Not only has this assumption not been conclusively proven by the literature[42] but in Chile, this approach has not even contributed to achieving its basic purpose: the diversification of ownership. With a highly concentrated media market, especially in radio and press, Chile shows poor signs of media pluralism and diversity.[43]

A final word must be said about a norm contained in the Telecommunications Act and applicable only to radio broadcasting that establishes criminal and civil liability for those who operate or exploit radio services without authorisation from the administrative body.[44] This norm adds to a wider system of speech crimes, including libel and slander, which has been widely criticised for being disproportionate sanctions which produce a chilling effect on free speech in democratic societies. The special rapporteur for freedom of expression of the Inter-American Commission of Human Rights has recommended their repeal.[45]

6. Press Freedom and Platform Regulation

Social media and video sharing are not subject to special regulation in Chile. As long as they qualify as media for legal purposes, they are subject to the rules contained in the Press Act, a statute drafted in a pre-digital era. In fact, the Act provides a broad legal concept of media that includes all platforms that can disseminate texts, sounds or images intended for the public on a stable and regular basis, whatever the medium or instrument used. This concept was deliberately drafted to

---

[40] ibid cons 8 and 9.
[41] See n 21.
[42] A Harcourt and R Picard, 'Policy, Economic, and Business Challenges of Media Ownership Regulation' (2015) 6(3) *Journal of Media Business Studies* 1; R Horwitz, 'On Media Concentration and the Diversity Question' in P Napoli (ed), *Media Diversity and Localism: Meaning and Metrics* (New York, Routledge, 2006) 9.
[43] See n 23.
[44] General Telecommunications Act of 1982, art 36B.
[45] Comisión Interamericana de Derechos Humanos, Relatoría Especial para la Libertad de Expresión de la Comisión Interamericana de Derechos Humanos, Situación de la Libertad de Expresión en Chile Informe especial de país 2016 (2017), paras 46, 136 and 138. For critiques, see *Mapping Digital Media: Chile, Country Report* (London, OSF, 2012) 124–25; Singh (n 37) 165–66; Charney (n 11) 175–93.

include not only the press, but also television, radio and what at the time the Act was published (2001) was usually referred to as new media. The only requirements for an organisation to be qualified as media for legal purposes are regularity and stability in the production and dissemination of media content and the intention that this is directed to the public. Therefore, the application of this law to digital newspapers is unproblematic. The problem has arisen with intermediary services that do not publish content of their own but of others, like YouTube, Facebook or Twitter. The central question is whether these platforms are liable for speech crimes committed through their platforms or subject to the duties contained in the Act. Among these crimes are libel and slander, hate speech and public affronts against morality.

Some authors have argued that the Press Act cannot be applied to internet intermediary services. The argument is that this would be tantamount to holding bookstores liable for selling books containing libellous material, since these services are mere providers of physical infrastructure to access the network or mere distributors.[46] Others argue that in the case of intermediary services there is no link of subordination and/or dependence with their users. In contrast, this relationship exists between the media and their editors and contributors, which make them liable for the acts of third parties under the terms of the law.[47]

Courts have differed over whether internet intermediaries should fall within the concept of media for legal purposes. Sometimes they have confirmed that social media such as Facebook, Twitter and YouTube are *media* in terms of the Press Act.[48] Consequently, publications made on these platforms are subject to the limits and requirements of the Act. However, courts have not made social media liable for publications on their platforms infringing norms contained in the Act but only individuals that have published on them. A different approach has been taken towards search engines. Google, for example, has not been considered *media* in the terms of the Press Act, because courts have found that search engines are not responsible for the content published on the sites they provide to users.[49] In contrast, websites that comply with the requirements of regularity and stability in their publications qualify as media for the purpose of the Act.[50]

The legal uncertainty about the status of internet intermediaries has significant consequences for freedom of expression. Indeed, if the courts' characterisation of social networks as media is taken to extremes, then social networks would have to be held responsible for all content uploaded on their platforms whenever

---

[46] C Maturana, 'Responsabilidad de los proveedores de acceso y contenido en Internet' (2002) 1 *Revista Chilena de Derecho Informático* 24.

[47] M Hercovich, 'Responsabilidad de los ISP por contenidos ilícitos o infractores de terceros' (2013) 2 *Revista Chilena de Derecho y Tecnología* 132–33.

[48] Court of Appeals (Punta Arenas), Rol 882-2015; Supreme Court, Rol 450-2018; Court of Appeals (Concepción), Rol 8556-2021.

[49] Court of Appeals (Concepción), Rol 11611-2020.

[50] Court of Appeals (Concepción), Rol 5315-2020.

they commit some offence listed in the Press Act. Such a conclusion would be highly problematic, especially because it is likely to promote collateral censorship. Collateral censorship is not the product of direct state action against those who seek to exercise their freedom of expression but the consequence of rules that make internet intermediaries liable (civilly or criminally) when illegal content circulates or is published through their sites, platforms or services.[51] As a matter of fact, when rules exist that hold intermediary services liable for infringing content uploaded by third parties, they tend to censor and block more content than necessary to exempt themselves from liability. Thus, collateral censorship not only prevents the publication of undesirable content but also, by extension, content that can contribute to public discussion.[52] Moreover, this conclusion is problematic, since large content intermediaries such as Facebook and Twitter are based in the United States (US) and are subject to its jurisdiction.[53]

On the other hand, if one concludes that social networks should enjoy full immunity, the consequences also remain problematic from a freedom-of-expression perspective. In effect, full immunity for intermediaries means handing over to large companies full control over the delimitation of the exercise of freedom of expression, and thus implicitly accepting the application of the US model, where these companies are based.[54] Thus, the governance systems of the large platforms with their regulatory frameworks, control bodies, content moderation systems and cultural, political and legal frameworks would be applied in Chile to define the way in which freedom of expression is exercised in the digital sphere. The constitutional consequences of such an interpretation require a reconstruction of the Chilean regulatory framework in order to assess appropriate institutional responses to this problem.

7. Conclusions

Chilean media regulation is the combination of two regulatory frameworks that do not always fit well together. On the one hand, the press is subject to strong limits based on the importance that the system attributes to other rights, such as reputation. Against insistent recommendations from international bodies to decriminalise libel and slander, there has been no serious effort to do so, and it seems that this will not change any time soon. Additionally, even if the system

---

[51] M Meyerson, 'Authors, Editors, and Uncommon Carriers: Identifying the "Speaker" Within the New Media' (1999) 71 *Notre Dame Law Review* 116.
[52] F Wu, 'Collateral Censorship and the Limits of Intermediary Immunity' (2011) 87 *Notre Dame Law Review* 297.
[53] R Jijena, 'Contenidos y censura en Internet. Críticas al proyecto de ley de Chile de agosto de 1999' *Actas del 7º Congreso Iberoamericano de Derecho e Informática* (Lima, Universidad de Lima, 2000) 3.
[54] See K Klonick, 'The New Governors: The People, Rules and Processes Governing Online Speech' (2018) 131 *Harvard Law Review* 1598.

provides broader defences to the media (*vis-a-vis* individual speakers) against libel, defences are still limited to justification and no public interest defence has been incorporated. These are institutional factors that contribute to creating a chilling effect that distorts the democratic process, especially when it affects political speech. In contrast to conventional media, platforms are not easily coached into the system. There are no special rules designed to make platforms responsible for illegal content circulating on them. In practice, platforms enjoy full immunity, following the American model. Therefore, two parallel systems govern media freedom in Chile in relation to the limits of speech.

In contrast to limits, structural regulation of the media in Chile is highly liberalised. Media pluralism and diversity is a basic legal principle which is framed in strict liberal terms of non-interference. The system works under the assumption that media markets, if left on their own, will expand media ownership and promote content diversity. The fact is that Chile has a highly concentrated media market with weak signs of content diversity across its different platforms. This is a contentious issue. Historically, structural media regulation has been the subject of intense political confrontation, dividing those who defend a system of non-state interference, from those who believe that pluralism and diversity requires legal intervention. This makes structural regulation highly unstable. Especially now that a constitutional process is on its way, it is likely that this issue will re-emerge in the discussion. The outcome of that discussion could have profound implications on media regulation in Chile in the coming years.

11

The US Press: A Legal Framework of Complexity, Contradiction and Uncertainty*

LILI LEVI

1. Introduction

Despite the breadth of freedom of speech protection under the Constitution of the United States of America (US), the specific prohibition on laws abridging freedom of the press in the Press Clause of the First Amendment, and the assumption of US press exceptionalism in public discourse, the reality of American press protection has recently been one of complexity, contradiction and uncertainty. The American press today is fragile and under attack from all sides. Conservatives lambast the mainstream institutional press as ideologically liberal and intent on silencing conservative voices. Progressives criticise the press for being supine to power, blinded by 'bothsideism' and complicit in the spread of disinformation harmful to democracy. Courts retrench from press favouritism, calling for greater balance between speech and other interests. Economically, traditional journalism has been in free-fall for some time. The hollowing out of local and regional media has left significant news deserts.[1] As for public perception, the public's trust in the press has reached historic lows,[2] doubtless reinforced by former President Trump's characterisation of the press as 'the enemy of the American people'.[3]

---

* The American spelling and footnote citations in this chapter have been edited to conform to British style.

[1] PM Abernathy and T Franklin, 'The State of Local News 2022: Expanding News Deserts, Growing Gaps, Emerging Models' (*Local News Initiative*, 2022), https://localnewsinitiative.northwestern.edu/research/state-of-local-news/report/ (reporting on increased number of communities with diminished access to local and regional news and information).

[2] See, eg, M Brenan, 'Americans' Trust in Media Dips to Second Lowest on Record' (*Gallup*, 7 October 2021), https://news.gallup.com/poll/355526/americans-trust-media-dips-second-lowest-record.aspx.

[3] See, eg, MM Grynbaum, 'Trump Calls the News Media the "Enemy of the American People"' *The New York Times* (17 February 2017), www.nytimes.com/2017/02/17/business/trump-calls-the-news-media-the-enemy-of-the-people.html.

Press diminishment is quite convenient for those who wish to avoid oversight and accountability. Authoritarianism, corruption, illegality and even mere error thrive in obscurity. The public interest requires a courageous press willing and able to serve as the proverbial watchdog over government and the powerful.

Thus, I write this chapter to dissent from enthusiastic criticisms of the press and calls for its regulation. Perhaps counter-intuitively, I argue that existing constitutional protections under American law should be retained and even increased for the press, particularly with respect to newsgathering, in order to empower journalism in the service of the public interest. I focus on the Supreme Court's apparent loss of faith in the press, and the ongoing attempts to eliminate or reduce constitutional protections for press defendants in defamation cases, as two of the critical threats to press function today. I claim that the current call for regulation of social media – even if successful – should not be deemed to diminish the need for press protections. Instead of focusing on press control to improve the public sphere, therefore, I suggest a pivot in our attention – to improving the legal climate for accountability journalism and designing realistic and evidence-based ways to improve public perception of the American press's democratic functions.

This is not to deny press errors or partisanship, to assert that any regulation in any way affecting the press is by definition anti-democratic, undesirable and unconstitutional, or to engage in a comparative exercise evaluating US press law relative to other countries. It is, rather, to redirect the discussion from the harms and failures of the press to the legal support it needs in order to play its socio-legal roles most effectively. In this time of technological, social and political change, and in light of the growing worldwide threat of authoritarian leadership, it is particularly necessary to shore up the press in order to obtain the benefits of its democracy-protecting capabilities.

2. The Press and Its Protections under US Law[4]

American law contains a mosaic of constitutional protections, federal statutes and state law provisions that all affect the legal status of the press. This combination of legal rules has provided American news organisations and journalists with significant legal protection, particularly with respect to publication.[5] There has also been a non-legal tradition of practices reinforcing official press protections. Historically, this tradition has reflected a mutual dependence between the institutional press and government officials and politicians desiring coverage, a history of public and judicial goodwill, a set of political and access norms largely adhered to by government voluntarily, and at least public rhetoric signaling government appreciation

---

[4] I use the terms 'press', 'news organisations' and 'media' interchangeably in this chapter, as American law tends to do.

[5] A parallel regulatory regime applicable to broadcasting, described in section 3, is increasingly irrelevant to the current legal landscape affecting the press.

of the press's democratic role.[6] As discussed below, however, new stresses have already started creating doctrinal instability in this medley of protections, posing potentially grave threats to the press's legal status.

2.1. Theoretical Foundations of Constitutional Protection

The First Amendment[7] of the US Constitution specifically mentions both the freedoms of speech and press. The constitutional free speech guarantee has been read expansively at least since the latter part of the twentieth century,[8] while the Press Clause has received far less attention. Still, although no Supreme Court decision in a press case has rested solely on the Press Clause,[9] the Court's expansive readings of the First Amendment's Speech Clause for all speakers have either specifically included the press under their protective umbrella or simply failed to make any distinctions among speakers.

Virtually all First Amendment scholars agree that there is no single unifying theory of the First Amendment, and they emphasise different strands in First Amendment jurisprudence and theory.[10] It is clear, though, that political speech, broadly conceived, is always most extensively protected. With respect to the protection of the press and its published output, the most common theoretical justifications have focused on the role of the press as the Fourth Estate, monitoring government and serving to check the abuse of official power,[11] and its role as

---

[6] See, eg, R Andersen Jones and SR West, 'The Fragility of the Free American Press' (2017) 112 *Northwestern University Law Review* 567.

[7] The First Amendment of the US Constitution provides, inter alia, that 'Congress shall make no law ... abridging the freedom of speech, or of the press.' Although, in its terms, the First Amendment specifically protects speech and press against abridgement by Congress, the Supreme Court made clear that these freedoms 'are among the fundamental personal rights and "liberties" protected by the due process clause of the Fourteenth Amendment from impairment by the States'. *Gitlow v New York*, 268 US 652, 666 (1925). The First Amendment restrains both the federal and state governments, but it does not protect speakers against private parties.

[8] See, eg, DM Rabban, 'The Emergence of Modern First Amendment Doctrine' (1983) 50 *University of Chicago Law Review* 1205 (describing the history).

[9] See, eg, D Anderson, 'The Origins of the Press Clause' (1983) 30 *UCLA Law Review* 455.

[10] Some prominent scholars have identified at least three purposes for the First Amendment in the Court's constitutional cases: (1) protection of the marketplace of ideas in order to advance knowledge and discover truth; (2) protection of expression in order to promote human autonomy and self-expression; and (3) protection of communication in order to advance democracy and self-government. See, eg, RC Post, *Democracy, Expertise, and Academic Freedom: A First Amendment Jurisprudence for the Modern State* (London, Yale University Press, 2012) 6. Others have added the role of the press as the Fourth Estate, eg, VA Blasi, 'The Pathological Perspective and the First Amendment' (1985) 85 *Columbia Law Review* 449; VA Blasi, 'The Checking Value in First Amendment Theory' (1977) 2 *American Bar Foundation Research Journal* 521; P Stewart, 'Or of the Press' (1975) 26 *Hastings Law Journal* 631, 634 ('The primary purpose of the constitutional guarantee of a free press was ... to create a fourth institution outside the Government as an additional check on the three official branches').

[11] See, eg, Blasi, 'Checking Value' (n 10); Blasi, 'Pathological Perspective' (n 10); CE Baker, 'The Independent Significance of the Press Clause Under Existing Law' (2007) 35 *Hofstra Law Review* 955 (distinguishing between Speech Clause protection of individual expressive autonomy and Press Clause protection of the press's instrumental democratic role).

educator (and sometimes proxy or agent) of the public, disseminating informa-tion necessary for a self-governing citizenry and serving as a critical intermediary in the operation of the First Amendment's commitment to a 'free marketplace of ideas'.[12] The Supreme Court clearly communicated in its landmark cases during the Golden Age of the press – from the 1960s to the 1980s – that the press plays a unique and central role in American democracy.[13]

2.2. A Doctrinal Overview of Constitutional Protections

First Amendment freedom of speech jurisprudence has been described as an 'endless maze'[14] – complex, intricate and sometimes confounding.[15] *In toto*, however, the First Amendment free speech jurisprudence has served as a shield to protect against regulation of content and journalistic output. First Amendment jurisprudence has defined speech broadly, to include even symbolic expression and expressive conduct. The Roberts Court has interpreted the Free Speech Clause particularly expansively and in a libertarian vein, focused principally on protect-ing the autonomy rights of the speaker.[16] Although some categories of speech have been treated exceptionally – so that attempts to regulate them could proceed under significantly less demanding standards of constitutional review[17] – the traditional focus of the press on matters of public interest and concern has placed its work at the centre of constitutional protection of expression. Government restrictions on

---

[12] See, eg, R Andersen Jones and L Grow Sun, 'Freedom of the Press in Post-Truthism America' (2020) 98 *Washington University Law Review* 419 (addressing the press's role in the marketplace of ideas); SR West, 'The Stealth Press Clause' (2014) 48 *Georgia Law Review* 729 (describing the 'unique constitutional functions' of the press as gathering and disseminating news to the public and checking government and the powerful).

[13] See, eg, *Leathers v Medlock* 499 US 439, 447 (1991) ('The press plays a unique role as a check on government abuse'); *The New York Times Co v the United States* 403 US 713, 717 (1971) (Black J, concurring; stating that the press plays an 'essential role in our democracy'); *Mills v Alabama* 384 US 214, 219 (1966) ('The Constitution specifically selected the press, which includes not only newspapers, books and magazines, but also humble leaflets and circulars, to play an important role in the discussion of public affairs'). With such explicit encomia, the Justices recognised the press's constitutional and socio-political importance even when they grounded substantive protections on the Speech Clause or broad references to the First Amendment generally, rather than explicitly on the Press Clause.

[14] SH Shiffrin, *The First Amendment, Democracy and Romance* (Cambridge, Harvard University Press, 1990) 9.

[15] Here, I focus only on constitutional protections of the press rather than providing an overview of all of First Amendment doctrine. Even so, the overview provided must necessarily skim the surface and remain incomplete.

[16] See, eg, *United States v Alvarez* 567 US 709 (2012) (contemplating First Amendment protec-tion even for lies, at least so long as they did not cause extensive harm). By and large, the categorical approach to the protection of speech has discouraged the Supreme Court from engaging in balancing of speaker and hearer interests.

[17] Examples include obscenity, child pornography, fighting words and true threats. Attempts to regu-late commercial advertisements and speech that incites imminent lawless action are also subjected to less searching constitutional review. See generally, VL Killlion, 'The First Amendment: Categories of Speech' (Congressional Research Service, 16 January 2019), https://sgp.fas.org/crs/misc/IF11072.pdf.

expression due to its content – and particularly its viewpoint[18] – as well as over-broad or vague laws that burden and chill speech are virtually always subjected to the most stringent constitutional scrutiny.[19]

The press benefits from the presumptive unconstitutionality of prior restraints on publication, including licensing for print media.[20] Editors' decisions about the content they deemed newsworthy and appropriate to print also receive significant deference from the Court under the First Amendment. In *Miami Herald v Tornillo*,[21] for example, the Court rejected a state statute which granted a right of reply to any political candidates whose character or official record had been criticised or whose record had been attacked in a newspaper. In holding the statute unconstitutional, the Court focused on editorial freedom, finding that the statute 'fails to clear the barriers of the First Amendment because of its intrusion into the function of editors'.[22] Although the Court has not held that 'truthful publication is automatically constitutionally protected',[23] it has made clear that attempts to prosecute the press for such publications will be subjected to stringent constitutional scrutiny.[24]

Speakers, including the press, also receive constitutional protection if they publish defamatory statements.[25] In a case of great significance for the press, the Supreme Court effectively 'constitutionalised' state defamation law in *New York Times v Sullivan*[26] and its progeny. Prior to *Sullivan*, defamation was considered solely a matter of state law. Courts assumed that the Constitution would not protect defamatory publications, and state laws did not require plaintiffs in defamation

---

[18] See, eg, *Reed v Town of Gilbert* 135 S. Ct. 2218 (2015).

[19] Under the judicial review standard of strict scrutiny (which is applied to regulation of the viewpoint of expression and virtually always to regulations affecting the content of speech), the government has the burden of proving that its regulation is narrowly tailored to address a compelling governmental interest. Narrow tailoring is to be truly narrow, with the regulation being the least restrictive means to achieve the identified compelling government interest. Strict scrutiny has been said to be virtually always 'fatal in fact'. G Gunther, 'The Supreme Court, 1971 Term-Foreword: In Search of Evolving Doctrine on a Changing Court: A Model for a Newer Equal Protection' (1972) 86(1) *Harvard Law Review* 8 (coining the phrase).

[20] *Near v Minnesota* 283 US 697 (1931) (holding that prior restraints on publication are presumptively unconstitutional); *New York Times* (n 13) 714 (rejecting government attempts to prohibit publication of excerpts from the Pentagon Papers). Notably, the scope of the presumption to include judicial injunctions in addition to administrative preclearance systems.

[21] *Miami Herald Publishing Co v Tornillo* 418 US 241 (1974).

[22] ibid 258 ('A newspaper is more than a passive receptacle or conduit for news, comment, and advertising').

[23] *Florida Star v B.J.F.* 491 US 524, 541 (1989).

[24] See, eg, *Landmark Communications, Inc v Virginia* 435 US 829 (1978); *Smith v Daily Mail Pub Co* 443 US 97 (1979); *Oklahoma Publishing Co v District Court* 430 US 308 (1977).

[25] In order to avoid end-runs around the constitutional privilege associated with defamation law, the Court has also held that plaintiffs prove actual malice even in cases seeking recovery for intentional infliction of emotional distress. See, eg, *Hustler Magazine, Inc v Falwell* 485 US 46, 46–47 (1988); *Time, Inc v Hill* 385 US 374, 390 (1967). Similarly, in a line of cases dealing with the tort law of privacy, the Court took a press-protective reading of the relationship between privacy law and the First Amendment protections for press reporting. See *Cox Broadcasting Corp v Cohn* 420 US 469 (1975); *Florida Star* (n 23) 525.

[26] *The New York Times Co v Sullivan* 376 US 254, 254 (1964).

cases to show that defendants had published the defamatory statements at issue with any form of fault. In *Sullivan*, the Court was faced with a strategic attempt by Southern public officials to use defamation law as a club to curb nationwide coverage of the civil rights struggle in the 1960s.[27] Asserting 'a profound national commitment to the principle that debate on public issues should be uninhibited, robust, and wide-open',[28] the Court held that a public official could not recover damages for defamatory statements about his official conduct without proving actual malice.[29] Rather than an inquiry into ill-will, actual malice requires the plaintiff to prove, with convincing clarity, that the defendant published the defamatory falsehood about him or her 'with knowledge that it was false or with reckless disregard of whether it was false or not'.[30]

In subsequent cases, the Court extended the actual malice standard to defamation actions by public figures.[31] In *Gertz v Robert Welch*,[32] the Court permitted states to adopt their own standards of liability, including negligence but short of strict liability, for defamatory statements of public concern about private figures. Even in those circumstances, though, if a plaintiff wished to recover presumed or punitive damages, they would have to satisfy the requirement of actual malice.[33] Less constitutional protection is provided to defamatory statements about matters of private concern concerning private figures.[34]

---

[27] A Lewis, *Make No Law: The* Sullivan *Case and the First Amendment* (New York, Random House, 1991); KL Hall and MI Urofsky, *New York Times v Sullivan: Civil Rights, Libel Law, and the Free Press* (Lawrence, University Press of Kansas, 2011). *Sullivan* concerned trivial inaccuracies in an editorial advertisement calling for support of Dr Martin Luther King and the growing civil rights movement. Applying state law, the Alabama courts imposed a defamation verdict of US$500,000 on the newspaper. The plaintiff, who had not even been specifically named in the advertisement and whose reputation the ad likely burnished rather than tarnished in much of his community, was making a political point attempting to shut down out-of-state criticism of Southern violence against African Americans attempting to exercise their civil rights. This was only one case in a concerted effort to silence the press with respect to the civil rights struggle. By the time *Sullivan* was decided, *The New York Times* and other press outlets were facing an existence-challenging US$300 million in potential liability in defamation actions brought by Southern officials.

[28] *Sullivan* (n 26) 270.

[29] ibid 279–80.

[30] ibid 280.

[31] The Court extended the actual malice requirement to public figures in the companion cases of *Curtis Publishing Co v Butts* 388 US 130 (1967) (concerning a prominent football coach) and *Associated Press v Walker* 388 US 130 (1967) (concerning a retired US army general who had become active in anti-desegregation politics). The 'public figure' category has been deemed to include both general purpose public figures (such as those considered 'household names') and limited purpose (and even involuntary) public figures. A limited purpose public figure has been defined as a person who 'voluntarily injects himself or is drawn into a particular public controversy and thereby becomes a public figure for a limited range of issues', *Gertz v Robert Welch, Inc* 418 US 323, 361 (1974).

[32] *Gertz* (n 31).

[33] ibid 349.

[34] See *Dun & Bradstreet, Inc v Greenmoss Builders, Inc* 472 US 749 (1985) (plurality holding that a private figure plaintiff could recover presumed or punitive damages for publication of a defamatory statement by a non-media entity about a matter of private concern without having to prove actual malice). In addition to the uncertainty created by the range of the Justices' rationales (see, L Levine and S Wermiel, 'The Landmark Opinion That Wasn't: A First Amendment Play in Five Acts' (2013) 88(1) *Washington Law Review* 100), *Dun & Bradstreet*'s holding with respect to actual malice is not typically

Despite the significant constitutional protections the press has enjoyed under the Speech Clause, scholars have urged that limiting the press's protections under the First Amendment to the freedom of speech unduly limits the press's ability to fulfil its constitutional purpose fully. At least since Supreme Court Justice Potter Stewart argued for a structural interpretation of the Press Clause under which the institutional press would receive constitutional protection,[35] advocates have argued that the Press Clause should be rescued from its role as mere First Amendment surplusage, and that courts should see in the Press Clause broader protections for press functions than would otherwise be covered by the First Amendment's Speech Clause guarantee.[36]

Nevertheless, the Supreme Court has expressed doubt that the press should receive any constitutional privileges not also granted to all speakers.[37] The original meaning of the Press Clause – namely the Framers' understanding – is uncertain.[38] At the same time, the relevance of the views of the constitutional Framers to the interpretation of constitutional provisions today is a topic of great controversy, splitting originalists from more evolutionary interpreters of constitutional meaning. And the Supreme Court's most explicit statements dismissing a robust interpretation of the Press Clause themselves have a thin grounding in precedent.[39]

Ultimately – and especially given differences of scholarly opinion on the question – one might ask why the constitutional basis of press protection under the Press Clause should matter. At a minimum, one answer is based on the need to protect newsgathering. Grounding substantive press protections on the Speech rather than the Press Clause has meant that the most extensive protections have been limited to the press as speaker and publisher, rather than including its work in gathering news.

---

seen as relevant to news media in light of the presumption that press reporting typically relates to matters of public concern.

[35] Stewart (n 10).

[36] See, eg, SR West, 'Favoring the Press' (2018) 106 *California Law Review* 91; SR West, 'The "Press", Then and Now' (2016) 77 *Ohio State Law Journal* 49; SR West, 'Press Exceptionalism' (2014) 127 *Harvard Law Review* 2434; SR West, 'Awakening the Press Clause' (2012) *BYU Law Review* 1953.

[37] *Citizens United v FEC* 558 US 310, 352 (2010) ('We have consistently rejected the proposition that the institutional press has any constitutional privilege beyond that of other speakers', quoting *Austin v Michigan Chamber of Commerce* 494 US 652, 691 (1990) (Scalia J, dissenting).

[38] Scholars debate whether the Press Clause protects merely the right to publish using mass technology (see, eg, E Volokh, 'Freedom for the Press as an Industry, or for the Press as a Technology, From the Framing to Today' (2021) 160 *University of Pennsylvania Law Review* 459, 463), or the press as an institution (see, eg, Stewart (n 10), or the press function (see, eg, West, 'The "Press"' (n 36); West, 'Press Exceptionalism' (n 36); West, 'Favoring the Press' (n 36)). Even if the press largely meant 'printing press' rather than journalism in the early Republic, the press was still seen as a key element of democracy for the drafters of the Constitution. Indeed, protection of press freedom may have had greater salience at the time of the founding than the individual right to speak. See SR West, 'The Majoritarian Press Clause' (2020) *University of Chicago Legal Forum* 311; Anderson (n 9); R Andersen Jones, 'Press Speakers and the First Amendment Rights of Listeners' (2019) 90 *University of Colorado Law Review* 499.

[39] See, eg, S Gillers, *Journalism Under Fire* (New York, Columbia University Press, 2018) 23–32.

2.3. Distinct Constitutional Treatment of Newsgathering

The Supreme Court has interpreted the Constitution's protections for newsgathering as standing on much more uncertain and limited footing than issues relating to publication. First, the Court has frequently stated that the press is not immune from laws of general application.[40] If those laws do not target or single out the press *qua* press, the 'First Amendment does not require [their] enforcement against the press be subject to stricter scrutiny than would be applied to [their] enforcement against others'.[41]

Second, the Court's attitude toward newsgathering has been ambivalent. The Court's statement in *Branzburg v Hayes* that 'news gathering is not without its First Amendment protections' and its recognition that 'without some protection for seeking out the news, freedom of the press could be eviscerated',[42] constitute parsimonious recognition of the need for newsgathering protection. Although many appellate courts interpreted the Supreme Court's decision in *Branzburg v Hayes* as implicitly recognising a qualified constitutional reporter's privilege,[43] some rejected that reading[44] and the Supreme Court has never clarified the question. Journalists have gone to jail rather than revealing the identities of their sources.[45]

With respect to constitutional rights of access to government property, information, meetings or processes, the Supreme Court has recognised a constitutional right for the press and the public to access criminal trials.[46] Even when courts have recognised a public right of access to civil proceedings, practices such as secret settlements, protective orders that seal documents, and limits to the ability to examine exhibits have all served as impediments to reporting. Journalists have also been subject to subpoenas and government searches and seizures under warrant.[47]

---

[40] See, eg, *Cohen v Cowles Media* 501 US 663 (1991).

[41] ibid 664.

[42] *Branzburg v Hayes* 408 US 665, 681, 707 (1972). *Branzburg*, which consolidated three cases in which reporters sought First Amendment protection from grand jury subpoenas requiring them to identify confidential sources and testify as to criminal activities they may have witnessed, produced a fractured decision rejecting a privilege on its facts.

[43] See, eg, *Zerilli v Smith* 656 F.2d 705 (D.C. Cir. 1981). Many courts read the totality of the opinions in *Branzburg*, including Justice Powell's enigmatic concurring opinion, as together recognising a qualified constitutional reporter's privilege against compelled disclosure of confidential sources.

[44] See, eg, *McKevitt v Pallasch* 339 F.3d 530 (7th Cir. 2003); *United States Department of Education v National Collegiate Athletic Association* 481 F.3d 936 (7th Cir. 2007).

[45] For example, reporter Judith Miller spent 85 days in jail before she agreed to testify. See, eg, A Liptak, 'Reporter Jailed After Refusing to Reveal Source' *The New York Times* (7 July 2005), www.nytimes.com/2005/07/07/politics/reporter-jailed-after-refusing-to-name-source.html.

[46] *Richmond Newspapers, Inc v Virginia* 448 US 555, 576 (1980) (plurality opinion; access rights to criminal trials). The press has no special constitutional rights to access prisons or government documents. *Houchins v KQED, Inc* 438 US 1, 15, 16 (1978); *Saxbe v Washington Post Co* 417 US 843 (1974). Despite the Supreme Court's failure to address the matter, however, most state and federal courts have asserted a First Amendment right of the public to attend civil trials.

[47] See, eg, *Zurcher v The Stanford Daily* 436 US 547, 565 (1978), reh'g denied, 439 US 885 (1978). See also GP Leslie (ed), 'First Amendment Handbook' (*Reporters Committee for Freedom of the Press*,

In recent years, the government has even threatened reporters with prosecution under the Espionage Act for revealing leaked information or protecting whistleblower sources.[48] As for publication of illegally obtained materials, although the Supreme Court refused to enjoin the publication of excerpts of the 'Pentagon Papers' in *The New York Times Co v the United States*,[49] scholars have shown that the mythology of the case is in fact broader than the Court's actual holding.[50] And although the Court in *Bartinicki v Vopper*[51] held that a news organisation would not be deemed liable for its broadcast of an electronic communication illegally intercepted by a third party, it was constitutionally significant that the publisher played no part in the illegal interception, that the defendant's access to the information was obtained lawfully, and that the conversations dealt with a matter of public concern.

The bottom line on the constitutional front is that while the press benefits from very significant protections under the First Amendment, such protections are far from absolute and do not guarantee the press exceptional constitutional rights beyond those accorded to all speakers.

2.4. Complexity Added by State Law and Federal Statutes

In addition to federal constitutional law, both state and federal statutes impact news organisations and their journalistic functions. Journalists have benefited from a variety of statutory protections often extending beyond federal constitutional protections, albeit to varying degrees. For example, the large majority of states have reporter's privilege statutes which, in different ways and to varying degrees, protect reporters from being compelled to disclose the identities of their sources or confidential materials.[52] As a result of the significant differences among such reporter's privilege protections, however, there have been several attempts to lobby Congress to adopt a federal reporter's privilege statute.[53] None

---

2022), www.rcfp.org/resources/first-amendment-handbook/#confidential-sources-and-information. Journalists have also been subjected to warrantless searches of their electronic devices at US borders, surveillance of their activities, and arrests by law enforcement, particularly in covering political protests.

[48] See, eg, H Kitrosser and D Schulz, 'A House Built on Sand: The Constitutional Infirmity of Espionage Act Prosecutions for Leaking to the Press' (2021) 19 *First Amendment Law Review* 153, 178. See generally LC Bollinger and GR Stone, 'Opening Statement' in LC Bollinger and GR Stone (eds), *National Security, Leaks and Freedom of the Press: The Pentagon Papers Fifty Years On* (Oxford, Oxford University Press, 2021).

[49] *New York Times* (n 13).

[50] See, eg, Bollinger and Stone (n 48).

[51] *Bartnicki v Vopper* 532 US 514 (2001).

[52] See 'Reporter's Privilege Compendium' (*Reporters Committee for Freedom of the Press*), www.rcfp.org/reporters-privilege/ (comparing states' approaches to reporter's privilege); Leslie (n 47).

[53] Recently, eg, the House of Representatives unanimously passed H.R. 4330, the Protect Reporters from Exploitative State Spying (PRESS) Act, which would create a national privilege to protect reporters

of those attempts has yet borne fruit, largely because of concerns about how to define 'journalist' or 'reporter' for purposes of the statute's application. Because there is no uniform federal statute, source-protection varies in its robustness and breadth among the states.[54]

With respect to access to documents, several statutes on the federal level, including the Freedom of Information Act,[55] provide documentary access processes. However, the Freedom of Information Act system has been subject to stringent criticism, particularly with respect to press access.[56] Recent Supreme Court precedent approving limits to certain types of access is likely to make access harder for journalists seeking certain kinds of private corporate information.[57] As for state laws, while many states have enacted some variety of 'sunshine law' (freedom of information and open meeting laws), the jurisdictional variation and unpredictability problems that plague the reporter's privilege context exist with respect to documentary access for the press as well.

In terms of protecting the press against censorship-seeking litigation, 32 states and the District of Columbia have adopted statutes curtailing 'strategic lawsuits against public participation', commonly referred to as anti-SLAPP legislation.[58] Anti-SLAPP laws are designed to deter meritless lawsuits brought ostensibly over the defendants' exercise of their First Amendment rights but in fact to deter protected speech.[59] The most protective, such as legislation enacted by New York, provide for early dismissal of defamation suits unless the plaintiff can meet the actual malice standard.[60] There is a significant amount of jurisdictional

---

from having to reveal protected information including confidential sources and documents and information collected in the course of engaging in journalism, www.congress.gov/bill/117th-congress/house-bill/4330.

[54] In Wyoming and Hawaii, eg, there is no shield law. In seven states (Idaho, Iowa, Virginia, Mississippi, Missouri Utah and Virginia), there is no shield law, but courts recognise a qualified privilege. Twenty states, including Texas and Florida, have qualified shield laws, while 17 have adopted the strongest level of protection against the obligation to reveal sources, see Reporter's Privilege Compendium (n 52).

[55] Freedom of Information Act, 5 USC § 552. See also Federal Advisory Committee Act, 5 USC. App., and Government in the Sunshine Act, 94 PL 409.

[56] MB Kwoka, *Saving the Freedom of Information Act* (Cambridge, Cambridge University Press, 2021).

[57] See, eg, Food *Marketing Institute v Argus Leader Media* 139 S. Ct. 2356 (2019).

[58] George Pring and Penelope Canan described and criticised 'strategic lawsuits against public participation', dubbing them SLAPP suits. G Pring and P Canan, *SLAPPS: Getting Sued for Speaking Out* (Philadelphia, Temple University Press, 1996). See also, A Vining and S Matthews, 'Overview of Anti-SLAPP Laws' (*Reporters Committee for Freedom of the Press*), www.rcfp.org/introduction-anti-slapp-guide (linking to various states' anti-SLAPP statutes).

[59] They purport to do so in a variety of ways. Typically, they allow defendants to stay discovery once an anti-SLAPP motion has been filed and to secure rapid dismissal prior to discovery. Some offer winning defendants attorney's fees and costs. Some allow defendants immediate interlocutory appeals from a trial court's denial of an anti-SLAPP motion.

[60] New York expanded its anti-SLAPP law in 2020. N.Y. Civ. Rights § 70-a (McKinney). Now, plaintiffs may not recover damages in covered cases unless they show 'by clear and convincing evidence' that

variation among these statutory provisions, but reports indicate that most are broad enough to encompass suits brought against the press over critical report-ing. Still, a few anti-SLAPP statutes have been found unconstitutional under their states' constitutions on the ground that they interfere with trial by jury,[61] and there is disagreement among the federal circuits as to whether state anti-SLAPP statutes apply in federal court.[62] Although a bill proposing a federal anti-SLAPP law is currently pending in Congress,[63] no prior attempts have been successful thus far.

By contrast to statutory and common law protections that cover the press function, there are also numerous state and federal laws that constrain journal-istic newsgathering activity. Obvious examples include privacy laws (covering claims over intrusion, publication of private facts, or false light), misappropria-tion, infliction of emotional distress, interference with contractual relations, negligence, fraud, product disparagement laws, a variety of tort claims includ-ing tortious as well as criminal trespass, harassment, and the right of publicity. Journalists who do not follow law enforcement orders while at places such as crime scenes and demonstrations can be arrested and charged with, inter alia, interference or disorderly conduct.[64] With respect to undercover newsgathering, some courts have used fiduciary duty analysis to impose liability on news organi-sations whose reporters have engaged in undercover newsgathering by posing as employees of companies.[65] In addition, some state as well as federal eavesdrop-ping and surreptitious recording statutes limit reporters' ability to record others without obtaining consent.[66] Thirteen states prohibit the unauthorised placement or use of hidden cameras in private places, and doing so is a criminal act in a few states.[67]

---

the defendant made the statement knowing it was false or 'with reckless disregard' as to whether it was false, codifying the *New York Times Co v Sullivan* actual malice standard in state law. N.Y. Civ. Rights Law § 70-a(2) (McKinney).

[61] *Davis v Cox* 351 P. 3d 862 (Wash. 2015); *Leiendecker v Asian Women United of Minnesota* 895 N.W.2d 623, 637, 638 (Minn. 2017). The Washington legislature redrafted the state's anti-SLAPP law to address the Washington Supreme Court's concerns in *Davis v Cox*. See Vining and Matthews (n 58).

[62] Vining and Matthews (n 58).

[63] See, eg, M Masnick, 'Finally, Some Good News: Federal Anti-SLAPP Law Introduced' (*techdirt*, 19 September 2022), www.techdirt.com/2022/09/19/finally-some-good-news-federal-anti-slapp-law-introduced (describing bill).

[64] The availability of each of the causes of action in this laundry list depends on the jurisdiction at issue, eg, Florida does not recognise the false light cause of action.

[65] In the famous case of *Food Lion v Capital Cities/ABC* 194 F.3d 505 (4th Cir. 1999), which involved a hidden-camera exposé of unsafe meat sale practices in a supermarket, the court found ABC News liable for trespass and breach of the duty of loyalty because the network's reporters, as employees, owed fiduciary duties of loyalty to the company.

[66] For an overview, see First Amendment Handbook (n 47). While 38 states and the District of Columbia allow for 'one party consent' recording, '[t]welve states forbid the recording of private conversations without the consent of all parties'; ibid.

[67] ibid.

3. Federal Regulation of Broadcasting and Cable: The Rise and Decline of the 'Other' First Amendment Tradition

While, as noted above, the US does not regulate the print press,[68] Congress and the courts have historically allowed a degree of government regulation of radio and television that would not have been constitutionally permissible for other speakers. Due to the perceived differences between electronic media and print, constitutional scholars did not typically address this doctrinal inconsistency early on. They saw the First Amendment as protecting traditional speech and print, and broadcast law as a limited aberration – a specific response to the peculiar characteristics of mass electronic media. In the late twentieth century, however, some observers began to assert that the US was simultaneously operating under two parallel but inconsistent First Amendment traditions.[69] For some, the duality achieved the proper balance.[70] Others, though, saw in the Federal Communications Commission's (FCC) regulatory approach a subversive alternative that would open the door to a less libertarian and more regulatory path for the First Amendment.[71]

Neither of those two reactions was to prevail, however. The dual regime and First Amendment variation by medium diminished significantly over the years. Even in its heyday, broadcast regulation had a narrow ambit, and any expansive regulatory ambitions the FCC might have had for cable and the internet were quickly limited. While radio and over-the-air television were the central mass media in the late twentieth century, they are significantly diminished now. Today, the regulation of broadcasting and cable is even more 'light touch', both as to content and industry structure. Far from serving as a viable alternative to the libertarian First Amendment, then, the US experiment in administrative regulation of mass media speech has largely faded.

Still, a bird's eye view of regulatory history is instructive. Beginning in the early twentieth century, Congress established that radio (and later television) broadcasting would be licensed by the federal government and licensees would have no property rights in the broadcast spectrum assigned to them.[72] The FCC

---

[68] This does not mean that the press is exempted from rules of general application, see n 40 above. So long as the Court has not seen such laws as hiding discrimination against the press, they have not been subjected to the most stringent level of constitutional scrutiny.

[69] For important early discussions of the dual First Amendment tracks, see J Weinberg, 'Broadcasting and Speech' (1993) 81 *California Law Review* 1101; LC Bollinger, Jr, 'Freedom of the Press and Public Access: Toward a Theory of Partial Regulation of the Mass Media' (1976) 75(1) *Michigan Law Review* 16.

[70] See, eg, Bollinger (n 69).

[71] See, eg, JA Barron, 'Access to the Press: A New First Amendment Right' (1967) 80 *Harvard Law Review* 1641 (arguing that the First Amendment should impose affirmative duties of access to the press on monopoly newspapers).

[72] Communications Act of 1934, 47 USC § 301.

(successor to the Federal Radio Commission) was the independent administrative body tasked with broadcast licensing in the 'public interest, convenience and necessity'.[73] In the mid-twentieth century, the rules of the FCC were a powerful force affecting radio and television. Under the FCC's early rules, the initial licence terms were short, and even licensees that had made significant investments in their stations were compelled to participate in comparative hearings to prove to the Commission that their renewal should be deemed in the public interest.

In addition to its role as licensor, the FCC's expansive statutory mandate allowed it to adopt a broad range of broadcast regulations. Notably, the Commission adopted both content regulation and structural regulations.[74] Seeking to promote the goals of competition, diversity and localism, the Commission adopted content-focused rules such as the equal opportunities rule regulating political advertising,[75] the limited right of access to the air for federal candidates,[76] the fairness doctrine and its corollaries,[77] rules regulating on-air indecency,[78] the news distortion doctrine,[79] and children's television programming advertising rules.[80] On the structural side, the Commission adopted both national and local ownership regulations designed to promote diversity and localism – including limits on how many broadcast licences one entity could own nationally and locally, and limits on

---

[73] ibid §§ 1, 307, 309.

[74] For the FCC's compilation of its regulations for the public, see 'The Public and Broadcasting', www.fcc.gov/media/radio/public-and-broadcasting#CRITICISM. By structural regulations, I refer principally to regulations, such as broadcast ownership limitations, that were designed to impact the structure of the media industry in the service of diverse and efficient service.

[75] Communications Act of 1934, 47 USC, § 315 ('if any licensee shall permit any person who is a legally qualified candidate for any public office to use a broadcasting station, he shall afford equal opportunities to all other such candidates for that office in the use of such broadcasting station').

[76] ibid § 312(a)(7) (the FCC may 'revoke any station license or construction permit ... for willful or repeated failure to allow reasonable access to or to permit purchase of reasonable amounts of time for the use of a broadcasting station by a legally qualified candidate for Federal elective office on behalf of his candidacy').

[77] The fairness doctrine was an FCC policy that required broadcast licensees to cover controversial issues of public importance in their overall programming, and to do so in a fair manner, enabling the expression of contrasting viewpoints; In the Matter of Editorializing by Broadcast Licensees, 13 FCC Rept. 1246, 1246–1270 (1949); Applicability of the Fairness Doctrine in the Handling of Controversial Issues of Public Importance, 29 Fed. Reg. 10426 (1964). Ultimately, the FCC adopted two fairness doctrine corollaries: the personal attack and political editorialising rules. In *Red Lion Broadcasting Co Inc v FCC* 395 US 367 (1969), the Supreme Court upheld their constitutionality as a legitimate exercise of the FCC's Congressional authority. Thereafter, the Commission began to question the effectiveness of the fairness doctrine in the 1980s, and ultimately repealed it in 1987. *In re* Complaint of Syracuse Peace Council against Television Station WTVH Syracuse, New York, 2 FCC Rcd 5043 (1987), aff'd by *Syracuse Peace Council v FCC* 867 F.2d 654 (D.C. Cir. 1988).

[78] For discussions of the history of FCC indecency regulation, See, eg, L Levi, '"Smut and Nothing But": The FCC, Indecency, and Regulatory Transformations in the Shadows' (2013) 65 *Admin. Law Review* 509; L Levi, 'First Report: The FCC's Regulation of Indecency' (2008) 7(1) *First Reports*; L Levi, 'The Hard Case of Broadcast Indecency' (1993) 20 *NYU Review of Law & Social Change* 49.

[79] See, eg, L Levi, 'Reporting the Official Truth: The Revival of the FCC's News Distortion Policy' (2000) 78 *Washington University Law Quarterly* 1005 (describing policy).

[80] See, eg, L Levi, 'A "Pay or Play" Experiment to Improve Children's Educational Television' (2010) 62 *Federal Communications Law Journal* 275 (describing children's educational television rules).

a variety of media cross-ownership structures.[81] The Commission also exercised its statutory right to rule on proposed mergers in the broadcast industry.[82] All told, the FCC and its regulatory initiatives were seen as important both practically and doctrinally during the twentieth century.

Historically, the Supreme Court was deferential to Congress and the FCC's regulatory decisions regarding radio and over-the-air television. For example, in the 1943 opinion in *NBC v FCC*,[83] the Court rejected a First Amendment challenge to the FCC's chain broadcasting rules and affirmed that the Commission's right to regulate in the public interest extended beyond being a mere 'traffic officer'. Later, the Supreme Court in *Red Lion Broadcasting v FCC*[84] held that the FCC's fairness doctrine passed constitutional muster under the First Amendment, in marked contrast to the Court's highly editor-protective decision striking down a right-of-reply statute in *Miami Herald v Tornillo* in the print press context. In *FCC v Pacifica*, the Court upheld the Commission's broadcast indecency policy.[85]

The Court's deference to the Commission's broadcast regulation rules was based on two principal rationales: the scarcity of broadcast frequencies[86] and the unique pervasiveness and invasiveness of broadcasting to children.[87] Beginning with a fundamental attack on the scarcity rationale by Ronald Coase in 1959,[88] however, many began to question the viability of scarcity as the factor persuasively justifying differential treatment of the print and electronic media with respect to administrative regulation. After all, in what way is spectrum differently scarce than other valuable goods offered at no cost? The Supreme Court itself recognised the criticisms of the scarcity rationale.[89] And even in the context of broadcasting, three

---

[81] See, eg, L Levi, 'Reflections on the FCC's Recent Approach to Structural Regulation of the Electronic Mass Media' (2000) 52 *Federal Communications Law Journal* 581, 582–92, and sources cited therein.

[82] 47 USC §§ 214(a) and 310(d). This 'dual' review process adds FCC review to the typical antitrust review to be undertaken by the Department of Justice and the Federal Trade Commission in proposed mergers.

[83] *National Broadcasting Co v United States* 319 US 190, 216 (1943). The chain broadcasting rules were an attempt by the FCC to limit the ability of the broadcast networks to control their affiliated broadcast stations.

[84] *Red Lion* (n 77).

[85] *FCC v Pacifica Foundation* 438 US 726 (1978). See FCC, 'Obscene, Indecent and Profane Broadcasts', www.fcc.gov/consumers/guides/obscene-indecent-and-profane-broadcasts#:~:text=Broadcasting%20 obscene%20content%20is%20prohibited,may%20be%20in%20the%20audience for the Commission's current time channelling rules for indecent broadcast content; Levi, 'Smut and Nothing But' (n 78); Levi, 'First Report' (n 78); Levi, 'The Hard Case' (n 78).

[86] See, eg, *National Broadcasting* (n 83) 226.

[87] *Pacifica Foundation* (n 85).

[88] See, eg, RH Coase, 'The Federal Communications Commission' (1959) 2(1) *The Journal of Law and Economics*.

[89] *FCC v League of Women Voters of California* 468 US 364, fn 11 (1984) ('The prevailing rationale for broadcast regulation based on spectrum scarcity has come under increasing criticism in recent years .... We are not prepared, however, to reconsider our longstanding approach without some signal from Congress or the FCC that technological developments have advanced so far that some revision of the system of broadcast regulation may be required').

justices in *CBS v DNC* acknowledged the editorial freedom of broadcast licensees in their day-to-day decisions, including the right not to sell airtime.[90]

The FCC as well began to distance itself from both structural and content-focused regulation. As for content regulations, the Commission discarded the fairness doctrine and described its news distortion policy with significant limitations.[91] The Commission's focus regarding children's educational television regulations appears to be on commercial content;[92] and even indecency enforcement is rarely in the news.[93] What remains in place other than the children's educational programming rules is the regulation of political advertising under §§ 315 and 312(a)(7). Even in the political context, though, the FCC 'exempt programming' rulings have exempted much political programming from the equal opportunities rules. On the structural front, while the Commission has not completely eliminated its broadcast ownership rules, it has loosened them significantly[94] without running afoul of its obligations under the Administrative Procedure Act.[95] As for the need for FCC merger approval, the Commission has been approving media mergers with relatively mild approval conditions. As a result, although the FCC's regulation of broadcasting in the past at least theoretically had significant bite, the Commission's regulatory regime now is quite diminished.

Even when there was more extensive administrative regulation of broadcasters, both cable companies and, later, internet providers, were treated quite differently from the regulatory point of view. The Supreme Court addressed a constitutional attack on the cable must-carry rules in two *Turner Broadcasting v FCC* cases.[96] Rejecting the applicability of the deferential broadcast regulation review standard for cable, the Court applied intermediate scrutiny and upheld the FCC's must-carry rules. The Court's treatment of the internet stands in even greater contrast to the regulation of broadcasting and cable. Relatively early in the

---

[90] *Columbia Broadcasting System, Inc v Democratic National Committee* 412 US 94, 120–21 (1973) (*dictum* in part III of the plurality opinion).

[91] See FCC, 'Broadcast News Distortion' (*FCC*, 31 August 2022), www.fcc.gov/broadcast-news-distortion.

[92] In the Matter of Cunningham Broadcasting Corporation, et al, Notice of Apparent Liability for Forfeiture, FCC, 21 September 2022, www.fcc.gov/document/fcc-proposes-fines-violations-childrens-tv-programming-rules (approximately US$3.4 million fine).

[93] See, eg, D Oxenford, 'Indecency' (*Broadcast Law Blog*), www.broadcastlawblog.com/articles/indecency.

[94] For the current rules, see www.fcc.gov/consumers/guides/fccs-review-broadcast-ownership-rules. Under the Telecommunications Act of 1996, the FCC must review its rules governing broadcast media ownership every four years and determine whether they 'are necessary in the public interest as the result of competition' and must 'repeal or modify any regulation it determines to be no longer in the public interest'. Telecommunications Act of 1996, § 202(h).

[95] *FCC v Prometheus Radio Project* 592 US ___ (2021) held that the FCC's decision to modify or repeal some ownership rules was not arbitrary or capricious under the Administrative Procedure Act.

[96] *Turner Broadcasting System v FCC* 520 US 180 (1997) (*Turner I*); *Turner Broadcasting System v FCC* 512 US 622 (1994) (*Turner II*). The cable must-carry rules required cable operators to carry a certain number of local over-the-air television signals.

world wide web revolution, the Supreme Court refused to extend the regulatory approach of broadcast regulation to the internet in *Reno v ACLU*,[97] and treated internet speech indistinguishably from its most protective constitutional treatment of non-electronic speech.[98] This has meant that government attempts to regulate the content of online speech would be subjected to exacting constitutional scrutiny.

4. The Current Push for Social Media Regulatory Reform

At the start of the internet age, after a state court[99] had held an internet service provider liable for a defamatory post by a user on one of its message boards, Congress passed the internet service provider protective Section 230 of the Communications Decency Act. Section 230 has two provisions – one which immunises such providers from secondary liability for merely publishing information provided by third parties, and the other which permits them to engage in content moderation and filtering.[100] Since then, and now increasingly, there have been many calls to regulate social media speech by eliminating or significantly revising the Section 230 protections. Albeit for different reasons, President Biden and former President Trump have both consistently expressed opposition to the provision, with President Biden suggesting that Section 230 be 'revoked, immediately'.[101]

Some proponents of such changes argue that social media are the fulcrum from which much democracy-harming disinformation spreads, and that internet service provider immunity undermines the social media companies' incentives to stop the spread of disinformation. Other reform proponents express concern that the social media companies have discriminated against certain types of speech, and particularly conservative speech, in their private content moderation processes. Yet others emphasise the ways in which harmful speech on social media replicates social inequalities and disproportionately affects marginalised people and groups.

---

[97] *Reno v ACLU* 521 US 844, 868 (1997) (striking down under the First Amendment provisions of the Communications Decency Act protecting minors from indecent communications on the internet, establishing that internet speech is entitled to the high degree of First Amendment protection accorded to speech and print media, and asserting that the 'special justifications for regulation of the broadcast media' did not apply to 'the vast democratic forums of the internet').

[98] Since then, the Court has explicitly recognised the significance of digital speech to modern society and has characterised the internet as the 'modern public square'. *Packingham v North Carolina* 137 S. Ct. 1730, 1737–38 (2017).

[99] *Stratton Oakmont, Inc v Prodigy Services Co* 1995 WL 323710 (N.Y. Sup. Ct. May 24, 1995).

[100] 47 USC § 230.

[101] M Ingram, 'Section 230 heads to the Supreme Court' (*Columbia Journalism Review*, 6 October 2022), www.cjr.org/analysis/section-230-heads-to-the-supreme-court.php; D Cameron, 'Biden Issues Another Vague Call to "Reform" the Internet's Most Important Law' (*Gizmodo*, 10 September 2022), https://gizmodo.com/biden-issues-another-vague-call-to-reform-section-230-1849519743.

Supporters of Section 230 argue not only that the provision has allowed for the rapid growth of the internet and its innovations, but that eliminating the provision would diminish the platforms' ability to curate and moderate content, leading social media to become even more of a morass of harmful information, lies and expressive violence than it is currently.

In addition to their presence at the legislative level, these issues – the breadth of Section 230's immunity and the extent to which the First Amendment protects social media platforms' content-moderation decisions – are also squarely before the courts today. Justice Thomas has in the recent past called for the Supreme Court to 'consider whether the text of this increasingly important statute aligns with the current state of immunity enjoyed by internet platforms'.[102] Recently, the Court, in *Gonzalez v Google*[103] and *Twitter, Inc v Taamneh*,[104] chose to avoid addressing the question whether platforms should be deemed protected from secondary liability under Section 230 when, beyond hosting third party content, their algorithms make targeted recommendations of such content to their users.[105] The Court's grant of *certiorari* in *Gonzalez* and *Twitter* was striking since there was no pending circuit conflict for whose resolution the Court typically grants review and a large number of bills to reform Section 230 are still pending before Congress. Although the various internet platforms to which Section 230(c)(1) applies have material differences, a common thread is that their recommendation functions are critical both to their economic models and, by now, to the public's expectations about the curation of the firehose of information available online. A finding that the platforms could be subject to indirect liability for harms caused by their algorithmic recommendations of third-party content would constitute a radical shift and likely lead to fundamental changes in the architecture of the internet.

Also heading to the Supreme Court is a conflict among the circuit courts regarding the validity of state laws restricting internet service providers' ability to moderate content on their platforms. Both Florida and Texas recently enacted legislation purporting to restrict social media platforms' ability to moderate content and 'deplatform' or restrict users based on their political views, as well as imposing disclosure requirements on covered platforms with respect to their content moderation activities.[106] In *NetChoice v Moody*, the Court of Appeals for the 11th Circuit largely upheld a preliminary injunction preventing Florida's

---

[102] *Malwarebytes, Inc v Enigma Software Group USA, LLC* 141 S. Ct. 13, 14 (2020) (Thomas J concurring in denial of *certiorari*).

[103] *Gonzalez v Google LLC* 598 U.S. ____ (Sup. Ct. 2023).

[104] *Twitter, Inc v Taamneh* 598 U.S. ____ (Sup. Ct. 2023).

[105] Both cases were brought under the Antiterrorism Act, 18 USC § 2333, by families of victims of ISIS attacks who seek to hold Google and Twitter secondarily liable over algorithmic recommendations of ISIS recruitment materials.

[106] The Florida and Texas statutes are similar in their prohibition of viewpoint-based content moderation or content removal, but the Texas statute purports to regulate social media platforms' content moderation discretion and disclosure obligations even more extensively than Florida's statute.

Senate Bill 7072 from going into effect on the ground that the statute would likely be deemed an unconstitutional infringement of the platforms' First Amendment rights except as to some of its disclosure provisions.[107] By contrast, in *NetChoice v Paxton*,[108] the Court of Appeals for the Fifth Circuit rejected the platforms' First Amendment argument, asserted that their content moderation activities were not constitutionally-protected speech, and reversed a preliminary injunction that had been entered by the district court below to Texas House Bill 20.[109] Florida and NetChoice each petitioned for a grant of *certiorari* by the Supreme Court.[110] Given the conflict among the circuit courts regarding similar statutes, and in light of the Court's apparent desire to consider other aspects of Section 230, key issues will be decided by the high court this term.[111] It is also notable that three Justices of the Supreme Court have already asserted that '[i]t is not at all obvious how our existing precedents, which predate the age of the internet, should apply to large social media companies'.[112]

Of course, critics' worries – *inter alia* about viral disinformation, the possibility of political imbalance in content preferences of powerful and electorally unaccountable platforms, and unequal impacts of harmful speech on marginalised communities – are understandable. But I suspect that many of the proposed approaches to Section 230 reform are likely to lead to worrisome consequences and even hinder the press without clearly ensuring an improved public sphere. The current state attempts to regulate social media content moderation raise serious constitutional and policy questions, including concerning the propriety of government content and viewpoint review.

With respect to the Section 230(c)(1) immunity, an argument grounded on a purported distinction between hosting and recommending content raises difficult

---

[107] *NetChoice, LLC v Moody* 546 F. Supp. 3d 1082 (N.D. Fla. 2021), aff'd in part, vacated in part and remanded, 34 F.4th 1196 (11th Cir. 2022).

[108] *NetChoice LLC v Paxton* 49 F. 4th 439 (5th Cir. 2022).

[109] An Act Relating to censorship of or certain other interference with digital expression, including expression on social media platforms or through electronic mail messages, https://capitol.texas.gov/BillLookup/History.aspx?LegSess=872&Bill=HB20.

[110] *NetChoice LLC v Paxton*, Petition for a writ of *certiorari*, 21 September 2022; *Attorney General, State of Florida et al v NetChoice LLC*, Petition for a writ of *certiorari*, 21 September 2022. The Supreme Court has asked the Biden Administration for its views on the Florida and Texas statutes at issue in the two petitions for *certiorari*. A Howe, 'Justices Request Federal Government's Views on Texas and Florida Social-Media Laws' (*ScotusBlog*, 23 January 2023), www.scotusblog.com/2023/01/justices-request-federal-governments-views-on-texas-and-florida-social-media-laws.

[111] *Certiorari* was granted in supremecourt.gov/orders/courtorders/092923zr_q8l1.pdf. In addition to calls for Section 230 reform, the social media platforms have also recently been subject to challenge under competition law in the United States (not to mention Europe).

[112] *NetChoice v Paxton* 596 US ___ (2022) at 3 (Alito J, Thomas J and Gorsuch J, dissenting). Prior to its most recent decision, the Court of Appeals for the Fifth Circuit had stayed a district court's preliminary injunction preventing the law from taking effect, but the Supreme Court vacated that stay. While Justice Alito, writing for himself and two other Justices in dissent from the Court's grant of the application to vacate the stay of the Texas statute, disclaimed having 'a definitive view', he began his dissent by referring to 'the power of dominant social media corporations to shape public discussion of the important issues of the day', ibid 1. The dissenters agreed that the issues involved in the Fifth Circuit dispute 'will plainly merit this Court's review'.

questions. Deciding what is to go in a newspaper is a typical editorial function. So too, in a different way, is the newspaper placement decision of the vendor of a news kiosk. Are platform recommendations so materially different simply because they are algorithmic and at a scale far different from that of the twentieth century newspaper? How much should it matter that the newspaper editors' choices are at least aspirationally dictated by journalistic values, while the platforms' algorithmic decisions are directed both by assumptions about what people want to see or read based on their prior behaviour and the platforms' own financial interests in consumer engagement? How much, if at all, should it matter that newspapers have historically been a 'pull' medium, whereas social media such as Facebook is a 'push' medium? The platforms' recommendation functions are helpful and even necessary in order to curate the veritable sea of material online, but at the same time, is their current business structure optimal from the point of view of democratic discourse? Or is the desire for an optimal public sphere too likely to serve as a cover for aggregation of control by increasingly authoritarian public officials? It is true that newspapers and other publishers are not immunised from liability for their re-publication of defamatory content, so would eliminating Section 230(c)(1) simply even the playing field? Or is the sheer scale of online communications such that elimination of the protection would likely lead to excessive risk-aversity with respect to user-generated content on the part of the platforms? And are the platforms all sufficiently similar to deserve a single regulatory approach or do their differences counsel more granular analysis?

With respect to the state statutes prohibiting platform 'censorship', if the Supreme Court were to decide that platform decisions about what speech they disseminate is not First Amendment-protected expressive activity and that states can constitutionally preclude social media platforms from moderating much content,[113] there will predictably be a significant increase in the scale and scope of disinformation and otherwise harmful speech likely to spread on the platforms. To the extent that speech on the platforms triggers coverage over conventional media such as cable news, disinformation online is likely to flood even further the airwaves and cable channels which are already distorted by political disinformation under current law. This becomes particularly worrisome when considering the tools of technological fraud such as deepfakes. It also invites a degree of government control over the platforms' content and viewpoint decisions far beyond even that granted to the FCC in its heyday. Will this lead to a significant chilling effect on the platforms? The largest internet platforms have adopted community norms and terms of service that restrict some speech that would otherwise be legal under US law.

The combination of user pressure, fear of negative publicity, advertiser brand effects concerns, and regulatory threats have increasingly led the platforms to

---

[113] As they purport to apply to the activities of companies incorporated elsewhere, the Texas and Florida statutes also seem to implicate questions of extraterritorial application of state laws, a question beyond the scope of this chapter.

restrict some 'lawful but awful'[114] speech. How does the inevitability of moderation cut? Even if the legislation in question is limited, will the algorithms learn to permit even hate speech and harassment for fear of the anti-censorship statutes? To the extent that the First Amendment protects editorial discretion, is such legislation clearly unconstitutional? Or are the major online platforms now so powerful and ubiquitous that we should treat them as akin to common carriers? Should their oligopolistic character impose public, fiduciary duties on them? Or does the history of early internet social media suggest that the barriers to successful entry online are less significant impediments than market power in the offline world? Are the regulatory rationales for the state legislative initiatives too likely to spread to the press or to news-disseminating entities that some officials do not see as sufficiently press-like? Is a better approach to engage in structural regulation, focused on antitrust and competition law, consumer protection, and privacy,[115] rather than the Florida and Texas speech regulation paths?

These are all highly contested matters. At a minimum, social media regulatory initiatives should not distract us from what is needed to protect the function of the press in generating effective accountability journalism. It is true that most young people – and perhaps now most people, with no age modification – get their news online, often from social media or by 'googling' for information.[116] Most people do not encounter news by buying a physical newspaper or even visiting a newspaper's web page. This should not lead to the conclusion, however, that Section 230 reform is likely to solve or even ameliorate the major problems afflicting the press today. To be sure, the relationship of social media and the press is complex and fraught. The online world undercut the traditional economic model of the institutional press, and social media companies have only recently begun to commit to helping journalism. A recent Pew Research Center survey reports that while the vast majority of journalists use social media in their work, most think that social media is having a negative impact on journalism as a whole.[117] But forcing social media to stop recommending content and/or limiting their ability to engage in content monitoring and moderation will not solve the press's

---

[114] E Goldman and J Miers, 'Online Account Terminations/Content Removals and the Benefits of Internet Services Enforcing Their House Rules' (2021) 1 *Journal of Free Speech Law* 191, 194); A Chander, 'Section 230 and the International Law of Facebook' (2022) 24(1) *Yale Journal of Law & Technology* 25.

[115] See, eg, J Balkin, 'To Reform Social Media, Reform Informational Capitalism' in LC Bollinger and G R Stone (eds), *Social Media, Freedom of Speech, and the Future of Our Democracy* (Oxford, Oxford University Press, 2022).

[116] E Shearer, 'More than Eight-In-Ten Americans Get News from Digital Devices' (*Pew Research*, 2021), www.pewresearch.org/fact-tank/2021/01/12/more-than-eight-in-ten-americans-get-news-from-digital-devices/; M Walker and KE Matsa, 'News Consumption Across Social Media in 2021' (*Pew Research*, 2021), www.pewresearch.org/journalism/2021/09/20/news-consumption-across-social-media-in-2021/.

[117] J Gottfried et al, '3. Many Journalists Say Social Media Helps at Work, but Most Decry Its Impact on Journalism' (*Pew Research Center*, 14 June 2022), www.pewresearch.org/journalism/2022/06/14/many-journalists-say-social-media-helps-at-work-but-most-decry-its-impact-on-journalism.

(and therefore the public's) problems. Indeed, such developments might even exacerbate journalism's challenges – as predictable increases in disinformation, hate speech and harassment intimidate and deter sources, and a decline in curation raises the prospect of increased invisibility and decreased access to audiences, particularly for fringe or new journalism outlets. After all, today's scarcity is attention rather than bandwidth.

5. Modern Legal Threats to the US Press

The American media – already economically battered – is now functioning under a series of new threats. An anti-press attitude in the public at large, juries and judges; the decline in non-legal norms and customs protective of the press; the politicised attacks on the 'fake news' press by a former President and his allies; the fact that Congress has not yet passed federal anti-SLAPP legislation or a federal reporter's shield law; threats of prosecution for national security reporting based on whistleblower materials; reporter surveillance by government; and increased breakdowns in the operations of federal and state records access statutes and procedures are just a few elements of the combination of threats and challenges facing the press today. In light of space constraints, this chapter focuses on two of the most pressing current dangers, namely the decline of the Supreme Court's positive view of the press, and the associated possibility of radical changes to press protections against crushing defamation liability.

5.1. The New Negativity in the Public's and Courts' Views of the Press

Much ink has been spilled documenting the anti-press attitude of the public today. Juries have not been immune to this development. Congress too has not rushed to the defence of the press, at least to the extent that it has failed to pass press-protective legislation. Recently, Professors RonNell Andersen Jones and Sonja West have powerfully demonstrated, through a thorough empirical examination of the history of the Supreme Court's mentions of the press from 1784 to 2020, that the current Supreme Court is more sceptical of (and even hostile to) the press than at any time in its history.[118] The press has few supporters in its corner.

 Why does the Supreme Court's attitude matter? As Professors Jones and West have persuasively argued, much of the legal perception of the press and its status have been grounded on the Court's positive descriptions of the constitutional significance of the press function. If the Court no longer holds those views,

---

[118] R Andersen Jones and SR West, 'The U.S. Supreme Court's Characterizations of the Press: An Empirical Study' (2022) 100 *UNC Law Review* 375.

then it may be more disposed to shift ground away from its previous pro-press constitutional interpretations. The Court's attitude is also likely to seep down to the lower courts, thereby further limiting any interpretive benefit of the doubt that such judges might otherwise extend to the press. This is also likely to affect the press and the media bar's own views about what cases and issues are worth pursuing through the legal system. Legal culture matters, both in terms of doctrine and party behaviour. That the press has lost the protective umbrella of the Court's positive perception is also particularly problematic when seen as part of a whole system of increased distrust in the press in legislatures as well as in public opinion. One of the open questions is whether the Court's jaundiced view of the press can be reversed. If not, the next question is whether and how Congress and the states can step in to enhance appropriate press protections designed to further journalism's democratic promise.

5.2. The New Reliance on Disinformation as a Justification to Diminish Press-Protective Constitutional Law

The Supreme Court's protections of the press under the First Amendment are unstable and under sustained assault, with the strategic help of a rising and sophisticated plaintiff's defamation bar. Most recently, a new argument – based on the need to fight disinformation – has been deployed to justify eliminating or radically limiting the *New York Times v Sullivan* regime. This has begun to pose a powerful new threat, building on a series of pro-plaintiff shifts that had already been occurring before the disinformation argument started gaining traction.

For several years, defamation plaintiffs have been mounting a quiet attack on constitutionalised defamation law. While the substantive and procedural standards applied in defamation cases still generally reflect a defence-protective legal landscape for press defendants in defamation cases involving public figures,[119] there has also been developing a degree of pro-plaintiff recalibration in defamation doctrine as applied. Courts have rejected more defence motions for early dismissal in highly publicised cases than heretofore;[120] have issued

---

[119] See, eg, JM Cornett, 'Pleading Actual Malice in Defamation Actions After Twiqbal: A Circuit Survey' (2017) 17 *Nevada Law Journal* 709 (discussing how some courts have applied stringent 'plausibility' pleading standards on motions to dismiss in actual malice cases). In addition, many state laws include news-protective privileges, including, eg, the fair and accurate report privilege. A few jurisdictions also have a 'neutral reportage' privilege, seeking to protect a news organisation's re-publication of newsworthy charges about public figures if they were made by responsible people and institutions, on condition that the publisher reported them neutrally, without endorsing the truth or falsity of the statements. See *Edwards v Audubon* 556 F.2d 113 (2d Cir. 1977). Not unexpectedly, there are differences among the jurisdictions with respect to the scope and coverage of the fair report privilege, and most states have not adopted the neutral reportage privilege.

[120] See, eg, *Palin v NY Times Co* 588 F. Supp. 3d 375 (S.D.N.Y. 2022); *Palin v New York Times Co* 940 F.3d 804 (2d Cir. 2019).

more anti-libel injunctions;[121] and have even permitted an increased number of criminal libel prosecutions in several states that still have criminal libel statutes on their books.[122] At least some courts are also beginning to adopt doctrinal interpretations designed to re-adjust the balance between the interests of the press and the plaintiffs' interests in privacy and reputation – and are adopting a critical stance toward media claims. This pro-plaintiff doctrinal attitude is also particularly evident in cases requiring the application of print-based defamation law to the online context. Due to an increase in high-profile defamation cases with high damage awards and plaintiffs' claims of billions of dollars in reputational harm, defendant press entities are also more open to high-figure settlements.[123]

As I have described elsewhere,[124] these pro-plaintiff shifts are now being weaponised with the use of the new argument grounded on the need to protect the public from disinformation. Changes in the media ecosystem and concerns about stemming disinformation in public discourse are fueling scholarly and judicial arguments to reverse or reform the *New York Times v Sullivan* framework.[125] Justices Thomas and Gorsuch have already called for a reconsideration and reversal of the actual malice rule and, it appears, much of the entire *Sullivan* framework.[126] The anti-disinformation frame could well tip the scales and generate a majority on the Court to dismantle almost 60 years of constitutionalised defamation law. This is quite worrisome today, particularly in light of the numerous strategic defamation suits brought by public officials and public figures and entities against the press for hundreds of millions (and even billions) of dollars in damages.[127] If these legal changes occur, the stratospheric – multi-million and even multi-billion

---

[121] See E Volokh, 'Anti-Libel Injunctions' (2019) 168 *University of Pennsylvania Law Review* 73 (arguing they are not presumptively prohibited constitutionally). Some courts have agreed that such injunctions can pass constitutional muster if appropriately narrowly tailored.

[122] E Volokh, 'The Return to Criminal Law as a Remedy: Libel' (*Reason*, 17 February 2021), https://reason.com/volokh/2021/02/17/the-return-to-criminal-law-as-a-remedy-libel.

[123] Looking beyond defamation, observers see Hulk Hogan's US$144 million win against Gawker in a breach of privacy suit over its post of a sex tape as a 'bellwether' for media liability more generally. See, eg, AM Gutierrez, 'The Case for a Federal Defamation Regime' (2021) 131 *Yale Law Journal*.

[124] L Levi, 'Disinformation and the Defamation Renaissance: A Misleading Promise of "Truth"' (2023) 57 *University of Richmond Law Review* 1235.

[125] DA Logan, 'Rescuing Our Democracy by Rethinking *New York Times Co. v Sullivan*' (2020) 81 *Ohio State Law Journal* 759.

[126] *McKee v Cosby* 139 S. Ct. 675 (2019) (Thomas J, concurring); *Berisha v Lawson*, 141 S. Ct. 2424, 2424–25 (2021) (Thomas J, dissenting); *Coral Ridge Ministries Media Inc v Southern Poverty Law Center* 597 US ___ (2022) (Thomas J, dissenting); *Berisha v Lawson* 141 S. Ct. 2424, 2425–29 (2021) (Gorsuch J, dissenting).

[127] Many of these suits assert monstrous amounts in money damages, such as the US$1.6 billion and US$2.7 billion damage claims respectively in two pending defamation suits against Fox News by Dominion and Smartmatic, the two major American election machine software manufacturers. Very high damages have even been granted, including US$8.2 million awarded to former judge and senatorial candidate Roy Moore over a television ad recounting accusations of misconduct with underage girls, US$3 million to a former University of Virginia administrator from *Rolling Stone* magazine over statements about her in a discredited story about an alleged gang rape at the school, and US$45 million and almost US$1 billion in two recent verdicts against conspiracy theorist Alex Jones of InfoWars in connection with his claims that an elementary school mass shooting was a government hoax.

dollar – damage claims by plaintiffs in some of these cases clearly pose the risk of existential harm to the funding of accountability journalism. Concerns about such outcomes could well increase the incentives for press defendants to settle, even if they continue to maintain the truth of their coverage – as ABC did when its parent company settled a defamation case for over US$177 million over the network's characterisation of the plaintiff's beef product as 'pink slime'.[128]

The new disinformation frame for defamation suits, which brings serious democratic costs without clear corresponding benefits, offers an illusory distraction and further politicises defamation. Defamation lawsuits cannot credibly stem the systemic tide of disinformation or predictably correct reputational harm, but they do threaten powerful chilling effects for the press, super-sized by our current socio-historical context. This reveals clearly that the call to reduce constitutional protections for the press in fact functions as a broader attack on the press, political speech and the fundamental right guaranteed by the US Constitution to criticise the government and the powerful.

5.3. What the Press Needs Now

First, what the press now needs is stability in protections under the First Amendment. To be sure, not every aspect of constitutionalised defamation law under *The New York Times v Sullivan* and its progeny must be preserved exactly as it is, encased in amber. Still, it would be a grave error to subject the already-beleaguered press to the hundreds of millions or even billions in potential defamation liability that it would face without the protections of the *Sullivan* framework. Such a change in the law would most advantage powerful political figures or officials, corporations with deep coffers, and others intent on strategic use of the law to stop the press from investigating and criticising them (or even just exacting revenge). The chilling effect on the watchdog role of the press would be predictable and considerable. Targeted arguments against the diminishment of the protections under *Sullivan* and its progeny are critical to the attempt to forestall radical shrinkage of defendant protections.

The American press would also benefit from enhanced newsgathering rights, particularly as it seeks to cover issues of public concern.[129] Helping improve the press's work as an agent of accountability advances the democratic project. The scope of such rights, the feasibility of establishing them, and whether they should

---

[128] C Hauser, 'ABC's "Pink Slime" Report Tied to $177 Million in Settlement Costs' *The New York Times* (10 August 2017). The US Dominion suit against Fox News was recently settled for US$ 787.5 million.

[129] This is obviously contested terrain, but I join Professor West and others in arguing that American history and the full arc of the Supreme Court's First Amendment press jurisprudence do not foreclose the recognition of such rights under the Constitution. See also PJ Charles and KF O'Neill, 'Saving the Press Clause from Ruin: The Customary Origins of a "Free Press" as Interface to the Present and Future' (2012) *Utah Law Review* 1691.

be grounded in the Constitution or statutory law are all contested issues beyond the scope of this chapter. While the Supreme Court has shied away from formally accepting preferential treatment of journalists, its principal reason for doing so – namely, the difficulty of defining the press – does not seem insuperable.[130]

Admittedly, that the Supreme Court seems particularly unsympathetic to the press, as described above, does pose an obstacle to the prospects of expanded press exceptionalism through the high court. Still, shifts in public perceptions of the press, increases in effective reporting in the public interest, better empirical data on which to rest their impressions of the press and its work, and richer historical arguments could possibly help shift the Court towards greater press-receptiveness in the future. Furthermore, even if the Supreme Court lags in ensuring further newsgathering rights, Congress and the states could begin to lead the way.

Most generally, what the US press needs now is increased legitimacy,[131] including improvement in public and judicial understanding of its contributions. Regarding how the press is perceived, cognitive science has already taught us some things about how people form opinions, how and when they change their minds, how they process claims of falsity and harm, and what can help to increase their trust in institutions. But there is much more to be learned. Both resources for those empirical inquiries and access to adequate information (including concerning social media operations) would be critical to advance that research. More reliable and consistent social science data to support effective responses to the loss of public trust, as well as a commitment by news organisations to tackle the problem and improve their own processes, could well serve to promote legal enhancements in press protection in the US going forward.

---

[130] See, eg, West, 'Awakening the Press Clause' (n 36).

[131] Of course, another obvious pressing need for the press is economic stability and access to audiences. The economic stability issue is too broad to be addressed here, although further examination of multiple funding models (including by social media (see, eg, M Minow, *Saving the News* (Oxford, Oxford University Press, 2021) 104–107) and an antitrust exemption for group negotiation by news organisations with social media platforms are warranted. The Journalism Competition and Preservation Act, S 673, which would have provided such an exemption, has recently been derailed over questions regarding platform content moderation. See J Sisco and B Bordelon, 'Ted Cruz Amendment Blows up Journalism Antitrust Bill' (*Politico*, 8 September 2022), www.politico.com/news/2022/09/08/content-moderation-blows-up-journalism-antitrust-bill-00055556.

PART IV

Oceania

12

Media Regulation and Press Freedom in Australia: Problems without Resolution

DAVID ROLPH

1. Introduction

Media regulation and press freedom have been the subject of intense policy debate in Australia over the last decade. There have been six major national public inquiries into aspects of media regulation and press freedom conducted in that period of time. These have been undertaken by different bodies: one was an inquiry undertaken by a former judicial officer; one by an expert committee; one by an independent statutory body; and three by parliamentary committees. The six reports generated by these inquiries have all sought to grapple with seemingly intractable problems of how to regulate media in a rapidly changing technological environment; how to reform and adapt existing media regulations, which is constituted around traditional media forms and not the reality of modern media; how to foster public interest journalism when the commercial model underpinning the mass media environment of the second half of the twentieth century has substantially eroded, if not disappeared entirely; and how to protect and enhance media freedom from threats to it, and encroachments upon it, by outside actors, most particularly by the state.

Taken together, the reports represent a substantial body of policy work. They make a significant number of recommendations aimed at improving media regulation and freedom in Australia, many of which would be far-reaching, if implemented. What is striking is that, despite all of this sustained policy work about these important issues, virtually none of the recommendations has been implemented. The consequence is that most of the seemingly intractable problems relating to media regulation and press freedom which existed a decade ago still exist and, if anything, have become more acute with the passage of time. This chapter examines these six reports and, in doing so, explores the current state of media regulation and press freedom in Australia. It considers what legislative responses have in fact occurred and what changes may need to be made to deal with the changed and changing media environment.

2. The Finkelstein Inquiry

The first major report into media regulation and press freedom in Australia was the Report of the Independent Inquiry into the Media and Media Regulation. It came to be known as the 'Finkelstein Inquiry'. In mid-September 2011, the then Minister for Broadband, Communications and the Digital Economy, Senator Stephen Conroy, appointed former justice of the Federal Court of Australia, Raymond Finkelstein QC, to inquire into the media and media regulation. Matthew Ricketson, Professor of Journalism at the University of Canberra, was also appointed to assist with the inquiry.[1] The impetus for the inquiry was the *News of the World* phone hacking scandal and the establishment, in mid-July 2011, by the then British Prime Minister, David Cameron, of the Leveson Inquiry into the culture, practices and ethics of the press.[2] Given that the majority of the print media in Australia is owned by News Ltd, the Australian subsidiary of News Corporation, which was also the parent company of News International, the owner of the *News of the World*, there were understandable calls in Australia for the establishment of a similar inquiry, even though there were no concrete allegations that journalists at News Ltd newspapers had engaged in similar practices to their *News of the World* counterparts.[3] There were particular concerns expressed that News Ltd newspapers, particularly the national broadsheet, *The Australian*, and the Sydney tabloid newspaper, *The Daily Telegraph*, were biased in their reporting of public policy issues, such as climate change.[4] Under the terms of reference, Finkelstein was required to investigate into:

- the effectiveness of current media codes and practices in Australia, particularly in light of the transition from print to digital and online platforms;

- the impact of technological change on the business model supporting quality journalism and news reporting by traditional media organisations and how such activities could be supported and media diversity enhanced;

- ways to strengthen substantially the independence and effectiveness of the Australian Press Council, including in relation to online publications and particularly in relation to the handling of complaints; and

---

[1] Hon R Finkelstein QC, *Report of the Independent Inquiry into the Media and Media Regulation* (28 February 2012) [1.1], https://apo.org.au/sites/default/files/resource-files/2012-02/apo-nid28522.pdf.
[2] ibid [1.4].
[3] ibid [1.5].
[4] ibid [1.6].

- any other related issues affecting the ability of the media to operate according to regulations and codes of practice and in the public interest.[5]

It is important to note that there were important issues not within the Finkelstein Inquiry's terms of reference. The inquiry did not extend to a consideration of whether there should be restrictions imposed on foreign ownership of the Australian press or other changes to the laws relating to press ownership.[6] The timeline for the inquiry was short, considering the breadth of the issues to be canvassed, with the Report due by February 2012, less than six months after it was established.[7] The Report was delivered on time, on 28 February 2012.

There was a public call for submissions.[8] In addition, Finkelstein wrote to publishers, editors and academics soliciting submissions.[9] Ultimately, approximately 11,000 submissions were received, of which about 9,600 were co-ordinated by an advocacy group.[10] Public hearings were held,[11] at which 41 people gave evidence.[12] The inquiry also undertook a visit to the office of *The West Australian* newspaper to observe the making of a daily newspaper. Finkelstein described it as 'a most enlightening experience'.[13] Finally, the inquiry conducted an academic roundtable on freedom of expression and its relationship to freedom of the press.[14]

The Report of the Finkelstein Inquiry commenced with a consideration of 'the democratic indispensability of a free press'. It canvassed the historical background to the emergence of a free press in England.[15] It then examined the well-known rationales for freedom of speech and freedom of the press, beginning with 'the search for truth'[16] and 'the marketplace of ideas', then turning to the necessity of freedom of speech for citizens' participation in representative democracy[17] and the role of free speech in individuals' self-fulfilment and autonomy.[18] It considered the rationale of a free press specifically as 'the fourth estate'.[19] The Report reached the unsurprising conclusion that, which rationale is relied upon, freedom of speech is not absolute.[20] It then turned to consider the rationale for a free press, giving most attention to the 'social responsibility'

---

[5] ibid [1.2].
[6] ibid [1.2].
[7] ibid [1.2].
[8] ibid [1.8].
[9] ibid [1.10], Annexure B.
[10] ibid [1.11].
[11] ibid [1.12].
[12] ibid [1.14].
[13] ibid [1.15].
[14] ibid [1.16].
[15] ibid [2.8]–[2.13].
[16] ibid [2.14]–[2.28].
[17] ibid [2.29]–[2.34].
[18] ibid [2.35]–[2.40].
[19] ibid [2.41]–[2.46].
[20] ibid [2.47]–[2.51].

theory, the idea, in essence, that, because the press is an institution enjoying certain protections and privileges, it owes a responsibility to the society in which it operates. It explored the history of the social responsibility theory of a free press, as well as some critiques of it.[21]

Drawing upon the work of several theorists, the Report then identified a number of roles played by news media in contemporary democracies: information, investigation, analysis, social empathy, public forum and mobilisation.[22] It concluded that, although there was substantial agreement that a vital press was necessary for a functioning democracy,[23] there was equally a widespread belief that the press wielded significant power, with which came significant responsibility.[24] However, as the Report noted, whilst there was consensus about these issues of principle, there was significant difference as to the limits to be imposed, when they should be imposed, who should impose them and how they should be imposed.[25] It noted the particular concern about government regulation of the media, which may seek to advance the interests of the incumbent party by preventing scrutiny and limiting criticism. It equally noted, however, the proprietors of commercial news organisations, having their own interests to advance.[26]

The Report then turned to examine the Australian newspaper industry's structure and performance. It set out the history of newspapers in Australia,[27] focusing on the increasing concentration of newspaper ownership. It noted that, at the beginning of the twentieth century, there were 21 daily newspaper titles in the six state capital cities, with 17 independent owners. The peak occurred in 1923, when there were 26 daily newspaper titles in those cities, with 21 independent owners. The decline in newspaper titles and the concentration in newspaper ownership had become pronounced by the mid-twentieth century, with the growing challenge of radio and television as sources of news and current affairs.[28] By 1960, there were only 14 daily newspaper titles in the six state capital cities, with only seven independent owners.[29] The Report noted that, in 1984, there were 56 daily newspapers, published across Australia but that, by 1992, this had declined to 49 titles.[30] By 2012, only Sydney and Melbourne had competing daily newspapers. Most state capital cities, urban and regional centres, had only one daily newspaper. Only 11 titles comprised the major metropolitan and national newspapers. There were only three owners for these titles. The Report also noted that the overwhelming majority of these titles had existed since the 1930s.[31]

---

[21] ibid [2.52]–[2.88].
[22] ibid [2.90].
[23] ibid [2.89].
[24] ibid [2.90]–[2.91].
[25] ibid [2.92].
[26] ibid [2.93].
[27] ibid [3.3]–[3.4].
[28] ibid [3.7].
[29] ibid [3.6].
[30] ibid [3.8].
[31] ibid [3.9].

In relation to the 58 regional newspapers, although most of these began as independent concerns, by 2008, only two of them were.[32] At the time of the Report, there were four major newspaper publishers. The largest, owning 65 per cent of the total circulation of the metropolitan and national daily newspapers, or 58 per cent of all daily newspapers, was News Ltd. The second largest, owning 25 per cent of the total circulation of the metropolitan and national daily newspapers or 28 per cent of all daily newspapers, was Fairfax Media. (Fairfax Media no longer exists, after it merged in July 2018 with Nine Entertainment Co, a major media company, the principal asset of which is the commercial television network, Channel Nine.) The remainder of the newspaper market is divided between WA Newspapers, which is the major newspaper proprietor in Western Australia, and APN, which owns newspapers in regional New South Wales and Queensland.[33] The Report concluded that 'Australia's newspaper industry is among the most concentrated in the developed world'.[34]

The Report then tested the proposition that the advent of the internet was responsible for the decline in newspaper circulation in Australia. It noted that newspaper circulation had begun to decline noticeably from the late 1950s onwards, with the arrival of television in Australia, a trend which continued with the passage of time. The closure of all afternoon tabloid newspapers by the late 1980s demonstrated this.[35] The Report also considered the impact of the internet on advertising revenue. It is reflective of the time at which the Report was written, but which looks curious when viewed from this current vantage point. The Report notes that there had been some decline in newspaper classified advertising but that this may be in part due to the effects of the Global Financial Crisis of 2008.[36] The Report still talked about the prospects of newspapers deriving a revenue stream from online advertising,[37] but noted the challenges of seeking simply to translate 'offline' advertising online.[38]

The Report unsurprisingly found that declining newspaper readership accompanied declining newspaper circulation. It recorded that, in 2006–07, 82 per cent of Australians aged 14 years and over had read a national or metropolitan daily newspaper in the preceding week. By 2010–11, that figure had dropped to 72 per cent. The Report noted that newspaper readership was strongly correlated with age, with the decline being lowest amongst those aged 65 years and older.[39] In addition, it noted that the decline in newspaper readership was strongly correlated to the extent of internet use.[40]

---

[32] ibid [3.10].
[33] ibid [3.11].
[34] ibid [3.12].
[35] ibid [3.36]–[3.38].
[36] ibid [3.52].
[37] ibid [3.53]–[3.56].
[38] ibid [3.58].
[39] ibid [3.67].
[40] ibid [3.68].

The Report canvassed a range of survey evidence that confirmed that a signifi-cant reason for internet use by Australians was to access news online, particularly national rather than local or international news. This use, though, consistently ranked behind email, instant messaging and banking transactions.[41] However, research from a variety of sources also confirmed that internet users tended to spend less time and engaged less with online news.[42] In addition, the Report noted that multiple surveys confirmed that there was a low willingness amongst Australians to pay for online news content.[43]

The Report then turned to consider media standards. At the outset, it recorded that the prevailing, although not unanimous, view amongst Australian media executives was that there was no problem with Australian media standards and that existing accountability mechanisms were sufficient.[44] The Report framed its discussion by observing that there was 'much to celebrate about the Australian news media', pointing in particular to journalists' coverage of natural disasters and overseas conflicts.[45] Nevertheless, the Report noted that there were real prob-lems with public confidence in the media. It recorded that, in 21 surveys over the period from 1966 to 2011, there had been a marked decline in Australians' posi-tive perceptions of the media on the issues of trust, performance, bias, power and influence and ethics.[46]

On the issue of trust, however, the Report noted that there were significant differences in the levels of trust between institutes and outlets, with the national broadcaster, the Australian Broadcasting Corporation (ABC), consistently ranked as the most trusted media organisation in the country.[47] It recorded that Australians generally, and even Australian journalists themselves, consistently thought poorly of the accuracy of the Australian media.[48] It identified the emerging problem of an increasing reliance upon public relations material in news reporting as a signifi-cant challenge to high quality journalism.[49] The Report further noted the media had been identified by the Australian public as one of the four major centres of power in Australian life, alongside the national government, business and trade unions.[50] Survey evidence consistently demonstrated that Australians were concerned at the disproportionate power and influence wielded by the media in Australian public life.[51]

The disparity between community expectations and media ethics was exposed in the survey evidence canvassed in the Report. On the issue of whether it was

---

[41] ibid [3.73]–[3.74], [3.78]–[3.80].
[42] ibid [3.83]–[3.84].
[43] ibid [3.100]–[3.101].
[44] ibid [4.1]–[4.5].
[45] ibid [4.6]–[4.7].
[46] ibid [4.11], [4.14], [4.18], [4.21], [4.23], [4.26]–[4.34].
[47] ibid [4.15].
[48] ibid [4.23].
[49] ibid [4.24].
[50] ibid [4.43].
[51] ibid [4.44]–[4.45].

unethical to take a photograph of a person in their backyard from outside the property without the person's consent, 92 per cent of Australians thought it was, whilst only 38 per cent of professional journalists surveyed did. On the ethics of pretending to be sympathetic to a person in order to secure an interview, 68 per cent of journalists thought it was right and only 28 per cent thought it was never right, whereas 70 per cent of Australians thought it was never right and only 29 per cent thought it was right.[52] The Report asserted, however, that those who received their news online tended to have higher levels of trust in it and higher levels of distrust in traditional media outlets. It concluded: 'Why this should be so is not yet clear.'[53]

The Report then canvassed the privileges the media enjoyed, and the restrictions imposed upon them, under Australian law. As to the media's privileges, the Report included protections against journalists' sources,[54] the 'information provider' defence to misleading or deceptive conduct,[55] exemptions from the Privacy Act 1988 (Cth),[56] media-specific defences to Commonwealth and state offences[57] and privileges for court reporting.[58] In relation to restrictions on freedom of speech and freedom of the press, the Report listed official secrets legislation,[59] terrorism and sedition offences,[60] racial discrimination laws,[61] classification laws,[62] the principles of *sub judice* contempt, suppression and non-publication orders,[63] defamation,[64] copyright[65] and confidential information.[66]

The Report then turned to examine the regulation of broadcasting in Australia, taking the understandable view that, given media convergence, it was no longer feasible to attempt to discuss newspapers in isolation.[67] It noted that print and online media were essentially self-regulated, whereas radio and television were heavily regulated by statute.[68] It identified the reasons ordinarily given for the differential treatment of broadcasting, notably the need to allocate finite spectrum, as well as the perceived power that broadcasting has to influence

---

[52] ibid [4.56].
[53] ibid [4.77].
[54] ibid [5.15]–[5.18].
[55] ibid [5.19]–[5.23]. As to the 'information provider' defence to misleading or deceptive conduct, see Australian Consumer Law (Cth), s 19.
[56] Finkelstein (n 1) [5.24]–[5.30].
[57] ibid [5.31].
[58] ibid [5.37]–[5.41].
[59] ibid [5.37]–[5.38].
[60] ibid [5.59]–[5.61].
[61] ibid [5.62]–[5.64].
[62] ibid [5.65]–[5.70].
[63] ibid [5.71]–[5.80].
[64] ibid [5.90]–[5.110].
[65] ibid [5.111]–[5.112].
[66] ibid [5.113]–[5.116].
[67] ibid [6.1].
[68] ibid [6.2]. As to the history of broadcasting regulation in Australia, see ibid [6.7]–[6.15]. The principal legislation regulating radio and television in Australia is the Broadcasting Services Act 1992 (Cth).

public attitudes.[69] The Report then considered the complaints handling procedures of the broadcasting regulator, the Australian Communications and Media Authority (ACMA),[70] as well as those of the national broadcasters, the ABC and the Special Broadcasting Service (SBS).[71] It concluded that the ACMA's procedures did not provide a sound model, given that complaints took four months, on average, to resolve.[72] In beginning to develop its own response to the problem of regulating a converged media environment, the Report rejected the idea that any public funding would undermine the independence of a media regulator, pointing in support of the independence of publicly funded broadcasters like the ABC and the BBC.[73]

The Report then contrasted the regulation of broadcasting with the self-regulation of the print media. It raised to dismiss the market as an accountability mechanism.[74] It then canvassed journalists' codes of ethics[75] and ombudsmen or readers' editors[76] as other forms of accountability mechanisms. However, the most significant accountability mechanism for print media is the Australian Press Council (APC). Before examining the APC, the Report canvassed the history and operation of press councils in the United Kingdom, New Zealand, Ireland and South Africa.[77] It then detailed the history of the APC.[78] The Report then turned to the APC's current constitution, membership and functions.[79] It noted that the three principal functions of the APC are the development of media standards, the issuing of policy statements and the determination of complaints.[80] A key feature of the APC's complaints handling process is that a complainant has to waive their right to take legal action between a complaint about a publication can proceed.[81] In assessing the effectiveness of the APC, the Report noted that there were limitations affecting this. Nevertheless, the Report did identify the APC's structure as a significant problem. Because the APC was a self-regulatory body, it was funded by, and is therefore dependent upon, the will of media organisations. Media organisations can withdraw from, or not subscribe to, the APC's jurisdiction. They can withdraw funding. They can bring to bear formal or informal pressure on the APC's decision-making.[82]

Having canvassed the APC's operation, the Report concluded that 'few people outside the media contend that self-regulation or, at a minimum, the current

---

[69] Finkelstein Report (n 1) [6.26]–[6.28].
[70] ibid [6.40]–[6.40].
[71] ibid [6.50]–[6.59].
[72] ibid [6.60].
[73] ibid [6.67].
[74] ibid [7.5]–[7.9].
[75] ibid [7.33].
[76] ibid [7.35]–[7.50].
[77] ibid [8.10]–[8.61].
[78] ibid [8.64]–[8.85].
[79] ibid [8.86]–[8.91].
[80] ibid [8.92].
[81] ibid [8.98].
[82] ibid [8.109].

form of self-regulation, is adequate'.[83] It identified 'the better view ... that there must be some effective means of raising standards of journalism and of making the media publicly accountable'.[84] Beginning to think about public account-ability mechanisms, the Report recommended an enforceable right of reply.[85] It canvassed, but ultimately dismissed as unworkable, an enforceable right of access to the media.[86]

The Report then turned to examine directly the issue of regulation. It began by canvassing theories for regulation, albeit briefly. It identified two broad ration-ales for regulation: to address market failure and to pursue social or equity objectives.[87] The Report suggested that, rather than conceiving of regulation as a dichotomy between self-regulation and government regulation, regulation should be thought of as a spectrum, with these options as the opposite ends but with a variety of different blends and formulations in between.[88] It considered the relative advantages and disadvantages of government regulation and self-regulation.[89] It canvassed co-regulation as an intermediate pathway.[90] The Report then examined regulatory design, observing that this was essential to the efficacy of any regulatory system which might be recommended.[91]

The Report then turned to consider proposed reforms directly. It asked first whether there was a problem which needed addressing through reform. The Report identified market failure as a significant consideration. Given that news generated additional social benefits beyond the private benefits to the media and consumers, there was information asymmetry between the media and consumers – consumers were not in a position to determine for themselves whether the news they were receiving was accurate – and the concentration of media ownership, there were, in the Report's view, multiple indicators of market failure in the Australian media market, warranting intervention.[92] The other major considera-tion was the lack of public trust in the media.[93]

The Report concluded that self-regulation had failed to address irrespon-sible reporting. It also concluded that the APC had failed, for a combination of reasons: 'lack of awareness of its existence, lack of funding, lack of enforcement powers, lack of reach'.[94] The Report noted the special problems presented by online

---

[83] ibid [8.123]. For further consideration of the efficacy of press self-regulation, see Hon R Finkelstein and R Tiffen, 'When Does Press Self-Regulation Work?' (2015) 38 *Melbourne University Law Review* 944.

[84] Finkelstein Report (n 1) [8.127].

[85] ibid [9.49].

[86] ibid [9.51]–[9.67].

[87] ibid [10.4].

[88] ibid [10.14].

[89] ibid [10.23]–[10.25].

[90] ibid. [10.26]–[10.27].

[91] ibid [10.29].

[92] ibid [11.3]–[11.5].

[93] ibid [11.7].

[94] ibid [11.12].

publications and the incongruity of different regulatory regimes applying to the same content in different media.[95] It then stated that the costs of ineffective regulation of the media are borne not by the media but by those who are the target of inaccurate and unfair reporting who have no meaningful redress at law and by the community more generally, which depends upon the media for accurate news for a functioning democracy.[96] The Report suggested that a regulatory regime should be designed which transferred back the costs from individuals and the community more generally to the media themselves, in order to provide the media with an incentive to improve their standards.[97]

Of the possible regulatory options, the Report rejected self-regulation as the ineffective *status quo*. Equally, it rejected the licensing of the press, as an excessive form of governmental intervention with the prospect of censorship.[98] The Report was clear that any regulatory regime needed legal backing in order to be effective.[99] Ultimately, the model advocated by the Report was what it styled 'enforced self-regulation', being 'an independent system of regulation that allows the regulated parties to participate in the setting and enforcement of standards, ... but with participation being required, rather than voluntary'.[100] Thus, the Report recommended the establishment of an independent statutory body, the News Media Council (NMC), to oversee the enforcement of news media standards.

Such a body would take over the functions of the APC and the ACMA.[101] It recommended that the NMC should be independent of the executive.[102] There should be an independent body responsible for appointments to the NMC.[103] The NMC should have a full-time chair and 20 part-time members.[104] The chair should be a retired judge or another eminent lawyer, whether practising or non-practising.[105] The part-time members should be equally male and female,[106] and half should be drawn from the media whilst the other half should be members of the public.[107] The Report recommended that the NMC should be funded out of consolidated revenue, rather than from a levy on industry.[108] In terms of the NMC's functions, the Report was emphatic that the NMC should not be concerned with the promotion of freedom of speech as '[t]here are ample bodies

[95] ibid [11.13].
[96] ibid [11.17].
[97] ibid [11.19].
[98] ibid [11.26].
[99] ibid [11.27].
[100] ibid [11.32].
[101] ibid [11.44].
[102] ibid [11.45].
[103] ibid [11.46].
[104] ibid [11.47].
[105] ibid [11.50].
[106] ibid [11.49].
[107] ibid [11.48].
[108] ibid [11.53].

and persons in the community who do that more than adequately'.[109] Rather, it should be concerned with the setting of standards, the investigation of alleged contraventions of those standards[110] and educating the media and the public about those standards.[111] The NMC should also, in the Report's view, undertake a periodic assessment of the state of Australian news media, to allow for informed and serious analysis of media performance.[112] As to the jurisdiction of the NMC, the Report recommended that it 'should have supervision of the standards of all news media on all platforms'.[113]

The Report grappled with the difficulty of defining the 'news media' for the purposes of the NMC's jurisdiction.[114] It also considered that the NMC should have jurisdiction over any internet publisher which has a 'more than tenuous connection with Australia'.[115] The Report recommended that the NMC should have the power to order the publication of a correction or a right of reply, the power to require the withdrawal of a publication, to direct the publication of an NMC determination and to direct where and when such publications should occur.[116] It recommended against allowing the NMC to impose fines or order compensation as such a course would raise constitutional problems.[117] To enforce its decisions, the NMC should have the power to apply to a court of competent jurisdiction for an order compelling compliance, in default of which the media outlet would be held in contempt of court.[118] During such a court process, the Report recommended that there may be judicial review of the NMC's decision but that otherwise there should be no internal or external appeals or reviews of the NMC's decisions.[119]

Unsurprisingly, the Finkelstein Inquiry produced a strong, swift and adverse reaction from the Australian media.[120] Broadly, it was perceived as inimical to

---

[109] ibid [11.55].

[110] As to the Report's recommendations about the NMC's complaints handling procedures, see ibid [11.70]–[11.73].

[111] ibid [11.52], [11.55].

[112] ibid [11.56]–[11.57].

[113] ibid [11.58].

[114] ibid [11.59]–[11.67].

[115] ibid [11.69].

[116] ibid [11.74].

[117] ibid [11.76].

[118] ibid [11.77].

[119] ibid [11.78]–[11.79].

[120] See, eg, S Brook, 'Put Simply, Mooted Muzzle Would Not Work' *The Australian* (3 March 2012) 8; B Hall and J Lee, 'New Media Watchdog Plan Angers Publishers' *The Canberra Times* (3 March 2012) 6; L Tingle and A White, 'Labor Plan to Control the Media' *The Australian Financial Review* (3 March 2012) 1; C Berg, 'Free Press to be Sacrificed for Political Retribution' *The Sunday Age* (4 March 2012) 15; A Bolt, 'Thought Police can Only Stifle Debate' *The Daily Telegraph* (5 March 2012) 13; N Christensen, 'Fears Sites Will Go Offshore' *The Australian* (5 March 2012) 5; M Day, 'Free Press Not Open to Political Meddling' *The Australian* (5 March 2012) 24; M Gawenda, 'Findings All Very Good in Theory' *The Australian* (5 March 2012) 28; A Meade, 'Inquiry Upsets the Networks: TV could Be Brought under Mega Watchdog' *The Australian* (5 March 2012) 28; E Simper, 'New Cop Not the Solution' *The Australian* (5 March 2012) 24; A White and J Chessell, 'Politicians "Running a

freedom of the press, attempting to address a foreign problem without an analogue in Australia and a distraction from the serious political difficulties which beset the Gillard Labor Government. There was some public support for the proposed NMC,[121] but this was a minority view. The release of the Finkelstein Inquiry's Report generated a temporary fillip in support for the APC.[122] The Gillard Labor Government never moved to implement the Finkelstein Inquiry's recommendations. Indeed, Gillard herself was deposed as the leader of the Australian Labor Party, with Kevin Rudd being returned as Prime Minister of Australia before the 2013 Federal election.

3. The Convergence Review

Another initiative of the Gillard Labor Government in relation to media regulation was the commissioning of the review into Australia's media and communications policy framework. Known as the Convergence Review,[123] the report was prepared by a committee comprised of Glen Moreham (the former managing director of IBM Australia and New Zealand), Malcolm Long (the former managing director of Australia's multicultural public broadcaster, the SBS) and Louise McEvogue (an international digital executive who had worked in Australia, the United Kingdom and the United States). The committee was appointed by the then Minister for Broadband, Communications and the Digital Economy, Senator Stephen Conroy, in March 2011. In addition to extensive consultations with key industry leaders and organisations and public consultations, the committee received 340 written submissions. The fundamental approach of the Convergence Review was to remove unnecessary and expensive regulation. In reimagining the Australian media and communications regulatory regime, the Convergence Review sought not only to answer the question, 'Why regulate?' but also to answer the question, 'Who should be regulated?'

Jihad" Against News' *The Australian Financial Review* (5 March 2012) 2; G Henderson, 'Lawyers and Academics Propose More Regulation? It's Hardly News' *The Sydney Morning Herald* (6 March 2012) 11; D Kemp, 'Finkelstein Media Recommendations Would Poison our Democracy' *The Australian* (6 March 2012) 14; J Albrechtsen, '"Never Waste a Crisis" and Other Inexorable Laws of Political Nature' *The Australian* (7 March 2012) 12; T Andrews, 'Finkelstein Report Threatens to Muzzle Free Speech' *The Australian Financial Review* (7 March 2012) 63; P Kelly, 'Naïve Hubris Pervades Media Inquiry' *The Australian* (7 March 2012) 12; C Jones, 'Media Reform "Like Cuba"' *The Advertiser* (9 March 2012) 9; H Mitchell, 'There Is No Pressing Case to Be Made for Reform' *The Sydney Morning Herald* (9 March 2012) 8; J Roskam, 'A Failure to Defend Liberty' *The Australian Financial Review* (9 March 2012) 50; D McLure, 'Aussies can Decide for Themselves about the Media: A Step Towards Pravda' *The Geelong Advertiser* (10 March 2012) 40; H Ergas, 'Watchdog can Muzzle Government's Critics' *The Australian* (12 March 2012) 12.

[121] See, eg, S North, 'Finkelstein's "Monster" Not So Big and Scary' *The Sydney Morning Herald* (13 March 2012) 11; R Tiffen, 'Finkelstein Gets a Bad Press' *The Age* (14 March 2012) 13.

[122] See, eg, K Simpson, 'Publishers Aim to Bolster APC for Better Regulation' *The Sydney Morning Herald* (9 March 2012) 8.

[123] As to the terms of reference of the Convergence Review, see Australian Government, *Convergence Review, Final Report* (March 2012), Appendix A.

The Report strongly recommended a movement away from what it character-ised as a 'black-letter' approach to media regulation. It noted that Australian media were currently regulated by highly detailed legislation based on specific delivery platforms, which had an inbuilt obsolescence. Instead, the report recommended a principles-based approach to regulation, coupled with an independent regulator. Such an approach, in the Report's view, would allow for greater adaptability to meet the challenges posed by media convergence as well as enhancing transpar-ency and clarity.[124] An independent regulator which could apply, amend or remove regulatory measures was, in the report's view, the preferred option. In addition, the Report recommended the establishment of a separate, industry-led body to over-see news and journalistic standards across all platforms.[125] The Report traversed a range of other issues, including the allocation and management of broadcasting spectrum and Australian content standards for television, radio and public and community broadcasting.

At the outset, the Report made clear the need for a new approach to regu-lation, noting that the existing regulatory arrangements had been overtaken by developments in communication technologies. It used television as an obvious illustration: commercial television remains heavily regulated in Australia, under the Broadcasting Services Act 1992, because of its use of broadcasting spectrum, yet it is technologically possible now to start a television service online, which would be unencumbered by this regulation. The thrust of the Report was avow-edly deregulatory. The Report identified the three areas warranting continuing government intervention as diversity in media ownership and control, content standards and Australian content. The alternative regulatory model proposed by the Report focused on significant enterprises, rather than specific media outlets and platforms. In the Report's view, the type of content, the size of the audience and the revenue generated should be the bases attracting regulation. Thus, the Report contemplated that blogging and user-generated content should be outside the ambit of regulation.[126]

The Report made some key recommendations underpinning its new approach to media regulation. First, it recommended that Parliament should avoid enact-ing legislation which favoured or disadvantaged any particular communications technology, business model or delivery method for content services. Instead, the focus of legislation should be on establishing the parameters within which the independent media regulator can operate. Second, the Report recommended that there should be no licensing requirement or other barrier to entry for the supply of content or communication services, except where there was a finite resource, such as radio-communications spectrum. Third, the focus of media regulation should be on large enterprises providing professional content services to a signifi-cant number of Australians. The Report recommended that such large enterprises

---

[124] ibid 14.
[125] ibid 15.
[126] ibid 11.

should have proposed changes in their ownership scrutinised, should be required to meet community expectations about content standards and should contribute appropriately to the availability of Australian content. Such large enterprises should be identified by the control they have over the content they deliver, a threshold of a large number of Australian users of their content and a threshold of a high level of revenue derived from the supply of professional content to Australians.[127] The independent regulator should be able to determine and review the criteria for what constitutes a large enterprise.[128]

The Report suggested that the thresholds for content service providers being subject to the proposed regulatory framework should start at AUS$50 million per annum in Australian-sourced revenue, with 500,000 users per month.[129] The Report rejected the suggestion, made in some submissions, that the Review was attempting to regulate the internet. It took the position that any enterprise which had a significant presence in Australia should be accountable in Australia.[130] Beyond direct regulation, the Report recommended that the regulator should have the power to promote the development of the media sector, engage with industry in developing solutions to problems, report on the state of the media market, protect users, such as through complaints processes, inform users through public education processes and provide advice and propose initiatives to government.[131]

The Report was asked to consider the recommendations of the Finkelstein Inquiry in its development of its own approach to content standards. The Report concluded that the Finkelstein Inquiry's recommendation of what it character-ised as 'a statutory authority that would regulate news and commentary' should be 'an option of last resort'.[132] The Report argued that its recommendation for an industry-led solution was more likely to produce immediate results, as well as providing a better long-term solution. Instead, it recommended a two-fold approach to media regulation, which was, in its view, technology-neutral and flex-ible. First, it recommended that there should be a new communications regulator, which should be responsible for all compliance matters relating to media content standards, except in relation to news and commentary. For news and commentary, the Report recommended that there should be an independent, self-regulatory news standards body which should be responsible for enforcing a media code aiming at ensuring fairness, accuracy and transparency in professional news and commentary.

In relation to this news standards body, it recommended that content service providers should be required to join such a body and to fund it, along

---

[127] ibid 10.
[128] ibid 13.
[129] ibid 12.
[130] ibid 13.
[131] ibid 16.
[132] ibid 37.

with a financial contribution from government (of at least a third of its running costs),[133] given the public interest in such a body. The Report also recommended that those news and commentary providers who were not content service providers should be strongly encouraged to subject themselves to this new body. The Report recommended that the news standards body needed to have 'credible sanctions' and the power to order the prominent publication of its findings. As to the interaction between the communications regulator and the news standards body, the Report recommended that the news standards body should be able to refer a news or commentary provider to the communications regulator where that provider had engaged in persistent or serious breaches of the media code and that the communications regulator should be able to request the news standards body to conduct an investigation.[134] This approach, the Report argued, was consistently with its twin concerns of ensuring consistency across platforms and deregulation.[135]

The Report recommended that the news standards body should be independent of government. Thus, legislation should not dictate its form, structure and operation. However, the Report recommended that there should be legislation requiring content service providers to become members of the news standards body and to prescribe requirements for what constitutes a content service provider. It identified the structural weakness of the APC as the ability of members to opt out of its jurisdiction at any time and to defund it. The Report suggested that content service providers' retention of privileges under Commonwealth law, such as special defences against liability for misleading or deceptive conduct and exemptions from privacy legislation should be contingent upon membership of the news standards body.[136]

The Report identified convergence as a significant issue, rendering existing media regulation in Australia incoherent. It pointed in particular to the blurring of boundaries, whereby traditional media platforms had significant and increasing online presence, the emergence of online platforms, which fell outside coverage by existing media regulation, the explosion in mobile content, which was poorly regulated by existing media regulation, and social media sites, aggregators and user-generated content hosts, which were only regulated when people complained about content.[137] The Convergence Review was less controversial than the Finkelstein Inquiry, which was understandable, given the orientation of its recommendations. However, like the Finkelstein Inquiry, it did not lead to legislative changes, leaving the difficult policy conundrum of regulating a converged media environment unresolved.

[133] ibid 52.
[134] ibid 38.
[135] ibid 50.
[136] ibid 51.
[137] ibid 40.

4. The Senate Select Committee on the Future of Public Interest Journalism

The third inquiry undertaken in Australia within the last decade on a topic of media regulation and press freedom was the Senate Select Committee on the Future of Public Interest Journalism. The Committee was established by the Senate in mid-May 2017. Under its terms of reference, it was to inquire into the current state of public interest journalism in Australia, including the role of government in facilitating such journalism; the adequacy of competition and consumer laws to deal with the market power of search engines, social media platforms and content aggregators; the impact on public interest journalism of search engines and social media platforms circulating 'fake news'; an examination of fake news, propaganda and disinformation in Australia and overseas; and the future of public and community broadcasters in delivering public interest journalism, in regional Australia and to culturally and linguistically diverse groups.[138] The majority report was produced by Labour and Green Senators. There was a brief minority report from the Liberal National Party Government Senators. What follows is a distillation of what the majority report found. The Report noted that the APC had been invited to participate in the inquiry but did not make a submission and did not appear to give evidence at a public hearing. It described this non-engagement as 'profoundly disappointing'.[139]

The Report began by identifying media trends since the Finkelstein Inquiry Report. In particular, it noted that the scale and speed of technological changes had depleted the capacity of traditional media outlets to conduct public interest journalism and that this capacity had not been replaced by online media content providers.[140] It noted that traditional media outlets were still struggling to monetise online content,[141] and internet technologies' disruption of traditional media's business models had led to accelerating job losses.[142] The fragmentation of media markets was also accelerating.[143] The Report noted that these changes had particular impacts in relation to certain forms of journalism, such as local, regional and rural reporting,[144] 'journal of record' journalism,[145] foreign affairs,[146] public health,[147] indigenous affairs[148] and content for culturally and

---

[138] *Senate Select Committee on the Future of Public Interest Journalism, Report* (February 2018) [1.1].
[139] ibid [1.29]–[1.30].
[140] ibid [2.4].
[141] ibid [2.7], [2.14].
[142] ibid [2.7], [2.21]–[2.23], [2.25].
[143] ibid [2.17]–[2.18].
[144] ibid [2.33]–[2.40].
[145] ibid [2.41]–[244].
[146] ibid [2.45].
[147] ibid [2.46]–[2.47].
[148] ibid [2.48]–[2.50].

linguistically diverse communities.[149] The Report noted the rise of the phenomenon of fake news, connecting it with the 2016 United States Presidential election and the Brexit referendum,[150] but observed that, for all the references to fake news in the submissions, that there was little evidence advanced for fake news in Australia.[151]

The Report then turned to examine the opportunities presented by changing technologies. It noted that internet technologies had increased and internationalised audiences for content and reduced barriers to entry.[152] It also noted that, by this time, there was evidence of positive growth for traditional media outlets as a result of online technologies, in part through increased online subscriptions for established mastheads and in part from monetisation of content and diversification of revenue.[153] The Report then considered the effectiveness of tax incentives to drive philanthropic investment in public interest journalism, accepting that there was evidence both in the United Kingdom and the United States suggesting that this approach was effective in supporting high quality journalism.[154] It noted that there had been little experience of this approach in practice in Australia, with the *New Daily* and *The Saturday Paper* being the two ongoing exceptions.[155] The Report further recorded that the crisis in traditional journalism had led to innovative partnerships between media organisations that might previously have been rivals or between media organisations and universities or journalism schools or centres.[156] Increased diversity of opinion was also identified as a significant benefit of internet technologies over traditional media outlets, which tended to have a strong 'gatekeeping' function.[157]

The Report then turned to examine the relationship between aggregators and the news media. Given their size, power and influence, the Report understandably focused on Google and Facebook.[158] The Report canvassed but ultimately did not recommend the implementation of a levy on aggregators like Google and Facebook as part of an attempt to make them pay an amount to a jurisdiction from which they derived substantial benefits. It did, however, suggest that this policy option was worth considering in the future.[159] The Report noted that Google and Facebook had already altered their practices, in an attempt to minimise the likelihood of such a levy being imposed on them.[160]

---

[149] ibid [2.51]–[2.53].
[150] ibid [2.62].
[151] ibid [2.70].
[152] ibid [3.3]–[3.4].
[153] ibid [4.14].
[154] ibid [3.27]–[32.8].
[155] ibid [3.33].
[156] ibid [3.37], [3.40], [3.43].
[157] ibid [3.44].
[158] ibid [4.2]–[4.3].
[159] ibid [4.64].
[160] ibid [4.63].

The Report then turned to canvass the experience in other countries in subsidising, in different ways, public interest journalism. It considered Germany, Austria, Belgium, the United Kingdom, Norway, Sweden, France, Italy, Spain, the United States, Canada, the Philippines and Indonesia.[161] It then examined the extent to which the Commonwealth Government in Australia already supports public interest journalism, pointing in particular to the public funding of the two national broadcasters, the ABC and SBS.[162] The Report's first recommendation was for adequate Commonwealth funding for the ABC and SBS.

The Report turned to consider the possible uses of the Australian taxation system to encourage philanthropic support of public interest journalism. It identified the most obvious means of doing this by extending deductible gift recipient status to media organisations undertaking public interest journalism, meaning that donations to those organisations would confer a tax deduction on donors.[163] Another option was research and development tax write-offs for media organisations engaging in public interest journalism.[164] A further option was allowing consumers a tax deduction for their news media subscriptions.[165] Ultimately, the Report recommended both the expansion of deductible gift recipient (DGR) status and the tax deductibility of news media subscriptions.[166] The Report then assessed the extent to which public interest journalism was impeded by substantive laws in Australia, noting the effect of national security legislation,[167] defamation laws,[168] inadequate protections for journalists' sources[169] and whistleblowers[170] and copyright law.[171] The Report recommended a review of laws impinging upon public interest journalism and in particular recommended defamation law reform.[172]

5. Digital Platforms Inquiry

Almost five years (and three prime ministers) later, the next large-scale review of media regulation and press freedom by a public body independent of government was commissioned. The statutory body, the Australian Competition and Consumer Commission (ACCC),[173] was directed by its responsible Minister, the

---

[161] See generally ibid, ch 5.
[162] ibid [6.4]–[6.40].
[163] ibid [7.12].
[164] ibid [7.26]–[7.27].
[165] ibid [7.39].
[166] ibid, Recommendations 4 and 5.
[167] ibid [7.47]–[7.54].
[168] ibid [7.56]–[7.64].
[169] ibid [7.70]–[7.72].
[170] ibid [7.65]–[7.69].
[171] ibid [7.73]–[7.77].
[172] ibid, Recommendations 6 and 7.
[173] The ACCC is constituted under the Competition and Consumer Act 2010 (Cth) Pt II.

then Treasurer (and later Prime Minister), Scott Morrison, to inquire into the impact of digital search engines, social media platforms and other digital content aggregation platforms on the state of competition in media and advertising markets, in particular in relation to the supply of news and journalistic content and the implications for media content creators, advertisers and consumers. The ACCC was given 18 months within which to finalise its report.[174] It received 60 submissions in response to its issues paper, released in late February 2018, and over 120 submissions in response to its preliminary report, released in mid-December 2018. As a statutory authority, the ACCC was empowered to, and did, issue statutory notices to various bodies for information and documents.[175] The ACCC also held forums for interested stakeholders. The final report was released in June 2019 (by which time the Minister who commissioned it was the Prime Minister).

The rise of these digital platforms had occurred with astonishing rapidity, within the space of 15 years. The Report recorded that 70 per cent of Australians used Google Search on a daily basis, whilst 58 per cent used Facebook daily, 29 per cent used YouTube daily and 22 per cent used Instagram daily. It also noted the booming online advertising market, with Google and Facebook generating the overwhelming majority of online advertising revenue.[176] The Report noted that digital platforms have a significant impact on news and journalism, even though they did not themselves produce journalism. Digital platforms perform key roles in the supply of consumption of content: by providing platforms for publication and marketing for media businesses, allowing media companies to reach new audiences, by collating and curating news, but also being a rival supplier of advertising opportunities, challenging commercial media outlets in particular. They have transformed the way in which Australians consume news, with the Report noting that, as at 2019, 43 per cent of Australians obtained their news primarily online.[177] The media environment the Report depicted was a disrupted one: one in which the classified advertising revenue which underpinned newspapers and the advertising revenue commercial radio and television relied upon being diverted away to digital platforms, with no replacement stream identified.[178]

As a competition regulator, the ACCC was concerned with the market power of digital platforms. It had no difficulty in concluding that Google had substantial market power in relation to search services and search advertising and was likely to retain this in the medium term.[179] It also readily concluded that Facebook has substantial market power in relation to social media services and display

---

[174] As to the terms of reference of the Digital Platforms Inquiry, see Appendix A.

[175] As to the power of the ACCC to issue notices to provide information and documents, see Competition and Consumer Act 2010 (Cth), s 95ZK.

[176] Australian Competition and Consumer Commission, *Digital Platforms Inquiry, Final Report* (June 2019) [1.2].

[177] ibid [1.4].

[178] ibid [1.5].

[179] ibid [2.3], [2.6].

advertising, which it was likely to retain in the short to medium term.[180] The extent of time users spent on these platforms, as well as the breadth and depth of data collected by Google and Facebook, made these digital platforms attractive to advertisers.[181] Given the substantial market power of Google and Facebook, traditional media outlets were compelled to engage with them but, in those negotiations, the digital platforms had substantial bargaining power,[182] making it difficult for traditional media outlets to secure a commercially beneficial deal.[183]

The ACCC concluded that digital platforms actively participate in the 'online news ecosystem' and perform several of the same functions as traditional news outlets: by selecting and curating news content, by evaluating content according to specific criteria; and ranking and arranging content for display, by displaying advertising services (although not yet creating its own content).[184] Consequently, in the Report's view, digital platforms are more than mere distributors or pure intermediaries of news content in Australia. However, the ACCC noted that virtually no regulation applies to digital platforms.[185] The problem is compounded, in the Report's view, by the sector-specific approach to the regulation of Australian media and Australian media content. Digitalisation and the rise of online news and media sources exposed the inconsistent regulatory treatment of the Australian media, according to the ACCC.[186] In particular, the ACCC viewed the inadequate addressing of media convergence as presenting a problem to competition within the Australian media sector.[187]

Under its terms of reference, the ACCC was required to consider the impact of digital platforms on the choice and quality of news and journalism to consumers. It accepted that there were a number of benefits to be derived from providing high-quality news and journalism: holding the powerful to account; campaigning for social goals; keeping a journal of record; and providing a forum for ideas. Because high-quality news and journalism contributes to politics, the economy and society more generally, the ACCC reasoned that there was a public interest in maintaining high journalistic standards.[188] In seeking to define 'public interest journalism', the ACCC adopted the meaning settled upon by the Cairncross Review on a sustainable future for journalism, being journalism which 'has the primary purpose of recording, investigating and explaining public policy and issues of public interest or significance with the aim of engaging citizens in public debate and informing democratic decision making'.[189]

---

[180] ibid [2.4], [2.7].
[181] ibid [2.5].
[182] ibid [2.8.1].
[183] ibid [3.7].
[184] ibid [4.2.1]–[4.2.3].
[185] ibid [4.3.2]–[4.3.6].
[186] ibid [4.5].
[187] ibid [4.4].
[188] ibid [6.2.1].
[189] ibid [6.2.2].

The ACCC expressed the view that this definition of 'public interest journalism' was broad, but did not extend to 'celebrity gossip, opinion pieces detailing personal experience of a new diet or car, coverage of fashion launches and reporting of sport results'. It emphasised that it was not suggesting that such journalism was without value but rather that it was concerned to identify types of journalism without which Australian society as a whole would suffer a detriment.[190] Because the ACCC was asked to consider quality and choice in journalism, it turned to explain how it conceived of those two terms. It suggested that high quality journalism would need to meet minimum standards of accuracy, objectivity and transparency. It accepted that not every item of what qualified as public interest journalism would necessarily constitute high quality journalism.[191] In relation to the concept of choice, the Report noted that historically, Australia had tried to address choice through diversity of ownership. Increasingly, however, it noted that there was a concerted effort to view choice through the prism of the plurality of voices available in the media.[192]

The ACCC noted that a significant part of Australia's media landscape was regional and local news, across different platforms. However, problems were presented because the populations were smaller, the journalists were fewer and the advertising revenues to underwrite such journalism were less substantial, compared to major metropolitan media.[193] It also noted the rise of what it described as 'digital natives' – media outlets which only existed online, in contrast to traditional media outlets, which existed before the internet was invented and have been migrating online.[194]

The Report noted that online publication had several advantages over traditional media formats, most obviously lower production and distribution costs.[195] It also led to the rapid decline in classified advertising, which had historically underpinned public interest journalism in print.[196] The Report pinpointed the ways in which digital platforms challenged the business model of traditional media outlets: by being significant rivals for advertising spend, whilst at the same time being key providers in the advertising supply chain; by facilitating the 'atomisation' of journalism and the dilution of brand value, whilst also providing new opportunities for low-cost content production. In terms of the adverse impact of atomisation and self-curation of news, the ACCC recorded its own survey evidence, in which it found that, whilst 66 per cent of adults identified the source of a news story as important, only 45 per cent of 17-year-old schoolchildren did.

---

[190] ibid [6.2.2].
[191] ibid [6.3.1].
[192] ibid [6.3.2].
[193] ibid [6.5.2].
[194] ibid [6.5.4].
[195] ibid [6.6.1].
[196] ibid [6.6.2].

The Report also noted that online publication allowed government, corporations and other organisations to bypass journalists and to provide content directly to the public, thereby avoiding the traditional 'gatekeeping' function served by the media.[197] It then canvassed the various funding models available to respond to the challenges posed by online publication: subscriptions, crowdfunding, direct support, microtransactions, philanthropy, collective subscriptions and pay-per-view live events.[198] Beyond the decline in advertising revenue, the Report recorded that there were other indicators of the impact of the rise of online publication on public interest journalism. It noted that the Australian Bureau of Statistics estimated that, between 2006 and 2016, the number of people employed as journalists fell by nine per cent, but the figure was 26 per cent for print journalists.[199] The ACCC also reported the results of its own quantitative data survey, which showed that the decline in resources for the media had affected certain types of public interest journalism more than others. Its survey revealed that, between 2001 and 2018, across 12 metropolitan daily and national newspapers, there had been a 26 per cent decline in the number of local government stories, a 40 per cent decline in the number of local court reports, a 30 per cent decline in the number of health stories (although that will no doubt have since been reversed) and a 42 per cent decline in science reporting.[200] Because of the ACCC's concern about the decline of local and regional newspapers, it recommended that a grants programme should be established to support such media outlets.[201] It also recommended that the tax settings should be changed so that support of public interest journalism was recognised as a charitable purpose.[202]

The Report did note that some aspects of digital publication were of variable effect. An undesirable consequence of the atomisation of news and journalism content was the real possibility of 'echo chambers' or 'filter bubbles', whereby users were only exposed to a particular type of content, reinforcing the users' own preconceptions and predispositions. Paradoxically, in this way, digital publication may be inimical to media plurality. Nevertheless, the ACCC did not recommend any direct government action to address a concern about digital 'echo chambers' or 'filter bubbles'.[203] The Report then explored the effect of the atomisation of news on public interest journalism. It noted that consuming a news item in isolation, detached from its source, furthered consumers' concerns about the authenticity of news – not merely 'fake news' but also the possibility of sponsored content not identified as such. It also recorded survey evidence

[197] ibid [6.6.3].
[198] ibid [6.6.4].
[199] ibid [6.7.2].
[200] ibid [6.7.3].
[201] ibid, Recommendation 10.
[202] ibid, Recommendation 11.
[203] ibid [6.11.2].

demonstrating that Australians used digital publications for certain types of news – 41 per cent for celebrity stories, 35 per cent for lifestyle news, 23 per cent for crime and justice stories – whereas traditional media was used for other forms of news – 66 per cent for 'news of the day' and 63 per cent for news about Australian politics. Thus, even though social media is increasingly important for Australians, traditional media also continues to play a significant role in media consumption.[204]

The Report noted that 'information disorder' – disinformation, misinformation and malinformation – were threats to public interest journalism in Australia, to varying degrees. (The ACCC concluded that malinformation, being the spread of accurate information by bad-faith actors with the intent to injure, particularly politically, was not a significant problem in Australia.) It reported survey evidence which suggested that Australians were concerned about fake news, with only 36 per cent of Australians thinking their compatriots could spot fake news, whilst 67 per cent believed that they personally could. The opportunities for disinformation and misinformation were heightened on digital platforms, with a concomitant concern – 66 per cent of Australians – about the quality and reliability of online news and journalism.[205]

In terms of addressing the impact of digital platforms on the consumption of journalism, the Report noted that many digital platforms were already themselves taking some steps to enhance the quality assurance of news content they disseminated,[206] and that steps were being taken to address similar issues in overseas jurisdictions.[207] It made concrete recommendations that the Commonwealth Government fund digital media literacy training in the community and in schools.[208] It further recommended that the ACMA should monitor digital platforms' voluntary practices to curb disinformation and misinformation,[209] as well as requiring digital platforms with over one million active users per month to implement an industry code of conduct to handle complaints about disinformation relating to news and journalism content.[210]

6. The Parliamentary Joint Committee on Intelligence and Security

The fifth inquiry into media regulation and press freedom in Australia in the last decade was the report produced by the Commonwealth Parliamentary Joint

---

[204] ibid [6.11.3].
[205] ibid [6.11.5].
[206] ibid [6.12.1].
[207] ibid [6.12.2].
[208] ibid, Recommendations 12, 13.
[209] ibid, Recommendation 14.
[210] ibid, Recommendation 15.

Committee on Intelligence and Security (PJCIS) following its inquiry into the impact of law enforcement and intelligence powers on the freedom of the press. The Report was released in August 2020. Unlike the earlier inquiries, which were broad-ranging in focus, the PJCIS inquiry was directed towards the more limited but nonetheless important issue of the impact of national security concerns on freedom of the press. In early July 2019, the then Commonwealth Attorney-General, Christian Porter, referred to the matter to the PJCIS.[211] The impetus for the inquiry was the Australian Federal Police's execution of search warrants on successive days in June 2019, in separate investigations, on the Canberra residence of Annika Smethurst and the headquarters of the national broadcaster, the ABC.[212] The Canberra home of Annika Smethurst, the political editor of the Sydney tabloid newspaper, *The Sunday Telegraph*, was raided by the Australian Federal Police (AFP), executing a warrant obtained following a story she wrote in which she reported that the Secretaries of the Departments of Home Affairs and Defence had formulated a plan to allow the security agency, the Australian Signals Directorate, to be able to monitor Australian citizens' emails surreptitiously. Subsequently, the High Court of Australia held that the search warrant was invalid.[213] On the following day, the AFP executed a warrant on the headquarters of the ABC arising out of a story published by journalists, Sam Clark and Dan Oakes, based on the 'Afghan Papers', dealing with alleged war crimes committed by Australian servicemen in Afghanistan. Subsequently, the Federal Court of Australia held that the search warrant was valid.[214]

Under its terms of reference, the PJCIS was to investigate the experiences of journalists and media organisations becoming subject to law enforcement or intelligence agencies, the impact of those agencies' exercise of their powers and functions on journalists' work and the reasons that journalists and media organisations became the subject of attention by such agencies. It was also asked to investigate whether any changes, and if so what changes, should be made to the thresholds for the exercise of those agencies' powers and functions in relation to journalists and media organisations, so as to achieve a better balance between press freedom, on the one hand, and criminal investigation and national security, on the other hand. In particular, the PJCIS was asked to consider whether contested hearings for warrants authorising investigative action into journalists and media organisations and increased thresholds for security agencies accessing electronic data on journalists' devices were appropriate.[215]

The Report noted that, since 2001, the Commonwealth Parliament has been incredibly active in legislating about national security. It has passed over 75 pieces

---

[211] Parliamentary Joint Committee on Intelligence and Security, *Inquiry into the Impact of the Exercise of Law Enforcement and Intelligence Powers on the Freedom of the Press* (August 2020) [1.1].

[212] ibid [1.5].

[213] *Smethurst v Commissioner of Police* (2020) 272 CLR 177, [2020] HCA 14.

[214] *Australian Broadcasting Corporation v Kane* (2020) 377 ALR 711, [2020] FCA 133.

[215] Parliamentary Joint Committee on Intelligence and Security Inquiry (n 211) xi.

of national security legislation. Although it suggested that all of these changes were appropriate, having gone through the usual parliamentary processes, the Report acknowledged that the submissions to the inquiry raised concerns about the volume, pace and impact of these legislative reforms.[216] The level and constancy of legislative changes made laws more complex and therefore more difficult to advise upon and implement,[217] giving rise to potential inconsistencies in interpretation and application.[218] In the view of media representatives, the reforms contributed to a 'culture of secrecy'.[219] In addition, journalists felt that the execution of search warrants on homes and offices had an undoubted 'chilling effect' on investigative journalism generally.[220] The Report noted the slow decline of Australia on the Reporters Without Borders' World Press Freedom Index, ranked 19th in 2018, 21st in 2019 and 26th in 2020.[221] In response to this, the first recommendation of the committee was that the AFP should notify journalists when an investigation has concluded and when journalists are no longer persons of interest.[222]

The Report noted that the terms of reference for the Committee were broad, but that the PJCIS was not able to provide a comprehensive response to the issues raised, because it was not a general policy or legislative drafting body.[223] Given the complex and interrelated problems posed, the PJCIS suggested that the Government and 'major media stakeholders' should work co-operatively towards a solution,[224] but specifically refrained from recommending the mechanism by which this should be effected.[225]

The PJCIS then turned to the difficult issue of journalists and media organisations being able to review or contest warrants. Media outlets understandably submitted that allowing them to contest warrants after they had been executed failed to strike an appropriate balance between the competing interests.[226] Before a warrant can be issued against a journalist, a submission must be sought from the Public Interest Advocate (PIA).[227] However, a wide range of submissions were critical of the lack of transparency around the role of the PIA.[228] The PJCIS canvassed the international experience of dealing with warrants issued against journalists on national security grants, examining the position in the United Kingdom[229] and Canada.[230] Ultimately, the PJCIS made only a modest proposal, having accepted

---

[216] ibid [2.47].
[217] ibid [2.49].
[218] ibid [2.51].
[219] ibid [2.50].
[220] ibid [2.74]–[2.76].
[221] ibid [2.85].
[222] ibid, Recommendation 1.
[223] ibid [3.38]–[3.39].
[224] ibid [3.42], [3.207]–[3.211].
[225] ibid [3.43].
[226] ibid [3.52].
[227] Telecommunications (Interception and Access) Act 1979 (Cth), s 180X.
[228] Parliamentary Joint Committee on Intelligence and Security Inquiry (n 211) [3.65]–[3.69], [3.75].
[229] ibid [3.86]–[3.104].
[230] ibid [3.105]–[3.111].

that there were legitimate law enforcement concerns limiting press freedom.[231] It recommended that the profile and scope of the role of the PIA should be expanded.[232] Specifically, it recommended that a PIA be required to consider an application made by law enforcement or by the Australian Security Intelligence Organisation when seeking an overt or covert warrant that relates to a person working in a professional capacity as a journalist or media organisation when the warrant is related to the investigation of an unauthorised disclosure of government information.[233]

The PJCIS considered that warrants could continue to be issued against journalists and media outlets but that the PIA should be required explicitly to represent the principle of public interest journalism when making its submission to the issuing authority.[234] In addition, it recommended that the PIA should be required to make a submission in every case where a warrant is sought against a journalist or media organisation.[235] The PJCIS acknowledged that there were inconsistent definitions of what constituted 'journalism' and who qualified as a 'journalist' under the various Commonwealth secrecy offences. It recommended that public interest journalisms should be introduced as a defence to Commonwealth secrecy defences.[236] In relation to the protection of journalists' source, the PJCIS noted that 'shield laws' across Australia were not uniform and the differences between the states and territories gave rise to a 'chilling effect'. Therefore, it recommended the harmonisation of shield laws across Australia.[237] However, in relation to the direct application of shield laws to secrecy offences, the PJCIS was of the view that the expanded role of the PIA would overcome much of the concern about the absence of such direct protection.[238]

7. The Senate Press Freedom Inquiry

The impetus for the sixth inquiry was also the AFP raids on Smethurst's Canberra home and the ABC's Sydney headquarters. In the month after the execution of these search warrants, the Senate referred the issue of media freedom to the Environment and Communications References Committee. Although, at the time, the centre-right Liberal-National Coalition Government had a majority in the House of Representatives, it did not control the Senate. Consequently, it was unable to block this reference. Indeed, the Committee was chaired by Greens Senator, Sarah Hanson-Young, and was comprised of a majority of non-government

[231] ibid [3.118].
[232] ibid [3.120]–[3.122].
[233] ibid [3.122].
[234] ibid [3.123].
[235] ibid [3.125].
[236] ibid [3.198].
[237] ibid [3.311]–[3.313].
[238] ibid [3.310].

senators. Under its terms of reference, the Committee was to inquire into disclosure and reporting of sensitive and classified information, including the issue of warrants against journalists, and whistleblower protections.[239] The Committee called for submissions, receiving 48 of them. It also conducted public hearings over five days.[240] The Committee issued its final report in May 2021.

The Report accepted the importance of national security and freedom of the press, but concluded in light of the evidence given before the Committee that the balance in Australia had favoured the former at the expense of the latter in recent decades.[241] In light of this, it recommended a wholesale review of Commonwealth secrecy offences.[242] It made the further specific recommendation that, in this review, the Commonwealth Attorney-General's Department should examine the best way to protect journalists and media organisations who make, in good faith, public interest disclosures about special intelligence operations. The Report recommended that the standard to be applied should require that the disclosures for which liability would be imposed should be 'genuinely likely to result in serious harm'.[243] It further recommended that the relevant criminal offence should be amended to remove the evidential onus on journalists and media organisations to demonstrate that an unauthorised disclosure was in the public interest, with the onus instead being placed on the prosecution.[244]

The Report then canvassed media concerns that the Commonwealth freedom of information (FOI) regime was deteriorating. It accepted the criticisms that the long delays in processing FOI requests and the extensive redactions in government documents ultimately released impedes the media's ability to report on government activity as matters of legitimate public interest. The Report accepted that government departments clearly evinced a lack of respect for open government, which defeated the purpose of the FOI regime.[245]

The Report also strongly recommended the implementation of reforms to the Public Interest Disclosure Act 2013 (Cth), to protect whistleblowers more effectively.[246] Similarly, it suggested that shield laws should be strengthened and modernised 'to set a high standard' and to work towards the harmonisation of the diverse protection of journalists' sources under Commonwealth, State and Territory law.[247] The Report recommended that press freedom should be an explicit consideration when determining whether security agencies should be able to obtain search warrants against journalists and media organisations.[248] Finally,

---

[239] ibid [1.3].
[240] ibid [1.5]–[1.6].
[241] ibid [2.41]–[2.44].
[242] ibid, Recommendation 1.
[243] ibid, Recommendation 6.
[244] ibid, Recommendations 7 and 8.
[245] ibid [2.83]–[2.86].
[246] ibid, Recommendation 10.
[247] ibid, Recommendation 11.
[248] ibid [6.95].

the Report turned to consider proposals to strengthen press freedom in Australia. It made the broad recommendation that the Commonwealth Government should initiate an independent review of law enforcement and national security laws with a view not only to reducing duplication and inconsistencies but also with aligning those laws with Australia's international human rights obligation, in particular the right to freedom of expression.[249]

8. Concluding Remarks

It is clear that media regulation and press freedom have been the subject of sustained policy work in Australia over the last decade. The problems identified are well-known and well-rehearsed, but are complex and do not admit of ready solutions. The concentration of media ownership in Australia remains a perennial problem. In part, the viability of commercial media in Australia has always been challenging because of Australia's relatively small, geographically dispersed population. The advent of internet technologies has allowed new entrants in the market, but have also allowed existing media organisations to extend their reach from traditional media online. The regulatory problem of media convergence remains unaddressed in Australia. The same regulatory regime which pertained more than a decade ago – with print media largely self-regulated, with radio and television co-regulated and with online media largely unregulated – persists without substantial modification.

The issue of media convergence is only likely to become more acute into the future, as the importance of traditional media continues to decline. The challenge of imagining a regulatory environment for online media predominates will not disappear. The dissipation of the funding models which underpin traditional media and, in turn, subsidised investigative journalism in the twentieth century also needs to be addressed. The reports also illustrate an ongoing anxiety, by no means unique to Australia, about how to reconcile the need for national security in an international environment which is characterised by insecurity with the equally important need in a liberal democracy to ensure that the state, particularly the executive, is held accountable. The tension between national security and freedom of speech and freedom of the press remains fraught. These reports demonstrate an awareness of the social necessity of public interest journalism, as well as its resource-intensive and somewhat uncommercial nature. Having identified the problem, none of these problems has offered a definite solution.

For all of the attention given to the issues of media regulation and press freedom in these reports, there has been little translation into legislative action. The single, notable exception is the development of the News Media Bargaining Code. The News Media Bargaining Code came out of the ACCC's Digital Platforms Inquiry.

---

[249] ibid, Recommendation 16.

It now finds a legislative basis in the Competition and Consumer Act 2010 (Cth) Pt IVBA. The News Media Bargaining Code requires platforms, like Facebook and Google, to negotiate a code with traditional news publishers based in Australia, under which platforms provide a fee to those news publishers for their use of Australian news content. The initial reaction of platforms to the introduction of the legislative requirement for an industry code in this form was not positive. In mid-February 2021, Facebook blocked Australians' access to news content.[250] This lasted a few days, before Facebook relented. Over the last two years, Facebook and Google in particular have been negotiating fee agreements with traditional news publishers in Australia. However, given that the outcome has to be negotiated, the platforms have not been able to reach agreement with all traditional news publishers and remain unimpressed by the policy.[251] The News Media Bargaining Code represents a small step in addressing the challenges presented by the new and continually shifting media environment. Larger steps will no doubt be required in the future.

---

[250] S Meixner, 'Facebook News Ban Drops Reader Traffic to News Stories by 13 Per Cent Within Australia, Chartbeat Data Shows' (*ABC Online*, 18 February 2021), www.abc.net.au/news/2021-02-19/ facebook-referral-traffic-down-news-ban-morrison-frydenberg/13171568.

[251] Z Samios and N Bonyhady, '"Punitive" and "Untidy": Meta Talks Tough on Media Bargaining' *The Sydney Morning Herald* (1 March 2023), www.smh.com.au/business/companies/punitive-and-untidy-meta-talks-tough-on-media-bargaining-20230301-p5comw.html.

13

One Body to Rule Them All: Press Regulation in New Zealand

URSULA CHEER

1. Introduction

This chapter interrogates press freedom as a conceptual and practical concern in New Zealand today. Aotearoa New Zealand is involved in a hyperactive review of its complex and piecemeal system of press regulation. In the last 10 years, we have reviewed or launched reviews of new media vis-a-vis news media, extreme online content, video-on-demand services, hate speech provisions and social cohesion, and the manifestation of our public media entities. Our Prime Minister has even become involved in international efforts to regulate internet content. However, although these reviews have been characterised by initial enthusiasm, this has generally been followed by a stepping back from radical or comprehensive change.

Contemporary New Zealand press regulation has been focussed on legacy media – it is a byzantine system made up of statutory regulation established under classification, broadcasting, and other legislation,[1] as well as voluntary self-regulation.[2] Each piece of our regulatory jigsaw developed largely independently from the rest, and the whole has been augmented by piecemeal mutations following reviews or outcries that prompted special state responses intended to plug gaps.[3] The Government now believes the regulatory system, such as it is, is not sufficiently consistent and integrated, and is not capable of adapting to changes in the way individuals rely on and interact with media content. The multifarious scheme has also been described as an uneven playing field because some media remain subject to no regulation at all.[4] A broad, harm-minimisation focussed review will,

---

[1] The Films, Videos, and Publications Classification Act 1993; the Broadcasting Act 1989.
[2] Including the New Zealand Media Council (www.mediacouncil.org.nz) and the Advertising Standards Authority (www.asa.co.nz).
[3] Such as the Harmful Digital Communications Act 2015.
[4] See Cabinet Minute CAB-21-MIN-0179, 'Initiating a Broad Review of the New Zealand Media Content Regulatory System' (24 May 2021), www.dia.govt.nz/diawebsite.nsf/Files/Proactive-releases/

it is anticipated, contribute to the Government's priority of supporting a socially cohesive New Zealand.[5] Nevertheless, it has been acknowledged that the harm-minimisation objectives of review have to be balanced with other fundamental human rights, including freedom of expression.[6]

2. Theory of Press Freedom

In Aotearoa New Zealand, the free press is considered to be the cornerstone of democracy.[7] We have seen the practical consequences of this in an extensive 2010 review carried out by the Law Commission into the legal and regulatory environment in which news media and other communicators operate in the digital era.[8] In its 2013 report, the Commission outlined how New Zealand inherited and adopted press freedom theory that accords our media status as a cornerstone of democracy. It described how the 'news media' evolved sporadically over centuries, assisted by technological developments, but also impacted by a clash of social, political and economic influences. Mass media stimulated the growth of public opinion, which in turn began to impact how governments acted and democratic institutions developed. The Commission identified the nineteenth and twentieth centuries as the period when the idea that the press has a central role in the democratic process took root and became fundamental to the vindication of an independent and free press. Thus, '[a]n individual's fundamental right to freedom of expression became conflated with "freedom of the press"'.[9]

Therefore, although mostly off-shore and privately owned in Aotearoa New Zealand,[10] our press is expected to perform core democratic functions under the terms of a social contract between it and the public it serves.[11] Although the Law Commission examined closely the question whether mainstream media still carry out such a role in the face of continued technological disruption and the associated disruption of traditional funding models, it concluded that it does.[12]

$file/Cabinet-material-about-the-initiation-of-the-media-content-regulatory-review.pdf; 'The News Media Meets "New Media": Rights, Responsibilities and Regulation in the Digital Age' (New Zealand Law Commission R128, 2013) ch 1, 30, www.lawcom.govt.nz/sites/default/files/projectAvailableFormats/NZLC%20IP27.pdf.

[5] Cabinet Minute CAB-21-MIN-0179 (n 4).

[6] See Department of Internal Affairs, 'Media and Online Content Regulation', www.dia.govt.nz/media-and-online-content-regulation.

[7] The term 'press' does not refer only to the print media in New Zealand. The terms 'press' and 'media' are used interchangeably in this chapter and include broadcast and online media.

[8] See Law Commission, 'Regulatory Gaps and New Media 2010', www.lawcom.govt.nz/our-projects/regulatory-gaps-and-new-media?id=725.

[9] 'The News Media Meets "New Media"' (n 4) s 3.16.

[10] See the 2021 Aotearoa New Zealand Media Ownership Report by the AUT research centre for Journalism, Media and Democracy (JMAD), www.jmadresearch.com/new-zealand-media-ownership.

[11] 'The News Media Meets "New Media"' (n 4) s 3.10–3.16.

[12] ibid ch 3.

It determined there remains 'a public interest in continuing to recognise the news media as a special class of publisher with distinguishing rights and responsibilities arising from the functions they perform'.[13]

If media is to be privileged as a special class of publisher under press freedom theory, there must be some assurance that it does in fact employ such freedoms to perform core democratic functions. Put another way, the press must exercise its freedoms responsibly by engaging in news gathering and publication that are accurate, fair, balanced and in the public interest. Ultimately, press responsibility requires a system of regulatory oversight, both to encourage adequate performance and to provide complaints processes for those who suffer significant harm. Thus, true freedom of the press presupposes an effective system of press regulation.

It is unsurprising then, that at the end of its review, the New Zealand Law Commission recommended the creation of a new grand media complaints body, the News Media Standards Authority (NMSA), to provide New Zealanders with a consistent set of news media standards and a one-stop-shop for adjudicating complaints across all news producers. NMSA would be independent of government and the industry, and membership would be voluntary, but available to a broad group of news producers. This recommendation, as with recommendations from the Leveson Inquiry in the United Kingdom, was strongly resisted by New Zealand media and ultimately not adopted by government.

The Law Commission also employed the concept of the social contract between press and public in another of its recommendations – it advocated for a new standard legal definition of news media based on the function of the publisher, rather than the publishing platform, for use in any relevant statute.[14] To be eligible for statutory exemptions and privileges available to the news media, an entity or individual would have to meet the following criteria: a significant element of their publishing activities involves the generation and/or aggregation of news, information and opinion of current value, they disseminate this information to a public audience, publication is regular and not occasional, and the publisher is accountable to a code of ethics and a complaints process.

Although this recommendation, which could embrace digital as well as legacy media, was also not specifically adopted in New Zealand, it has had some influence on the law. For example, in *The Director of Human Rights Proceedings v Slater*,[15] the Human Rights Review Tribunal had to determine whether a media

---

[13] ibid s 3.22. See also, for the UK, the 'Leveson Report': Rt Hon Lord Justice Leveson, *An Inquiry into the Culture, Practices and Ethics of the Press* (London, The Stationery Office, 2012) Vol 1, Part B, 'The Press and the Public Interest', chs 1 and 2, 53–68, https://assets.publishing.service.gov.uk/government/uploads/system/uploads/attachment_data/file/270939/0780_i.pdf; and for Australia, the 'Finkelstein Report': Hon R Finkelstein QC, *Report of the Independent Inquiry into the Media and Media Regulation* (28 February 2012) ch 2: 'The Democratic Indispensability of a Free Press', https://apo.org.au/sites/default/files/resource-files/2012-02/apo-nid28522.pdf.

[14] 'The News Media Meets "New Media"' (n 4) s 3.101.

[15] *Director of Human Rights Proceedings v Slater* [2019] NZHRRT 13.

exemption from the data protection provisions of the Privacy Act could apply to a blogger, Mr Slater. Interpreting the Privacy Act exemption, it found it was not all-encompassing or open-ended, and proceeded to read in a requirement that the privileges and exemptions of the news media under the Act were to be exercised *responsibly*. This meant 'news activity' which could trigger the exemption was to be understood as 'news activity conducted responsibly':[16] on that basis, most of the blogs under consideration were not protected by the exemption. The Privacy Act has since been updated and the new 2020 version now allows the exemption to apply to responsible media only. 'News entity' under the 2020 Act means an entity (including an individual) whose business, in whole or part, consists of a news activity; and that is, or is employed by an employer that is, subject to the oversight of named existing news media regulatory bodies, or any other body prescribed as a regulatory body by regulations made under the Act.[17]

Press freedom theory continues to have weight in New Zealand law and policy. In its most recent 2021 regulatory review, the Government remains beguiled by the idea of a regulatory scheme that delivers responsible media, while guaranteeing press freedom as well.[18] However, it is notable that the concept of responsible media has expanded to embrace social responsibility as well, and the bounds of that concept remain tantalisingly unclear.

3. Constitutional Press Freedom

Since 1990, Aotearoa New Zealand's unwritten Constitution has included a form of Bill of Rights.[19] The Bill of Rights Act is not supreme law, and contains no judicial strike-down power – it operates as an interpretative direction for the judiciary and other state servants. Nonetheless, enactment of the Bill has elevated the rights consciousness of the New Zealand public, the media and the legal fraternity. New Zealand courts balance rights in the European style and have not adopted the hierarchical approach to protecting speech which dominates the approach in American law.[20] Section 14 of the Bill of Rights Act provides: 'Everyone has the right to freedom of expression, including the freedom to seek, receive and impart information and opinions of any kind in any form.'

The Court of Appeal has said that section 14 is 'as wide as human thought and imagination'.[21] 'Freedom of the press' is not expressly included in this provision, however, freedom of expression and freedom of the press are regarded

---

[16] ibid [92].
[17] Privacy Act 2020, ss 7 and 8(b)(x).
[18] See Cabinet Minute CAB-21-MIN-0179 (n 4).
[19] The New Zealand Bill of Rights Act 1990 (hereafter: Bill of Rights Act).
[20] A Koltay, *Freedom of Speech* (Budapest, CompLex, 2013) 109.
[21] *Moonen v Film and Literature Board of Review* [2000] 2 NZLR 9 [15].

as inextricably bound together:[22] New Zealand courts strongly recognise the importance of press freedom, for example: 'The right of freedom of the press is no more and no less than the right of all and any member of the public to make comment.'[23] In media law cases, the concepts are treated as synonymous. Of course, freedom of expression existed as a legal principle of New Zealand law well before the Bill of Rights Act, and certainly our judges referred to the principle before 1990.[24] However, incorporation in the Bill of Rights Act made it normative for freedom of expression to be expressly raised in media law cases, and prompted the principle to be at the forefront in parliamentary and administrative processes.

However, no rights in the Bill of Rights Act are absolute. The section 14 provision does not confer freedom to publish anything at all.[25] This is captured in section 5 of the Act, which states: 'the rights and freedoms contained in this Bill of Rights may be subject only to such reasonable limits prescribed by law as can be demonstrably justified in a free and democratic society'. There are many limits on freedom of speech and hence on press freedom in New Zealand. These include laws relating to defamation, contempt of court, breach of confidence and invasion of privacy. Parliament and the courts must attempt to ensure that these limitations on freedom of expression meet the requirements of section 5 of the Bill of Rights Act.

The Bill of Rights Act was intended to have only vertical effects: it applies to the three branches of government and bodies exercising public functions,[26] and on the face of it, only protects private citizens from the state.[27] In spite of this, it is clear that the New Zealand judiciary gives the Bill horizontal effect when resolving disputes between private citizens and when developing the common law, including press law.[28] Because this process does not produce directly enforceable rights, the horizontal effect is usually regarded as weakly or strongly indirect.[29] It is given content in two ways, though sometimes in combination: our judges state they are

---

[22] See, eg, New Zealand Media Council, *Statement of Principles*, Preamble, www.mediacouncil.org.nz/principles.

[23] *Solicitor-General v Radio New Zealand Ltd* [1994] 1 NZLR 48 (HC) 61 per Eichelbaum CJ and Greig J. See also, *Television New Zealand Ltd v Attorney-General* [1995] 2 NZLR 641 (CA) 646 per Cooke P.

[24] See J Burrows, 'Freedom of the Press Under the New Zealand Bill of Rights Act 1990' in P Joseph (ed), *Essays on Constitution* (Brookers, Wellington, 1995) 287. See also the discussion by Thomas J in the Supreme Court in *Brooker v Police* [2007] NZSC 30 [171]–[231], as to the role and purpose of Bills of Rights.

[25] Tipping J in *Hosking v Runting* [2005] 1 NZLR 1 [231].

[26] The New Zealand Bill of Rights Act 1990, s 3. See A Geddis, 'The Horizontal Effect of the NZBORA, as Applied in *Hosking v Runting*' (2004) *New Zealand Law Review* 68. See also, A Geddis, 'The State of Freedom of Expression in New Zealand: An Admittedly Eclectic Overview' (2008) 11 *Otago Law Review* 657.

[27] See P Rishworth, 'Human Rights' (2005) 1 *New Zealand Law Review* 87.

[28] *Simunovich Fisheries Ltd v Television New Zealand Ltd* [2008] NZCA 350 [89].

[29] J Norton, '*Hosking v Runting* and the Role of Freedom of Expression' (2004) 10 *Auckland University Law Review* 245, 249.

simply bound by the Bill as the judicial arm of the state, or that they are implicitly required to take account of the values expressed in the Bill.

Section 14 of the Bill of Rights Act is applied in a number of ways that can impact press freedom. First, judges use it when they are developing the rules of common law. An example is a recent leading defamation media case, *Durie v Gardiner*, where the Court of Appeal recognised a very significant public interest defence and referred to the Bill of Rights as justification for doing so.[30] Similarly, in the leading invasion of privacy case, *Hosking v Runting*,[31] a defence of 'legitimate public concern' was recognised to ensure that the scope of privacy protection would not exceed such limits on freedom of expression as are justified in a free and democratic society.

Second, statutes require interpretation, and the Bill of Rights Act provides that in interpreting them the courts should, as far as possible, settle on a meaning that is 'consistent' with the Bill of Rights freedoms.[32] An example of this is *Gravatt v Auckland Coroner's Court*,[33] where suppression under the Coroners Act 2006[34] of the identities of health professionals responsible for the care of a patient who had died was successfully challenged. Whata J held none of the statutory grounds were triggered, and the reasons provided by the coroner for suppression were too generalised and had failed to demonstrate why the principles of open justice and freedom of expression should be outweighed.

Third, many rules, of both common law and statute, confer discretionary powers on the court (or other officials). An example is provided by the Broadcasting Standards Authority (BSA), a statutory regulatory body discussed further below that resolves complaints against New Zealand broadcasters applying discretionary powers conferred by the Broadcasting Act 1989. The BSA has stated that '[t]he law and common sense require us to be cautious before restricting freedom of expression. The New Zealand Bill of Rights states this should only occur when it is "demonstrably justified in a free and democratic society".[35] To summarise, New Zealand's constitution provides protection for media freedom indirectly through statutory recognition of freedom of expression, which is interpreted broadly and clearly to include freedom of the press.

4. Press Regulation

There exists in Aotearoa New Zealand no special legislation devoted to regulating the press in an overarching manner. No single statutory provision defines a

---

[30] *Durie v Gardiner* [2018] NZCA 278, [2018] 3 NZLR 131 [56(d)].
[31] *Hosking* (n 25).
[32] Bill of Rights Act 1990, s 6.
[33] *Gravatt v Auckland Coroner's Court* [2013] NZHC 390, [2013] NZAR 345.
[34] Coroners Act 2006, s 74.
[35] Broadcasting Standards Codebook 2022, 'Introduction, Freedom of Expression' www.bsa.govt.nz/broadcasting-standards/broadcasting-code-book-2022/codebook-introduction-2.

journalist for legal purposes, although a number of statutes do contain definitions. For example, the Evidence Act 2006 provides for journalist source confidentiality to be claimed before a court if a person is a journalist. A journalist means a person who in the normal course of that person's work may be given information by an informant in the expectation that the information may be published in a news medium, and a news medium means a medium for the dissemination to the public or a section of the public of news and observations on news.[36] This somewhat circular definition also entitles New Zealand journalists to claim special rights against search and seizure and surveillance.[37] Other provisions are more exacting, such as those which grant media rights to remain in court for reporting purposes. These seek to grant the rights only to responsible media by defining journalists as those who adhere to codes of ethics and complaints procedures.[38] As outlined above, the Law Commission attempted in its 2010 review of the law and new media to make responsibility a requirement of a uniform statutory definition of media, but was unsuccessful. There are social, political and legal acceptance that the New Zealand media exercises the important function in a democracy of informing the citizen, but also that it has the potential to behave unfairly, offensively or excessively by, for example, invading privacy, damaging reputations and conducting partisan campaigns. This potential has been recognised, and accordingly a number of different public complaints forums have been established.

I have already observed that New Zealand has a complex and piecemeal system of press regulation. For largely historical reasons, broadcasters are regulated differently from the print media. Complaints relating to radio and television are provided for in a statutory regime under the Broadcasting Act 1989. This set up the BSA and gives legal force to codes of practice developed in consultation with broadcasters themselves. The scheme is promoted by government as a form of co-regulation. In contrast, the print media regulates itself through the New Zealand Media Council, a private body funded by newspaper proprietors and journalists through their unions. The Council does not have total coverage of the print media, nor does it have any legal powers. A voluntary body, the Online Media Standards Authority, was also set up by broadcasters to deal with complaints about online publication by broadcasters only. However, after two years, it folded its role into the Media Council in 2017. Responsibility for complaints about the main providers of content of video on demand was handed to the Media Council in 2018.[39]

Media that publish commercial and advocacy speech are subject to a different form of self-regulation again, in the form of the Advertising Standards

---

[36] Evidence Act 2008, s 68(5). See also the Privacy Act 2020, ss 7 and 8(b)(x), discussed above.
[37] See Search and Surveillance Act 2012, ss 136, 140 and 142.
[38] See Criminal Procedure Act 2011, s 198.
[39] See www.mediacouncil.org.nz/news/press-council-to-launch-new-video-on-demand-classifications-code. The main providers covered were TVNZ, RNZ, Mediaworks, Māori Television, Lightbox, Netflix, Stuff, NZME and Amazon.com.

Authority (ASA).[40] Advertising complaints go directly to an Advertising Standards Complaints Board and there is no requirement to complain to a broadcaster in the first instance. It is regrettable that media regulatory bodies proliferate in New Zealand and jurisdiction is now distributed haphazardly between them. The most obvious weakness is that the system is unnecessarily complex for those who need to complain. Further significant weaknesses are inconsistency between the various bodies, and gaps in their coverage. All of these issues have been identified by various government reviews over the years, but no significant reform has been attempted or completed. However, from a press perspective, it could be argued that the continued existence of complaints bodies at least ensures the press does not become a licensed profession. The main complaints bodies are examined below.

4.1. Broadcasting Standards Authority

The BSA[41] is a Crown entity that consists of four members appointed by the Governor-General on the recommendation of the Minister of Broadcasting. The BSA's main sources of funds are money appropriated by Parliament,[42] and levies on broadcasters.[43] Every broadcaster is responsible for maintaining, in programmes and their presentation, standards which are consistent with:

a)   the observance of good taste and decency; and
b)   the maintenance of law and order; and
c)   the privacy of the individual; and
d)   the principle that when controversial issues of public importance are discussed, reasonable efforts are made, or reasonable opportunities are given, to present significant points of view either in the same programme or in other programmes within the period of current interest; and
e)   any approved code of broadcasting practice applying to the programmes.[44]

The BSA has as one of its functions the encouragement of broadcasters to develop codes of broadcasting practice in relation to the protection of children, the portrayal of violence, fair and accurate programmes and procedures for correcting factual errors, safeguards against the portrayal of persons in a manner that encourages denigration of or discrimination against sections of the community, restrictions on the promotion of alcohol, the presentation of appropriate warnings

---

[40] See www.asa.co.nz.
[41] The BSA maintains an excellent website which contains an overview of its functions, a guide to how to make a complaint, information about and the text of its Codebook (covering free-to-air television, pay TV, and radio). A search facility for decisions from 1994 to the present is provided at www.bsa.govt.nz.
[42] Broadcasting Act 1989, s 31.
[43] ibid ss 30A–30G.
[44] ibid s 4(1). See *Ransfield v Radio Network Ltd* [2005] 1 NZLR 233 (HC).

in respect of programmes, and the privacy of the individual.[45] In addition, the BSA may issue advisory opinions to broadcasters about broadcasting standards and ethical conduct,[46] and conduct research and publish findings on matters relating to standards.[47]

There is currently one Codebook, standardised as much as possible to cover radio, free-to-air television, and pay television.[48] There is also a separate code covering election programmes.[49] The Codebook contains eight ethical require-ments that deal with social responsibilities, balanced and accurate reporting in news, current affairs and factual content, and rights to privacy and fair treatment. Each standard is accompanied by associated interpretative guidelines. The guide-lines and commentary inform how each standard is interpreted, and are designed to allow flexibility for applying the standards so they can be interpreted as required by particular circumstances or context, including the platform on which the content was broadcast.[50]

If a complainant is not satisfied with a response to a complaint by a broad-caster, the complaint may be referred to the BSA.[51] If it relates to alleged infringement of privacy, the complainant may complain directly to the BSA in the first instance.[52] The BSA may determine a complaint without a formal hearing.[53] In all cases the BSA should consider the complaint with as little formality and technicality as the law permits.[54] If the BSA decides that a complaint is justified, it has considerable statutory powers of enforcement. It may direct the broad-caster to publish an approved statement, to stop broadcasting programming or advertising for up to 24 hours, or refer the complaint back to the broadcaster; and for privacy breaches, it may order the broadcaster to pay the individual compensation of up to NZ$5,000.[55] Decisions of the BSA may be appealed to the High Court, which will treat the decisions as if they were made in the exercise of a discretion.[56]

---

[45] Broadcasting Act 1989, s 21(1)(e).

[46] ibid s 21(1)(d).

[47] ibid s 21(1)(h).

[48] In effect from 1 July 2022: *Broadcasting Standards Codebook.* www.bsa.govt.nz/broadcasting-standards/broadcasting-code-book-2022/the-codebook.

[49] *Election Programmes Code of Broadcasting Practice*, www.bsa.govt.nz/broadcasting-standards/election-code.

[50] See Broadcasting Standards in New Zealand Codebook, 'Introduction, Standards, Guidelines and Commentary', www.bsa.govt.nz/broadcasting-standards/broadcasting-code-book-2022/codebook-introduction-2/#e568.

[51] Broadcasting Act 1989, s 8; *TV3 Network Services Ltd v Prime Minister (Rt Hon Helen Clark)* HC Wellington CIV-2003-485-1655 and CIV-2003-485-1816, 10 February 2004.

[52] Broadcasting Act 1989, s 8(1A).

[53] ibid s 10(1).

[54] ibid s 10(2). In *TV3 Network Services Ltd v Prime Minister (Rt Hon Helen Clark) v TV3* BSA 2002-157-158, 7 October 2002, the High Court noted that the process is intended to be a straightforward, 'non-technical' process for laypeople.

[55] Broadcasting Act 1989, s 13.

[56] A complainant becomes a respondent when a broadcaster appeals an Authority decision into the Court system: *Moonen v Broadcasting Standards Authority* (1995) 8 PRNZ 335 (HC).

The BSA notes it received 206 complaints in 2021 – a 52 per cent increase on 2020. The Authority issued 160 decisions and determined 181 complaints in 2021 – a 44 per cent and 40 per cent respective increase on the previous year.[57] It issued 160 decisions in the 2020–2021 period and upheld just under 10 per cent of complaints. The uphold rate has hovered at that figure for the last few years. It is a much lower rate generally than the near 27 per cent upheld for the 2011–2012 period,[58] and the average uphold rate of approximately 25 per cent over the 10 years to 2010. The BSA has suggested the reduction may flow from a more robust and integrated analysis of freedom of expression, adopted in 2011,[59] that these statistics are positive indicators that generally broadcasters' understanding of the standards is improved,[60] and more recently, that the Covid pandemic increased engagement by the public with broadcasting, especially during lockdown periods.[61]

Complaints about accuracy, balance, and good taste and decency predominate, as well as fairness. The BSA Annual Report of 2021 shows that most complaints still concern news, current affairs and talk radio.[62] In the 2020–2021 year, the most successful complaints were about privacy (over half, five out of nine, were upheld). The least successful complaints in the same period were accuracy complaints (only four out of 78 were upheld). This may well reflect, as noted by the BSA, increasing concerns about accuracy during the Covid pandemic, concerns that were not justified. This means the BSA's role as a fact checker has recently become more prominent.

The Authority applies the standards using contemporary social values and conditions. An example where the Authority has demonstrated a socially responsive approach to its role has been in relation to complaints about the increasing use of te reo Māori, the Māori language, in broadcasting. Te reo Māori is an official language of New Zealand. The BSA has held that complaints about the use of te reo Māori do not raise any issues of potential harm as envisaged by the standards, and signalled it will not determine such complaints in future. Broadcasters welcomed the clarity and confirmation of their practice.[63] The 2021 Annual Report discloses that the Authority considers the co-regulatory system is working well in the circumstances, and that BSA decisions continue to contribute much to the standards of ethical journalism in New Zealand broadcasting. One commentator has summarised it well with this conclusion:

> The BSA has a very important task to perform in ensuring the broadcasters subject to it meet appropriate standards in a democracy. It has … one of the most difficult

[57] BSA Annual Report (2021), Chair's Report, 5.
[58] ibid 11.
[59] BSA Annual Report (2012) 15.
[60] BSA Annual Report (2019) 12.
[61] BSA Annual Report (2021) 5, 13.
[62] ibid 17.
[63] *KS and Television New Zealand Ltd* (2020-135) and *Vorwerk and Discovery NZ Ltd* (2020-158). See BSA Annual Report (2021) 25.

tasks of any New Zealand tribunal. It has to satisfy a wide range of people – broadcast-ers, complainants, the public, lawyers and judges – in both its decisions and the way it communicates them. It has to operate in a media environment which is changing at high speed. It has to combine common sense with legal compliance, and reality with logic. It has to operate with an Act written 32 years ago.[64]

The BSA Chair has noted its involvement in the current general media regula-tory review.[65] The BSA believes the regulatory system has not kept pace with changing habits, resulting in fragmentation, gaps and overlaps, and supports the development of a new framework based on how audiences consume content.[66] The Chair has also expressed the view that '[b]etter regulation does not have to be the enemy of free expression'.[67]

4.2. New Zealand Media Council

In 1972, a Press Council was formed in New Zealand based on the English model. Unlike the BSA, the Council, renamed the New Zealand Media Council in 2018, has no legislative backing but is a purely voluntary organisation with no legally enforceable punitive powers. It is financially supported by four metropolitan newspapers, 22 regional newspapers, three Sunday newspapers, nine commu-nity newspaper interests, one business weekly, seven magazine interests (three of which are student magazines), nine video on demand interests, 10 broadcasters that have online content and 20 digital members.[68]

The Council has considerably extended its membership and functions over the years. It accepted membership of non-newspaper digital media in 2014.[69] It launched a Video on Demand Code in 2018, and now operates a video on demand committee that deals with complaints about content and classifica-tion of video on demand.[70] The Council is large and consists of 11 permanent members: an independent chairman (thus far always a retired judge), five persons representing the public, and five industry representatives. The Media Council's main objective is to provide the public with an independent forum for resolv-ing complaints involving the press, and it is also concerned with promoting press

---

[64] Emeritus Professor J Burrows, *External Review of Balance Decisions* (23 May 2021) Conclusion at 16, www.bsa.govt.nz/assets/Uploads/External-Review-of-Decisions-Balance-Standard.pdf.

[65] See n 6 above.

[66] See BSA Annual Report (2021) 5.

[67] Judge Bill Hastings, Chair's Report, ibid 5–6.

[68] See Membership, www.mediacouncil.org.nz/principles/#membership. All have agreed to abide by the Council's guiding principles.

[69] See 'NZ Press Council to Extend Coverage, Gain New Powers' (Press release, 23 March 2014). Membership fees depend on the size of the digital entity and its commercial or non-commercial status.

[70] See 'Press Council to Launch New Video-On-Demand Classifications Code' (18 December 2017), www.mediacouncil.org.nz/news/press-council-to-launch-new-video-on-demand-classifications-code.

freedom and maintaining the press in accordance with the highest professional standards. The Council also specifically endorses the principles and spirit of the Treaty of Waitangi and the Bill of Rights Act, but notes also that this is without sacrificing the imperative of publishing news and reports that are in the public interest.[71]

Most of the Council's time is taken up in considering complaints and, following an extensive independent review,[72] it adopted a detailed complaints procedure.[73] All complaints against a print or digital publication must first be made to the publication concerned in order to give the editor the opportunity to deal with the matter first. Most complaints are dealt with on the papers only, but there is provision for both sides to be heard, and the Council conducts the hearing not unlike judicial proceedings. Publishers named in any complaint are expected to publish the Council's decision, giving it fair prominence. Decisions must be published unedited and unaccompanied by editorial comment, though publications can comment on the decision elsewhere. The Council reserves the right to direct a right of reply, correction or retraction. In egregious circumstances, if unanimous, the Council may censure a publication. Such censure must be published in the publication or website giving due prominence. If a complaint is not upheld, the publication may determine whether to publish the decision and where it should be published.

The range of complaints dealt with by the Council is vast and includes: inaccuracy, distortion and failure to verify facts; lack of balance; unprofessional and unethical conduct; subterfuge; bias; misrepresentation; censorship and suppression of facts; breach of confidence and failure to observe embargoes; some aspects of letters to the editor; refusal to allow a right of reply; offensive or sensational language, particularly in headlines; unnecessary publication of the names of persons or schools involved in sensitive matters; invasions of privacy; intrusions into private grief; wrongful or unnecessarily upsetting use of photographs; racist reporting; the insensitive reporting of suicide and tragedy; and lack of good taste generally. Complaints have been received about published articles, but also about pictures, cartoons, advertisements and billboards; and also breaches of good journalistic practice in obtaining information.

The Council's Statement of Principles currently cover accuracy, fairness and balance; privacy; children and young people, comment and fact; aspects relating to columns, blogs, opinion and letters; headlines and captions; discrimination and diversity; confidentiality; subterfuge; conflicts of interest; photographs and graphics, and corrections.[74] The Principles may be used by complainants when they wish to advise the Council of their complaint. However, a complainant may

---

[71] See Preamble to the Principles, www.mediacouncil.org.nz/principles.
[72] I Barker and L Evans, *Review of the New Zealand Press Council* (NPA, EPMU, MPA, 2007), www.mediacouncil.org.nz/media/website_posts/10/Press-Council-Barker-Evans-Review-2007.pdf.
[73] See www.mediacouncil.org.nz/complaints.
[74] Statement of Principles, www.mediacouncil.org.nz/principles.

nominate other ethical grounds for consideration too.[75] The Council's decisions lack the penalties which a court of law or the BSA can impose, in that, apart from the Council website database, decisions against a publication only receive publicity in the relevant publication itself. However, conscious of the perceived weakness of its sanctions and following a significant private review,[76] the Council adopted powers to direct where an adjudication should appear in a publication, based on a requirement for fair prominence. All electronic copy that persists and is deemed to be conveying inaccuracy must be noted as having been found incorrect and why. Where the potential harm outweighs the need to keep the public record intact, the Council may go so far as to require the removal of story elements or the taking down of a story in its entirety.[77]

In 2021 the total number of complaints ruled on by the Council was 199, mark-edly more than any other year. Of these complaints 72 went to the full Council and 127 were ruled insufficient grounds to proceed. A further 12 complaints were resolved informally. Uphold rates of the Council still vary somewhat year by year. Of the 72 complaints that were considered by the full Council, eight were upheld in full; two were upheld by a majority; five were upheld in part; one was not upheld by a majority; and 56 were not upheld. A five year comparison of complaints reveals that numbers of complaints received by the Council have more than doubled in that period. It appears that the Covid pandemic, as with BSA complaints, was in part responsible. The Council now appears to receive and adjudicate more complaints than the BSA.[78]

The Council itself has stated that an independent press plays a vital role in a democracy, and that the proper fulfilment of that role requires a fundamental responsibility for the press to maintain high standards of accuracy, fairness and balance, and it also requires public faith in those standards. Two recent decisions strikingly illustrate this. In *Tom Frewen v Stuff*,[79] the Council considered the now common practice of some media attempting to pass off sponsored, branded or native content on their webpages – in other words, advertising, as genuine news. This content is presented as headlines from 'promoted stories' together with curated images which make it appear the stories are local or of concern to local readers. In *Frewen*, the example promoted investment in Bitcoin and revealed how to go about it, but had no local or news connection at all.

The Council stated firmly it will take jurisdiction in such cases, and native advertising will be judged under the standards applied to the form it emulates – that of genuine news. All news, even content masquerading as news, must reflect the principle that editors are responsible for what appears in their publications. The headline in this case breached the regulator's principle requiring accuracy.

[75] Preamble to the Principles, www.mediacouncil.org.nz/principles.
[76] Barker and Evans (n 72).
[77] Publication of Adjudications, www.mediacouncil.org.nz/complaints.
[78] Information received from the Council Chief Executive, 30 June 2022.
[79] *Tom Frewen v Stuff*, Case No 2632, 19 December 2017.

It was a total fiction and did not match the advertising linked to. The Council also found a breach of ethical requirements requiring professionalism and suggested to meet such standards, media sites need to be transparent and earn the trust of their readers by using visual cues to delineate where news stops and advertising begins.

A decision of the Council in 2022 censured a different attempt to embed advertising as editorial. *New Zealand Dermatological Society, Inc v Stuff* involved an article that advised readers about sunscreen use and used advice received from experts,[80] including the complainant. Various brands of sunscreen were depicted and some were presented as if recommended by the complainant, together with a plus sign which triggered a link facilitating purchase of the brand on a retail site. The complainant had not given permission for her quotes to be used to promote sunscreen products.

The Council again strongly flagged the complaint because it raised a general industry issue of whether such stories compromise the independence of the media. It found the format blurred the lines between advertising and editorial content, and this put editorial standards in peril. The fact that the editor and the lifestyle editor had been asked to include certain material by their advertising department was straying 'into perilous territory' and also 'troubling'. As with the *Frewen* decision, requirements for accuracy, fairness and balance had been breached. Using uncharacteristically strong language, the Council expressed the hope its ruling would prompt debate about media independence and the need to be free from commercial obligations.

In spite of these two powerful decisions, overall as a media complaints body, the New Zealand Media Council suffers from an ongoing lack of potency and a tendency to be regarded as typically light-handed self-regulation that some journalists do not take seriously. Its perceived effectiveness is undercut when it is compared to the BSA. Industry funded regulators also suffer from limited resourcing that can become strained when complaints increase, and are hampered by dependence on voluntary membership.

4.3. Advertising Standards Authority

Commercial speech in the form of advertising and advocacy speech is also self-regulated in New Zealand, and for the sake of fullness, the scheme is traversed briefly here.[81] On 1 July 1993 responsibility for advertising standards became a matter for the ASA. The Authority was formed in 1973 as the Committee of Advertising Practice by the Newspaper Publishers Association, the NZ Broadcasting Commission and the Accredited Advertising Agencies Association, and, following

---

[80] *New Zealand Dermatological Society, Inc v Stuff*, Case No 3216, February 2022.
[81] See www.asa.co.nz/ and the ASA's Codes.

a name change, was incorporated in 1990. Any media owner or organisation representing media owners, any communications agency or organisation representing communication agencies and any advertiser or organisation representing advertisers, is eligible for membership.[82] The ASA now has 14 member organisations representing advertisers. Funding of the ASA is by means of annual member subscriptions and levies determined by the ASA.

The ASA promotes its system of voluntary self-regulation by developing and promulgating codes which the members undertake to uphold. Currently the advertising codes are the Advertising Standards Code and five sector codes where advertisers are expected to take particular care; Alcohol, Children and Young People, Finance, Gambling and Therapeutic and Health advertising.[83] If an advertisement is found to have breached one or more of the codes, the advertiser, advertising agency or media in question are requested to withdraw or amend the advertisement. The ASA reports it had 97 per cent compliance in the 2021 year.[84]

The codes cover the entire range of advertising activity. The Advertising Standards Code is a general collection of the rules that apply to all advertisements and covers social responsibility and truthful presentation. It contains broad provisions that focus on a variety of concerns, including privacy, consent, decency, offensiveness, safety and misleading or deceptive advertisements. Misleading advertising is the issue most often complained about, followed by issues relating to social responsibility and then taste and decency. In 2021, advocacy advertising was the most complained about category of advertisement, with 36 per cent of those being Covid-related.

The ASA has flexibility, allowing it to pivot to take account of technological developments. For example, in 2021, it opened up a new category of influencer advertising for complaints resolution, and found the most common complaint in that category was insufficient identification. That year was also the first year when digital advertising overtook television advertising as the most common medium complained about.[85] Any member of the public who considers that an advertisement has breached the advertising codes of practice may make a complaint, free of charge. If a complaint is upheld, the breaching advertiser is required to withdraw the advertisement with immediate effect and media members of the ASA are required not to publish or broadcast the breaching advertisement. In Decision 95/334, the Advertising Standards Complaints Board (ASCB) acknowledged that neither the ASA nor the ASCB had any power of enforcement and that its decisions were advisory only.[86] Any party to a complaint may appeal

---

[82] Rules of the ASA, Rule 12, www.asa.co.nz/about-us/rules-of-the-asa.
[83] See www.asa.co.nz/codes.
[84] ASA Annual Report (2021), www.asa.co.nz/wp-content/uploads/2022/05/ASA-Annual-Report-2021.pdf.
[85] ibid 6.
[86] ASCB Decision 95/334, 6.

a decision of the ASCB within 14 days of receipt of the written decision.[87] In *Electoral Commission v Cameron*,[88] the Court of Appeal confirmed that decisions of the ASCB are also subject to judicial review, and the ASA website now states that as a body with a public decision-making function, decisions of the Complaints and Appeal Boards are subject to judicial review under the Judicial Review Procedure Act 2016.[89]

The jurisdiction and practice of the ASA, which has now been operating for nearly half a century, have a low profile and are not often scrutinised. In 2021, the ASA noted the advertising landscape is changing rapidly, driven by new media developments, advances in technology, changing consumer behaviour and by wider concerns such as the Covid pandemic.[90] The ASA's workload is always expanding, but it continues to maintain that it responds nimbly to these new challenges. As a form of self-regulation, it remains prone to charges of possible bias and a tendency to light-handed adjudication. Additionally, although successful complaints result in orders for cessation of the promotion, these can lack effectiveness if they come near the end of the promotion, or after it is over.

This brief review of the three regulatory bodies reinforces the description of the regulatory landscape as byzantine and difficult for potential complainants to negotiate. The codes and principles share themes, but are not the same across all bodies. There is inconsistency in remedies and enforcement. All the regulatory bodies share some success in being accessible and cheap. However, all are coping with increasing numbers of complaints, and face intense pressure to excel as fact-finding bodies. Overall, the 'system' appears to be creaking at the seams and is not fit for purpose. Real reform would be timely.

5. Media Freedom

As discussed above, certain rights, privileges and exemptions are accepted as legitimately due to responsible media in Aotearoa New Zealand. These can only be claimed by professional journalists and media outlets, and have been usefully identified by the Law Commission. They include statutory rights to attend court hearings, including criminal proceedings from which the public have been excluded,[91] and Family and Youth Court cases where the public have no right to attend generally.[92] Media also have standing in criminal proceedings to be heard in relation to applications for suppression orders or applications to renew, vary or

---

[87] Rules of the Advertising Standards Complaints Board Complaints Procedures, Second Schedule, 6.
[88] *Electoral Commission v Cameron* [1997] 2 NZLR 421 (CA).
[89] See Appeals Process, Judicial Review, www.asa.co.nz/complaints/the-appeals-process/.
[90] ASA Annual Report (n 84) 2.
[91] Criminal Procedure Act 2011, ss 97, 198 and 199.
[92] Oranga Tamariki Act 1989; Children's and Young People's Wellbeing Act 1989, s 166.

revoke suppression orders; and to appeal.[93] Further, only they have the right to communicate electronically from the courtroom.[94] Genuine reporters also have a statutory right to attend local body meetings as members of the public and to report proceedings.[95]

Media are exempt from some publication constraints that apply to members of the public. Thus, newspapers and broadcasters are not bound by the Fair Trading Act 1986 provisions that impose liability for 'misleading conduct in trade',[96] and news media are not bound by the Information Privacy Principles in our data protection legislation, while they carry out newsgathering activities.[97] The offence of publishing statements on polling day liable to influence voters does not apply to publication of a party name in news relating to the election published in a newspaper or by a broadcaster.[98] Further, the Human Rights Act 1993 allows newspapers and broadcasters to accurately report racist statements made by another even though the maker of the statements might have infringed the Act.[99]

These statutory benefits are available to media alone, and depend on varied definitions of news media or news media activities, some more dated than others. I have already identified that the most recently crafted definitions reflect a government goal of granting statutory privileges only to responsible media. For example, the relevant definitions for court reporting purposes require media to be subject to a code of ethics and a complaints procedure.[100]

The question of whether statutory privileges can apply to new as well as legacy media has arisen in the context of journalist source protection in New Zealand, and been answered in the affirmative. Courts have attempted to protect journalistic sources as much as possible in New Zealand, and there is no record of journalists being held in contempt of court for refusing to disclose. Source protection has been enhanced by amendment to our Evidence Act, and courts have been called on to interpret the extent of protection provided. Section 68 of the Evidence

---

[93] Criminal Procedure Act 2011, ss 210 and 283.

[94] In-Court Media Coverage Guidelines 2016, Ministry of Justice, Cl. 5.2, www.justice.govt.nz/about/news-and-media/media-centre/media-information/media-guide-for-reporting-the-courts-and-tribunals-edition-4.1/appendices/10-8-in-court-media-guidelines-2016.

[95] Local Government Official Information and Meetings Act 1987, s 49.

[96] Fair Trading Act 1986, ss 9 and 15.

[97] Privacy Act 2020, ss 7 and 8(b)(x). However, it is important to note that the regulatory codes of the BSA and the principles of the Media Council contain customised accuracy and privacy standards.

[98] Electoral Act 1993, s 197(1)(g)(i); see also the Electoral Referendum Act 2010, s 31(2)(b).

[99] Human Rights Act 1993, s 61(2). These hate speech provisions were reviewed, see the Report: Hate Speech and Hate Crime Related Legislation, 26 November 2020, https://christchurchattack.royalcommission.nz/assets/Publications/Hate-speech-and-hate-crime-related-legsilation-Companion-legal-paper.pdf; Government response to the Royal Commission of Inquiry into the Terrorist Attack on Christchurch Masjidain Report, www.beehive.govt.nz/sites/default/files/2020-12/Government%20Response%20to%20RCOI.pdf. The review resulted in the Human Rights (Incitement on Ground of Religious Belief) Amendment Bill, www.parliament.nz/en/pb/bills-and-laws/bills-proposed-laws/document/BILL_130197/human-rights-incitement-on-ground-of-religious-belief. However, in February 2023, the Government withdrew the Bill and referred it to the Law Commission for further investigation, see www.beehive.govt.nz/release/government-takes-new-direction-policy-refocus.

[100] Criminal Procedure Act 2011, s 198(2).

Act 2006 contains a presumption of non-compulsion for journalists where disclosure of sources is at risk.[101] In *Police v Campbell*, Randerson J in the High Court[102] concluded the starting point is no obligation on journalists to disclose, but with potential for that prima facie immunity to be displaced. The Judge held protection should not be overridden easily, but no high threshold is to be assumed, such as requiring truly exceptional or compelling circumstances. Hence, the presumptive right to protection is not to be displaced lightly and only after careful weighing.[103] In this case, the Court was able to avoid mandating disclosure and the application was dismissed on the understanding that Mr Campbell would provide a statement to police on the basis of a 'will say' statement he presented to the Court.

Following *Campbell*, the provision was further tested in relation to new media, in a defamation claim, *Slater v Blomfield*.[104] In this civil case, a controversial blogger attempted to use the Evidence Act to resist a discovery order obtained by Mr Blomfield, who was suing for publication of various posts about himself on a blog. Blomfield wished to test the pleaded defence of honest opinion, and sought discovery of emails held by the defendant that belonged to Blomfield. The

---

[101] Section 68 of the Evidence Act 2006 provides:

Protection of journalists' sources

(1) If a journalist has promised an informant not to disclose the informant's identity, neither the journalist nor his or her employer is compellable in a civil or criminal proceeding to answer any question or produce any document that would disclose the identity of the informant or enable that identity to be discovered.

(2) A Judge of the High Court may order that subsection (1) is not to apply if satisfied by a party to a civil or criminal proceeding that, having regard to the issues to be determined in that proceeding, the public interest in the disclosure of evidence of the identity of the informant outweighs—

  (a) any likely adverse effect of the disclosure on the informant or any other person; and
  (b) the public interest in the communication of facts and opinion to the public by the news media and, accordingly also, in the ability of the news media to access sources of facts.

(3) The Judge may make the order subject to any terms and conditions that the Judge thinks appropriate.

(4) This section does not affect the power or authority of the House of Representatives.

(5) In this section—

informant means a person who gives information to a journalist in the normal course of the journalist's work in the expectation that the information may be published in a news medium;

journalist means a person who in the normal course of that person's work may be given information by an informant in the expectation that the information may be published in a news medium;

news medium means a medium for the dissemination to the public or a section of the public of news and observations on news;

public interest in the disclosure of evidence includes, in a criminal proceeding, the defendant's right to present an effective defence.

[102] *Police v Campbell* [2010] 1 NZLR 483 (HC).
[103] There is no such presumption under the Criminal Disclosure Act 2008 where source protection is not at issue, see, *Wright v Television New Zealand* [2022] NZCA 133, where media were required to disclose an interview recording despite giving an undertaking of confidentiality.
[104] *Slater v Blomfield* [2014] 3 NZLR 835.

blogger claimed journalist source protection, arguing that at the time of the blog posts, he was a journalist under the Evidence Act. After noting that the legislation provides an exemption from compellability rather than an entitlement to a particular type of privilege,[105] Asher J found that at the time of the posts, the blogger and his blog did fit the definition of a journalist and a news medium in the Evidence Act. Overall, the blog was not of such low quality that it was not reporting news.[106]

This case demonstrated that the journalist source privilege can apply to new media such as blogs.[107] However, the blogger was ultimately ordered to comply with the discovery order because the blog posts related to a private dispute and it seemed likely the emails were obtained illegally by the sources. This diminished the importance of protecting the sources in terms of public interest and there would be no real chilling effect from ordering disclosure which might affect media sources generally. Ultimately, the Judge found that the protection in the Act could be available to the blogger, but the lack of true public interest in the information removed the need for source protection. The latter requirement is likely be a common obstacle to bloggers claiming the benefit of the protection.

The provision was examined by the Court of Appeal in a further defamation case, *MediaWorks TV Ltd v Staples*, where the Court endorsed a robust, media-friendly interpretation of the public interest balancing process required by section 68.[108] Mr Staples had obtained an interim injunction against earlier publications by another party about his business and argued that MediaWorks acted illegally by broadcasting against the terms of that injunction, thus reducing any public interest it had in source protection. However, the Court returned to the importance of responsibility and emphasised that MediaWorks was an established media organisation that can be held to account through a regulatory process (the BSA). It found a strong specific public interest in the programmes complained about that justified the media having the ability to receive material from informants and being able to give undertakings of confidentiality in the knowledge that they and the informants could expect them to be upheld under section 68. Thus, the balancing process in *Staples* resulted in an outcome that protected the sources involved.

The *Staples* decision is a powerful general endorsement of public interest in the communication of facts and opinion to the public by the news media. It suggests that section 68 of the Evidence Act will be interpreted robustly to protect

---

[105] ibid [32].

[106] ibid [3]–[4]. This finding was controversial in the light of allegations made in a book *Dirty Politics*, published during the defamation proceedings by investigative journalist Nicky Hager (Nelson, Craig Potton, 2014).

[107] The definition in the Evidence Act does not require responsible journalism, and although the blogger later joined the Media Council, he did not belong to a regulatory body at the time the claim arose. *cf Craig v Stringer* [2016] NZHC 1956, where a blogger was found not to be a journalist within the terms of s 68.

[108] *MediaWorks TV Ltd v Staples* [2020] 2 NZLR 372 [27]–[43].

legitimate media reporting and sources in New Zealand. The decision identified two different forms of public interest that must be addressed in any section 68(2) balancing process. First, there is the narrow question of public interest in knowing the identity of the particular informant. This must be followed by investigation of the much broader question of the public interest in the free and safe communication of facts and opinion to the public by the news media, whereby sources are protected from having their identity exposed.[109]

6. Duties of the Media

There are no 'must carry' rules in Aotearoa New Zealand. Under the Radio-communications Act 1990, the Government allocates radio spectrum through a price mechanism to those who are prepared to pay the highest price. Tenders and auctions are used to allocate spectrum. Following initial allocation of spectrum, rights can be freely traded, and spectrum managers can make decisions about whether and how to get involved in the market.[110] Some spectrum is reserved to meet public policy objectives.[111]

The duties of New Zealand media as provided for in the standards and codes of the regulatory bodies have been outlined above. To these may be added duties relating to ownership and the market. There is no special regulatory scheme directed at preventing cross-ownership of media in New Zealand. However, the Commerce Commission monitors and prohibits mergers and acquisitions that substantially lessen competition under the Commerce Act 1986. The Act also prohibits anti-competitive agreements between businesses and makes it illegal for companies to abuse a dominant market position. The Commission will give a written clearance for an acquisition if it is satisfied that it will not have or be likely to have, the effect of substantially lessening competition in a market.[112] Lessening of competition in the market is the only relevant factor in achieving a clearance. Where no clearance has been obtained, it is illegal to acquire a business or shares in it if market dominance results.[113] Penalties for breach of the requirement can be very severe.[114]

Under the Commerce Act, it is illegal to 'enter into a contract or arrangement, or arrive at an understanding, containing a provision that has the purpose, or has

---

[109] ibid [39]. *cf Christian v NZME Publishing* [2021] NZHC 1278.
[110] See www.rsm.govt.nz/about/our-work/our-history.
[111] See www.rsm.govt.nz/about/our-work/public-policy-spectrum-reservations.
[112] Commerce Act 1986, ss 47 and 66.
[113] ibid s 47(1).
[114] ibid s 83(3) provides for pecuniary penalties payable to the Crown not exceeding NZ$500,000 in the case of an individual, or the greater of NZ$10 million or an amount based on commercial gain in every other case. Section 84 provides for the granting of injunctions, s 84A allows actions for damages, and under s 85, the Court may order divestiture of assets or shares.

or is likely to have the effect, of substantially lessening competition in a market'.[115] The provision also prohibits giving effect to such a contract, arrangement or understanding. In other words, both entering into and giving effect to such an agreement is illegal. In 2017, the Commission declined to grant clearance for the proposed merger of Sky Network Television and Vodafone New Zealand, because of the impact of the proposed merger on competition in both the broadband and mobile telecommunications markets.[116]

Also in 2017, the Commission refused to approve a merger between New Zealand's two largest newspaper networks and corresponding online news sites, NZME and Fairfax, under common ownership. The Commission was of the view that such a merger would be likely to substantially lessen competition in the advertising and reader market, specifically Sunday newspapers, online news and community newspapers in 10 regions. It also considered that the merger would not be of such a benefit to the public that it should be allowed. The merged company would have direct control of the largest network of journalists in the country, and employ more editorial staff than the next three largest mainstream media organisations combined. Its news media business would include nearly 90 per cent of the daily newspaper circulation in New Zealand and a majority of traffic to online sources of New Zealand news. The resulting concentration of media ownership was regarded as unacceptable.[117] The decision was appealed by the media companies to the Court of Appeal, which upheld the decision of the Commission and its right to take into account non-economic or out-of-market considerations when it is considering benefits to the public. The Court of Appeal held the Commission was within its jurisdiction when it considered a loss of media plurality could result from the proposed merger.[118]

Currently, the Commission is carrying out a review of the structure of the broadcasting transmission service sector in New Zealand. Historically, government owned transmission assets and networks in order to provide public radio broadcasting services and later television services. Those assets are now held by a dominant state owned enterprise, Kordia. The traditional broadcasting sector has been disrupted by streaming services supported by widespread availability of new technologies. Potential new entrants to the market face considerable barriers and this is now being monitored by the Commission.[119]

---

[115] Commerce Act 1986, s 27.

[116] *Vodafone Europe B.V. and Sky Network Television Ltd* [2017] NZCC 1.

[117] See https://comcom.govt.nz/news-and-media/media-releases/2017/commission-declines-nzme-fairfax-merger, and *NZME Ltd and Fairfax New Zealand Ltd* [2017] NZCC 8.

[118] Commerce Act 1986, s 67. See also, *NZME Ltd, Fairfax Lts and Stuff Ltd v Commerce Commission* [2018] NZCA 389, [2018] 3 NZLR 715, and https://comcom.govt.nz/news-and-media/media-releases/2018/commission-welcomes-court-of-appeal-ruling-on-nzmefairfax-merger.

[119] See *Broadcasting Services Market Review Report*, Network Strategies Report Number 41023 (1 June 2022), https://comcom.govt.nz/regulated-industries/telecommunications/monitoring-the-telecommunications-market/topic-papers-other-reports-and-studies/broadcasting-transmission-services-market-review.

There is no general statutory right of reply in New Zealand. However, specific statutes, like the Defamation Act 1992, contain provisions that may provide forms of reply in civil defamation claims. For example, section 25 of that Act provides that anyone who claims to have been defamed in a news medium may, within five working days of becoming aware of the publication, request the person responsible for the publication to publish a retraction or a reasonable reply in the same medium, with substantially similar prominence and without undue delay. Where the person agrees to publish that retraction or reply, that person must also offer to pay the requester the cost of publishing the reply (if that is what is asked), the requester's solicitor-client costs in connection with the publication of the retraction or reply, all other expenses incurred by the requester, and compensation for any pecuniary loss suffered by the requester as a direct result of the publication complained of. For this purpose the term 'reply' means a statement of explanation or rebuttal or of both explanation and rebuttal. The publication of such a retraction or reply is to be taken into account in assessing any measure of defamation damages (Section 29(b)). There is little incentive to defendants to comply with the provision, because the publication of an agreed statement as part of a negotiated settlement is also possible outside the Act, offers more complete protection (the Act does not say that publication of the retraction or reply is a complete defence), and the defendant is not saddled with the obligation to pay costs.

The Defamation Act also provides that in any defamation proceedings the plaintiff may seek a recommendation from the court requiring the defendant to publish a correction of the matter that is the subject of the proceedings, and the court may make such a recommendation (section 26). The recommendation may cover content, timing and prominence of the correction (section 27). Failure to publish will be taken into account in the assessment of damages where the court gives final judgment in favour of the plaintiff, and the plaintiff will be awarded solicitor and client costs, unless the court orders otherwise (section 26(3)). Once the defendant has published, the plaintiff will be awarded solicitor and client costs and is entitled to no other remedy or relief in the proceedings. Thus, if a correction is published as recommended, general damages for loss of reputation, hurt feelings and the like, and punitive damages, may not be awarded as well. The proceedings are deemed finally determined (section 26(2)). Originally, the court was to have full power to order rather than recommend a correction. However, it was argued by the media that correction orders were a restraint on freedom of speech, in that they can force a news medium to publish matter with which it does not agree. The objections of the media were sufficiently convincing to cause the Act's provisions to be watered down. However, the court can still dictate the content of the correction (section 27(1)).

It is not apparent that corrections are being sought in preference to damages. Only one order has ever been made, that was tailored to mandate and prescribe an apology and correction to be sent in a letter to all recipients of a defamatory letter in a small community some years before, and to be published, at the cost of the defendants, in the Public Notices section of two local newspapers within one month of the date of the judgment.[120] If the defendants elected not to comply, they would be liable for damages of NZ$100,000, the total sum sought by the plaintiff. The judgment was appealed, but after negotiations, the matter was settled, with the defendants recording in a statement that they did not accept the findings in the original judgment.

The Harmful Digital Communications Act 2015 gives power to the District Court to order corrections or rights of reply to applicants claiming breach of the digital communication principles contained in the Act.[121] However, under this legislation, before complaints reach the District Court, applicants must apply to Netsafe, an agency that attempts to mediate the dispute. The Act was not passed to remedy harmful digital publication by media, but to reduce general digital stalking and the publication of cyber-porn. It contains significant protections for freedom of expression that should make it difficult to complain about media online publication. Netsafe has stated that the legislation is unclear as to its application to media. Therefore, it appears unlikely that the Act will result in significant, if any, rights of reply orders against media.[122]

7. Press Freedom and Platform Regulation

As observed above, New Zealand does not have a grand media regulator. However, the growth of new media and possible gaps in our regulatory regime have been under continuous review in recent years. In 2013 the Law Commission recommended the establishment of one over-arching regulator known as the News Media Standards Authority (NMSA).[123] The Authority was to be a 'one-stop shop' covering three previously separate media platforms – print media, broadcasters, and online, and anything between. The Commission also recommended a new and consistent statutory definition of 'news media', which would include new media. Membership would be voluntary but non-members would still be covered by other laws such as those relating to defamation and privacy. They would also be subject to new laws recommended by the Commission covering speech that causes serious harm online.[124] The Government accepted the latter recommendations, but not

---

[120] *Newton v Dunn* [2017] NZHC 2083, (2017) 14 NZELR 621.
[121] Harmful Digital Communications Act 2015, ss 19 (1)(d) and 19 (1)(e).
[122] See 'Netsafe Washes its Hands of Avery "Harm" Complaint' (*Newsroom*, 18 September 2018), www. newsroom.co.nz/netsafe-drops-avery-digital-harm-complaint.
[123] See 'News Media Meets "New Media"' (n 4).
[124] The Harmful Digital Communications Act 2015. See Harmful Digital Communications: The Adequacy of the Current Sanctions and Remedies, Ministerial Briefing, Law Commission (15 August 2012),Law Commission releases ministerial briefing for its review of regulatory gaps and the new media | Law Commission.

the more major recommendations about media regulation generally. It concluded there was no pressing need for statutory or institutional change of the regulatory bodies at that time.[125]

Other reviews followed, one of which examined how all audiovisual publications could be regulated.[126] This produced proposals to amend the Broadcasting Act under a Digital Convergence Bill to ensure on-demand content met classification and content standards. The proposed changes would not affect user-generated content, such as Facebook or YouTube videos and would exclude news and current affairs. Under this Bill, the BSA would produce a code of practice to support its new jurisdiction. However, at the end of 2017, a new administration announced a halt to this work in order to carry out further consultation.[127] It then launched a general appraisal of media regulation, incentivised by a perception of increasing online harmful content.[128]

Alongside these busy reviews, private media in New Zealand, including the proprietors of online publishing platforms, have, as elsewhere, been subjected to increasing pressure to moderate and remove harmful content on the internet. Private publishers, including all forms of news media, have always practised some degree of censorship, usually motivated by commercial imperatives. However, incentivised by our own terrorist tragedy,[129] New Zealand's Prime Minister, Jacinda Ardern, and French President, Emmanuel Macron, have called on Heads of State and Government and leaders from the tech sector worldwide to adopt the Christchurch Call, a commitment by governments and tech companies to eliminate terrorist and violent extremist content online.[130] This movement recognises that respect for freedom of expression is fundamental and that a free, open and secure internet offers benefits to society. However, it persists in seeking international acceptance of increased self-regulation online essentially based on a moral imperative alone.

Finally, early in 2020, the Government directed the development of a business case on the merger of our public media services, Television New Zealand and Radio New Zealand, to form a new public media entity.[131] The merger was announced,

---

[125] See www.lawcom.govt.nz/sites/default/files/governmentResponseAttachments/News-media-meets-new-media-government-response-to-law-commission-report%20%28D-0503423%29.PDF.

[126] 'Content Regulation in a Converged World', Discussion Document (Ministry for Culture and Heritage, 25 August 2015), Content Regulation in a Converged World submissions (Nov 2015) | Ministry for Culture and Heritage (mch.govt.nz).

[127] See government announcement at www.beehive.govt.nz/release/digital-convergence-bill-put-hold.

[128] Proactive release of Cabinet material about the initiation of the media content regulatory review, 2 July 2021, www.dia.govt.nz/media-and-online-content-regulation.

[129] See the Royal Commission of Inquiry into the terrorist attack on Christchurch mosques on 15 March 2019, https://christchurchattack.royalcommission.nz.

[130] See www.christchurchcall.com.

[131] 'Government Announces Business Case Study to Evaluate Proposed Merger of TVNZ, RNZ' (*1News*, 7 February 2020), www.tvnz.co.nz/one-news/new-zealand/government-announces-business-case-study-evaluate-proposed-merger-tvnz-rnz.

and a draft Bill published. The new entity was to be called Aotearoa New Zealand Public Media.[132] The Government's stated goals in this project were manifold but not well communicated to the public – they were to better align government investment across platforms, ensure flexibility to respond to future demographic and technological changes, and reduce inefficiencies, to ensure a more sustainable long-term funding model, and focus on under-served and under-represented audiences while continuing to provide for existing audiences.

Details about the proposal were not well promulgated. Aotearoa New Zealand Public Media was to be an autonomous Crown entity, to have obligations under a statutory charter, and be required to engage with Māori and work with the Māori media sector, to give effect to the Crown's responsibility under the principles of te Tiriti o Waitangi – the Treaty of Waitangi. Aotearoa New Zealand Public Media would be editorially independent, and Ministers would be unable to direct the entity or remove board members because of editorial matters. Content would have to be made freely available and accessible to all New Zealanders and be predominantly free of charge. The entity would have obligations to work collaboratively across the media sector, to support a diverse, capable, and resilient media ecosystem.

It was envisaged that existing regulatory systems would continue to apply to the new entity, but it would also have unique ethical and cultural obligations imposed by a statutory Charter, that would require editorial independence, impartiality, and balance, and the provision of reliable, accurate and comprehensive regional, national, and international news and information. The House of Representatives would review the Charter and Aotearoa New Zealand Public Media's performance against it. All services provided commercial-free by Radio New Zealand would continue to be provided commercial-free.

The new entity was to be in operation from 1 March 2023. However, following a strong negative response to the proposal during consultation on the new Bill, early in an election year, the Government announced the merger would not proceed because planning had been too rushed, and stated that support for public media needed to be at a lower cost and without such significant structural change.[133] More than NZ$16 million had been spent on the proposal. Unsurprisingly, the private media sector greeted the news with more positivity than public media.[134]

---

[132] Aotearoa New Zealand Public Media Bill 2022, 146-1, www.parliament.nz/en/pb/bills-and-laws/bills-proposed-laws/document/BILL_125298/aotearoa-new-zealand-public-media-bill.

[133] Prime Minister Rt Hon C Hipkins, 'Government Takes New Direction with Policy Refocus' (8 February 2023), www.beehive.govt.nz/release/government-takes-new-direction-policy-refocus. Some for the promised extra funding would still go to RNZ.

[134] 'TVNZ, RNZ and NZ On Air Respond to Purging of Merging' (*The Spinoff*, 8 February 2023), https://thespinoff.co.nz/live-updates/08-02-2023/tvnz-rnz-and-nz-on-air-respond-to-purging-of-merging.

8. Conclusion

This chapter has revealed that Aotearoa New Zealand is apparently awash with reformatory zeal where media is concerned. A great flood of regulatory water has flowed under the bridge, driving before it good ideas and bad. Experience demonstrates that reform initiatives do not occur in a political vacuum and tend to produce only piecemeal reform, depending on whether the government of the day is focussed on supporting economic and business interests, or has other goals such as strengthening cultural and social cohesion as well. The thoughtful, thorough and comprehensive vision of the Law Commission, of one body with regulatory oversight for all news media content in New Zealand, remains attractive but as elusive as ever.

14

Conclusions

This volume reviews the press regulation and jurisprudence of a number of countries with fundamentally different legal, political and economic systems. A meaningful comparative analysis at the level that a volume of this kind can reach is not really possible. We have not sought to do more than to place the countries side by side, by presenting similar issues, and to leave any comparison to the reader. Even so, some general conclusions still can be drawn.

This is certainly a more difficult task than in the case of Volume 1, where European legal systems were presented, which are somewhat similar, and which are harmonised by the law of the European Union in all the Member States and by the case-law of the European Court of Human Rights. The conclusion of that volume was that a common European concept of freedom of the press actually exists, that the foundations of the national legislations are the same or very similar, even if there are significant differences in detail (and that Russia can be considered a special case, not only because of its non-EU status but also because of its undoubted democratic problems).

This volume does not focus exclusively on fully democratic states either, but even in countries where there are problems with the political system, the issue of press freedom – and at least its formal protection – is present in public life and in the legal rules. The book also presents democracies that are relatively young (South Africa, Chile) and where, as a consequence, press freedom protection is not yet fully developed. The book also presents well-established democracies where press freedom protection is outstanding, but where it is also not a completely closed issue, and legislators and courts have to deal with it constantly, under pressure from social, market and technological changes. Press freedom is equally important everywhere, and is the cornerstone of the democratic system, or of the aspirations towards it.

It is by no means certain, and this volume can serve as a lesson in this respect, that the extent to which press freedom is protected depends exclusively or primarily on the existence of constitutional and other legal guarantees. What is certain is that the texts of legislation can sometimes obscure the reality of the situation. In Australia, for example, there is no constitutional provision on freedom of the press, but no one would think that the Australian press is not free as a consequence (which is not to say that there may not be problems there waiting for a solution). The First Amendment to the United States' (US) Constitution explicitly refers to press freedom, but the US Supreme Court has consistently refused to recognise special constitutional protection for the press, yet the press is obviously also entitled to a high level of protection for free speech, and at the level of the US states this protection may be even stronger than the Supreme Court's practice would lead us to believe.

However, nowhere does legislation and judicial decisions paint the full picture. Laws have to be interpreted and inevitably only a small number of contentious cases reach the courts. Freedom of the press requires a healthy political culture, a demanding public and the necessary economic background that allows it to operate. Press laws exist in only a small number of the countries surveyed, which is both good and bad news for the press: laws can both broaden the protection of press freedom and limit it. Press self-regulation, on the other hand, exists in many of the countries presented (examples are Chile, South Africa, New Zealand, Israel and South Korea) and faces similar challenges in all of them. Although self-regulation can replace or complement legal (statutory) regulation, the question is how effective and independent it can be.

The regulation of other media beyond the press (traditional broadcasting and its digital versions) is also addressed in several chapters. It can be seen that the regulation of these services is much more detailed everywhere, for historical and technological reasons, and stems from the belief that the media of moving images and sound have a greater impact on their audience and are therefore more dangerous than the press. (In the age of the internet, this argument is losing its persuasive force, but this volume does not address these issues, focusing on the press.)

Freedom of the press can be seen as a separate right from freedom of expression, with its distinct content. Those who exercise freedom of the press (primarily journalists and editors, and indirectly the owners of publishing houses) may exercise more rights and be subject to stricter regulation than the right to freedom of expression generally grants to anyone. All the democratic states covered in this volume grant some form of privilege to the press. These prerogatives vary from one country to another, of course, but the approach is common: the press has a key role to play in a democratic society and must therefore be guaranteed the ability to play that role. This is why the widely known protection of sources, or the protection against searches and seizures, privileged access to the courtroom, protection against surveillance and, above all, protection of the press publishing content of public interest against the general rules on defamation and privacy are justified.

Recognition of the democratic role of the press could even lead to a requirement of social responsibility. This social responsibility is widely invoked in some countries, but is not actually required by law. The press is free to choose the issues it wishes to cover and even to avoid public issues altogether. If it chooses to cover public issues, it can do so mostly within the limits of freedom of expression.

But fairness, accuracy, impartiality, objectiveness and journalistic ethics are not required by law. Some of these may be imposed by the courts or self-regulation in some cases, in the absence of legal provisions. At most, the law may provide for the possibility of a reply (when untrue factual statements are published concerning the claimant), as in Chile and South Korea (and almost all of Europe except the United Kingdom). This is all very well and fosters the hope that a strictly protected press, with these protection and privileges, will indeed contribute to the proper functioning of democracy.

The regulation of press freedom can no longer be discussed without taking into account the regulatory issues of the internet and, more specifically, of online platforms (in particular social media and video-sharing portals). Some chapters in this volume also cover these issues, although they do not focus on them. While the operation of these platforms has a fundamental influence on the press, the approach to their regulation is fundamentally different from that of the press. This book covers the current regulation of the press, but some chapters also look at the regulation of online platforms. This is a key issue also for future regulation of the press. The European Union has detailed legislation on this subject,[1] but it does not address all the issues involved. Comprehensive attempts at regulation are completely lacking elsewhere.

The internet expanded the possibilities of public communication considerably, allowing virtually anybody to publish his or her opinion without significant cost. The various online forums, blogs, chatrooms, comment streams and social media sites, are full of opinions on important matters (and trivial ones). The internet has started to dismantle the obstacles standing between professional journalists and independent opinion leaders, and has contributed to the democratisation of the public sphere, at least in a sense that it has made possible the emergence of more voices in the public space.

The internet thus also has an impact on professional journalism. First, the internet news services and social media platforms have greatly transformed earlier reader/user habits and turned a considerable section of the public away from professional media products, thereby undermining the economic foundations of the latter.[2] Second, the news aggregator sites and social networking websites (also) profit from the content produced by professional journalists, without any real effort on their part (that is content production), thereby disrupting the earlier business models.[3] Furthermore, changes to the habits of users do not necessarily expand the number of people meaningfully contributing to public debates (or the

---

[1] Regulation (EU) 2022/2065 of the European Parliament and of the Council of 19 October 2022 on a Single Market For Digital Services and amending Directive 2000/31/EC (Digital Services Act) [2022] OJ L277/1.

[2] R Foster, *News Plurality in a Digital World* (Oxford, Reuters Institute for the Study of Journalism and University of Oxford, 2012) 16–24.

[3] B Rossi, 'The Reinvention of Publishing: Media Firms Diversify to Survive' *The Guardian* (30 January 2017), www.theguardian.com/media-network/2017/jan/30/reinvention-publishing-media-firms-diversify-survive.

number of opinions expressed): blogs that can be considered independent forums usually do not attract large crowds,[4] and the most powerful and popular websites are mostly the online versions of dominant offline news outlets that have also managed to exploit their economic power on the online markets.[5] On the other hand, less fortunate media outlets have to struggle to survive.

The world of news services is thus changing, but not necessarily in the way one might have hoped. The biggest loser in the market restructuring is the primary 'home' of serious journalism, the press. Though the voices replacing the press are indeed numerous, their power is negligible and their function is not the same as that of professional journalism. The spare-time breed of writers or (on the contrary) elite opinion leaders disguised as 'independent bloggers' are incapable of investigative journalism due to their obvious financial constraints, and the main-stream media products adapted to the internet do not especially contribute to the growth of the diversity of content and opinions. Some authors are arguing already that the internet will lead to the demise of professional media.[6]

In an essay published in 1995, Eugene Volokh sought to predict the future path of the transformation of the online public sphere.[7] He welcomed the phenomenon he called 'cheap speech', as he believed it would eliminate the existing technological scarcity and enable any person to articulate an opinion on public matters cheaply (or even for free) and without any intermediary (television, radio or press), thereby moving the democratic process of decision-making onto broader and more direct foundations.[8]

Almost three decades later, it seems unclear whether such 'cheap speech' is indeed a welcome development. The opportunities afforded by online mass communication and the emergence of social media platforms have challenged the business model of traditional journalism and the enforcement of profes-sional standards. Due to the drop in revenue from advertising and the material weakening of the press, investigative journalism has lost its prominent role and has been replaced by sensationalist and impulse-based content production. User habits have also changed, and lengthy and thorough articles (if written at all) have a difficult time finding (sufficient) readership. These phenomena facilitate the spread of disinformation, while the decline of local news services enables the spread of local corruption and the deterioration of public political discourse,

---

[4] J Curran, 'The Internet of Dreams: Reinterpreting the Internet' in J Curran, N Fenton and D Freedman (eds), *Misunderstanding the Internet*, 2nd edn (London, Routledge, 2016) 23–25; M Hindman, *The Internet Trap: How the Digital Economy Builds Monopolies and Undermines Democracy* (Princeton, Princeton University Press, 2018).

[5] Curran (n 4) 23.

[6] RW McChesney and J Nichols, *The Death and Life of American Journalism: The Media Revolution that Will Begin the World Again* (New York, Nation Books, 2009); A Keen, *The Cult of the Amateur: How Today's Internet is Killing Our Culture* (New York, Currency, 2007).

[7] E Volokh, 'Cheap Speech and What It Will Do' (1995) 104 *The Yale Law Journal* 1805. See also E Volokh, 'What Cheap Speech Has Done: (Greater) Equality and Its Discontents' (2021) 54 *UC Davis Law Review* 2303.

[8] Volokh, 'Cheap Speech and What It Will Do' (n 7) 1849.

making a mockery of election campaigns and breeding extremism.[9] Some studies found that anonymous 'trolls', who challenge reasonable public discourse on numerous forums, cannot be disciplined or banned, and there is no adequate solution to the problems they raise. Trolls therefore keep provoking and insulting others and making it impossible to engage in a thoughtful and progressive debate. Moreover, this state of affairs does not even represent a problem for the social media platforms but rather a benefit, as their economic interests seem to be better served by heated and active interaction than by calm and reasonable discussion of public affairs.[10]

Indeed, social media, as a new means of consuming news, seem not to be conducive to revealing any truth.[11] Whether or not it comes from an authentic or reliable source, all news is presented in Facebook's news feed in the same way as gossip and scandals; sensationalist titles and reports are much more popular than pieces of actual journalism (which are difficult to read on mobile devices anyway), and even the existing products of real journalistic effort get lost in the endless and continuously updating flood of information. The market of traditional media is occupied by personalised news feeds and the freely available mass of junk news.[12] Social media have conquered the production and consumption of news. The general consensus on a commonly accepted 'truth' and some common ground that connects members of society has been weakened or even eliminated – every social group, if not each and every person, has its own 'truth' on the internet.[13] The professional requirements of accuracy and the verification of facts have also fallen victim to the decline of the institutionalised press.[14] In this changed market environment there is no pressure to meet popular demand, and it is increasingly difficult to enforce legal liability; these were the two main means of holding the press accountable by or on behalf of the public. Meta and Google – the two biggest online companies – have not only occupied the news and traditional journalism, they have occupied everything, from political campaigns to the banking system, from the entertainment industry to trade. Not even government or national security functions the same way as it used to in the pre-social media era.[15] In such a

---

[9] RL Hasen, *Cheap Speech: How Disinformation Poisons Our Politics – and How to Cure It* (New Haven, Yale University Press 2022).

[10] L Rainie, J Anderson and J Albright, *The Future of Free Speech, Trolls, Anonymity and Fake News Online* (Pew Research Center, 2017), http://assets.pewresearch.org/wp-content/uploads/sites/14/2017/03/28162208/PI_2017.03.29_Social-Climate_FINAL.pdf.

[11] See P Coe, 'Redefining "Media" Using a "Media-as-a-Constitutional-Component" Concept: An Evaluation of the Need for the European Court of Human Rights to Alter its Understanding of "Media" within a New Media Landscape' (2017) 37(1) *Legal Studies* 25, 42–44.

[12] M Taibbi, 'Can We Be Saved From Facebook?' (*Rolling Stone*, 3 April 2018), www.rollingstone.com/politics/politics-features/can-we-be-saved-from-facebook-629567.

[13] K Viner, 'How Technology Disrupted the Truth' *The Guardian* (12 July 2016), www.theguardian.com/media/2016/jul/12/how-technology-disrupted-the-truth.

[14] L Levi, 'Social Media and the Press' (2012) 90 *North Carolina Law Review* 1531, 1555–72.

[15] E Bell, 'Facebook Is Eating the World' (*Columbia Journalism Review*, 7 March 2016), www.cjr.org/analysis/facebook_and_media.php.

landscape, it seems to have become the responsibility of governments to promote the production of content and news, and to guarantee equal access to information through grants and regulations in order to strengthen democracy.

Social media platforms open the gates to the spread of false news, that is the deliberate dissemination of false information.[16] Despite appearances, this is not a malfunction that could be dealt with by an appropriate intervention but a nearly inevitable consequence of the very nature of such platforms.[17] Accurate profiling is made possible by huge volumes of data and information collected about users in bulk, and such profiles can be used to deploy algorithms that display targeted advertisements and select pieces of content to be presented to users – a decisive factor is the goal of triggering a psychological need to return to the platform with increasing frequency. Another factor is the architecture of such platforms, including the nature of communication through them, as they facilitate the spread of sensationalist content that can be consumed quickly but which is not interesting for a long period. False news has always existed, even before the existence of media and at earlier stages of technical advancement. The difference is that such news now becomes available quickly and *en masse*, and that the new information platforms do not simply disseminate false news randomly but provide an ideal environment for it to spread.[18] Traditional media outlets use citizen journalists and social media generally as sources of news. Thus, in the same way that bloggers may regurgitate false or misleading information obtained, for instance, from the traditional media or other bloggers, the traditional media may do the same in respect of information obtained from social media.[19]

These are issues that the legal systems in this volume will also have to deal with, sooner rather than later. Concerns about the state of the democratic public sphere are felt around the world, but so far regulation has done little to address them. This book paints a very diverse picture of the state of regulatory approaches to press freedom in countries beyond Europe, a diversity that has some common features. These common features allow us to talk about press freedom within a common conceptual framework and to identify the problems accordingly. Of course, the book is not just about the *problems* of press freedom: centuries of struggle for this right have led to reassuring and well-established legal solutions in many countries. We must consider this a great achievement, even if, by its very nature, this struggle can never end. The authors of this volume are therefore driven by the conviction that their joint efforts can contribute to the further strengthening of press freedom, which we all cherish.

---

[16] L Levi, 'Real "Fake News" and Fake "Fake News"' (2018) 16 *First Amendment Law Review* 232.
[17] P Bernal, *The Internet, Warts and All: Free Speech, Privacy and Truth* (Cambridge, Cambridge University Press, 2018).
[18] ibid.
[19] Coe (n 11) 414–15.

INDEX

abuse of process (right to freedom violated), 195 (case law)

access to documents (United States), statutes covering, 25

Act on Information Disclosure by Public Agencies 1996 (Korea), 144

actio injuriarum (South Africa), 185–95
damages and defences for, 192–5
elements of, 186–93
'of and concerning', 191–2

'actual malice' principle (Korea), 141–2 (case law)

Adelson, Sheldon (Israel), 113–14

advertising (Israel), 108–9
digital, 108
expenditure of, 108
'native', 108–9

advertising (New Zealand):
editorial, as, 316 (case law)
genuine news, as, 315–16 (case law)

Advertising Standards Authority (ASA), (New Zealand), 309–10, 316–18
codes, 317
commercial and advocacy media, controlled by, 309–10
complaints resolution, 317–18
formation and composition of, 316–17

Advertising Standards Complaints Board (ASCB) (New Zealand), 317–18

African Regional Symposium on Telematics for Development (1995), 161

African Telecommunications Policy Study Group, 160–1

Africell DRC (Africa), 156

aggregators (Australia) and news media, relationship between, 289

Altshuler, Tehilla Schwartz, 12–13
Israeli press freedom, on, 11

Anglophone uprising (Cameroon), 166, 173

Anti-Communist Act case, (Korea) (1967), 132

anti-SLAPP legislation, 17
United States press and, 254–5

anti-trust law (Israeli) and media concentration, 112

Anuradha Bhasin v Union of India (2020), 95

Apple Daily Ltd v the Commissioner of the Independent Commission against Corruption, (2000), 54

Apple Daily newspaper outlet, 71–2

Arnab Ranjan Goswami v Union of India (2020), 96–7 (case law)

Ashwini Kumar Ghose v Arabinda Bose (1953), 91

attorney-client privilege (South African Airways), 180–1 (case law)

audiovisual publications, regulation of (New Zealand), 326

Australian Broadcasting Corporation (ABC), 278, 280

Australian Competition and Consumer Commission (ACCC),
digital platforms and, 290–5

Australian newspaper industry:
Finkelstein Inquiry, considered in, 276–7
internet's effect on, 277

Australian Press Council (APC), 280–1

Australian taxation's support of public interest journalism, 290

Bartinicki v Vopper (United States) (2001), 253

Basic Law (Hong Kong), Article 23, 59

Basic Law: Human Dignity and Liberty (Israel), 100, 103

Bennett Colman and Co and others v Union of India and others, 84–5 (case law)

'bi-material entities (Israel) as private mass media, 123

Bill of Rights (BOR) (Hong Kong), 48

Bosasa Operations (Pty) Ltd v Basson (2013), 180–1

Boycott Law (Israel), 103

Branzburg v Hayes (United States) (1972), 252

Brij Bhushan Sharma v Delhi (1950), 83 (case law)

British Mandate (Israel), laws left over from at independence, 100

British mandated Press Ordinance (1933), 11
speech rights and, 105

broadcasting:
  Finkelstein Inquiry, considered in (Australia), 279–80
  practice codes (New Zealand), 310–11
  standards (New Zealand), 310
  transmission service (New Zealand), review of, 323
Broadcasting Act 2020 (Korea), 144
Broadcasting Complaints Commission of South Africa (BCCSA), 181–2
broadcasting media:
  disclosure of information under (Korea), 144–5
  regulation of (South Africa), 181–2
broadcasting regulation (Israel), 110
broadcasting regulation (United States), 256
  internet and, 259–60 (case law)
  press regulation and, differences between, 256
Broadcasting Standards Authority (BSA) (New Zealand), 309, 310–13
  Codebook, 311
  complaint handling procdeure, 311–12
  freedom of expression, restriction of, 308
  statistics of complaints received, 312

Cable Broadcasting Council (Israel), 111
cable must-carry rules (United States), 259–60 (case law)
Canadian Broadcasting Corporation v New Brunswick (Attorney General) (1996), 210–11
Canadian Charter, freedoms in (1982), 209
Canadian courts' approach to free press, 211–12 (case law)
Canadian Supreme Court on public interest defence, 219–20
Canan, Penelope, on SLAPPS, 18
'capacity-communication-power' nexus (Foucault), 164
cell phone boom (Africa), 166–7
censorship:
  collateral (Chile), 243
  governance of (China), 28
  informal control of (China), 29
Channel 14 (Israel), ban on broadcasting on elections, 126
'cheap speech', 332
children's books (Hong Kong), publication of, 69–70 (case law)
Chilean Constitution 1980, enactment and content of, 229
Chilean media system, pluralism in, and competition law, 240–1

Chilean Supreme Court, CNTV decision on religious pluralism overruled, 238–9
Chinese Communist Party (CCP), governance structure and control of, 24–5
Chinese media:
  public-facing and official-facing roles, 26–7
  public opinion, moulding, 27
choice (Australia) and diversity of ownership, 293
Citizen, The, v McBride (2010), 190–1 (case law)
civil defamation claims (New Zealand), forms of reply in, 324
Code of Ethics of Press Council (Israel), 120, 122
Commerce Act 1986 (New Zealand), 322–3
Commerce Commission (New Zealand), 322, 323
commercial and advocacy speech (New Zealand), ASA regulates, 309–10
commercial television regulation, 110–11
commercialisation (China), media governance and sector and, 30–2
commercialised media (China), competition encouraged by, 32
Commission on the Freedom of the Press (Hutchins Commission), 6, 8
Commissioner of Police v Television Broadcasts Ltd (2016), 54–5
common law (Hong Kong), 47–8, 50–2
  Chinese system 'triumph over', 63–5 (case law)
  July 1997 onwards, 48, 55
  twentieth century development of, 51
Commonwealth Parliament (Australia), national security legislation passed by, 296–7
Commonwealth secrecy offences, review of (Australia), 299
communication (Africa):
  Information Society and, 163
  weaponisation of (Foucault), 164
competition (China), commercialised media encourages, 32
Competition Law (Chile):
  pluralism in media system, and, 240–1
  rules for external pluralism, 233
confidentiality of information sources (India), 86
Consejo Nacional de Televisión (CNTV) (Chile), 236–9
  composition and function of, 236–7
  official recognition of, 236

pluralism in television, enforcement of, 237
political pluralism and, 237–8
consent (Israel) and privacy invasion, 121
'constitutional action against the offender'
    (Chile), 231
contempt (India):
    civil and criminal, 91–2 (case law)
    test for, 92–3 (case law)
Contempt of Courts Act 1971 (India), 91–2
content service providers, Convergence
    Review on, 286–7
Convergence Review (Australia), 284–7
    committee for, 284
    content service providers, on, 286–7
    Finkelstein Inquiry recommendations
        considered, 286
    independent regulation proposed, 285
    media regulation, on, 285–6
    news standards body, recommendation for,
        286–7
    principle-based approach to regulation, 285
    television, revised regulation of, 285
corrections (New Zealand):
    breach of digital communication, for, 325
    defendants to publish, 324–5
corruption (China) in media profession, 33–4
Cory, Justice, on good reputation, 217
Court of Final Appeal (CFA) judgment
    (China) (2021), 63–5 (case law)
    Chan on, 65
criminal and civil offences (Chile), committed
    through media, 234
Criminal Procedure Law (Powers of
    Enforcement – Communication
    Data) 5768-2007 (Israel), 118–19
criminal trials (United States), public and
    press access to, 252
critical:
    culture (China), 36–7
    journalism (China), effect of, 37

Dagenais/Mentuck test (Canada), 214–15
    (case law)
damages (India) under civil law, 92
damages (South Africa):
    Constitutional Court on, 192
    interdict, entitlement to, 193
    patrimonial loss, claim for, 192–3
*Debi Prasad Sharma and Others v the King
    Emperor* (1944), 91–2 (case law)
decentralisation (China), effect of, 32–3
decision-makers (Israel) and media controllers,
    connections between, 113

Declaration of Principles (Africa) (2003),
    162–3
Declaration of the Independence of the State
    of Israel (1948), 102
defamation:
    actions by public figures (United States), 250
        (case law)
    Canada, in, 217
    China, in, 39
    defendent to publish correction
        (New Zealand), 324–5
    media (New Zealand), 308 (case law)
Defamation Act 1992 (New Zealand), 324
defamation (Korea):
    cases prioritised by courts, 138
    definition, 141
    lawsuits, statistics of, 142
    news media and, 135, 141
Defamation Law 5725-1965 (Israel), 120
defamatory:
    remark (Canada), classification of, 222
        (case law)
    statements, constitutional protection for
        publication of, 249–50 (case law)
digital communication (New Zealand), breach
    of, corrections or right of reply
    for, 325
Digital Media and Marketing Association
    (South Africa), 182
'digital natives' (Australia), 293
digital platforms (Australia):
    choice and quality of news and journalism,
        impact on, 292
    market power of, 291–2
    'online news ecosystem', participation in, 292
    rise and impact of, 291
Digital Platforms Inquiry (ACCC) (Australia),
    290–5
    market power of, 291–2
    recommendations of, 295
    responsibility for, 290
digital publications (Australia), atomisation of
    news and, 294–5
Director of Human Rights Proceedings v Slater
    (New Zealand) (2019), 305–6
disasters, state secrets list removed from
    (China), 38–9
disclosure of information (Korea) under the
    Broadcasting Act, 144–5
disinformation (United States) and
    Section 230, 260–1
disputes and SLAPPs distinguished, 19–20
dissent, silencing of, SLAPP's use of for, 18–19

Durie v Gardiner (New Zealand) (2018), 308
duty and subversion, 11

*Edmonton Journal v Alberta (Attorney
    General)* (Canada) (1989), 214
Egyptian administrative court's ruling on
    internet blackout, 171–2
Eko, Lyombe, on press freedom, 10–11
Electoral Commission v Cameron
    (New Zealand) (1997), 318
electronic mail forums (Africa), 166
English weekly journal (Cross Roads), banned
    from circulation in Madras, 82–3
    (case law)
Environment and Communications
    References Committee (Australia),
    298–9
essential care guarantee (Chilean
    Constitution), 231
Evidence Act 2006 (New Zealand), 309
    Section 68, 319–22 (case law)
executive authorisation without judicial
    oversight, 68–9
expression (United States), constitutional
    protection of, 248–9

Facebook, market power of (Australia),
    291–2
Facebook Bill (Israel), 127
fair comment:
    defamation defence (South Africa), 195
    defence (Canada), 220 (case law)
    test (Hong Kong), 53–4 (case law)
'Fairness Doctrine' (United States) binding in
    Israel, 110
fake news (South Korea), 145
FCC v Pacifica Foundation (United States,
    1978), 258–9
Federal Communications Commissions
    (FCC) (United States), 256–9
    (case law)
    broadcast regulated adopted by, 257–8
    (examples)
    content-focused regulation, distancing
    from, 259
First Amendment (United States
    Constitution):
    freedoms of speech and press in, 247–8
    protection for newsgathering, 252 (case law)
Fiss, Owen, 4, 5, 6
follow-up stories (South Korea), right to
    demand, 138, 139

free expression guarantee (South Africa), 182
    (case law)
free press:
    Finkelstein Inquiry, considered in
        (Australia), 275–6
    right to (India), right to circulation included
        in, 84 (case law)
free press (Canada), 206–7, 210–11
    Canadian courts' approach to, 211–12
        (case law)
free press (Chile):
    defences for, 227–8
    fundamental right, as, 228
    history and development of, 226–7
    limits to, 230–1
    political benefits of, 227
free speech:
    clause (United States), 248
    development of (South Africa), 176–7
    journalists' right to (India), 96–7 (case law)
Free Speech and Free Press Clause (Korean
    Constitution), 133
freedom:
    to express opinions (Chile), 229–30
    social media enhances, 42
    of speech, history of, 50–1
    to travel (India), 86 (case law)
freedom of expression:
    Africa, in, 163
    Commonwealth (Australia), 299
    right to a good name and, balance between
        (Israel), 121
    social networks and (Chile), 241–2
freedom of expression (Canada):
    democratic society, in, 214 (case law)
    open court principle and, 214 (case law)
    post-Charter, 209–10
    post-*Irwin Toy*, 212–13
    pre-Charter, 208–9
freedom of expression (New Zealand):
    BSA and, 308
    fundamental rights, as, 304
freedom of expression (South Africa),
    179–80
    Constitution (1996), in, 178
freedom of information:
    Israel, in, 105–6
    Korea, in, 144–5
Freedom of Information Law 5758-1998
    (Israel), 105–6
freedom of press (Canada), 211
    newsgathering and, 216

freedom of press (India), 81–2 (case law)
confidentiality of sexual offences and
victims, 88
definition, 75
English weekly journal (Cross Roads),
banned from circulation in Madras,
82–3 (case law)
freedom of speech, is part of, 82 (case law)
post-independence period, 80–1
'reasonable' restrictions, 82
repesentative democracy, in, 76 (case law)
resistance to, 83–4 (case law)
restriction of by right to privacy, 87
(case law)
state administration effectiveness and, 76–7
freedom of press (Israel):
Basic Law: Human Dignity and Liberty, not
mentioned in, 103
defences for, 120
digital age, in, 126–7
right to privacy and, 121–2
freedom of speech (India):
ancient and medieval and colonial periods,
in, 77–9
freedom of press, is part of, 82–5
fundamental rights, as, 77, 79, 81, 82, 83
Indian Constitution, in, 81
freedom of speech (South Korea), 130
Constitutional Court defines, 134
press freedom, and, distinguished, 136
fundamental rights, 56, 65
free press, as (Chile), 228
freedom of expression as, 304
freedom of speech (India), to, 77, 79, 81, 82, 83
protection of (Hong Kong), 55

gag orders (Israel), 124
**General Telecommunications Act 1982
(Chile), responsibility for radio
broadcasting,** 240
Gertz v Robert Welch **(1974),** 250
Gonzalez v Google **(United States) (2023),** 261
**good reputation (individual's), importance of
(Cory),** 217–18
Google, market power of (Australia), 291–2
government policies (India), criticism of, 83
(case law)
**Government Press Office (GPO) (Israel) and
speech rights,** 105
governmental:
agencies (Egypt), access to
telecommunications, 169

censorship and press freedom, 10–11
Grant v Torstar, **(Canada) (2009),** 218–20
libel defences in, 222
Gravatt v Auckland Coroner's Court **(2013),**
308

Habermas, Jürgen, on pluralism, 8
Han, Judge, on press freedom, 133–4
**Harare Telecommunication Development
Conference,** 161
harm to society, 10
**Harmful Digital Communications Act 2015
(New Zealand),** 325
**harmful speech (United States) and
Section 230 of Communications
Decency Act,** 260–1
health professionals' identities, 308 (case law)
Hill v Church of Scientology of Toronto **(1995),**
217–18
HKSAR v Lai Chee Ying **(2021),** 63–4, 71
HKSAR v Mo Man Ching Claudia **(2021),** 72
HKSAR v Ng Hau Yi Sidney **(2021),** 69–70
HKSAR v Ng Kung Siu **(1999),** 56–7
**Hong Kong Bill of Rights Ordinance
(HKBORO),** 49
enactment of (1991), 52
Hong Kong Courts:
jurisdiction of removed by NSL, 63
national security, jurisdiction to determine,
62–3
NPC or NPCSC authority, questioning of, 56
(case law)
**Hong Kong Special Administrative Region
(HKSAR),** 48, 49
NPC legislates for, 60
prohibition on acts of treason, laws on
enacted under, 59
Hosking v Runting **(New Zealand),** 308

**Implementation Rules (Hong Kong),
journalistic sources, on,** 68
**Independent Communications Authority of
South Africa (ICASA),** 181
**independent press's role in democracy
(New Zealand),** 315–16 (case law)
**independent regulator (Australia), proposal
for,** 285
India Press Act 1931, 79
**Indian Constitution, freedom of speech under
(Article 19(1)(a)),** 81
*Indian Express Newspapers v Union of India and
Others* **(1986), 76, 83–4** (case law)

Indian Express v Union of India (1985), 76,
　　81–2
　right to freedom of trade and business,
　　considered in, 85
Indian Penal Code, 90
Indian Press Council, 14
**information and communication technologies
　　(Cameroon) and repression,** 169–70
**Information and Communications Network
　　Act (Korea) (ICNA),** 146
**information and communications
　　technologies (ICT) (China),** 24
　impact and ownership of, 40–2
**information and network technologies
　　(Egypt), privatisation of,** 169
'information disorder' (Australia), 295
**Information Technology Act 2000 (India),
　　regulation of illegal online content,**
　　94–5
**'intentional' impairment of rights
　　(South Africa),** 176
**intermediary services' (Chile) liability for
　　speech crimes,** 242
Internal Security Act 1950 (South Africa), 14,
　　183–4
**International Covenant on Civil and Political
　　Rights (ICCPR),** 49, 52
　Hong Kong law, incorporated in, 52–3
　ratification of (1976), 52
internet:
　access provision (Africa) (1990s), 165–6
　blocking orders (India), petition against, 95
　　(case law)
　broadcasting regulation, and (United States),
　　259–60 (case law)
　disconnectivity (Africa), creation of, 165
　government control of (Africa), 155
　material (Korea), temporary measures to
　　prevent, 146
　newspaper circulation, effect on (Australia),
　　277
　providers (Korea), regulation of, 146
　services (Cameroon), suspension of
　　(letter 006/DG), 172–3
　shutdowns (South Africa), 155–6
　telecommunications infrastructure's
　　connection to (Africa), 159
internet blackout (Egypt) (2011), 170–2
　Egyptian administrative court's ruling on,
　　171–2
internet connectivity (Africa), 160–1
　adoption process of, 161–2

internet platforms (United States):
　immunity of, and Section 230, 261
　　(case law)
　recommendations, aspects of, and
　　Section 230, 262–3
**internet service providers (United States),
　　moderation of content, state laws
　　restriction of,** 261–2 (case law)
**internet (United States) and broadcasting
　　regulation,** 259–60 (case law)
**Interpretation and General Clauses Ordinance
　　(IGCO) (Hong Kong),** 54
　Part XII, protection of journalistic sources
　　under, 67
invasion of privacy (New Zealand), 308
　　(case law)
**investigative journalism (China),
　　circumstances favour,** 36
Irwin Toy Ltd v Quebec (Attorney General)
　　(1989), 211–12 (case law)
Israel Broadcasting Authority (IBA), 107
Israel Hayom **(Israeli newspaper),** 114,
　　115, 123
Israeli Commercial Broadcasting Law, 111
**Israeli courts' criticism of Declaration of the
　　Independence of the State of
　　Israel,** 102
Israel Democracy Index 2022, 116–17
Israeli media market:
　control of, 112–13
　journalists and, 116
Israeli newspapers, closure of, 101–2
**Israeli Public Broadcasting Corporation
　　(IPBC),** 107–8

Jenin, Jenin **(Israeli film),** 101
Jeynes v News Magazines Ltd (2008), 188
*Jorawer Singh Mundy v Union of India and
　　Others* (2021), 93
journalism (Africa), practice and nature of,
　　154–5
journalism (Australia):
　atomisation of and digital publication,
　　294–5
　digital platforms' impact on, 292
　high quality, standards of, 293
　taxation's support of and, 290
**journalistic material referred to in
　　Implementation Rules,** 68
journalistic privilege, extent of, 118
**journalistic professionalism (Israel), decline
　　in,** 116–17

journalistic sources:
  confidentiality of, 117–19
  NSL, under, 67
  Protection Act 2017 (Canada), 216
  protection of (New Zealand), 319–22
    (case law)
  protection of under IGCO Part XII, 67
journalists:
  definition of (New Zealand), 309
  freedom of expression and (South Africa),
    180–1 (case law)
  privilege of and criminal investigations
    (Korea), 140–1
  right to free speech (India), 96–7 (case law)
  statutory protection of (United States),
    253–4
journalists (Australia):
  law enforcement, subject to, 276
  protection of, 299
  reviewing or contesting warrants, 297–8, 299
journalists (Israel):
  eviction of by police, 125–6
  Israeli media market and, 116
  Libeskind on, 116
  movement restrictions, 125–6
  Press Council, withdrawl of from, 117
  rights of and media owners' rights, 122–3
  violence against, examples of, 124–5
judicial review subject to ASCB decisions,
    (New Zealand), 318 (case law)
jurisdiction (South Africa), 186–7
Justice KS Puttaswamy v Union of India
    (2017), 93

Kesari (**Marathi newspaper**), 78–9
Knesset Elections Law (Propaganda Methods)
    (1959), 126–7
Kol Ha'am v Minister of the Interior (**1953**),
    101–2
Korea:
  Constitution (1987), press freedom in, 132–3
  Courts on press freedom, 135–6
  democratization of, 129
  media in, indirect laws affect, 140
  Press Ethics Commission, 139
Korea Forum **article libel case,** 141 (case law)

Lai Chee-Ying v Commissioner of Police
    (2022), 67–8
Laugh It Off Promotions CC v South African
    Breweries International (**2005**), 179
law, Mill on, 10

Law on Repression of Terrorism (Cameroon)
    (2014), 169–70
leaked information (United States), reporters'
    revealing of, 253 (case law)
Lebel, Justice, on facts in public domain,
    222–3
Leung Kwok Hung v HKSAR (**2006**), 68–9
libel defences in *Grant* (**Canada**), 222
Liberal Democracy Index (South Korea and
    United States), 129
Libeskind, Kalman, on journalists, 116

malice standard (United States) extended to
    defamation actions, 250
Maneka Gandhi v Union of India (**2021**), 86
Manohar Lal Sharma v Union of India (**2021**),
    86, 94
marketisation of press (China), 31
mass media:
  Africa, in, 160
  Aotearoa New Zealand, in, 304
  federation (Chile), 235
  nationalisation of (Egypt), 168
  state monopoly, and (Chile) 230
maximal enfranchisement, 9–10
meaning in defamation law, (South Africa),
    188–91
  English decisions, 188–9 (case law)
  exact meaning of words, 189
  judicial determination of, 189
  layers of, 190–1 (case law)
  plaintiff's proof for, 189
  pleading of, 190
  principles of, 188–9
media:
  concentration and ownership (Israel), 112
  controllers and decision-makers, connections
    between (Israel), 113
  criminal and civil offences committed
    through (Chile), 234
  exemption from data protection provisions of
    Privacy Act, 305–6
  Finkelstein Inquiry and (Australia), 278,
    283–4
  law regulation (Chile), 228
  organisations subject to law enforcement, 296
  owners (Israel), rights of, and journalists'
    rights, 122–3
  platforms subject to Press Act rules (Chile),
    241–2
  portals (South Korea), court rulings on,
    147–8

press, distinguished from, 2–3
profession (China), corruption in, 33–4
regulation, Convergence Review on, 285–6
social media's liability for harmful content is
    not (Israel), 127
system (Chile), pluralism in, 233
trends (Australia), Senate Select Committee
    on the Future of Public Interest
    Journalism, in, 288–9
watchdog role (Africa), 154
media (Aotearoa New Zealand):
public, 326–7
statutory benefits of, 318–19
media (China):
commercialised press and, 45
localisation of, 32
loosening of party's grip, effect of on, 32
Party, state disciplined by, 35
President Xi on, 23
Media Council 2017 (New Zealand), 309
media freedom:
Australia, in, 298
Chile, in, 228, 230
media governance (China), 24–6
Chinese Communist Party's control of, 24
commercialisation changes to, 31–2
control shifted to Party, 26
judicial remedies, absence of, 27–8
lawlessness in, 27–30
media (Israel), 106–8
phases of, 106–7
practice characteristics, 116
media organisations (Australia):
protection of, 299
reviewing or contesting warrants, 277–8
**media sector (China), commercialisation and
    diversity of,** 30–1
Media Works TV Ltd v Staples **(New Zealand)
    (2020),** 321–2
M.E.H. v Williams **(Canada) (2012),** 215
**mergers and acquisitions (New Zealand),
    Commerce Commission monitors,**
    322
Miami Herald v Tornillo **(United States)
    (1974),** 249, 258
military censorship (Israel), 123
journalists' evasion of restrictions, 124
Mill, John Stuart, on law, 10
Mineral Sands Resources (Pty) Ltd v Reddell
    (2022), 195
mobile phones (Africa):
catalyst for change, are, 167

orality and, 167
**Moon, Jae-wan (Korea), on a democratic
    nation 134**
multi-channel television regulation, 111

**National Association of Radio Broadcasters
    of Chile,** 239–40
**National Communication Council of
    Cameroon (1991),** 170
**National Flag Ordinance (Hong Kong),
    constitutionality of,** 56–7
    (case law)
national security (Australia), importance of,
    299
national security (Hong Kong), 62
Courts' jurisdiction to determine, 63
**National Security Law 2015 and 2020 (NSL)
    (Hong Kong),** 48–50, 58, 61, 62
Article 42, 73
CFA and, 64–5
dual system of legislation, 59–60
offences under, 61–2
press freedom norms under, 66
NBC v FCC **(United States) (1943),** 258
neican 26–7
legacy press, 11
Netanyahu, PM (Israel), 114–15
Sarna, quarrel with, 120
NetChoice v Moody **(United States) (2022),**
    261–2
NetChoice v Paxton **(United States) (2022),**
    262
New York Times v Sullivan **(1964),** 249–50,
    266, 267, 268
New Zealand Bill of Rights Act 1990, 306
Section 14, 306, 308
horizontal and vertical effects of, 307–8
*New Zealand Dermatological Society Inc v
    Stuff* **(2022),** 316
New Zealand media, cross-ownership of, 322
New Zealand Media Council, 309, 313–14
complaints procedure, 314–15
statement of principles, 314
news (Australia):
atomisation of and digital publication,
    294–5
digital platforms' impact on, 292
news gathering and press freedom, 216
news gathering (United States):
First Amendment, protection for, 252
    (case law)
statutory restraints for, 255

news (Korea), erasure of, courts' caution over, 142–3
news media:
defamation and (Korea), 135, 141
politics and, relationship between, 115
news media (Australia):
aggregators and, relationship between, 289
Finkelstein Inquiry, considered in, 276
News Media Council (Australia), 282–3
News Media Standards Authority (NMSA) (New Zealand), 305, 325
Newspaper Promotion Act (Korea), 137
newspapers:
circulation, internet's effect on (Australia), 277
Hebrew, 107
media outlets and restriction of press freedom, 70–1
regulation of price and usage of (India), 84–5 (case law)
television and film (China), regulations and rules for, 28–9
Ng Ka Ling v Director of Immigration (No 1) **(1999),** 55–6, 64
Ng Ka Ling v Director of Immigration (No 2) **(1999),** 56, 64
1980s' states of emergency (South Africa), 184–5
NM v Smith **(2007),** 197–8, 199
non-jury trial certificate, issue of, 65–6 (case law)
Nova Scotia (Attorney General) v MacIntryre **(Canada) (1982),** 213
NPC legislation for HKSAR, 60
NPCSC, Article 64, 62
NZME and Fairfax newspaper networks, merger between refused (New Zealand), 323

'objectionable matter', definition, 80
objectivity (press freedom), 8–9
'one country, two systems' (Hong Kong) (2014), 58–9
experiment, 55–6 (case law)
White Paper on, 58–9
online:
content (India), removal of, 93 (case law)
news (Australia), considered in Finkelstein Inquiry, 278
public sphere (Volokh), 332
Online Media Standards Authority (New Zealand), 309
'online news ecosystem' (Australia), digital platforms' participation in, 292

online publication (Australia):
advantages of, 293
provision of contact directly to public, 294
public interest journalism, impact on, 294
online publications (India), 92–3 (case law)
privacy of, 93 (case law)
open court concept (Canada), 213–14 (case law)
freedom of expression and, 214 (case law)
'open court doctrine' (Canada), 207
open court principle:
freedom of expression (Canada) and, 214 (case law)
privacy can be exception to, 215 (case law)
Open Government Information Regulations (OGIR) (China), 37–8
orality and mobile phones, 167

Parliamentary Joint Committee on Intelligence and Security (PJCIS) (Australia) (2020), 295–8
purpose of and reason for inquiry, 296
Party, the (China):
control of social media, 43–4
loosening of grip on media, 33
Pegasus (spyware), misuse of, 94 (case law)
Penal Code (Israel), Article 117, 117–18
personality rights, 176
photojournalists (Israel), eviction of by police, 125–6
platform control (United States), 263–4
pluralism, Habermas on, 8
pluralism (Chile):
Chilean media system, in, and Competition Law, 240–1
external, competition rules for, 233
media system, in, 233
political, in CNTV and TVN, 237–8
religious, CNTV decision overruled, 238–9
television, in, 237
police (Israel):
eviction of journalists and photojournalists, 125–6
Israelis, spying on, 119
Police v Campbell, **(New Zealand) (2010),** 320
political speech (United States), protection of, 247–8
political system, press in (Communist China and Soviet Russia), 5
politics (Israel) and news media, relationship between, 114–15
Post, Robert, 9
pluralism, on, 8

press:
  coverage (Israel) and privacy protections, 121
  India, in, laws covering, 92
  Korea, in, definition and functions of, 147
  media, distinguished from, 2–3
  political systems (Communist China and
      Soviet Russia) in, 5
  private enterprises as, 6
  production (United States), reduction of,
      266–8
  public and, social contract between, 305
  public service, duty for, 5–6
  watchdog, as, 54 (case law)
  wrongdoing in public office, discovery of by, 4
Press Act 2001 (Chile), 13, 231–2, 236
  rules, media platforms subject to, 241–2
Press and Registration of Books Act 1867
      (India), 89
Press Arbitration Act 2005 (Korea), 13, 138–9
Press Arbitration Commission (Korea), 139
press (Chile):
  function and regulation of (1990s), 232
  limits and duties of, 233–4
  right to reply against, 230
press (China):
  commercialised media and, 45
  marketisation of, 31
Press Clause (United States), 247, 251
Press Council Act 1956 (India), 89–90
Press Council Act 1978 (India), 14
Press Council (Israel), Journalists' Union's
      withdrawal from, 117
press freedom, 6–7
  disasters removed from state secrets list
      (China) (2003), 38–9
  govermental censorship and, 10–11
  Israel, in, 99, 100
  New Zealand, in, 305, 306–7
  theory (Aotearoa New Zealand), 304
  United Kingdom and United States, in, 7
  see also freedom of press
press freedom (Hong Kong), 53–5 (case law)
  norms under NSL, 66
press freedom (Korea):
  courts on, 135–6
  Korean Constitution (1987), in, 132–3
  negative freedom, is, 134
  1945–8, during, 131
  speech freedom and, distinguished, 136
Press (Objectionable Matter) Act 1951
      (India), 80
Press Ordinance (Israel) (1933), 14–15, 109

press regulation, 3
  broadcasting regulation and, differences
      between (United States), 256
  establishment and operation of
      (New Zealand), 303–4
  Israel, in, 109
press (United States):
  anti-SLAPP legislation and, 254–5
  Courts' negative views of, 265–6
  defamation cases, disinformation argument,
      266–8
  legitimacy need, 269
  newsgathering rights, 268–9
  protection need, 268
  threats to, 265
Prevention of Publication of Objectionable
      Matter Act 1976 (India), 80
principle of openness, (Canada), 213
Pring, George, on SLAPPs, 18
print media, regulation of (South Africa), 181
prior restraints on publication (United States),
      presumptive unconstitutionality of,
      249 (case law)
Prisons Act, 184
privacy:
  banning of publications and, 214
  invasion (Israel), forbidden without consent,
      121
  online publications, of (India), 93 (case law)
  open court principle, exception to, can be,
      215 (case law)
  protection and press coverage (Israel), 121
Privacy Act (New Zealand) (2020):
  data protection provisions and media
      exemption, 305–6
  updating of, 306
privacy (South Africa), 179, 196–7
  Constitution (1996), in, 178
  defences for, 199–200 (case law)
  fault, proof of, 197–8 (case law)
  publication is risk of, 197
  test for, 196
private:
  enterprises, press as, 6
  information (South Africa), disclosure of,
      relief for, 198
  mass media, 'bi-material' entities, as, 123
  media (New Zealand), regulation of, 326
privatisation (Egypt), information and
      network technologies, for, 168
privileged occasion (defamation defence)
      (South Africa), 193–4

production order from Royal Canadian
Mounted Police to Vice Media,
216–17 (case law)
Promotion of Equality and Prevention of
Unfair Discrimination Act 2000
(South Africa), 182–3
Propaganda Ministry (China), 25
Protection of Personal Information Act 2013
(South Africa), 183
public:
broadcasting regulation (Israel), 110
domain, facts in (Lebel), 222–3
figures, defamation actions by
(United States), 250 (case law)
opinion (China) controlled by society, 35–6
opinions supervision (POS) (China), 24, 34,
36, 39–40, 41
press and, social contract between, 305
service, press's duty to perform, 5–6
trust and press, 5
public interest:
Chile, in, 234–5
Israel, in, 121
risk, 215 (case law)
Public Interest Advocate (PIA) (Australia),
297–8
public interest defence (Canada), 218–20
(case law)
criteria, Canadian Supreme Court on,
219–20
public interest journalism (Australia), 298
Australian taxation's support of, 290
news categories not included in, 293
online publication's impact on, 294
publication (South Africa), 187–8
publications (Canada), banning of and
privacy, 214
publishers' platforms (Australia), 301

R Rajagopal v State of Tamil Nadu (1995), 87
(case law)
R v Denis (Canada) (2019), 212–13
R v Vice Media, (Canada) (2018), 216–17
racism and racist expression, treatment of,
103–4
radio and television broadcasters (Chile),
rules for, 230
radio broadcasting, FCC control of (United
States), 256–7
radio broadcasting (Chile):
concessions, corporations with foreign
capital, obtaining, 240

exploitation of services, liability for, 241
regulation and restrictions on, 239–41
radio services (Chile), exploitation of, liability
for, 241
reasonable publication (South Africa), 194–5
Red Lion Broadcasting v FCC (1969), 258
regulation (Australia):
Finkelstein Inquiry, considered in, 281
principles-based approach to, 285
Reno v ACLU (United States) (1997), 260
Report of the Independent Inquiry into
the Media and Media Regulation
(2011) (Finkelstein Inquiry):
aims of, 274–5
Australian media's reaction to, 283–4
Australian newspaper industry considered
in, 276–7
broadcasting considered in, 279–80
Convergence Review's consideration of, 286–7
establishment of News Media Council, 282–3
failure of self-regulation, 281–2
'free press' considered in, 275–6
impetus for, 274
media considered in, 278–9
news media considered in, 276
online news considered in, 278
proposed reforms in, 281
regulation considered in, 281
remoteness principle in, 10
self-regulation of print media in, 280–1
submissions received, 275
timeline for, 275
repression (Cameroon) and ICT, 169–70
reputation (Canada), 217–19 (case law)
good, Cory on, 217–18
right of privacy (Israel):
freedom of the press and, 121–2
public's right to know and, 121–2
right of reply for breach of digital
communication principles
(New Zealand), 325
right to:
circulation included in right to free press, 84
(case law)
constitutional remedies (India), 86
dignity (South Africa), 179 (case law)
be forgotten (online content) (India), 93
(case law)
freedom of trade and business (India), 85
(case law)
good name and freedom of expression,
balance between, 121

know, public's, and right to privacy (Israel),
    121–2
reply requirements, 13
right to privacy (India), 85–6 (case law)
    freedom of press restricted by, 87 (case law)
Romesh Thappar v State of Madras **(1950),**
    82–3
RWDSU v Dolphin Delivery Ltd **(Canada)
    (1986),** 213

S v Cornelissen **(1994),** 180
safeguarding public debate (Korea), 142
*Sakal Papers (P) Ltd and Others v Union of
    India,* 84–5 (case law)
**Second Authority for Television and Radio
    (Israel),** 110–11
Second Authority Law (Israel), 111
**Section 230 (Communication Decency Act,
    United States),** 260–1
    disinformation and harmful speech and,
        260–1
    internet platforms and, 261 (case law), 262–3
    regulation of social media and, 260
sedition law (Hong Kong), 51–2
seditious publication offences, 69–72
    (case law)
**self-regulation, failure of in Finkelstein
    Inquiry,** 281–2
self-regulation voluntary schemes, 14
self-regulatory laws (free press Korea), 139
self-regulatory systems examples, 15–16
Senate Press Freedom Inquiry (Australia),
    298–300
**Senate Select Committee on the Future
    of Public Interest Journalism
    (Australia) (2018),** 288–90
    aggregators and news media, relationship
        between discussed, 289
    Australian taxation's support of public
        interest journalism, 290
    media trends discussed in, 288–9
    public interest journalism in other countries
        canvassed, 290
'severe espionage offenses' (Israel), 124
**sexual offences victims (India), confidentiality
    of, and freedom of press,** 88
Sherman Estate v Donovan **(Canada) (2021),**
    215
**Shin Bet Law (Israel) monitoring of
    communication companies'
    information,** 119
'Silicon Mountain' (ICT start-up, Cameroon),
    174

Sim v Stretch **(Canada) (1986),** 222
Slater v Blomfield **(New Zealand) (2014),**
    320–1
Snyder v Phelps **(2011),** 18
social media, 43
    freedom, enhanced by, 42
    state control, evasion of, and, 42
social media (China):
    Party's control of, 43–4
    private ownership of, 42
**social media (Israel) liability for harmful
    content,** 127
social media (United States):
    regulation, 264–5
    regulation of and Section 230, 260
**social networks (Chile) and freedom of
    expression,** 241–2
society (Africa), deterritorialisation of, 162
society and harmful speech, 10
society (China), public opinion controls, 35–6
**South African Airways, withdrawal from
    aircraft purchase,** 180 (case law)
South African Constitution (1996), 178–81
    dignity, privacy and freedom of expression,
        on, 178
**South African Newspaper Press Union code
    of conduct,** 184
speech:
    crimes, liability for intermediary services,
        (Chile), 242
    freedom *see* freedom of speech
    press freedoms and (United States), 76–7
    rights, 104–5
state administration and freedom of press,
    76–7
state control, social media evades, 42
**State Council Regulations on the
    Management of Publications
    (China) (2001),** 28
**state laws (United States), internet service
    providers' moderation of content,
    restriction of,** 261–2, (case law)
statutory and administrative law (Korea),
    137–9
    principal statutes for, 137
**strategic lawsuits against public participation
    (SLAPPs),** 17–20, 121, 195
    Canan on, 18
    disputes and, distinguished, 19
    dissent, silencing of, and, 18–19
    Pring on, 18
    usage of, 17–18 (case law)
    see also anti-SLAPP legislation

Sullivan doctrine influence (Korea), 141–2
Sunstein, Cass, 4–5, 6
Supreme Court of Korea acceptance of erasure
    of news articles, examples of, 143

Taussig, Shuki, on Israeli media practice, 116
te reo Māori (official language), complaints
    about use of, 312–13
Tel Aviv shooting (April 2022), 126
Telecom Egypt, powers under
    Telecommunication Regulation
    Law (2003), 168–9
telecommunication regulation (Korea), 146
telecommunication statutes (Korea), 146
telecommunications (Egypt), government
    agencies' access to, 169
telecommunications infrastructure (Africa),
    internet, connection to, 159
Telecommunications Law (Israel), 111
Television Act 1970 (Chile), 236
    pluralism rules in, 237
television (Chile):
    multichannel regulation, 111
    regulation of, 236–9
television news (Israel), 107
test of balancing (Hong Kong), 54–5 (case law)
The New York Times Co v the United States
    (1971), 253
Tilak, Bal Gangadhar, 78–9
title to sue (South Africa), 186
Tom Frewen v Stuff (New Zealand) (2017),
    315–16
Tong Ying Kit v Secretary for Justice
    (Hong Kong) (2021), 65–6
Tool, The (Israel), 119
truth and public benefit (defamation defence)
    (South Africa), 194
Tse Wai Chun Paul v Cheng Alert and Others
    (1995), 53–4
Tshabalala-Msimang v Makhanya (2007),
    199–200
Turner Broadcasting v FCC cases
    (United States) (1997), 259
TVN (Chile public service broadcaster), 236
    political pluralism duty, failed in, 238

regulation and operation of, 239
Twitter, Inc v Taamneh (United States)
    (2023), 261

United Nations Millennium Development
    Goals (2000), 159–60
United States Supreme Court, FCC regulatory
    decisions considered, 258–9

V-Dem global democracy list, 129, 149
Van Breda v Media 24 Ltd (2017), 182
Volokh, Eugene, on the public sphere, 332

warrants, journalists' reviewing or contesting
    of, 297–8, 299
watchdog, 34, 66, 99, 134, 170
    media, 116, 154
    press, 135, 142, 268
    public, 4, 12, 15, 54, 94, 206
whistleblower sources, reporters' protection
    of (United States), 253 (case law)
whistleblowers, protection of (Australia), 299
WIC Radio Ltd v Simpson (Canada)
    (2008), 220
wiretapping (Israel), 118–19
Wiretapping Law, 5739-1979, (Israel), 118
World Bank on information revolution and
    economic development, 159
World Summit on the Information Society
    (WSIS), 162–3
    communication (Africa) and, 162, 163
wrongdoing in public office, discovery of by
    press, 4
wrongful dismissal of Israeli Arab journalist
    (Israel), 122–3
'wrongful' impairment of rights
    (South Africa), 177

Xi, President, on media (China) (2016), 23

Yedioth Ahronoth (Israeli newspaper), 107,
    112, 114, 117, 120, 122

Zenawi, Meles (Ethiopian Prime Minster),
    cartoon of, 156